North Africa

Morocco, Algeria and Tunisia
including Gibraltar, Pantelleria and the
Pelagie Islands and Malta

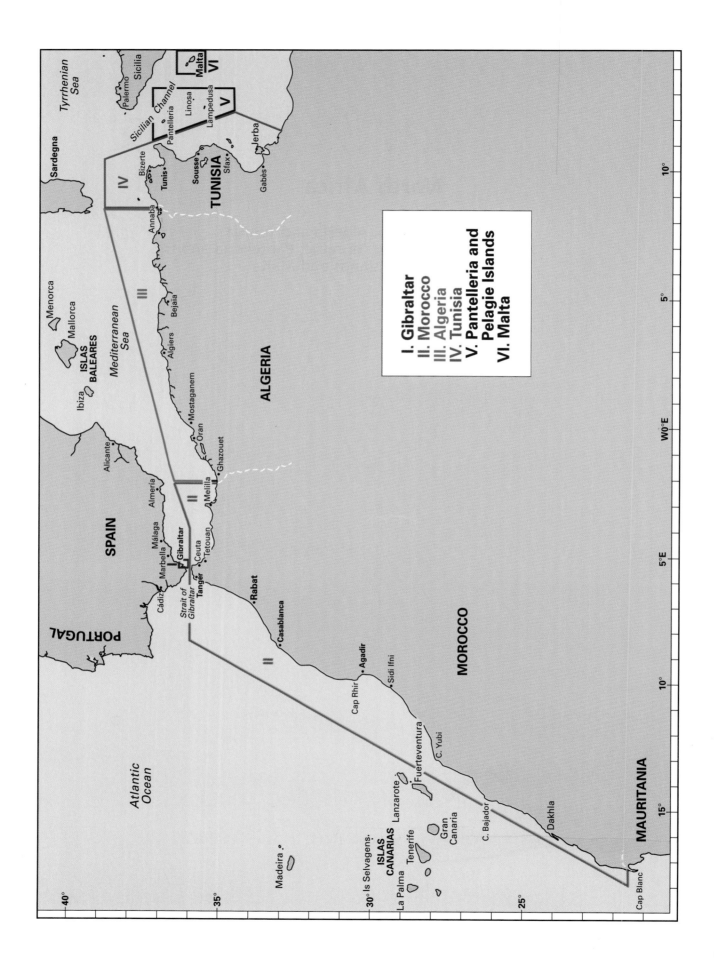

North Africa

Morocco, Algeria and Tunisia
including Gibraltar, Pantelleria and
the Pelagie Islands and Malta

ROYAL CRUISING CLUB
PILOTAGE FOUNDATION

Graham Hutt

Imray Laurie Norie & Wilson

Published by
Imray Laurie Norie & Wilson Ltd
Wych House The Broadway St Ives
Cambridgeshire PE27 5BT England
☎ +44 (0)1480 462114
Fax +44 (0) 1480 496109
www.imray.com
2005

© Text: Royal Cruising Club Pilotage Foundation 1994, 2000, 2005
© Plans: Imray Laurie Norie & Wilson Ltd 1994, 2000, 2005
© Photographs: Hans van Rijn 1991; Graham Hutt 2000, 2005

First edition 1991
Second edition 2000
Third edition 2005

ISBN 0 85288 840 6

British Library Cataloguing in Publication Data.
A catalogue record for this title is available from the British Library.

CORRECTIONAL SUPPLEMENTS

This pilot book will be amended at intervals by the issue of correctional supplements. These are published on the internet at our web site www.imray.com and also via www.rccpf.org.uk and may be downloaded free of charge. Printed copies are also available on request from the publishers at the above address. Like this pilot, supplements are selective. Navigators requiring the latest definitive information are advised to refer to official hydrographic office data.

CAUTION

Whilst every care has been taken to ensure that the information contained in this book is accurate, the RCC Pilotage Foundation, the authors and the publishers hereby formally disclaim any and all liability for any personal injury, loss and/or damage howsoever caused, whether by reason of any error, inaccuracy, omission or ambiguity in relation to the contents and/or information contained within this book. The book contains selected information and thus is not definitive. It does not contain all known information on the subject in hand and should not be relied on alone for navigational use: it should only be used in conjunction with official hydrographic data. This is particularly relevant to the plans, which should not be used for navigation.

The RCC Pilotage Foundation, the authors and publishers believe that the information which they have included is a useful aid to prudent navigation, but the safety of a vessel depends ultimately on the judgment of the skipper, who should assess all information, published or unpublished.

WAYPOINTS

This edition of the *North Africa* pilot includes the introduction of waypoints. The RCC PF consider a waypoint to be a position likely to be helpful for navigation if entered into some form of electronic navigation system for use in conjunction with GPS. In this pilot they have been determined by actual observation. All waypoints are given to datum WGS 84 and every effort has been made to ensure their accuracy. Nevertheless, for each individual vessel, the standard of onboard equipment, aerial position, datum setting, correct entry of data and operator skill all play a part in their effectiveness. In particular it is vital for the navigator to note the datum of the chart in use and apply the necessary correction if plotting a GPS position on the chart.

The attention of the navigator is drawn to the 'important note' paragraph on page 12 of the Introduction.

We emphasise that we regard waypoints as an aid to navigation for use as the navigator decides. We hope that the waypoints in this pilot will help ease that navigational load.

POSITIONS

Positions given in the text and on plans are intended purely as an aid to locating the place in question on the chart.

PLANS

The plans in this guide are not to be used for navigation - they are designed to support the text and should always be used together with navigational charts. Even so, every effort has been made to locate harbour and anchorage plans adjacent to the relevant text.

It should be borne in mind that the characteristics of lights may be changed during the life of the book, and that in any case notification of such changes is unlikely to be reported immediately. Each light is identified in both the text and where possible on the plans (where it appears in red) by its international index number, as used in the *Admiralty List of Lights*, from which the book may be updated when no longer new.

All bearings are given from seaward and refer to true north. Scales may be taken from the scales of latitude. Symbols are based on those used by the British Admiralty - users are referred to Symbols and *Abbreviations (NP 5011)*.

Contents

THE RCC PILOTAGE FOUNDATION

In 1976 an American member of the Royal Cruising Club, Dr Fred Ellis, indicated that he wished to make a gift to the Club in memory of his father, the late Robert E Ellis, of his friends Peter Pye and John Ives and as a mark of esteem for Roger Pinckney. An independent charity known as the RCC Pilotage Foundation was formed and Dr Ellis added his house to his already generous gift of money to form the Foundation's permanent endowment. The Foundation's charitable objective is 'to advance the education of the public in the science and practice of navigation', which is at present achieved through the writing and updating of pilot books covering many diffent parts of the world.

The Foundation is extremely grateful and privileged to have been given the copyrights to books written by a number of distinguished authors and yachtsmen including the late Adlard Coles, Robin Brandon and Malcolm Robson. In return the Foundation has willingly accepted the task of keeping the original books up to date and many yachtsmen and women have helped (and are helping) the Foundation fulfil this commitment. In addition to the titles donated to the Foundation, several new books have been created and developed under the auspices of the Foundation. The Foundation works in close collaboration with three publishers – Imray Laurie Norie and Wilson, Adlard Coles Nautical and On Board Publications – and in addition publishes in its own name short run guides and pilot books for areas where limited demand does not justify large print runs. Several of the Foundation's books have been translated into French, German and Italian.

The Foundation runs its own website at www.rccpf.org.uk which not only lists all the publications but also contains free downloadable pilotage information.

The overall management of the Foundation is entrusted to trustees appointed by the Royal Cruising Club, with day-to-day operations being controlled by the Director. All these appointments are unpaid. In line with its charitable status, the Foundation distributes no profits; any surpluses are used to finance new books and developments and to subsidise those covering areas of low demand.

PUBLICATIONS OF THE RCC PILOTAGE FOUNDATION

Imray
The Baltic Sea
Norway
North Brittany and
 the Channel Islands
Faroe, Iceland and
 Greenland
Isles of Scilly
The Channel Islands
South Biscay
North Biscay
Atlantic Islands
Atlantic Spain & Portugal

Mediterranean Spain
 Costas del Azahar,
 Dorada & Brava
Mediterranean Spain
 Costas del Sol & Blanca
Islas Baleares
Corsica and North
 Sardinia
Chile

Adlard Coles Nautical
Atlantic Crossing Guide
Pacific Crossing Guide
On Board Publications
South Atlantic Circuit
Havens and Anchorages for the South American Coast
The RCC Pilotage Foundation
Supplement to Falkland Island Shores
RCC PF Website www.rccpf.org.uk
Cruising Guide to West Africa
Supplements
Passage planning guides

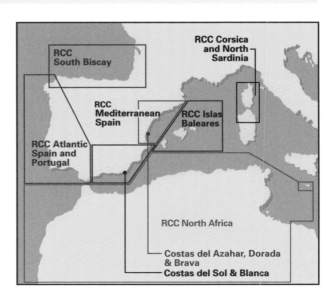

Foreword

The origins of this book go back to 1991 when Hans van Rijn provided, through the RCC Pilotage Foundation, cruising information for the south western Mediterranean shore. In 2002 Graham Hutt revised that work and extended it to include the Atlantic coast of Morocco. Until then many sailors bound for the Canary Islands passed well offshore to avoid an unknown coast line. Now many more yachts visit North Africa, with increasing numbers from North Europe, and further afield, joining French and Italian sailors to cruise or to over-winter.

Graham Hutt has extensive knowledge of the area, gained through visits in his own yacht and from his numerous contacts in the three North African countries, Gibraltar and the two island groups included here. In this book he provides both up to date pilotage information and sufficient description of each country to enable the first time visitor to better appreciate the culture and customs of those countries.

Cruising in North Africa is different to cruising in Europe and skippers should be prepared for this, both mentally and in their boat preparation and navigation. They must accept that changes may happen rapidly, both politically and in the infrastructure. In particular they should be aware that vigorous sea conditions near the Atlantic coast harbours may significantly affect depths of water available.

They should also be aware of the variety of chart datums in use by national hydrographic offices. Locations and waypoints to WGS84 have been introduced in this edition as an aid to navigating but attention is drawn to the notes on this subject in the Introduction. We invite yachtsmen to send us their observed WGS84 positions, as well as other updating matters, so that we can gradually extend our knowledge of positions to a common datum.

This pilot is by yachtsmen for yachtsmen. The Pilotage Foundation congratulates and thanks Graham Hutt for his continuing work, and also thanks the yachtsmen who have alerted us to changes taking place. We welcome feedback and contributions from those currently sailing these fascinating Atlantic and Mediterranean coasts so that we may continue to update this book when practicable.

Martin Walker
Director
RCC Pilotage Foundation
July 2005

Preface

The Arab countries of the Maghreb and Middle East have held a fascination for me over the past 37 years, since my first trip along the coast in 1966 from Tanger to Tripoli. I have lived in the Mediterranean for the past 25 years, owning different yachts over that time and sailing with my wife Anne and children: Ruth, Sera, Mark, Andrew and Ghada, as well as with many friends. We first lived aboard the 65 foot schooner *Arwen Palantir*, which took us on several trips along the North African coast, Syria and Turkey. Then *Orion*, a small delightful 29 foot Stella, on which we saw the Aegean and again, eastern Turkey. *Smoocher*, a friend's Golden Hind 32 took us to Beirut during the war years when the airport was closed and to the Greek Islands. Finally, the 48 foot sloop *Safwana*, which has experienced just about every port, anchorage and harbour in the Western Mediterranean and beyond, between Malta and the Canaries – many several times – over the past 16 years.

It is now six years since I completed the revision of Hans Van Rijn's *North Africa* for the 2nd edition. Many changes have since taken place necessitating this 3rd edition. There has been an incredible increase in the number of yachts visiting the shores of Tunisia and Morocco in the past two years, mostly from Italy and France. Algeria is once again being visited, though not without difficulty.

The addition of the Atlantic coast of Morocco in the last edition resulted in many more yachts visiting the ports along that coast. This is very encouraging, especially since it has been this section of the book which has needed the most revision, as many changes have taken place recently. New harbours have opened,

Europa Point, Gibraltar   *Graham Hutt*

facilities improved, some entrances silted and others changed completely.

It is a privilege to have been asked by the Pilotage Foundation to produce this edition, principally based on my own research over three summers and a winter cruising the coast of North Africa from the Atlantic to Malta since 2000.

However, this is not the work of one individual, and could not have been done without the input of many skippers who contributed information following their visits to these shores.

My thanks go to all who assisted with information and perspectives and to my wife and children who sailed for part of the time on recent trips to North Africa and who put up with great inconveniences at home during the preparation of this edition.

Finally, I would like to thank the Pilotage Foundation for entrusting me again with this project.

Graham Hutt
July 2005

2nd edition acknowledgements

Morocco The Ministry of Tourism: Moulay Hachem Kacimi and Mustapher El Aloui who arranged access to updated information and photographs of new port developments from the Chef de la Division Exploitation du Ports.

Cheikh Azouz and Amal Ghamrasni, in the Ports Technical Division, for their help in obtaining aerial photographs and charts.

Ali Belhaj for assisting with new chart information and verification of new ports.

Annette Ridout for photographs of northern Moroccan ports.

Serena Van Buskirk, who assisted with the historical information and insights.

Tunisia Mon. Houcine Sghaier, President Director General, Agence des Portes, et des Installations de Pêche.

Gibraltar
The Gibraltar Tourist Board for their help and to Di Stoddard who compiled the information.

3rd edition acknowledgements

Editorial assistance
Di Stoddard, who meticulously checked the text for both second and third editions and assisted with editing, spending many hours doing battle with her computer and the photocopier.

To Ros Hogbin of the RCC Pilotage Foundation who checked and assisted with editorial matters and proof readers: Petra and Jan Willem Versol (Morocco, Gibraltar), Mark Hutt (Algeria), Kit Power (Tunisia) and Walter Camilleri (Malta).

Thanks to the following who assisted by contributing information:

Morocco Andrew Firebrace, Yacht *Hecuba*. Yvonne & Bartek, Yacht *Tadorna*. Peter Honey, Yacht *Lillebolero of Duquesa*. Grahame & Lynne Brown, Yacht *Minaret* (who also contributed pictures of the Atlantic coast of Morocco). Petra and Jan Willem Versol, Yacht *Witte Raaf* (who also contributed a web site with information on Morocco). Jan Folkert Klazinga, Yacht *Ahab*, David Palmer Yacht *Zelenazaba*.

Algeria Jean Pierre David, Yacht *Futile*. Robert Dessureault, Yacht *Sortilege*.

Tunisia Françoise & Claire Goubert, Yacht *Samoa*. Kit Power, RCC Pilotage Foundation. Karim Ghannouchi, Captain of Sidi Bou Said Marina. Fadhel Rahoui, The Tunisian National Tourist Office, Tunis for information, pictures and brochures.

Malta Malta Tourist Authority for the supply of pictures and information.

Pantelleria and the Pelagie Islands Antonio Venanzio, Yacht *Red Fox*. Roberto, Carabinieri Marina Police

Gibraltar and N Morocco Alan Robinson, Alfer Sea School Gibraltar and to the many others too numerous to mention who contributed nuggets of information.

Photo credits used with permission are as follows:

Minaret: Grahame and Lynne Brown, yacht *Minaret*.
MTA: Malta Tourist Authority and Malta Maritime Authority.
TNTO: Tunisian National Tourist Authority.
Abdelmouttalib El Ghoulbzouri, Morocco.
Roberto: Officer of the Carabinieri, Italy.
Non-attributed pictures are either from my camera or from the previous edition.

The Author's yacht *Safwana*. 14m Hartley Fijian
Graham Hutt

INTRODUCTION

From the veranda of my house in Spain, on top of a hill overlooking Morocco and the Straits of Gibraltar, the awesome Mount Jebel Moussa looms in the background, close to the Spanish enclave of Ceuta. The vast continent of Africa is only fifteen miles away, but the significance of the separation, politically, economically and culturally, is indicated by the turbulent tidal waters flowing between the two continents.

Quickly giving way to calmer, non-tidal warmer waters once into the Mediterranean, the coast of North Africa: the Maghreb, opens out to present an unspoilt and challenging cruising ground, with miles of deserted beaches, quiet anchorages, sheer green mountainous coasts and ports with an ancient history, where yachtsmen will find a warm welcome. A cruise along the Maghrebian coast offers an insight into a totally different culture, but with a history closely linked to Europe. The Islamic culture has preserved a history almost locked in time in many places, especially further inland.

Whilst North Africa, apart from the East coast of Tunisia, was little visited in the past, cheap charter flights and a general reduction in airfares and travel costs, has meant that tourist facilities have been greatly improved, and without any deterioration of the sites of great historic interest.

Morocco

The Moroccan coast is virtually untouched by tourism and the majority of ports that can be visited are small fishing communities. Many ports have been in use for hundreds, and in some cases, thousands of years. Others are larger new commercial harbours, providing good shelter. Although not especially equipped for yachts, facilities are always made available and, more importantly, a typically friendly welcome awaits the visitor once the formalities are completed. Virtually the whole coast of Morocco, from its most eastern Mediterranean port of Ras el Ma, to the Atlantic port of Agadir, can be transited by day-hopping. The Atlantic coast is especially interesting, providing access to the fascinating interior of the country which has the most impressive Islamic monuments in the Maghreb. In spite of its Western orientation and considerable number of European tourists, Morocco retains a strong identity and vigorous culture, relatively unchanged for over a thousand years. One consequence of this is that harbours have not grown in size with the increasing number of visitors, so space is often tight.

Algeria

Algeria, is now a safe place to visit, though not without its difficulties. The political turmoil, which has resulted in endless bureaucracy on entry, is still in place, though changes are expected in the next two or three years that should improve matters.

The long Algerian coastline has many safe harbours offering good protection, though at present it is difficult to obtain a visa. There are many commercial ports without much traffic; a result of a declining economy. Several of the smaller harbours and anchorages are in beautiful quiet settings. A hospitable reception will be found almost everywhere, once clearance procedures have been completed. Moreover, steady easterlies in the summer make the Algerian coast a logical route for westbound yachts even if currently it is difficult to stop there.

Tunisia

Tunisia offers the most varied and established cruising area of all, with many harbours, from small fishing ports to several marinas. The landscape consists of isolated mountains in the north and shallow, tidal coastal areas in the south where the desert meets the sea. Few yachts venture S of Mahdia. The winters are mild and, as there are enough ports with good protection should the weather deteriorate, it is possible to continue cruising in the winter. As a result, an increasing number of yachts spend the winter in one of the four Tunisian marinas. There are many interesting historical sites to visit, reminders of the fact that this part of North Africa was once an important Roman province. Overland trips to the Berber dwellings in the south provide for interesting desert excursions to view a way of life unchanged through the centuries.

Libya

I had hoped to include Libya in this edition, having first learned the joy of sailing around Tripoli in the '60s. I worked hard to make this a reality, meeting with several top officials and diplomats, but in the end it proved impossible. Political will is there at the top but it could be some years before the result of nearly forty years of isolation is translated into a warm and friendly welcome to yachtsmen, despite the fast thawing political situation. It is, however, no longer unsafe for the adventurous to visit.

Gibraltar, Malta and the Pelagie Islands

Due to their proximity to North Africa, the islands of Malta, the Pelagie Islands and Pantelleria are included. Gibraltar, being close to Morocco, and Malta, only hours from Tunisia, offer excellent bases for provisioning and buying equipment as well as having international airports for crew changes. The Spanish enclaves of Ceuta and Melilla are also included because of their location on the African continent and their sailing attraction.

AIM OF THIS PILOT

The principal aim of this book is of course to present accurate pilotage information to assist navigation.

Although only a short distance from Europe, the Maghreb represents a huge leap in cultures and my desire is also to enable the yachtsman visiting for the first time to feel informed, know what to expect and to quickly adjust in order to fully enjoy and appreciate the rich culture and history of the area. The adventurous yachtsman will find information on almost every port in North Africa, from the eastern Tunisian border with Libya to the southern Moroccan Atlantic ports bordering Mauritania, a coastline of around 2,300 miles.

The plans have been simplified in order to present relevant information only. The harbour information is based on experience gained from visiting the ports.

Almost any visitor to North Africa will want to see the many historical sights all over the region. For this reason, more historical information is included than would normally be the case in a nautical pilot and sailing handbook.

SOCIO–CULTURAL GUIDELINES

Islam is the official religion in the Maghreb. Unlike in Europe, politics, religion and language are inextricably linked in Arab Muslim countries. Arabic itself is considered the language of the religion and is full of expressions, phrases and proverbs taken from the Qu'ran, which are in everyday use. The political nature and law of the Arab world is also based on Islam. Some countries invoke Shariah law, based on the teachings of the Qu'ran, while others have a more secular approach, or a duel system. Dress and most aspects of life are prescribed according to the Qu'ran and this practice is little changed since the 7th C. Islamic beliefs, observances and laws are well described in the travel guides listed, but a few relevant notes are included here.

Language

Arabic is the official language in the Maghreb, but in most places French is also spoken. Along the coast of Morocco many of the older people speak Spanish and the young guides in Tunisia and particularly Morocco often speak several other European languages. In commercial ports, the officials will usually speak a little English. Signs in Algeria are usually only in Arabic, while in Tunisia and Morocco they are in both Arabic and French. The Berber languages are widely spoken in Morocco and Algeria and there are many dialects: Kabyle, Soussi, Tamazight, Tashalhyat, as well as Derija, the colloquial Arabic. Though each country has its own dialect there is a lot of overlap. Classical Arabic is the written form uniting the whole Arab world. Its vocabulary and form is quite different from the colloquial languages spoken.

It will help considerably in dealing with officials and for the first steps ashore to speak at least a little French.

Kelibia, Tunisia: one of many ancient fortresses around the coast   *Graham Hutt*

Roman mosaic floor in Volubulis, Morocco   *Graham Hutt*

Islamic architecture: King Hassan II mosque, Casablanca
Graham Hutt

Religion

There are five calls to prayer every day, announced from the minarets. Friday is the weekly holy day. The most important annual celebration is Ramadan, the month of fasting, when Muslims do not eat, drink, smoke or have sex between sunrise and sunset. One should be discreet in public about eating, drinking and smoking during this period in order not to cause offence. Many restaurants are closed during the day and shops and markets only open later in the afternoon. The evenings give way to celebrations and special pastries are made during this period. Several lesser feasts or *Eids* are celebrated to commemorate events in their history. The next Ramadan begins on 4 October 2005. Each year it is approximately 11 days earlier.

It is forbidden for Muslims to eat pork or blood and all meat is prepared in a special *Halal* prescribed way. Though alcohol is widely available and wine and beer industries thrive in the Maghreb, strict Muslims do not indulge.

Cultural differences

There are substantial differences between the way Europeans behave, think and believe, and the way a Muslim does. Devotion to extended family, the call to prayer, obedience to the Qu'ran and Islamic teaching are but a few. It is easy to observe behaviour and draw conclusions based on our own culture, misinterpreting differences. In the Maghreb for example, as in many Mediterranean countries, holding hands and walking arm in arm is as customary amongst men as with women, and is in no way an indication of orientation.

It is common to see devout Muslims praying in public if they cannot get to a mosque. This highlights an important aspect of Muslim life: they are proud to be Muslims and to display the fact. Although many Christians make a public confession of their faith in various ways, few would so publicly worship God as an individual, in the way a devout Muslim does.

Perhaps one of the most remarkable and pleasant aspects of the Arab culture, is the hospitality afforded to a complete stranger. In areas where few yachtsmen visit, you will be invited to visit homes and receive a warm welcome by the whole family. Arabs have a deep sense of responsibility to care for strangers and provide hospitality. It is not uncommon to arrive in some ports and be invited to an official's home for cous-cous. This is a genuine act and they will be honoured by your accepting the invitation: it is disrespectful to decline.

Attitudes towards women

The relationship between men and women in the Arab world is quite different from that in the west. In public they lead different lives and this is continued in the home when guests are around.

Films, television and the inconsiderate behaviour of some tourists have helped to reinforce the idea that western women are promiscuous. Some men are quite curious about western women, who can be made to feel uncomfortable by their attention, and this is particularly true in some tourist centres. Considerate behaviour and dress code for women and men will command respect from locals and consequently avert any potential problems.

In order to really enjoy the pleasures of the Maghreb and the hospitality of the people, it is necessary to suspend prejudice and respect their culture.

Fundamentalism

Many westerners express fear about visiting any Muslim country because of the events of 9/11. You are more likely to win the lottery than be confronted with this problem. Most Moslems are not fanatics and object to the way they are perceived because of the actions of a minority. Even in Algeria, which has suffered more than any other country in the Maghreb, the least affected parts have been the northern coastline and not a single incident has been reported affected seagoing vessels.

Security

One of the most pleasant aspects of visiting North Africa is the security. The surveillance of every port and vessel is high everywhere and there is virtually no theft. Yachts can be left unattended for trips inland without any problems whatsoever in most places. There are some exceptions and these are noted where appropriate. More problems are attributable to other yachtsmen, than to locals. For latest information and advice on travel to any particular country, see the British Foreign Office web site. http://www.fco.gov.uk/servlet (Travel Advice by Country).

Peaceful men of Morocco   *Graham Hutt*

Dghaisa, traditional water taxi of Malta   *Graham Hutt*

Bakhshish

This could be a problem for those who are untravelled and has the potential to ruin your visit if not appreciated.

Bakhshish is money paid as a tip, often to speed up a bureaucratic process. It is a common practice throughout the world, though not so evident in Europe and North America. It usually involves a very small amount of money, a small gift: a packet of cigarettes, in a country where salaries are very low. It is best to respect this practice as part of the local tradition. Keep it in perspective as a minor issue and avoid making value judgements about it. Try to think of giving bakhshish as analogous to tipping in restaurants, or as a gift to people who have helped you. After all, there are few other charges to pay.

In its mildest form bakhshish involves pressure on you to pay for unsolicited services. For instance, on returning to your parked car someone will appear out of nowhere and ask for a fee for 'looking after it'. Since you only need to pay the equivalent of a few pence and, after all, he must have been watching it to have noticed your return, it is better to give something and abandon any sense of resentment at paying a few pence for a service you did not request. It can be used to advantage by asking for somebody to keep an eye on your yacht, bike or car. It will only cost you a dollar or two for a day, but will ensure your security and give food to someone who has a very small wage to survive on.

There is a more serious form of bakhshish which may involve paying to do what you are in any case entitled to. When police or customs officials come on board, they may well expect a gift of cigarettes, money, wine or spirits. Some will blatantly ask for it. This is perfectly normal, especially in Morocco and southern Tunisia. Although they will never coerce you to give, it will save a great deal of aggravation and possibly hours of your time if you are prepared to comply. It is wise to carry on board cartons of cigarettes especially for this purpose. The governments, having accepted that this offends some tourists, are trying to reduce this behaviour, especially from port officials.

Photography

In tourist areas, photography is usual and not a problem. Inland, taking pictures of people can be offensive. It is wise to ask first, but in any case be discreet. Beware of taking pictures in possibly sensitive areas: police buildings, military areas, gunboats etc.

Hammams

The Arab word *hammam* means 'healthy spot' and in the Maghreb this is the name for the public steam baths which are found in every town and village. Rather like a Turkish bath, it is a very interesting and refreshing experience to visit a *hammam*. They are always clean, (especially when compared to some marina showers!), and very inexpensive. Many of them have trained masseurs. A swimsuit is needed but generally soap and towels are supplied and you splash yourself with buckets of hot and cold water. Where *hammams* are found they are listed under the port description but, although often inconspicuous, they are everywhere. There are either separate hours or separate *hammams* for men and women.

MARITIME INFORMATION

Suitable types of yacht

These cruising grounds do not require a particular type of vessel, although a good engine is essential as there are periods in summer without wind – and you will frequently encounter strong winds when entering a harbour in the early evening, when the wind is often at its maximum before dying down at sunset. A few additions or modifications may be worthwhile to ensure a more comfortable time on these shores. See *Yacht equipment recommended* on page 14.

The shallower waters in the south of Tunisia will be out of reach of deep keeled yachts.

In common with climatic changes everywhere, short-lived severe gales are becoming a more common feature even in summer. These are usually sudden and unexpected squalls, especially in the area S of Sicily and along the N coast of Tunisia. Yachts should be prepared to encounter such winds, at least on rare occasions.

Meteorology

It should be noted that visual signs and methods of forecasting using clouds and barometer, as is usual in Northern Europe, often do not give the same indications in the Mediterranean, as you travel E from the Straits of Gibraltar. It is common to see a fast falling or rising barometer, with no resulting change in conditions. Similarly, cloud formations that we would usually associate with rain or storms approaching, often clear in minutes, leaving blue skies. Sudden winds or squalls can appear very quickly without any warning. These unannounced changes are normally short-lived. This situation changes near the Straits of Gibraltar and on the Atlantic coast of Morocco, where weather patterns are more predictable and long range forecasts are usually quite accurate. Winds along the North African coast and in the Straits of Gibraltar are often very localised. Winds of up to force 8 are often present at Tarifa, whilst in Gibraltar or Tanger, just a few miles away, they can be negligible.

Winds

The N coast of Africa can be divided into sections with varying general wind conditions.

1. **The Atlantic Coast of Morocco**
   The northern sector of this coast maintains a predominantly SW airstream, occasionally swinging to the NW or NE. In the winter months, strong gales frequently sweep through the area, as depressions move NNE from the Canaries through the Straits of Gibraltar and continue in a NE direction across Spain. In summer, the wind tends to be steady by day from SW, dropping at sunset. Further south, around Essaouira and beyond, winds are predominately from the NW, reaching 20kts by day and dying down at night. Gales are rare in summer months.

2. **The Straits of Gibraltar**
   Winds are almost always either E or W, equal in duration. If wind strength by day reaches around 20kts, it almost always drops at night. In winter, winds are predominantly E or W, but with frequent

swings to the SW, which usually indicates a depression with rain. Very occasionally in winter, NE winds carry very cold air to the area, usually accompanied by a long period of settled weather.

3. **The coast of Morocco and Algeria to Oran**
   Roughly from Ceuta to Oran in Algeria, E and W winds are about equal in frequency in the summer. As in many parts of the Mediterranean, quite often there is too little wind to sail in the summer and the winds do not dictate any favourable sailing direction. In the winter, winds from the W sector are more common.

4. **The coast of Algeria from Oran E to Cap Bon**
   From Oran eastward, W winds predominate in the winter. In spring and through summer, a steady E wind blows in a zone of 25M off the Algerian coast. Around midday it can reach up to 25kts and at sunset it usually dies down. Therefore a summer cruise along the N coast of Algeria can best be planned from E to W. In October, winds from the W sector become more frequent, until they predominate in the winter. Around Bizerte, Tunisia, strong NW winds are common in the summer and NW to E winds are usual in the Gulf of Tunis. Strong, warm, southerly winds of short duration frequently blow at night near the coast.

5. **From Cap Bon to the Libyan Border**
   On the E coast of Tunisia the wind regime is markedly different from the other areas, with onshore E winds in the summer and offshore W winds in winter. The summer sea breeze usually starts in the morning from the NE and after veering to the SE dies down around sunset. In springtime it can reach up to Force 5-6. In winter the situation is reversed with mostly westerlies.

   Between Sfax and Jerba winds are invariably from the E in spring and summer. The winter winds in this area are more evenly distributed around the clock, with a slightly higher percentage of W winds.

Levante cloud over Gibraltar creates gloomy conditions in the town   *Graham Hutt*

Strong wind hazards

Summer gales, once a rarity, are now more common, especially around Bizerte and to a lesser extent, Gabès, Tunisia though usually short lived. Winter gales on the N coast of Tunisia are generally stronger and more frequent than on the coast of Algeria and are most often from the NW. In NE Tunisia, especially around Cap Bon, sudden wind shifts are likely. On the E coast of Tunisia, gales are rare in summer and infrequent in winter but strong easterlies build up a nasty sea around Kelibia, making it difficult to enter the port. Bizerte and Pantelleria have the strongest average winds all year round. Local depressions develop over the Gulf of Gabès in winter and strong winds are common. Occasionally gales are recorded.

Scirocco is the name widely used in the Mediterranean for southerly Sahara winds which bring hot air laden with red dust. Fortunately it does not occur very often nor does it last very long. It is essential to clean off the resulting dust from sails as soon as possible or it will leave a stain.

Winter gales are more frequent in the Straits of Gibraltar and, in recent years, have brought torrential rain that can last for several days at a time, sometimes with wet unsettled weather lasting for weeks from January to March. These are the result of seasonal depressions moving NNE from the Canaries.

Rain

Rainfall varies considerably in the region from less than 200mm yearly in Gabès to 330mm in Sousse, 420mm in Tunis to almost 800mm in Annaba and Algiers and around 1200mm in Aïn Draham up in the mountains on the N coast of Tunisia. Around the Straits of Gibraltar and the Moroccan Atlantic coast, the weather pattern has changed markedly recently: annual rainfall has doubled in the past three years, after many years of drought. Fortunately for sailors, practically all of it falls in winter. 2004 was an exceptional winter with most depressions moving NW of the Straits towards Portugal, resulting in very little rain.

Waterspouts

Waterspouts generally occur in the vicinity of thunderstorms and most commonly at the end of summer. They can cause considerable damage. Their paths seem to follow the clouds and it is usually possible to sail out of their way. In the area around Algiers, many waterspouts are often seen together.

Visibility

Fog is rare, but occasionally occurs in summer in the Straits of Gibraltar, where it can be a nuisance. It is a phenomenon associated with an easterly (levante) wind and usually forms suddenly around 10am as the land temperature rises, clearing soon after midday in the Eastern Straits. Hazy conditions with a visibility of around four miles are common in summer along the Tunisian E coast and the Atlantic Moroccan coast. Visibility is reduced in a scirocco.

'Flying Saucer' clouds: Indication of strong E winds to come in 2–3 days
Graham Hutt

WEATHER FORECASTS

Radio

The Italian Maritime authorities 'Meteomar' operate a VHF weather station on Ch 68 which can be received from the Islas Baleares and Tabarka through to the S Adriatic sea and can be picked up in Malta. This alternates between English and Italian throughout 24 hours with occasional breaks for updating. It is not always accurate in forecasting local conditions, but generally gives a reliable outlook over a 3-day period.

Monaco 3AC

Probably the next most useful general weather forecast for the North African coast is given by Monaco Radio on SSB, although it will have to be interpreted to predict winds along the Tunisian coast.

Monaco 3AC broadcasts on 8728 and 8806kHz usB at 0715 and 1830 in French and English. The texts are those broadcast by INMARSAT-C for the western part of METAREA III. Monaco also broadcasts on 4363kHz at 0903 and 1915 LT in French and English and at 1403 in French only. Texts are as the latest Toulon NAVTEX broadcast.

UK Maritime Mobile Net

The Net, covering the Eastern Atlantic and the Mediterranean, can be heard daily on 14303kHz USB at 0800 and 1800 UT. On Saturday morning the broadcast sometimes contains a longer period outlook. Forecasts will be a rehash of what the Net leader has gleaned from various sources. No licence is required to receive on any frequency.

The Algerian SSB stations in Oran, Algiers and Annaba are difficult to receive, even along the coast, and are a partial retransmission of French weather forecasts.

In several Algerian and some Tunisian ports, weather forecasts, which will be gladly supplied to yachts, are available from the capitainerie, *marine marchande* or sometimes a small *Météo* office in the port. These are mentioned in the port descriptions.

All weather forecasts for Tunisia are in French.

Tunis Radio and Sfax Radio provide a good, although not always accurate forecast on SSB and this is probably the best for winds along the Tunisian coast. The National Broadcast Authority has a useful report on Radio Tunis Ch 2 (Chaine International) on medium wave. Also useful for obtaining information on winds out at sea are the transmissions of the Italian station Radio Due which are retransmitted in Tunisia.

For the area of Gibraltar, including a 5-mile radius covering Northern Morocco, good forecasts can be obtained from Gibraltar Radio throughout the day on FM92.6MHz and AM1458kHz. These stations can only be received if you are in the immediate vicinity of Gibraltar.

Accurate forecasts can be obtained from the local harbour authorities.

Radio fax and teleprinter

Northwood (RN) broadcasts a full set of UK Met Office charts out to 5 days ahead on 2618.5, 4610, 8040 and 11086.5kHz. (Schedule at 0236, surface analysis at 3-hourly intervals from 0300 to 2100 and 2300.) Deutscher Wetterdienst broadcasts German weather charts on 3855, 7880 and 13882.5kHz. (Schedule at 1111, surface analysis at 0430, 1050, 1600, 2200.)

DWD broadcasts forecasts using RTTY on 4583, 7646 and 10001.8kHz (in English at 0415 and 1610), 11039 and 14467.3kHz (in German at 0535). Note that 4583 and 14467.3kHz may not be useable in the Mediterranean. The most useful services are forecasts up to 5 days ahead at 12-hourly intervals and up to 2 days ahead at 6-hour intervals. Alternatively, a dedicated receiver 'Weatherman' will record it automatically: see www.nasamarine.com.

NAVTEX AND INMARSAT-C

NAVTEX and INMARSAT-C are the primary GMDSS modes for transmission of all Marine Safety Information. Broadcast times for weather are as follows

Transmitter	Times (UTC)
Tarifa – G (518kHz)	0900 and 2100
Cabo la Nao – X (Valencia) (518kHz)	0750 and 1950
Las Palmas – I (518kHz)	0920, 1320, 1720
Cagliari – T (518kHz)	0710 and 1910
August – V (518kHz)	0730 and 1930
La Garde – W (Toulon) (518kHz)	1140 and 2340
La Garde – S (Toulon) (490kHz)	0700 and 1900
INMARSAT-C METAREA III	1000 and 2200

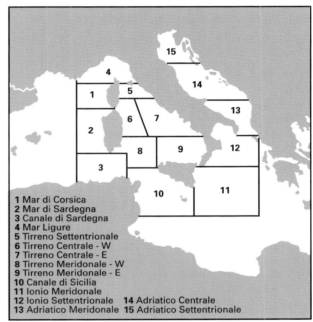

1 Mar di Corsica
2 Mar di Sardegna
3 Canale di Sardegna
4 Mar Ligure
5 Tirreno Settentrionale
6 Tirreno Centrale - W
7 Tirreno Centrale - E
8 Tirreno Meridonale - W
9 Tirreno Meridonale - E
10 Canale di Sicilia
11 Ionio Meridonale
12 Ionio Settentrionale   14 Adriatico Centrale
13 Adriatico Meridionale   15 Adriatico Settentrionale

Italy. Forecast areas

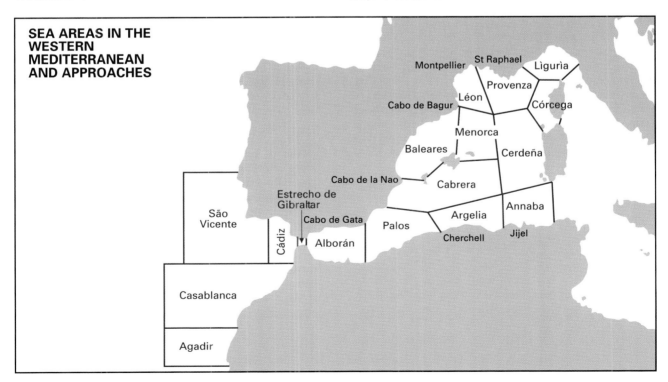

SEA AREAS IN THE WESTERN MEDITERRANEAN AND APPROACHES

Forecast frequencies and times

Time (UT)	Station	Frequency	Language
0715, 1715	Monaco Radio	8728.2kHz	French/ English
0805, 1705	Tunis Radio	1820kHz	French
0630, 1230	Radio Tunis	962kHz	French
0500, 1335, 2035	Radio Due	846kHz	Italian
0933, 1733	Sfax Radio	2719kHz	French

The forecast on Tunis Radio (SSB) starts with the AVURNAV, the *Avis Urgence aux Navigateur*, the Notice to Mariners.

The weather report begins with a general description of the weather systems followed by the 24-hour forecast for the three regions of Tunisia:

Zone du Nord, the coast from Tabarka to Cap Bon

Zone du Nord Est, the coast from Cap Bon to Mahdia and

Zone du Golfe de Gabès, the coast from Mahdia to Zarzis.

At the end of the forecast, the outlook for the following 24 hours is given.

The wind speed is given in knots, wave height in feet and visibility in nautical miles.

Internet

Many sites provide weather information and most, even the official sites, do change from time to time. As a good starting point, the RCCPF recommends Frank Singleton's site at www.franksingleton.clara.net Also see technical matters at www.rccpf.org.uk. Skippers are urged to use the Internet as a supplementary source of information and to ensure that GMDSS forecasts can be obtained on board.

GRIB coded forecasts (Saildocs)

This is a service set up by sailors in the USA. It enables arrow diagram forecasts, for up to 5 days ahead, and other information to be obtained in email form (or by Marine HF and HAM radio). The data is highly compressed, so that a great deal of information can be acquired quickly and at low cost – even using a mobile phone connected to a laptop computer. For details see websites above. There is no charge for this service. In addition Saildocs can provide the text to any web page stripped of all pictures and dropdowns. This is useful for getting texts of forecasts from the Spanish Met service site from which downloads are very slow.

SEA CONDITIONS

Currents

An E-going current sets along the coast from Gibraltar into the Mediterranean, stemming from the flow of Atlantic water into the Mediterranean, replacing water lost through evaporation. Within the Straits, during prolonged periods of easterly or westerly wind, currents caused by a combination of tidal flow, surface wind and standing current, can reach up to 6kts at HWS. This is more fully explained in the section *Transiting the Straits* on page 33.

Once into the Mediterranean, currents can reach 2kts around some promontories in the Al Hoceïma area, Morocco. Between Melilla and Jebha, 1.5M offshore, an unexplained W-going current is experienced, which can be used to advantage if going W. Off the Algerian coast, it runs E at between 0.5 and 1kt.

In the Sicilian Channel there is a constant SE current averaging about 1kt in summer. This can mean a rough ride heading W around Cap Bon, with its predominantly NW wind against this current. Currents off the Tunisian coast are weaker and less predictable but they can affect navigation when on passage from Pantelleria or Lampedusa.

The Atlantic coast of Morocco has a S-going current averaging 0.5kt.

Tides

Tidal ranges on the Moroccan coast from the western Straits of Gibraltar to the Canaries is around 3m, with little difference in timing from Gibraltar, which is a standard port. At Gibraltar it is around 1m, reducing rapidly once clear of Europa Point heading E, becoming negligible 10M into the Mediterranean, until Tunisia is reached.

South from La Chebba, on the SE coast of Tunisia, the range is again noticeable and in Gabès the spring range is 1.8m. In the shallow waters around the Kerkennah Islands the range can be 1m and appropriate allowances must be made. There are also strong tidal currents in the channels around the islands. Strong onshore winds can increase the range. In the Ajim Channel between the island of Jerba and the mainland, tidal currents are even stronger and navigation is made more difficult by the lack of reliable buoys.

Though rare, the *marrobbio*, a tidal surge with a period of between 10 and 26 minutes, can raise the water level during undisturbed weather. There are also gradual fluctuations during winter, when the mean level in the central Mediterranean can fall as much as 0.5m below normal. These differences are often associated with barometric pressure: high pressure causes lower water levels and vice versa. A range of around 1m can be experienced in otherwise non-tidal waters due to these barometric pressure differences, which are more noticeable in the eastern Mediterranean. Take this into account when exploring some of the smaller fishing ports with critical depths.

Swell

In summer, the Mediterranean is usually calm, except during prolonged periods of strong E or W winds. A daily wind at the western end usually dies around sunset. However, there are occasional gales which can very quickly whip up huge steep seas, though these are usually short lived. In July and August flat calms are often experienced, lasting for days. In winter, gales are more frequent and occasionally last for several days, whipping up high seas.

On the Atlantic coast of Morocco, a long swell from the SW or NW prevails. In summer this can be between 1 and 2m. In winter it is often 3 to 5m.

In the Straits of Gibraltar, the sea conditions depend very much on the state of the tide and wind direction. Strong E or W winds can create high seas at HW.

MARINE LIFE

In comparison with other parts of the Mediterranean, marine life along the Maghreb coast is relatively rich and sea pollution is far less. The countries are not as developed as in Europe, conservation measures have been taken by the governments and the coast is not as densely populated as the northern shores of the Mediterranean. The fishing fleets of the Maghreb are made up of small vessels which do not scour the seabed as effectively as the larger boats of the Italian or Spanish fleets and both Morocco and Algeria have a continental shelf too narrow to support large scale fishing activity. Tunisia, on the other hand, which is possibly one of the richest fishing grounds in the Mediterranean, has a very wide continental shelf. It still has potential for further exploitation and this is why many new fishing ports have been built recently and why their fishing fleet is expanding. Along the Moroccan and Algerian coast sardines, mackerel, various kinds of sea bream, grey mullet, red mullet, prawns, bonito, swordfish, tuna and shark are common. Along the E coast of Tunisia the mackerel disappears and red mullet become rare but octopus are abundant along with grouper and dentex.

Dolphins are common in the Straits of Gibraltar and along the Moroccan and Algerian coasts, where several pods of differing species live. Some of these families are up to 40 strong. Whenever transiting the Straits or crossing from Spain to Morocco, they will accompany your yacht, weaving in and out and crossing your bows at great speed. Pilot whales and occasionally other species of whale and shark will also be seen in the area. Hammerhead sharks, tuna and swordfish are often seen in the area between Ceuta and Cabo de Negro.

Fishing methods

Single boats trawl off the coast and on the edge of the continental shelf in depths up to about 400m.

Large circular nets are set for sardines and mackerel. The main boat, with a crew of sometimes up to 30, lays a floating net in a large circle. One or two of the small auxiliary boats enter the net and attract the fish with powerful lights. Then the bottom of the net is closed and hauled in.

Long lines, with a multitude of short lines furnished with baited hooks, are used mainly for swordfish. The long line is kept afloat with small pieces of styrofoam every 150m or so. Usually only the end buoys are lit and the fishermen patrol the length of the line.

Floating nets are usually laid close to the shore, around harbour entrances and in bays. This is real subsistence fishing as the catch is minimal. It also presents a hazard to sailing boats, particularly in Tunisia as the nets are easily caught around the propeller.

The traditional fishing technique of the Kerkennah Islands uses traps made of palm fronds to divert the fish into nets. The palm fronds are planted more or less permanently in the shallow banks, at right angles to the coast line.

In the S of Tunisia, baked clay pots are used to catch octopus. The pots are strung together and laid on the sandy bottom. Octopus prefer to seek protection in a hole and since the sandy bottom does not provide this,

Dolphins always accompany yachts passing through the Straits   *Graham Hutt*

they crawl in the clay pot. Other fishermen still use the ancient net throwing method in the shallows off the shores of southern Tunisia.

Tunny nets

The coast of North Africa and Morocco in particular, is famous for its tuna fishing and has been for thousands of years. Tunisia derived its name from the industry. Early coins from the ancient city of Lixus in Morocco bear the tuna fish engraved on them, proof of the importance of this industry as far back as Carthaginian times (around the 4th century BC). Tuna was preserved for export in vast factories, which derived salt from the nearby salt pans, in an age when ice was not available. These pans are still in use today, just below the ruins of Lixus and extending to the port of Larache in N Morocco.

This unique sense of ongoing history is a most endearing feature of North Africa. However, the industry also presents a navigational hazard to watch out for. Tuna (tunny) nets are often laid 4M out to sea from the shore. It has been reported that in the area of El Jadida, Morocco, they can extend further. They are laid out from April to December and are often placed in the same position from one year to the next. These nets consist of a heavy steel cable connected to floats and a deep-weighted net, which pulls down the floats so that they may be almost invisible. Usually, one can assume they are present when small boats are close inshore, with larger ones further out to sea – if they are obviously not trawling. The end marker usually has a flag, either on a buoy, or fixed to a short mast on a small dinghy. These also, often cannot be seen until one is almost upon them.

The nets are supposed to be clearly marked. However, in practice it is very difficult to spot them until a mile or less away and they are almost never lit at night. It is not possible to pass them on the landward side, so substantial deviations have to be made if your vessel is close inshore. They are laid every year between Ceuta and Marina Smir, Morocco, between Cap Spartel and Asilah and near to Larache, as well as along parts of the coast of Algeria and Tunisia.

Daunting as this may seem, don't feel intimidated by this hazard, for once you are used to spotting the tell-tale signs of these nets, there really is no problem in avoiding them. Wherever they are normally set, a note is included under the appropriate harbour.

Harpoon fishing

There are many places where harpoon fishing can be rewarding for an experienced snorkel diver. Most probably this will be a more reliable way to catch fish than trolling or fishing with a rod. As in Europe, harpooning when scuba diving is considered unethical and is forbidden. The attitude to harpooning when snorkelling is ambivalent. In most harbours, locals will be seen with harpoons snorkelling from the breakwaters. It is unlikely that official permission would be given if asked for, so it is best to proceed with discretion.

In 1990 new rules were issued in Tunisia for divers who come specifically for harpoon fishing. These foreign visitors can only receive permission when working from a Tunisian flagged boat. Applications can be sent through a local Tunisian diving club or the FAST (Fédération des Activités Subaquatique de Tunisie), BP 284, 1004 Tunis ☎ 239659.

To what extent yachtsmen cruising Tunisian waters will be affected remains to be seen.

The following are some of the good areas for snorkelling:

Morocco Cabo de Negro, El Jebha (bream, sea bass), Al Hoceïma and Ras-el-Ma.
Algeria Beni-Saf, Habibas Islands and the coast E of Bejaïa as far as Annaba.
Tunisia Cap Carthage (sea bass), around Cap Bon and La Chebba.

Scuba diving

Diving bottles on board a yacht are a problem to customs officials in many countries, including the Maghreb and diving is sure to attract attention from authorities. This is because the equipment is usually associated with a commercial activity requiring a licence, including diving on wrecks. As long it is only to observe or photograph, it may be allowed but any other activity will certainly require official permission. It is best to check beforehand with local officials to avoid any problems. Diving schools operate in several ports in Tunisia, Gibraltar, Ceuta and Malta and it is possible to participate in daily diving trips, especially in the summer months. Diving bottles can be filled and tested in Gibraltar. In Ceuta, several ports in Tunisia and in Morocco, wherever coral or sponge fishermen operate, one can arrange to get bottles filled.

Coral and sponge fishing

Recent laws to assist conservation have meant that harvesting coral and sponge are now licensed activities and few hold the necessary permission. Instead, a

Tunny nets often extend for miles from the coast and pose a navigational hazard   *Graham Hutt*

Sealife in the Mediterranean around Lampedusa   *Roberto*

healthy new tourist industry has developed by taking scuba divers to see and admire the coral reefs in situ.

Flora and fauna

The flora and fauna of North Africa is closer to that of Southern Europe than to the rest of Africa; the Sahara has been an impassable barrier for most plants and animals. In the S of Tunisia and Libya, the Sahara almost reaches the shore but in Morocco, Algeria and Northern Tunisia the coastal areas support a good variety of plant and animal life.

The flora has adapted itself to the cool and humid winters when snow only falls on the high mountains and the mild and wet spring when plants grow quickly. During the long hot and dry summer most of the vegetation wilts or dies and the land looks dry and barren.

The most common vegetation is the maquis. The typical Mediterranean scrubby underbrush; *Erica arborea*, dwarf palm, cytisus, holly, evergreen oak and pine trees are the primary vegetation. The prickly pear (*Opuntia*) has been introduced from America and eucalyptus from Australia is perhaps too successful in reforestation projects.

The majority of the population lives in the coastal plains and most of the soil is cultivated. In the spring there are big orange and yellow-coloured flower beds interrupted by blue lupins and yellow lathyrus. Since the plains have been cultivated for centuries, it is hard to imagine what the original landscape looked like but most likely it was made up of grassland, wild olive trees and cork oaks. Today all olive trees are cultivated but some of the original wild cork oak forests remain. The sandy soil on which they thrive has little value to mankind.

The pine and cedar covered slopes of the Rif Mountains in Morocco resemble the Sierra Nevada but, as in Spain, human habitation has taken its toll. Pine forests have been cut for building material or firewood and grazing goats have cleared low shrubs and trees. Through reforestation programmes, financially supported by the developed countries, a continuous effort is made to halt soil erosion, but the effect is offset by the increased need for farmland to feed the rapidly growing population in all of the Maghreb countries.

Numerous species of birds cross the Mediterranean strip as they migrate to and from northern Europe. Small animals like the weasel, otter and genet (genetta, a cat common in Southern Europe), are resident. Until the beginning of this century lions were found in NE Algeria and Tunisia but are now extinct. In the Middle and High Atlas of Morocco, leopards survive alongside more common red foxes and jackals. Wild boar are common in the N of Tunisia and Algeria, where hunting is allowed.

Typical domestic animals of North Africa are goats and sheep which are still kept by migrating shepherds. Dromedaries, mules and donkeys are particularly common in Morocco and Tunisia.

NAVIGATIONAL INFORMATION

Buoyage

Buoyage is practically non-existent in Morocco and Algeria. Parts of the Tunisian shallows are buoyed using the Cardinal system, whilst elsewhere anything from rusty oil drums to plastic bottles are used to mark channels, wrecks or reefs. Except for those which are important to commercial shipping, the position, characteristic (particularly lights), even the existence of buoys cannot be relied on.

Lights

Every effort has been made to acquire accurate information on lights. However maintenance is poor and, for instance in Tunisia, though the Navy is responsible for lights, it has no institutionalised way of reporting defects. Do not expect the lights to correspond exactly with the information in this or any other book. Generally, lighthouses and harbour lights in the bigger commercial ports are reliable but in the small ports and even the marinas they are not, so exercise extreme caution during night entries.

Radio beacons

Since the accuracy of GPS – even given the cautions below – is well above that which can be derived from radio beacons, this information is of diminishing value and many stations are no longer maintained.

A note on depths around harbour entrances

Depths where known are shown on the harbour plans. It should be noted, however, that these can and do change. This is especially true where onshore gales are a regular feature, where harbour entrances are open towards the gale sector, and near rivers. This applies particularly to the Atlantic Moroccan coastline where W gales are common and the E Tunisian coastline where harbours face NE gales. Although most ports and harbours are dredged, there is no certainty about the depth to which dredging has taken place or when it was last done. Always proceed with caution, paying attention to the depth sounder on entry to any harbour.

IMPORTANT NOTE ON WAYPOINTS AND LOCATION CO-ORDINATES

Waypoints have been added in this edition to assist with passage planning and harbour approach. These are of limited value and should be treated with caution due to the situation described below.

The World Geodetic System 1984 (WGS84) is now the standard datum for all new charts and therefore the system selected on most GPS receivers. However, most charts of the S Mediterranean – even recent reprints – have not been issued using this datum. There is often a note giving the necessary information to correct a GPS position to the chart, but the correction is usually different for each chart and often different on the same chart where several ports are printed on the same sheet. French SHOM charts, British Admiralty, Italian and American charts of the same area all use a different datum. On many charts the datum cannot be established at all.

This means that a latitude and longitude derived from a GPS receiver selected to WGS 84, though accurately giving the yachts position to within a few metres, may display a difference of 300m or more when plotted on the chart and referenced to land. In several areas along the Moroccan Atlantic coast and in Tunisia the error is 1.5 miles, though this degree of error is unusual. This problem, though not important offshore, obviously becomes critical when sailing in shallow or confined waters.

In view of the datum uncertainties, the author considers that within 500 metres of any danger, waypoint navigation should be discarded and other means, such as transits or leading lines used. This should allow sufficient margin of error around any waypoint regardless of datum (though there are exceptions where the error is greater).

Co-ordinates contained in this edition have, where possible, been referenced to a physical location on which a GPS WGS 84 datum fix has been obtained. Waypoint names indicate the nearest port location and will usually be 2–4 miles off the port.

Harbour 'Location' co-ordinates will be in the harbour entrance unless otherwise stated and should not be considered as waypoints.

Latitude and longitude graticules shown on plans are derived from the current official chart.

This problem of relating satellite fixes to charts will be resolved when all charts have been re-issued to the WGS 84 datum.

A note on the British Admiralty chart covering the Atlantic coast sums up the official Admiralty advice under the heading:

Satellite derived positions

'Positions obtained from satellite navigation systems such as GPS are normally referred to the World Geodetic System 1984 datum. The differences between GPS positions and positions on this chart cannot be determined. Mariners are warned these differences MAY BE SIGNIFICANT TO NAVIGATION and are therefore advised to use alternative sources of positional information particularly when closing the shore or navigating in the vicinity of dangers.'

A further caution on this and many charts in use states: '. . . positions on plans on this chart differ from each other by varying amounts. Positions should be transferred by bearing and distance from common charted objects, NOT BY LATITUDE AND LONGITUDE.'

Exercise extreme caution using a good lookout, sighted objects, depth sounder and seaman's instinct rather than relying on GPS.

CHARTS

European charts are used and listed, although countries of North Africa maintain their own hydrographic offices. The British Admiralty offers complete coverage of the North African coast at a scale of 1:300,000; its coverage of individual countries at larger scales is variable. The other two main European sources of charts are the Service Hydrographique et Océanographique de la Marine of France (SHOM) and the Instituto Hidrografico de la Marina of Cádiz, Spain. Reference to these organisations and their products will be British Admiralty, French and Spanish. See Appendix for details.

Morocco

The Spanish with their interest in Morocco, are an important source of information. Admiralty charts are updated but do not include some well-established harbours. Moroccan charts exist but are difficult to find. Much of the harbour information contained here is based on old charts, updated by hand with information gained from visits.

Algeria

Algeria is well covered by British Admiralty charts though these are not updated to WGS 84 datum. Its hydrographic service publishes charts which are available through the Ministry of Transport in Algiers.

Tunisia

French charts cover Tunisia in great detail but many of the surveys were made more than a century ago and there has been little up-dating during the past thirty years. Neither ports built within the last ten years nor changes to older ones, to say nothing of new conspicuous marks, appear. Nevertheless, navigation around the Kerkennah Islands or in the Gulf of Bou Grara should not be attempted without French charts. British Admiralty charts, although mainly to a smaller scale than the French charts, are more up to date and the range includes useful larger scale charts of areas important to shipping.

Tunisia does not have a hydrographic office but copies of French charts are available from the Service de Topography. The main office is near Tunis international airport, about 600m E of Stade Olympique in El Menzah and next to the *Météo* office which has a conspicuous satcom dome on the roof, and a branch is located at Sousse on Avenue Bourguiba, opposite the Monoprix.

Notices to Mariners

The *marine marchande* in Tunisia issue *Avis aux Navigateurs* on a regular basis. These notices are distributed to their offices in major ports and to the British embassy and are read before the weather on Tunis Radio and Sfax Radio. The contents deal with buoys, lights, tunny nets laid, firing exercises etc.

In Morocco, notices to mariners along with weather fax information is provided daily and posted in the customs house and harbourmaster's office.

Daily notices are posted on the notice boards of the marinas in Gibraltar.

A NOTE ABOUT THE HARBOUR INFORMATION

1. Co-ordinates of ports are taken from about midway in the entrance and given under 'Location'. These should not be taken as waypoints.
2. Description of lights has sometimes been changed from the Admiralty List of Lights when their description is not clear or simply incorrect.
3. Light characteristics are based on the author's observations and from information provided by yachtsmen.
   Positions given are from the Admiralty List of Lights which may differ slightly from the positions shown on the charts.
4. When two charts are quoted for a port the first one is scaled at 1:300,000 and the second is scaled at 1:60,000.
5. Distances are given to various ports.
   For Morocco Mediterranean coast from W to E.
   For Morocco Atlantic coast N to S
   For Algeria from W to E.
   For Tunisia the route is from W to E and then N to S after Cap Bon.
6. Spelling of names is taken from the Admiralty charts as long as their spelling agrees with Michelin map 172 for Algeria and Tunisia. Common differences are noted.
7. Co-ordinates for harbour entry lights are only given for the large commercial ports.
8. Some Admiralty charts give the tides as 'not exceeding 0.6m.' In practice, however, the tides are usually less and can really be ignored, except on the Atlantic coast and further S in Tunisia.
9. Prices for harbour dues and hauling out are only given as an indication. They are often negotiable and frequently change. Check the latest information on the internet where possible.
10. Bearings are true and from seaward.
11. Depths are in metres.
See French terms used on charts in glossary.

PLANNING YOUR CRUISE

Time zone

Algeria, Gibraltar, Malta and the Pelagie Islands use CET i.e. UT (GMT) +2 in summer and +1 hour in winter. Morocco uses GMT all year round. Tunisia uses CET summer and winter.

Budgeting and finance

The quiet unpolluted beaches and interesting sights to visit in the Maghreb provide rich cruising grounds for the adventurous, even those on a low budget. The cost of living and travel in Morocco and Tunisia (though not in Algeria - due to the exchange rate) can be kept surprisingly low. Many harbours do not charge for mooring, or ask minimal fees, and most marina charges are less than half the rate experienced in the rest of the Med. Also, local produce from the market is very cheap, leaving money available for inland travel.

The waters are comparatively rich in fish and, in season, giant prawns, grouper, swordfish, tuna, octopus and shark can be caught, as well as more common species such as mullet, sardines and mackerel. It is also cheap to purchase fish in the fishing harbours if you are prepared to barter early in the mornings.

Credit cards can be used almost everywhere to draw cash from banks on presentation of a passport. In the larger towns and tourist areas ATM machines are fitted in many banks. Travellers cheques are taken in most banks. Cash in dollars, Pounds Sterling and Euros are acceptable almost everywhere in banks and in many souk shops. Remember to take your bank details if you want to make an electronic transfer to a local bank.

It is useful to take whisky and cigarettes as a form of currency or to give as gifts.

Health advice

Vaccinations are not checked, even if theoretically required. It may be advisable though to be up-to-date with whatever is recommended by health authorities and travel agencies. Take any personal medicines or enquire about generic availability abroad via the internet. Many drugs are cheaper in North Africa than in Europe and available without prescription. Though not a requirement, limited health insurance can be inexpensive and many yacht insurance policies include health cover for crew, particularly in the event of injury while on board. This can include repatriation to home country for treatment.

Cruising grounds

Gibraltar is presented first, since many yachts are based there because of easy access to the UK, or prefer to stock up there or in nearby Spain. It is a good departure point for going into the Med along the N coast of Morocco, S down the Atlantic coast to the Canaries and across the Atlantic or N towards the Bay of Cádiz and Portugal. Others winter in Malta and depart from there to the cruising grounds in the Pelagie Islands and along the Tunisian coast. Algeria, though included, is still currently not a pleasant place to cruise because of the long time it takes to complete formalities in each port. Personal safety, however, seems no longer to be an issue.

Anchoring

There is no law prohibiting anchoring anywhere along the North African coast apart from in restricted areas as marked on charts. There is also no charge made for anchoring, as is common in Europe. However, in practice anchoring often arouses suspicion because smuggling is common, especially around the shores of Morocco and there is a fear of terrorist activity. Trafficking and illegal immigration has also added to the problem. Unless specific requests have been made at a nearby port, it is unwise to anchor. Even then, at night, it is likely to encourage a military boat to investigate. In Tunisia, there is less of a problem than elsewhere, because the authorities are more used to yachts. More information is included under each country section. In any event, as a rule, never anchor before clearing customs.

YACHT EQUIPMENT RECOMMENDED

Fenders and warps

In most of the harbours, yachts lie alongside a quay, so good fenders, warps and anti-chafing gear are necessary. A builder's plank, with a hole at either end so that it can be suspended outside the fenders is often useful when against a concrete wall. In marinas, mooring is usually bows or stern-to a quay or pontoon, with a line tailed from the quay.

Batteries

With sun all the year round, solar panels to keep the batteries charged will be useful, especially in some of the fishing harbours in Morocco, where it is difficult to get an electricity supply.

Water

A large water container or two should be carried for use in the harbours where a hose connection is far away.

Anchoring equipment

Although most anchorages are sand with good holding, very few provide overall protection and there can be sudden wind shifts. Consequently, anchor gear must be heavy enough for the boat. Bruce, CQR and Danforth type anchors work well in most anchorages and a Fisherman will be useful in weedy or rocky areas. Typical depths are between 3 and 6m and anchorages deeper than 10m are rare.

Insects

Flies can be a pest; mosquitoes are less of a problem. Good screens will keep both out and also help to keep cockroaches or rodents from boarding, although these are rarely a problem except in Malta.

Navigation

GPS navigation position finders are now very cheap, and will be a great advantage on the North African coast, where buoys are often out of position and lights change signature before charts can be updated, or simply do not function at all.

Communications

The GSM mobile phone system is installed in Morocco, Malta, Tunisia and Gibraltar, providing a link to the world even some miles offshore. With a computer interface, this can also provide Internet and email facilities. Ensure that the International Roaming Facility is activated for use abroad. GSM call rates are usually cheaper than using local hotel phones.

Items to carry
Tools and equipment to hook up to continental type electrical fittings. Take a long hosepipe and a selection of fittings and jubilee clips. Large water and fuel containers may be useful if in a small harbour or at anchor and needing supplies locally which are not available in the harbour.

Photocopies of ship's papers and crew lists which can be left with officials; see sample crew list in appendix.

A good sun awning; summer temperatures are higher than in the northern Mediterranean.

All charts, maps, guide books, and a French dictionary; all are difficult if not impossible, to obtain in North Africa.

AVAILABILITY OF SUPPLIES AND PROVISIONS

Fuel
Generally, fuel is available in all harbours, although it may have to be supplied in cans. This can always be arranged and carried by the locals for a small fee.

Water
The quality of tap-water is generally good along the North African coast as far as taste and bacteria-count is concerned but local circumstances and personal metabolism determine whether one can actually drink it unboiled. In Tunisian and Moroccan ports, quality is invariably good, but in some Algerian ports it is suspect. Avoid taps with no pressure. Bottled mineral water is widely available in Morocco and Tunisia but not in Algeria. Water is available by hosepipe in most of Tunisia, Malta and Gibraltar. In Algeria and Morocco it is available in some ports, but in others must be carried a short distance in cans. Again, there are always locals willing for a very small fee to take it to your yacht.

For more specific information look under the general information section of each port.

Gas
Camping Gaz is available almost everywhere. In Ceuta and Gibraltar all types of gas bottles can be conveniently and cheaply filled. In Morocco, Algeria and Tunisia, gas is widely used and bottled butane, propane or a mixture of both is widely available and cheap. All three countries have bottles with left-handed external thread as used on older English Calor Gas propane bottles. This is the same fitting as used on European propane bottles. Bottles with different fittings will be difficult to get filled in the Maghreb unless taken direct to the refineries.

Bottles can be filled in gas plants in Tanger, Bizerte and Gabès but sometimes foreign types, including Camping Gaz bottles, are refused.

In Algeria no foreign gas bottles are accepted.

In Tunisia, marina personnel in Al Kantaoui and Monastir fill from local bottles as a service to marina clients.

Although, technically, to purchase a bottle locally, a contract with the gas company is required, in practice it is often possible to avoid the bureaucracy.

Be careful about the type of gas. For detailed advice on fittings and procedures, contact the Boating Industry Liaison Section of Calor Gas Limited, Appleton Park, Slough SL3 9JG England ☎ 01753 40000.

Electricity
All marinas have 220v (or thereabouts) available. Many ports and harbours have no shore power officially, but often can make an arrangement for a small fee. It is a good idea to be self-sufficient with solar panels and an inverter if planning to anchor a lot or visit the more out of the way harbours, or be prepared to run your engine on a regular basis.

Provisions
A plentiful supply of fresh food is available everywhere. Fruit and vegetables are seasonal. Since deep freeze facilities are not generally used, meat too is always fresh – often alive waiting to be purchased and butchered. Freshly caught fish can be seen on the quays and in the markets. Local bread is delicious and at its best within a few hours of baking. It is baked throughout the day and, since there is no preservative added, it goes stale quickly and cannot be stored. Dry provisions like flour, sugar, rice and pasta, etc. are readily available, except in Algeria where they may be scarce. Canned food is not so easily obtained, so stock up in Gibraltar and Malta and in the large towns. In Tunisia, large hypermarkets have recently opened and are listed under the ports. Ice is available in almost every harbour, since it is used by the fishermen to keep their catch fresh and is usually manufactured in the harbours.

A wide range of locally produced soft drinks are very good value and many people find them better tasting than their European equivalents. Lager beer is also available in all towns, as well as locally produced wine. Spirits are usually very expensive. Whisky in Algeria is over 100 pounds a bottle! (A good bargaining currency in some places.)

YACHT REPAIR FACILITIES

Lift-out facilities
Most marinas are equipped with travel-hoists for hauling out boats, especially in Tunisia, Gibraltar, Malta and two in Morocco. Almost all the fishing ports in Tunisia have large travel hoists, though they may not be used to handling yachts. Almost every fishing harbour has a slipway with blocks, props and wedges that can be used in an emergency. In addition, on the Atlantic coast of Morocco, yachts can be careened on a mudflat or in harbour, as the tide range is up to 3m. In Marina Smir there are excellent haul out facilities. Kabila Marina has a light hoist for yachts up to 15 tons.

In Algeria, only Sidi Ferruch has a travel-lift (16 tons). In Tunisia there are travel-lifts in the marinas at Sidi Bou Saïd, El Kantaoui, Marina Jasmine and Monastir. There are now large travel-lifts, up to 250 tons in most larger fishing ports, though there is sometimes no high pressure hose available for cleaning. Water and electricity can generally be organised.

Primitive facilities but excellent workmanship at low prices *Graham Hutt*

Back in place: happy mechanics and an engine still going strong! *Graham Hutt*

Mechanical repairs

There are very competent engineers in most ports. As in most third world countries, mechanics take great pride in being able to fix almost anything. Rather than look for a spare part, which inevitably will not be available, a way will be found to either repair the old one or make a new component from scratch. This can even include a split engine block.

Spares

Almost all typical yacht spares can be obtained in the large towns and in many small harbours: ropes, fenders, bottle screws, wire rigging, bolts, 'U' clamps and anchoring gear for a boat of any size. Although you will not find stainless steel replacements, in an emergency, sturdy galvanised iron equivalents for most standing and running rigging parts can be found. Good quality polypropylene ropes of any length and thickness can be purchased in most hardware shops.

ENTRY FORMALITIES

Unlike sailing in Europe, where once cleared by customs you are free to travel anywhere without further formalities or contact with officials, in North Africa, things are different. In Morocco and Algeria yachts have to enter and clear each port visited with all the accompanying bureaucracy. Officials from the customs, immigration police, local police and harbour authorities will all visit your yacht on arrival. They are usually very courteous and the routine filling of forms is a friendly affair that does not take long in Morocco, but is a very protracted issue in Algeria.

Full details of your yacht and a crew list is necessary at each port, so carrying photocopies of the relevant information is very helpful. If the skipper's name is not on the owner's registration papers, a current notarised letter of authorisation from the owner is necessary to avoid problems. The officials like to see a ship's stamp on forms, although this is not strictly necessary.

If you intend to change crews or if an individual is leaving by land or air, it is important to inform the immigration department to avoid problems when you leave.

Further formalities at the next port are speeded up by informing the authorities of your next port of call, which leads to minimum hassle in Morocco. In Tunisia, once cleared, all that needs to be done in the next port is produce the clearance papers, without the need to complete further formalities. These are copied in each port. Nothing avoids extensive bureaucracy in Algeria.

A current radio licence for VHF and SSB equipment is required by most authorities, though almost never asked for.

Third party insurance may be asked for.

Pet 'passports' are required along with up-to-date health check documents, but are rarely asked for except in Malta where this is a big issue.

See sample crew list and boat details required in appendix.

See terms used in French and English for formalities in glossary.

Restricted items

Guns and large quantities of alcohol have to be declared. Spirits may be bonded onboard by the customs authorities until departure, if a suitable lock-up exists, or kept by the customs department until leaving. Guns, even a flare pistol, provoke a lot of paperwork when declared. Drugs are forbidden, except for medicinal purposes.

Visas

Specific visa requirement information should be obtained from the relevant embassies or consular officials in advance of travel, but most nationalities do not have any problem in Tunisia or Morocco. If a passport holder is not in possession of a visa, this is usually overcome by the authorities issuing a shore pass as they would for ships' crews while the passport is held until departure. Algeria is very different and most nationalities now require a visa before visiting, including Swiss and French nationals who were formerly exempt.

Insurance

On some entry formality forms, particularly in marinas, a yacht insurance policy number is required. There seems to be no legal requirement for insurance currently in North Africa and I have never heard of the policy being asked for. This may change in the future, as in most European marinas, where it is a requirement. Third party insurance is all that is required and is usually inexpensive.

VAT

There is no VAT requirement in North Africa. There is, however, a maximum period of time that a yacht can stay in any country before import duty has to be paid. This period varies from country to country and is alleviated by rules whereby a yacht wintering or laying up can apply for exemption during the time of immobility. These are rules of plombage, which mean that a yacht is not considered in a country while it is laid up: the yacht is exempt from the timing while not in use. This has to be arranged and agreed by the local customs authorities. Marina staff will always assist with this formality though smaller harbours may not be familiar with procedures.

Malta, having just joined the EU, should apply the normal EU rules whereby VAT must be paid on a vessel unless it has special exemption. To qualify for exemption, the vessel must have been launched before 1st January 1985 and have been in EU waters on 31st December 1992, with documentary evidence to prove these facts. A Single Administrative Document - SAD certificate is issued if these credentials are ascertained.

A boat registered outside the EU may stay in an EU port for up to six months before VAT must be paid,

Bartering for spices   *Graham Hutt*

although this time period can often be extended.

All the above rules are open to differing interpretations and flexibility and the practices vary considerably from one country to another.

Chartering

In Tunisia, chartering can only be arranged by a company with a Tunisian partner. In practice, privately chartered yachts based outside Tunisia have been allowed in and have even changed crews in some ports but all depends upon local officials and attitudes may change from year to year.

In Morocco and Algeria, a charter yacht is unlikely to encounter any problems, but crew changes must be notified to the immigration authorities.

Wintering

Many ports in Tunisia, the four marinas and Marina Smir in Morocco are well appointed and safe places to winter. Tunisia is by far the cheapest, with Monastir being the most popular followed by El Kantaoui and Sidi Bou Saïd, all of which are full each winter. It is possible to winter in Sidi Fredj in Algeria and in Marina Smir in Morocco, but these are expensive options. Other Moroccan ports are also available: Tanger, Casablanca and Agadir – but these are currently undergoing extensive alterations.

Gibraltar and Malta are other places to winter but need advance booking and are also expensive compared to Tunisia.

Internet facilities

Internet facilities abound all over the Maghreb and the other places covered in this book. Gibraltar, Malta, Morocco and Tunisia are most advanced with new facilities opening up every week. Prices per hour are exceptionally low in most places and although speed is not usually as fast as with the ADSL lines of Europe, they are more than adequate.

Eating out

Through the influence of tourism in Tunisia and Morocco and the French occupation in all three countries, a variety of restaurants will be found everywhere.

In Tunisia and Morocco, restaurants range from high class with French cuisine in the big cities to the most simple eating houses frequented by villagers. Interesting places which may not appear spotless, may serve the best meals; go by your nose but allow your system time to acclimatise before embarking upon something really adventurous. Desserts, apart from fresh fruit and flans, are not common in the more basic restaurants. Often restaurants will offer to send out for whatever is asked for from a local patisserie to eat with a *thé à la menthe* in Morocco or *thé noir* in Tunisia. Coffee is taken strong with a lot of milk or as espresso. Restaurants catering for tourists have a familiar menu of wine, starters, main dishes and desserts, similar to European cuisine.

Prices vary from as much as £10 per person for good French cuisine to as little as £1.20 for a meal in a local eating house. The better restaurants with a licence serve wine, which is often locally produced. Morocco Tunisia

Essaouira medina   *Minaret*

and Algeria all have flourishing wine industries. Lunch is usually served from 1200 onward and dinner from 2000. Small restaurants may only open at lunchtime.

In Algeria, restaurants are harder to find and cater mainly for the affluent, since eating out is not particularly cheap when the bill is paid with officially exchanged Algerian dinars. Ice-cream parlours are prolific in the Maghreb and the quality is quite good. In Malta, most restaurants cater for cheap tourist menus, whilst the Pelagie Islands cater almost exclusively for Italian fare.

Some typical dishes

Cous-cous, made of durum wheat and eaten with vegetables, chicken, meat or fish, is the most popular food in the whole Maghreb.

Bread is always eaten with any salad or appetiser and to soak up sauces. Chicken is always on the menu and good fish can be had along the coast.

Morocco

Harira, a spicy, thick, filling soup which can be a meal in itself.

Briouates, deep-fried pastry parcels filled with minced meat, prawn or chicken. Found in the better restaurants.

Tajine, meat and vegetables stewed in an earthenware pot and eaten with bread.

Cornes de Gazelle, batter covered almond pastries.

Tunisia

Brik à l'Oeuf, a thin pastry with a filling of egg, parsley and sometimes tuna fried in oil. Learn how Tunisians eat them or you will end up with a yellow mess.

Salade Mechouia, a relish from grilled or roasted peppers and tomatoes, garnished with olives and hard boiled egg.

Chakchouka, an egg dish with green peppers and harissa.

Ojja, a variety of chakchouka with a tomato base. Makes a tasty appetiser or light meal.

Harissa, a hot red pepper paste but not as hot as the Indonesian varieties. Mixed with some olive oil and eaten with bread, or as a dip for olives, it is a nice appetiser.

Baklava, puff pastry filled with ground nuts mixed with honey.

Shopping

Bartering is the normal and expected way to arrive at a price and the merchant has less respect for a buyer who does not barter. Rules are hard to formulate but here are some guidelines:

Do not get involved in serious bidding on an item that you do not really want to buy.

Determine for yourself what a certain product should cost or how much it is worth to you.

Do not feel embarrassed to leave a shop and compare prices in a neighbouring shop.

There is no bartering in government handicraft shops, food markets, supermarkets, non-tourist oriented clothing stores, restaurants and in taxis if they have a working meter – check this first.

The fixed-price government handicraft and tourist shops are well worth a visit to give you a general idea of the maximum price you can expect to pay in the souk after bartering.

Travel connections

International airports operate throughout North Africa, Malta and Gibraltar. Information is given in each country section. Tunisia operates charter flights from Monastir (Scanes) and Tabarka. Ferries operate from many ports to Europe and the internal transport system in the Maghreb is extensive, reliable and cheap.

For futher reading, see appendix.

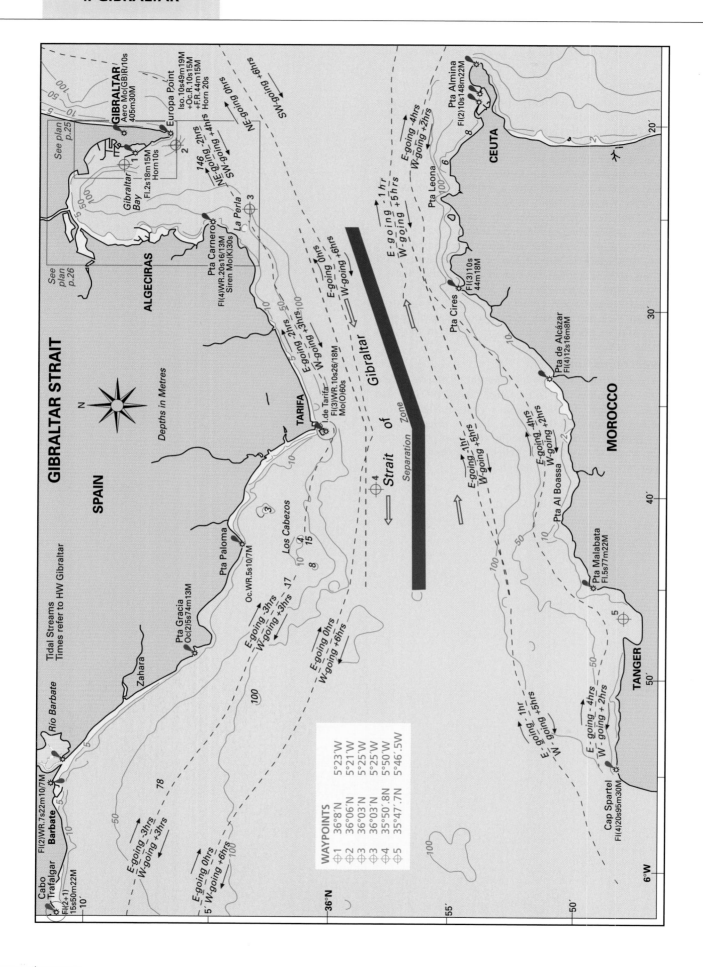

GIBRALTAR STRAIT

SPAIN

ALGECIRAS

GIBRALTAR
Aero Mo(GBR)10s
405m30M
Europa Point
Iso.10s49m19M
+Oc.R.10s15M
+F.R.44m15M
Horn 20s

Gibraltar
Bay
Fl.2s18m15M
Horn 10s

See plan p.25

See plan p.26

La Perla

Pta Carnero
Fl(4)WR.20s16/13M
Siren Mo(K)30s

146° - 2hrs
NE-going +4hrs
SW-going 0hrs

NE-going 0hrs
SW-going +6hrs

N

Depths in Metres

TARIFA

de Tarifa
Fl(3)WR.10s26/18M
Mo(O)60s

E-going -2hrs
W-going +3hrs

E-going 0hrs
W-going +6hrs

Strait

Separation Zone

of

Gibraltar

E-going - 1hr
W-going +5hrs

E-going -4hrs
W-going +2hrs

Pta Leona

Pta Almina
Fl(2)10s148m22M

CEUTA

Pta Cires
Fl(3)10s
44m18M

MOROCCO

Pta de Alcázar
Fl(4)12s16m8M

Pta Al Boassa

E-going - 1hr
W-going +5hrs

E-going -4hrs
W-going +2hrs

Pta Malabata
Fl.5s77m22M

E - going - 1hr
W - going +5hrs

E - going -4hrs
W - going +2hrs

Cap Spartel
Fl(4)20s95m30M

TANGER

Los Cabezos

Pta Paloma

Oc.WR.5s10/7M

Pta Gracia
Oc(2)5s74m13M

Zahara

Rio Barbate

Cabo
Trafalgar
Fl(2+1)
15s50m22M

Barbate
Fl(2)WR.7s22m10/7M

Tidal Streams
Times refer to HW Gibraltar

E-going -3hrs
W-going +3hrs

E-going 0hrs
W-going +6hrs

E-going -3hrs
W-going +3hrs

E-going 0hrs
W-going +6hrs

3

4

15

8

17

78

50

10

50

100

3

100

100

50

10

6

8

100

50

10

2

50

100

5

WAYPOINTS
⊕1   36°8'N   5°23'W
⊕2   36°06'N   5°21'W
⊕3   36°03'N   5°25'W
⊕3   36°03'N   5°25'W
⊕4   35°50'.8N   5°50'.W
⊕5   35°47'.7N   5°46'.5W

36°N

55'

50'

10'

6°W

I. GIBRALTAR

Introduction to Gibraltar

Gibraltar's location on the southern tip of the Iberian peninsula, its proximity to North Africa and its small (30,000) predominantly English speaking community, makes 'The Rock' invaluable to yachtsmen. It has an airport with several daily flights to the UK and is an ideal place to store, take on fuel, carry out repairs and explore Spain. It offers a safe place to lay-up and maintain ship, with all facilities available, including many European and US agencies represented for servicing and chandlery.

There are three marinas, all on the western side of the Rock in the Bay of Gibraltar (known as the Bay of Algeciras to the Spanish.) Two are within walking distance of the airstrip.

Major changes and improvements are underway at Sheppard's and Queensway Quay marinas, described below. A new marina complex is being built to replace the old Sheppard's Marina which will be moving N of the runway during 2005.

HISTORY

The Rock of Gibraltar has witnessed the unfolding of a chequered and very interesting history over the centuries from its vantage point at the intersection of two continents and two oceans.

Gibraltar claims to have some of the oldest inhabitants, with Neolithic human remains having been found.

Recent scientific announcements that there is no genetic link between these remains and humans, has not diminished claims by its tourist office to be the 'cradle of civilisation.' It has undoubtedly been a place of sojourn for many civilisations. For centuries the Rock served as an important landmark and provided shelter for mariners who came in their small ships, and as a place of worship: the latter evidenced by remains of Phoenician, Carthaginian and Greek pottery, amulets and artefacts bearing classical and Egyptian gods, found in caves at the foot of the Rock. The Phoenicians built settlements close to the Rock and the Romans built cities nearby, but neither they nor the ancient Greeks, built a city here.

The Rock was once named Moons Clap and, according to Greek mythology was, together with Moons Ably near Ceuta, (across the strait), one of the twin pillars of Hercules.

Around AD400, the decline of the Roman Empire led to invasions by Barbarians from the east and later Vandals and Goths, who swept through from Spain. Vandals marched on to conquer North Africa while from 414 the Goths occupied the Iberian Peninsula.

Gibraltar from the south   *Patrick Roach*

Gibraltar witnessed the beginning of one of the greatest moments in history: the Arab crossing and conquest of Spain from North Africa in the 8th century under Tarik ibn Zeyad, a Berber chief and Governor of Tanger. The Rock became known as Jebel Tarik: 'The Mountain of Tarik' which metamorphosed into its modern day name of Gibraltar.

The death of the Prophet Mohammed in 632 precipitated the rapid expansion of Islam. By the beginning of 8th century the Arabs had conquered the whole of the Iberian Peninsula with the exception of the Cantabrian mountains and the Pyrenees. Thus began the Moorish rule over Gibraltar and Spain which was to last more than six centuries. During this time, the peninsula was divided into Arab Kingdoms and by the 11th C, Gibraltar was under the dominion of the Arab Kingdom of Seville.

It was not until 1160 that the first town of Gibraltar and fortress were founded by Abdul Mamen, Caliph of Morocco and leader of the Almohads. A small walled city then grew up on the western side of the Rock on an area from the Tower of Homage to what is Grand Casemates Square today: the Medina al Fath or City of Victory.

By 1252, Arab influence was declining following inter-tribal skirmishes and fighting between Arabs and Christians. In 1309, the Spaniard Alonso Perez de Guzman and his troops laid siege to Gibraltar and took the upper Rock, from where they shelled the town. After a month, the garrison surrendered and the inhabitants were allowed to leave. Few remained and the Spanish were left to rebuild the fortifications and shipyard. In 1333 Gibraltar was recaptured by the Muslims and was once again under siege, this time led by Abdul Malik, Prince of Morocco. The garrison held-out for four months before finally capitulating. More sieges followed and in 1462 Gibraltar was recaptured by the Spanish, initially under the King of Castille but its strategic importance waned under the Spanish King Henry IV. As a result, his defences were weakened and more sieges and petty feuds followed. In 1474 the Catholic Queen Isabella came to the throne and in 1501 issued a decree declaring Gibraltar Crown Property. The following year she granted a Coat of Arms; the Castle and Key, with the inscription: 'Seal of the Noble City of Gibraltar, the Key of Spain.' The legacy of the Moors in architecture, art, science, cuisine and the names of many cities, towns and villages in Andalucía and beyond, remain to this day.

Gibraltar remained under Spanish rule until the beginning of the 18th century. In 1702 the King of Spain died childless, precipitating the eleven year 'War of Spanish Succession.' Britain first became interested in Gibraltar during the time of Cromwell, but it was during this struggle over the Spanish throne, between Archduke Charles of Austria and Philip of Anjou, (grandson of Louis XIV of France), that the English Lord Protector seized the opportunity of capturing the Rock. He sent a combined Anglo-Dutch fleet led by Admiral Sir George Rook, on behalf of Charles, which undertook a massive bombardment of Gibraltar. The acting Governor eventually surrendered. Philip eventually won the throne,

becoming Philip V, King of Spain but due to the collapse of the Archduke's cause, Gibraltar remained under British control. This was ratified under the Treaty of Utrecht in 1713 and Gibraltar became a British garrison. Peace was tentative and in 1727, the Spanish besieged the Rock, unsuccessfully. Spain was determined to regain Gibraltar and in 1779, began 'The Great Siege' lasting almost four years. The garrison demonstrated incredible fortitude and endurance and would have starved had they not received supplies from British fleets on three almost annual occasions. They were outnumbered almost five-to-one but against such odds, and using the Rock to its best advantage, they held their own. Tunnels were drilled into the Rock and a gun carriage was designed, facilitating the placement of guns high in the Rock face above their opponents. In November 1871 they launched a surprise counter-attack with devastating results. The Spanish realised that they could not starve out the Rock and changed tactics, assembling seemingly impregnable floating batteries consisting of naval vessels, from which they mounted a devastating assault, destroying most of the town. (Hence there is little evidence today of the original Spanish and Moorish architecture.) Even this challenge did not defeat the intrepid garrison who retaliated by raining down red-hot cannonballs, heated from their furnaces, which eventually penetrated and blew up the batteries ensuring an incredible victory and grand finale to the great siege as they took back supremacy of the Rock.

Recent history

In the 19th century, Gibraltar was rebuilt with even stronger fortifications and began to develop as a commercial centre comprising a fairly diversely cosmopolitan population of merchants. It was Nelson's home port and following the Battle of Trafalgar his body was brought here in 1805, pickled in a barrel of brandy. In 1830 Gibraltar became a Crown Colony.

At the beginning of the last century, with Germany increasing in military might, Britain responded by strengthening the Navy in Gibraltar and built a harbour and dockyard. It was from this base that the Straits were patrolled during the World Wars and the Allied warships repaired. An airfield was constructed and miles of tunnels were dug out of the Rock, creating a self-sufficient city with generators and telephone exchange, a hospital and food stores in case of another siege. In fact they were never utilised.

Out of the post-war years mushroomed a growing desire for self-government and in 1945 the Civil Council was reinstituted. In 1969 Britain issued a new Constitution granting autonomy in domestic affairs.

In 1963 Spain revived its claim on Gibraltar and began a campaign of increasing restrictions at the border culminating in 1969 with its complete closure. Gibraltar survived another 16 years of isolation before it was finally reopened following the death of General Franco. In the late 1980s and early 1990s the Rock became a haven for uncontrolled tobacco and drug smuggling. During this time the Spanish tightened their grip on the border in an attempt to stem the flow and imposed harsh sanctions on the people crossing to

Spain. This was resolved when the present government was elected and immediately banned the fast RIB craft which, travelling faster than any of the Spanish customs launches, conveyed most of the booty to Spain. However, even today political problems continue and the question of Gibraltar's future remains unresolved.

CULTURE

The 30,000 people of Gibraltar are a mixture of mainly Spanish, Italian, Maltese, British, Indian and North African nationalities. Spain contributes a large workforce which crosses the frontier daily to sustain companies in Gibraltar. In recent years many Indian businessmen have set up in Gibraltar, becoming a pillar of society. A large Jewish community has been there for centuries. All groups and religions co-exist peacefully in this multi-ethnic, multi-lingual society.

MARITIME INFORMATION

Weather

Around Gibraltar, weather usually conforms to the local area forecast, (unlike further E where local forecasting is notoriously difficult). Winds can be expected to be either E (Levante) or W (Poniente). The E winds bring a large cloud which hangs over the W side of the rock, often for several days, producing high humidity and miserable conditions. On rare occasions as low pressure and associated fronts move N from the Canaries in winter, strong SW winds bring rain and squally conditions, often closing the airport.

Forecasts: Radio Gibraltar (GBC) and British Forces Radio (BFBS) broadcast local weather forecasts from the RAF Met. Office. GBC includes a sailing forecast for a 5 mile radius from Gibraltar. GBC (91.3, 92.5mHz, 1458kHz. BFBS 1 (93.5, 97.8mHz. ☎ 54211) Storm warnings on F3E, on receipt. These are repeated throughout the day at half past the hour until evening. Tarifa Radio broadcasts area weather on Ch 16 at regular intervals in Spanish and English.

Gibraltar: Rounding Europa point. Note mosque behind the light   *Graham Hutt*

All the marinas post weather faxes on their notice boards daily.
See also www.bbc.co.uk/weather/coast/pressure/ and http://meteonet.nl/aktueel/brackall.htm for 5 day forecasts of the Med.

Tides

Gibraltar is a standard port and tidal information for the marinas is given under 'Gibraltar Port'. The maximum range is around 1m. Tide tables can be found on http://easytide.ukho.gov.uk

PLANNING YOUR CRUISE

Time zone

Gibraltar, like Spain runs to CET: UT+1 in winter and UT+2 in summer.

Money

The UK Pound Sterling is legal tender, along with the Gibraltar pound and of equal value, but only in Gibraltar. Beware of trying to exchange excess Gibraltar currency in the UK, as it is worth very little there. Euros can also be used in most shops but not in the Post Office where only local currency and sterling is accepted.

Banks: Gibraltar has well established banking services for both offshore and local customers with a full range of international banks, including several UK institutions. A full list of financial services is available from the Tourist Board. ☎ 74950. Banking hours are generally between 0900–1530 except Friday, when some are open later in the afternoon. There are also several Bureaux de Change agencies in Main Street; one at the airport and another in a circular office opposite the airport. Visa, Switch, American Express, Mastercard etc. are accepted almost everywhere, though not the post office and some government offices. ATMs at Barclays Bank in Main Street and Morrisons supermarket.

Local cruising information

Gibraltar is an excellent point for sailing in any direction, although a few people do get stuck here, sometimes for years, as witnessed by the number of aging live-aboard boats in Sheppard's Marina which have not moved for 10 or 20 years. With the airport close and daily flights to and from the UK, crew change-over is easily facilitated. Málaga airport is not much more than an hour away and Jerez airport is also another close option.

Sailing in and around Gibraltar Bay is often rewarded by the sight of dolphins and special dolphin cruises are organised daily from Marina Bay.

Harbour charges

These are currently under review for each marina and the best updates will be on the internet sites listed. Gibraltar remains a cheaper option than the Mediterranean marinas, although water is more expensive and usually metered. To offset this, fuel is cheap and VAT-exempt.

Security

There are no security concerns in any of the marinas in Gibraltar. Access to marina berths is either patrolled or is via a locked gate.

The Spanish claim to the Rock has implications, most noticeably at the border for those wishing to cross into Spain by land. There are often delays for those travelling by car but this rarely affects pedestrians. This situation has eased considerably over the past two years despite a lack of resolution to the political situation and the Spanish claim on the Rock. The number of smugglers operating from Gibraltar has reduced considerably in the past few years, leading to a calmer and less aggressive attitude on both sides of the border.

Marina facilities

These are generally similar to those in the UK and Spain: good water, electricity (220v to 240v) overland and air mailing facilities, internet facilities: either on site or nearby. Because Gibraltar is small, it is usually only a short walk to obtain anything from the shops in Main Street, though local bus transport is also available from one end of the Rock to the other. Spares can be sent to Gibraltar as 'Ships stores in transit' without the need to pay VAT.

Availability of supplies

Fuel
Diesel, petrol and water at the Shell or BP stations by the customs pier opposite Marina Bay.
Shell ☎ 48232 BP ☎ 72261
Gas
Available from New Harbours ☎ 70296.
Provisions
Morrisons supermarket (formerly Safeway) is a short walk from Queensway Quay and not far from Sheppard's or Marina Bay. It is on the Number 4 and 10 bus route (see below). Marina Bay has its own supermarket: Checkout, a branch of Tesco.

In Gibraltar's Main Street and its adjacent streets and alleyways, almost anything can be obtained. Peraltos Supermarket is tucked back behind the bus station. It has a good selection of tinned and frozen goods. Marks & Spencers have recently (2004) opened a small food department close to its main store in Main Street. The fish, meat and vegetable market is a covered market on the right as you pass through Casemates Gate. Fresh fruit and vegetables are best obtained from La Linea market, just across the border crossing to Spain, on Wednesday mornings.
Charts
Available from the Gibraltar Chart Agency, 11a Block 5 Water Gardens, Gibraltar ☎ 76293.
Chandlery
Just about everything for the boat is available at Sheppard's (temporarily at the old marina site ☎ 77183 Fax 42535) which has probably the best range of yacht chandlery in the Mediterranean W of Malta. There are also smaller chandlers located at Marina Bay.
Repair facilities
Sheppard's boatyard and repair facilities are currently reduced because of the closure and move to new premises (as described under Sheppard's). However, they are operating a 40-ton travel-hoist and 10-ton crane and engineering facilities from temporary premises near Queensway Quay. (Coaling Island) ☎ 78954.

Entry formalities

All yachts calling at Gibraltar must first proceed to the customs and immigration offices located a few metres from Marina Bay and marked on the chart. This includes yachts going to Queensway Quay which formerly had its own arrangements. This requirement is due to a higher state of security, owing to the new anti-terrorism considerations.

Gibraltar, like the UK, is not part of the Shengen agreement, which has different visa requirements to Spain. Check for latest information from the Gibraltar government web site www.gibraltar.gov.gi or contact the immigration department
☎ 46411 Email rgpimm@gibynex.gi

Crew intending to remain ashore, or obtain work in Gibraltar should inform Immigration Authorities of their intention to do so and supply an address. Changes of crew should also be notified to the authorities.

Wintering

All the marinas are safe for wintering and a cheaper alternative to Spain. It may be difficult to find a space for the next two years while major work is being undertaken at Sheppard's and Queensway Quay.

Internet facilities

The importance of access to the internet is currently being addressed in the marinas, with internet facilities being provided for each yacht. Internet cafés also abound in the town.

Mail

The main post office is in Main Street and will only accept local currency or sterling cash. UK mail usually arrives the following day, though postal services have frequently been disrupted by strikes over recent years.

Tourist information office

Offices in Cathedral Square off Main Street, ☎ 79450 Email tourism@gibraltar.gi www.gibraltar.gov.gi
Casemates Square and at the Frontier.
Detailed tourist information under 'Ashore.'

Useful Phone Numbers

(International code for Gibraltar 350). From Spain: 9567
Ambulance & Police ☎ 199
Fire ☎ 190
Operator ☎ 100
Health Centre ☎ 70112/78337 House calls ☎ 77003
St Bernard's Hospital ☎ 79700
Dentist, Neptune House, Marina Bay ☎ 78887
Airport: Flight enquiries ☎ 44737/75984
Customs ☎ 78879
Immigration ☎ 48531
Chandlers Sheppard ☎ 75148
Gibraltar Tourist Board ☎ 74950
Border ☎ 42777
Pumpkin Marine ☎ 71177
Med Marine Ltd ☎ 48888
Consulates ☎ 74950

VHF Ch

Port 16; 06, 12, 13, 14.
Pilots 16; 12, 14.
Lloyds Windy 08, 16; 12, 14 office hours.

Business hours

Shops are normally open Monday to Friday between 0930 and 1930. Many close between 1300 and 1500 and most close Saturday afternoons and Sundays.

Transport

A bus (No.10) runs from the bus station near Main Street and terminates at the Frontier. Other buses run between the frontier and Europa Point. The Tourist Information office has details of all bus routes in Gibraltar.

International travel

Gibraltar airport is located close to the frontier for flights to the UK and onward connections ☎ 73026. Málaga airport is little over an hour's drive up the coast (A7 or AP7 'peaje' toll road) for more destinations. Jerez airport is just over an hour away and provides very cheap charter flights to and from UK destinations.

Problems of using Gibraltar for flights other than to the UK is being addressed and a joint airport agreement is likely in late 2005. It is expected that major changes in routes will take place along with changes to the airport infrastructure to accommodate many more flights per day.

For those wishing to explore Spain, taxis await across the border and La Linea bus station is a short walk away. From here an excellent (and cheap) bus service networks the whole of Spain. If time is short the RENFE inter-city train service is a faster way to see the country. The nearest station is a few kms away in Algeciras, where there are also ferries to Tanger and Ceuta. There is a connecting bus between La Línea and Algeciras bus stations. From there you will have to walk or get a taxi to the port or RENFE.

Further reading

Official Guide of Gibraltar, issued by the Gibraltar Tourist Board and
A Guided Tour of Gibraltar by T J Finlayson.
Gibraltar Guidebook
Discover Gibraltar.

Approach and entry to Gibraltar

Gibraltar Bay leads to 3 excellent marinas and an anchorage, all separately described. Algeciras Port and its marina are located on the W side of the Bay. Shelter is good from all but S-SW winds.

G1 Gibraltar Bay (Bay of Algeciras)

Location
36°06′.6N 05°20′.6W (Europa Point)

Tide
Gibraltar is a standard port

MHWS	MHWN	MLWN	MLWS
1.0	0.7	0.3	0.1

Charts

	Approach	Port
Admiralty	793, 142, 1448, 144	
French	7298	7042
Spanish	445, 3500, 4451,4452	
Imray	M11	

Communications
See under each marina.
VHF Gibraltar Port control (North mole) Ch. 16, 6,12,13,14.

Lights
Approach
1. **Tarifa** 36°00′.1N 05°36′.5W
   Fl(3)WR.10s41m26/18M 113°-R-089°-R-113° White tower 33mMo(O)60s Masonry structure 10m
2. **Punta Carnero** 36°04′.7N 05°25′.5W
   Oc(1+3)WR.20s42m16/13M
   018°-W-325°-R-018° Siren Mo(K)30s
   Yellow round tower, green lantern 19m
3. **Gibraltar (Europa Point)** 36°06′.7N 05°20′.6W
   Iso.10s49m19M 197°-vis-042° and 067°-vis-125°
   Oc.R.10s15M F.R.44m15M 042°-vis-067° Horn 20s
   197°-W-042°-R(Oc&F-067°-W-125°
   White round tower, red band 19m
4. **Gibraltar Aeromarine** 36°08′.7N 05°20′.5W
   Aero Mo(GB)R.10s405m30M Entrance
5. **North mole east head** 36°09′N 05°21′.9W
   F.R.28m5M Tower

Gibraltar Bay and Gibraltar Port

Gibraltar is a major commercial port with excellent facilities. Its location adjoining Spain and with three marinas to choose from, presents a safe convenient haven for rest and repairs for yachts going into the Mediterranean, S to Morocco and the Canaries, or N towards the Atlantic and Portugal.

PILOTAGE

Approach to the Bay

By day

Gibraltar Rock rising to 406m is clearly visible except in fog, which is rare, though more frequent in summer. It is safe to enter the Bay of Gibraltar (Algeciras Bay) in almost any conditions but beware of squalls near the Rock once in the bay, particularly during strong easterlies when strong downdraughts occur off the rock. From the S and E, Europa point is prominent, with its lighthouse at the end. A short distance further up the point, the minaret of a new mosque will be observed. Strong currents and overfalls occur around the tip of the point when wind is against tide. (See section on Transiting the Straits on page 33.) From the W, Pt Carnero light lies at the SW entrance to the bay, near an old whaling station.

By night

The W side of the Rock is well illuminated by the town and to the east by the bright red lights marking the radio antennas on the north face, which is itself illuminated by spotlights. To the south is the lighthouse on Europa point, easily seen from NNE through to NNW, with a small red sector indicating the dangerous rocky shoreline to the W between Pta del Acebuche and Pta Carnero, which must be given a wide berth.

GPS

⊕2 gives clearance rounding Europa Point, ⊕3 clears the dangers coming from the W around Pta Canero. ⊕1 is off the detached mole leading to Queensway Quay Marina.

Entry to Gibraltar Port

The main port lies behind a detached mole running SSE with entry at either end. The harbour is not further described as it is a commercial port of little interest to yachts, except for access to Queensway Quay Marina. Depths throughout the port are in excess of 8m. Beware of ships anchored outside breakwaters.

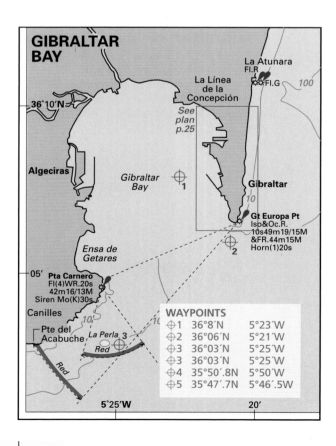

GIBRALTAR BAY

La Atunara
Fl.R
La Línea de la Concepción
Fl.G
100
See plan p.25
36°10′N
Algeciras
Gibraltar Bay
⊕1
Gibraltar
10
Gt Europa Pt
Iso&Oc.R.
10s49m19/15M
&FR.44m15M
Horn(1)20s
Ensa de Getares
⊕2
05′ Pta Carnero
Fl(4)WR.20s
42m16/13M
Siren Mo(K)30s
Canilles
10′
Pte del Acebuche
La Perla 3
Red
⊕
Red
5°25′W
20′

WAYPOINTS		
⊕1 36°8′N	5°23′W
⊕2 36°06′N	5°21′W
⊕3 36°03′N	5°25′W
⊕3 36°03′N	5°25′W
⊕4 35°50′.8N	5°50′W
⊕5 35°47′.7N	5°46′.5W

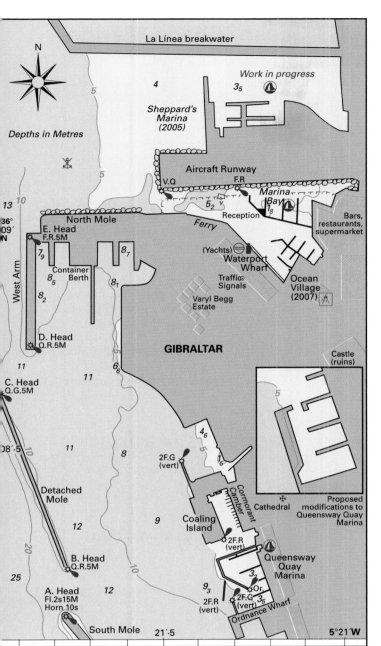

G2 Queensway Quay Marina

Location
36°08′.1N 05°21′.3W

Communications
Marina Control Centre (MCC) ☎ (00350) 44700
Fax 44699
VHF Ch 71 (call *Queensway Quay Marina*)
Email qqmarina@gibnet.gi
Ragged Staff Wharf, Queensway, Gibraltar VHF 73

The closest marina to Europa Point, currently undergoing extensive works to improve the design and infrastructure (2005).

The Marina

Queensway Quay Marina has the advantage of being some distance from the airport, with its noise, and close to the largest supermarket Morrisons (formerly Safeway) and Main Street, which is within walking distance. It provides 130 berths at present but current works will increase the berthing capability.

The marina itself has been in need of reconstruction due to design faults which allowed unacceptable surging with resulting damage to yachts. Changes to pontoon orientation failed to bring relief and now several major design changes are being made. These include replacement of the floating pontoon at the entrance with the construction of a solid mole on which will be built apartments. Queensway Quay Development includes luxury apartments, a restaurant and many business enterprises around the marina. Work on the extension began in mid 2004 and will not be completed before 2006. An early change will be to the marina entrance, which is being relocated on the N end of the marina nearer Coaling Island. Whilst work is underway, be prepared for the entrance and marina layout to be different to that drawn on the plans and expect some disruption, noise and dust for a while.

Berths and anchorages

Listed separately. Anchoring within the port is prohibited.

Entrance and formalities

Currently all inbound yachts must first report to the Immigration and Customs station; two huts located S of the airport runway, close to the Sheppard's and Marina Bay marinas, next to the fuelling station. A 'Q' flag is above the building. The short pontoon is very low so keep your fenders at waterline height. The staff officers do not offer assistance to yachts arriving.

Queensway Quay marina from W, before reconstruction in 2005
Patrick Roach

PILOTAGE

Head for Gibraltar bay as described previously and pass through either the N or S entrance of the detached mole. The marina is located inside Gibraltar Harbour between Gun Wharf and Coaling Island due W of the S end of the detached mole.

Berthing (current to mid-2005)

Visitors' berth on the first pontoon inside the marina to the south, or on the entrance floating pontoon near the fuelling berth. Longer stay berths are in the more sheltered northern end of the marina. Call up the duty Piermaster on channel 73 after clearing customs and he will allocate a berth and assist with lines. Mooring is stern-to concrete floating pontoons and accommodates vessels up to 35m in length. A limited number of deep-water berths varying from 3–7 metres in depth at LWS, with power points and water, are available along the southern wall of the marina.

Charges for a 12m Yacht

High season Apr–Oct
Day £10.95
Low season Nov–April
Day £7.65
Multihulls +50%
Plus metered electricity and water.
(Full information available on the web or by contacting the marina on email at the address given.)

Facilities

Every berth has access to a Service Module, with electricity, water, intercom and telephone. Access to the floating pontoons is by coded lockable gates and security is excellent. Car park by the Marina Control Centre (MCC). Office facilities available from the MCC include fax and photocopying, book swap and restaurant, showers and laundry.

Repairs Only available at Sheppard's Marina ☎ 75148/77183 *Fax* 42535.

Showers and *WC* Situated in the MCC. Facilities available for the disabled. Bath available for L3.50. These amenities close 30 minutes earlier than the rest of the establishment. Toilets for after hours' use can be found along the Main Quayside to the rear of the large anchor. Lock code available from Reception.

Security Access to pontoons (after hours) is by a coded digital lock.

Weather Daily reports are posted in the office. A weather station is on view at the MCC.

Transport Local buses from the bus station. No. 3 bus to the frontier from Line Wall Road near the Museum.

G3 Ocean Village Marina

Location
36°08′.9N 05°21′.4W

The Marina

A new marina complex is currently being built on the site of the old Sheppard's Marina S of Marina Bay and the airport runway and will have facilities for 140 luxury yachts from 10m to 30m. It will not be ready to receive yachts until 2006. Meanwhile Sheppard's retains its old moorings under a new company 'Temporary Moorings Ltd' while their new marina is being completed N of the airport runway, where all yachts will be moved later in 2005 (see below).

Berthing

At the time of writing, final plans for this new development are not finalized, new harbour plans have not been released and berthing charges are not yet known.

Tucked into a sheltered location, Sheppard's provides secure berthing in all weather conditions for 150 yachts. It is due to close in 2005 and re-open N of the runway.

G4 Sheppard's Marina (old)

Current location
36°08′.9N 05°21′.4W

Communications
VHF Ch 71
Harbour office ☎ (+350) 77183, 75148, *Fax* 42535
Email Sheppard@gibnet.gi
www.sheppard.gi

The Marina

Sheppard's was established as a yacht marina in Gibraltar in 1961. It was a pioneer project, not only in Gibraltar, but for many hundreds of miles around. Since then the company has developed and expanded successfully into several areas associated with the yachting trade including haulout yard facilities and one of the best stocked chandleries in the Mediterranean. It has, over the years, become a regular stopping point for all aspects of marine maintenance, equipment supply, berthing, repairs and fitting-out for Mediterranean or Atlantic-bound yachtsmen of all nationalities. It also offers new yachts sales and brokerage.

The boatyard has already closed and the marina is under the management of 'Temporary Moorings Ltd' whilst a new facility will be opened N of the runway, just to the R of the projection shown in the photograph on page 32.

Sheppard's activities will be carried out during 2005 from temporary facilities until these are transferred to the new marina as described under 'repairs'.

Gibraltar: Sheppard's, Marina Bay and the runway in late 2004. Changes due 2005   *Graham Hutt*

PILOTAGE

After clearing customs as described previously, proceed 50m E, where the marina will be seen.

Berthing

The visitors berth is at the end of the floating pontoon. (due to relocate 2005).

Charges for a 12m yacht

High season (June–November)
   Day £8.00

Low season
   Day £7.00
Multihulls +50%
Plus electricity and water
(Full information available on the web or by contacting the marina on email at the address given.)

Facilities

The 40-ton travel-lift and boatyard will not be operating until late 2005, following the move to the new marina. Other engineering and yard facilities available from temporary premises near Queensway Quay at Coaling Island. A 10-ton crane is available there for lifting small boats.

Water and *electricity* Accessible to each berth.

Repairs Facilities (see above) include workshops for mechanical and electronic repairs, rigging, light engineering and welding.

The chandlery (moved to new temporary premises near the marina) is very well stocked with electronics, spares, hardware, engines, generators, paints, inflatables and all materials needed for maintenance, repair and fitting out. The shop staff are knowledgeable about yachts and able to provide technical advice (☎ 75148).

Weather Posted daily at the office and broadcast as given in Maritime information section.

Sheppard's (new) Marina 2005

This new marina, being built N of the runway will offer yachtsmen a complete haul-out and repair yard to replace the old facility now closed. (Plan of proposed layout shown on plan page 27.) It will berth around 140 yachts from 6m–18m with a max draught of 3.5m on two pontoons within a secure basin.

Gibraltar showing new construction site for Sheppard's marina north (left) of the runway   *Patrick Roach*

G5 Marina Bay

Location
36°08'.9N 05°21'.4W

Communications
The Tower, P.O. Box 373, Gibraltar
☎ 73300 *Fax* 42656 VHF Ch 71
Email pieroffice@marinabay.gi
www.marinabay.gi

The Marina

Due N of Sheppard's (old) Marina and S of the runway, Marina Bay is an excellent location from which to visit Gibraltar or Spain. The ground tackle which fell into disrepair has mostly been replaced and facilities are excellent. This marina is the only one not undergoing radical changes. The marina can again take over 200 yachts. Nearby bars and restaurants along the quay and in Neptune House provide excellent food and a good social atmosphere.

PILOTAGE

The marina is 50m NE of the customs house.

Berthing

Call the marina office from the customs office and a berth will be allocated. A plan of the marina is shown in the customs house. Lines are tailed to the quay for bows/stern-to mooring. Larger vessels are berthed along the quays.

Note: Depths in the marina are around 2.5m but some areas are less. Make sure the berthing master knows your depth to ensure the correct location in the marina.

Charges for a 12m Yacht

High season May–Oct
Day £14.85
Low season Nov–Apr
Day £8.25
Cash discounts 10% 6 months 20% Annual 25%
Multihulls + 50%
Plus electricity and water
(Full information available on the web or by contacting the marina on email at the address given.)

Facilities

Water Available at every berth charged at 1p per litre.
Electricity Available at every berth charged at 15p per Kwh.
Repairs Mechanics can be brought to the yacht. Larger repairs and haul out facilities only available at Sheppard's Marina ☎ 77183 *Fax* 42535
Provisions Checkout supermarket near the main road entrance. Also see Provisions section in Availablity of Supplies on page 24.
Showers and *WC* On ground floor of Pier Office building. Facilities for the handicapped.
Launderette Near Checkout supermarket.
Dentist Mr. C. Linale, Neptune House. Marina Bay ☎ 78887
Security Security guards 24hr ☎ 40477.
Weather Daily bulletins are posted at the Pier Office. BFBS Radio ☎ 53416

Ashore

Eating out Enjoy the relaxed atmosphere of the waterfront restaurants within the marina complexes or the many restaurants, pubs and fastfood houses in the town, particularly in Main Street. A full list may be obtained from the tourist board.
Transport No 9 bus from the frontier to the bus station stops in Winston Churchill Avenue in front of the tower blocks at the northern end of Glacis Road, but it is only a 10 minute walk to the bus station and city centre.
Buses There are six local bus routes which run at approximately 15 minute intervals and cover most of the main tourist attractions. Details can be obtained from the tourist board ☎ 74950, Rock City Services ☎ 75660, or (Route 10 Safeway/Frontier) Calypso Tours ☎ 76520.
Hire cars May be arranged from the airport or from several car hire firms in the town and taken into Spain. Avis ☎ 75552/79200. Budget ☎ 79666. For full list contact the tourist board ☎ 74950.
Local taxis ☎ 70052/70027/79999 but are not permitted to cross the border into Spain.
Air services To the UK and Morocco (but not Spain).

To visit Spain, one may take a bus or taxi (or hire car) to the border where taxis wait on the Spanish side. La Línea Bus Station is fairly close and from here an excellent (and cheap) bus service networks the whole of Spain. If time is short, you may take advantage of the RENFE inter-city train service as a faster way to see Spain. The nearest station is in Algeciras where there and also ferries to Tanger and Ceuta. There is a connecting bus from La Línea to Algeciras bus station, from where you will have to either walk or get a taxi to the station or port.

Marina Bay marina (on left) and the old Sheppard's Marina
which will be moving to N of runway while space
renovated for Ocean Village marina   *Patrick Roach*

G6 Gibraltar Bay Anchorage

Location
   36°09′.2N 05°21′.6W

Located at the N end of the Bay N of the runway giving
good shelter except in W–SW winds.

ANCHORING

Anchorage is possible immediately north of the runway
in 4–6m sand with good holding. For safety reasons
yachts are prohibited from anchoring close to the
runway or on the flight path. Closer to the Spanish
shore of La Línea is a newly completed long jetty. The
anchorage has been considerably reduced by the placing
of buoys in the area. The anchoring area is further
restricted by the need for access to the new Sheppard's
complex which is being built E of the projecting mole
on the N side of the runway.

   Some surging can be expected during S winds.

   A better anchorage is NNW, near the La Línea
harbour mole.

ASHORE

Sites locally

There is a lot to see in Gibraltar with the many
monuments to its rich naval and maritime history to
visit, duty free shopping in the colourful, cross-cultural
High Street and souks. A trip to the top of the Rock can
be made by cable-car, taxi or a walk which takes around
an hour. Spain, Morocco and the Western Straits can be
seen on a clear day from the top, along with the famous
resident barbary 'apes', which are actually tail-less
monkeys from the Atlas Mountains of Morocco. It is
unknown how they came to be in Gibraltar, but in 1915,
the army took on their care in order to curb their
nomadic roaming. In fact, during the 2nd world war
their numbers declined almost to the point of
extinction, and it is said that Sir Winston Churchill
ordered more to be imported from Morocco, fearful of
the legend which deemed that Gibraltar would cease to
be British the day the apes left the Rock! St Michael's
Cave, half way up, is well worth a visit. Concerts are
sometimes held here and the acoustics are magnificent.
As Gibraltar is a mere 2 square miles in size, much can
be seen in a day. The quickest and most comprehensive
way to sample her history and spectacular views is to
take an Official Rock Tour which lasts approximately 90
minutes. (Or you can negotiate a tour of your choice,
which can include cable-car rides if desired.) Starting
from the frontier, the tour takes in visits from one end
of the Rock to the other. Highlights include:

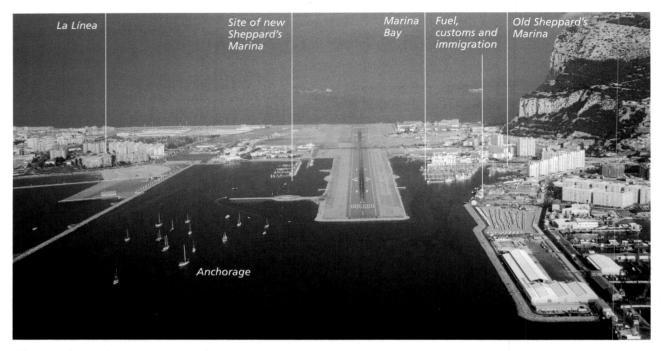

La Línea   Site of new Sheppard's Marina   Marina Bay   Fuel, customs and immigration   Old Sheppard's Marina

Anchorage

Gibraltar: The northern anchorage and entrance to Marina Bay

Catalan Bay, Water catchments, Europa Lighthouse, The Upper Rock Reserve, Jews' Gate, Saint Michael's Caves (the Cathedral Cave, a unique hall of crystallised nature thought to have been inhabited in neolithic times), O'Hara's Battery, the Apes' Den (a chance to be photographed with the Barbary Macaques monkeys), Military Heritage Centre, Great Siege Tunnels (excavated during the Great Siege of 1779–83 to permit the mounting of a gun on the north face). Gibraltar, a city under Siege, (optional: exhibition), Lime Kiln, Moorish Castle (the Tower of Homage, which dominates the hillside and approach to Gibraltar, dates back to AD1333 and displays battle scars sustained during ten sieges in the 14th and 15th century. It was refuge to hundreds in 1540 when Corsairs sacked the

Top of the Rock: famous for its barbary apes   *Graham Hutt*

town). The Gibraltar Museum & Moorish Baths, Parson's Lodge (optional: a historic battery guarding the entrance to Rosia Bay), Alameda Botanical Gardens.

Other tours can be arranged through travel agents or the tourist information offices. Worthy of mention are the Tunnel Tour of the Second World War tunnels, (☎ 54451). Many other places are of interest and may be encountered in Main Street, a colourful multicultural mixture of local shops and souks and British department stores such as Marks & Spencer, below a dignified colonial-style facade. Tour the Lower St Michael's Cave (☎ 55829 or 40561 Mr. Walker). It is possible to conduct your own walking tour of the city gates and fortifications, with the aid of the books listed. It is also possible to visit the main sites by local bus. A detailed bus routes sheet may be obtained from the tourist offices.

Further details of sites and other tourist information, including details of consulates, restaurants, natural history etc., can be obtained from the Gibraltar Tourist Board's excellent and comprehensive Fact Files which are issued free. The tourist board also provides a very good street map. Its offices are located at Duke of Kent House, Cathedral Square ☎ 79450, The Piazza, Main Street ☎ 79482, Four Corners, Winston Churchill Avenue, ☎ 50762, Arrivals hall, Gibraltar Airport ☎ 73026/47227. Customs hall at the border; Gibraltar museum, 18-20 Bombhouse Lane. John Mackintosh Hall, 308 Main Street. The staff are very friendly and extremely helpful.

Eating out

Everywhere you look in the town there is somewhere to eat, from pubs to expensive restaurants. The more expensive ones are in the marinas. For a refreshing stop while shopping or sight seeing in Main Street, visit Wesley House, the Methodist Church and Carpenter's

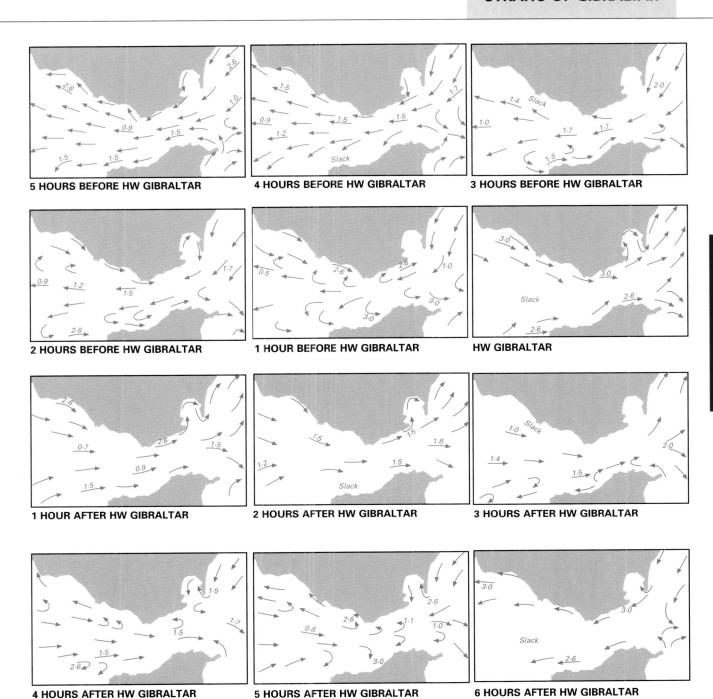

5 HOURS BEFORE HW GIBRALTAR

4 HOURS BEFORE HW GIBRALTAR

3 HOURS BEFORE HW GIBRALTAR

2 HOURS BEFORE HW GIBRALTAR

1 HOUR BEFORE HW GIBRALTAR

HW GIBRALTAR

1 HOUR AFTER HW GIBRALTAR

2 HOURS AFTER HW GIBRALTAR

3 HOURS AFTER HW GIBRALTAR

4 HOURS AFTER HW GIBRALTAR

5 HOURS AFTER HW GIBRALTAR

6 HOURS AFTER HW GIBRALTAR

Arms upstairs, which serves very reasonably priced home-made meals and snacks in a very welcoming atmosphere (open 0930–1400 Mon–Fri; closed August, Christmas and Easter weeks).

Transiting the Straits of Gibraltar

Many yachts will be using Gibraltar as the departure point for trips to Morocco. Many elements combine to produce a complex system of tides and current in the Straits, an appreciation of which will greatly help yachtsman heading west. Having spent many fruitless hours trying to make a passage westwards through the Straits some years ago, thoroughly convinced by the Admiralty tide tables that the current was with me, in fact I was losing ground while making 6 knots through the water. These paragraphs are included to assist the yachtsman transiting the Straits.

Eight miles separate Europe from Africa at its narrowest point in the straits. The water at the western end of the 30 mile stretch is some 2–3m higher than at the eastern end, thus causing a constant surface flow into the Mediterranean. This is due to evaporation in the Mediterranean, which is three times faster than the rate at which the combined waters from rivers flow into it and the fact that the Atlantic is tidal with a predominantly westerly swell, whereas the land-locked Mediterranean, is virtually non tidal. This produces a standing E-going surface current of between 1 and 2 knots. Differences in salinity between the Atlantic and the Mediterranean force the heavier water down, causing a sub surface current in the opposite direction. Wind also creates a surface current, depending whether it is E (levante) or W (poniente), which confuses the equation further. Then there are the tides, which are well documented in Admiralty tide tables. At the eastern end of the Straits the range is only half a metre and negligible once a few miles into the Mediterranean, whereas at Tanger, Morocco, the spring range is 3m. Barometric pressure differences also affect the height of water.

On the north side of the Western Straits is Tarifa. Winds in excess of 30 knots are said to blow there for 300 days of the year, whereas at the same time, winds at the eastern end may be negligible, resulting in conditions at one end of the Strait being very different from those at the other. Currents also vary in different parts of the Straits, and even run in opposite directions at the same time, as shown on the tidal chart. From these conflicting and confusing parameters some guidelines can be extracted.

Eastbound vessels

For yachts entering the straits from the west, there is no real problem going eastwards, unless there is a strong easterly wind, in which case passage will be rough, especially around Tarifa, where winds often reach 40 knots. If strong winds are forecast, stay in Tanger or Barbate until it drops, or anchor in the lee of Tarifa if strong E winds are encountered once on passage. During periods of light easterly winds, sea mist or fog may be persistent in the Straits, especially during the mornings. The best time to depart for the trip east is soon after LW. From Tanger, keeping close inshore, the light and increasing E-going current off Punta Malabata will be useful. If going to Gibraltar, most vessels cross to Tarifa from Punta Malabata, or from Ciris, 12 miles further east.

Westbound vessels

In strong westerlies it is almost impossible to make headway west, due to the combined E-going current that can, with unfavourable tide, reach 6 knots or more, with heavy steep swell and overfalls off Ceuta Point, Tarifa and Punta Malabata.

In good conditions, to make use of the favourable current, set off from Gibraltar 2 hours after HW. Keeping close inshore, a foul current of around a knot will be experienced off Punta Carnero. A favourable W-going current 4 hours after HW will assist passage during springs, although this is weak and E-going at neaps. Crossing from Tarifa to Tanger it is usually wise to use the engine to make a fast passage to combat the increasing E-going current, or anchor in the sheltered W side of Tarifa and wait for the next favourable tide, around LW to make the crossing. It is possible, using the engine, to make a fast passage from Gibraltar without encountering heavy adverse currents.

From Ceuta, the timing is similar: set off 2 hours after HW, keeping close inshore to make use of the counter current.

Gibraltar to Ceuta

Crossing from N to S and vice versa can normally be undertaken at any state of tide, since winds through the Straits are predominantly E or W, although it is important to leave enough sea room to counter the tide and currents. Remember, in general, a combined current of 1-2 knots is usually E-going, in addition to tidal effects. Beware of rough over-falls and stronger currents around Europa Point and Ceuta Point. Entering Ceuta harbour, this is particularly noticeable one mile NE off the entrance.

The above information is based on several articles regarding tides, current and wind effects in the Straits of Gibraltar, as well as many hours testing out the theories in over 50 journeys transiting them. The currents in the Straits are still full of surprises and for sailing purists who do not want a motor-assisted transit, this can be very challenging.

II. MOROCCO

Capital Rabat
Commercial capital Casablanca
Population Approximately 30 million

Introduction

Although less than eight miles separate Europe from Morocco and the African continent, Morocco is completely different from the European mainland and one of the world's most fascinating places to visit. The Rif mountains bordering the Mediterranean coast may appear deserted but they are dotted with small villages and isolated fishing communities wherever there is a small bay or narrow strip of beach. Further inland are the great cities of the plains, old capitals of powerful Sultans whose territories once stretched from Mauritania to the Pyrenees and from the Atlantic to Tunisia. Further S rise the majestic Atlas Mountains, home to the original Berber inhabitants, where many of the old rulers began their conquests. Beyond are the High Atlas mountains which give way to the Sahara desert.

Morocco has retained its traditional values and lifestyle more than any of the other North African countries of the *The Maghreb* (meaning 'the place where the sun sets: the furthest western land of the Islamic world'). It is an intriguing and delightful place: a country where visitors are welcome but where the government has not encouraged the sort of tourism that has destroyed the cultural fabric, as in so many towns elsewhere. There are no 'concrete jungles' here, as along the coast of Spain, Italy, France and Greece. Where tourist accommodation has been built, almost nowhere has it impinged on the ancient parts of the towns. In Tanger for example, the hotels are mainly along the seafront, completely separate, but within easy reach of the old part of the town. Likewise, the ports remain very Moroccan: typical busy fishing ports going about their business as they have for centuries. Do not expect to find luxurious well-appointed marinas as seen in Europe. However, two such marinas: Marina Smir and Kabila, are described and are well located for excursions to Chefchouen and Tetouan. More marinas are planned.

HISTORY

One of the most fascinating aspects of Morocco is the sense of ongoing history, which is clearly evidenced everywhere, both in the nature of the port activities and the historical constructions. The continuing and practical use of donkeys, working alongside the most modern vehicles, provokes a feeling of timelessness. The story you see in the architecture and the ruins around the ports, is one of a rise and fall of empires: Phoenician, Roman, Portuguese 16th-century global maritime trade, 20th-century French/Spanish colonial empires and Moroccan dynasties. Over time, their prominence and prosperity has ebbed and flowed like the tide.

Phoenician trading posts are evident along the entire coast of Morocco and the Romans built quite a large city near Volubilis, but Morocco was not subjugated to any central authority before the 7th century AD. The Berber tribes each had their own territories in the Maghreb region. Only after the Arab conquest in the 7th and 8th centuries did some sort of central rule emerge, possibly helped by the first successful invasion of Southern Spain in 711 by Muslim-converted Berbers. The Moors, as they were called, continued north until halted at the Pyrenees in 731 by Charles Martel. In 680, the Governor of Kairouan (in present day Tunisia), Oqba Ibn Nafi, had reached the Atlantic coast of Morocco and introduced the Islamic religion to the indigenous Berbers. When Islam split into Sunni and Shi'ite sects in the 8th century, many of the latter moved west from Damascus and eventually arrived in Morocco. Among them was Moulay Idriss who was accepted as the new leader by the inhabitants of Volubilis which at that time was still a major city. In 791 Moulay Idriss was poisoned by Sunni Muslims but his short reign marks the first Moroccan dynasty, the Idrissids. Moulay's son Idriss II ruled Morocco from the north to the oases south of the Atlas for over 20 years and founded Fes as his new capital. Situated between the other two great cities of western Islam, Cordoba in Spain and Kairouan in Tunisia, Fes became a flourishing trading as well as religious centre. The power of the Idrissids weakened after a short time and the sultanate fell apart again in separate principalities. In the 11th and 12th centuries Morocco was ruled by two great Berber dynasties, the Almoravids and Almohads

Today's aspiration for a Greater Morocco with regard to the Western Sahara goes back to the Islamic Golden Ages under these dynasties. The Almoravids set up Marrakech as their new capital and, having lost territory in Spain to the Christians, their leader Youssef bin Tachfine restored Muslim control as far N as Valencia in 1107. The Almohads, driven by religious zeal, eventually overthrew the Almoravids. Under Yacoub el Mansour they defeated the Christians in Spain again in 1195 and for the first time in history the Maghreb was one huge empire from the Atlantic to Tunisia and Spain to Senegal. With the wealth this brought, a new capital was built in Rabat and many new mosques and minarets were built in cities as far apart as Sevilla in the north and Marrakech in the south. When the Almohads tried to push the Christians north of the Pyrenees they were defeated in 1212 and a gradual decline set in until the Moors were finally defeated in Spain with the fall of Granada in 1492.

In the following centuries the Portuguese set up seaports on the Atlantic Coast and the Maghreb became

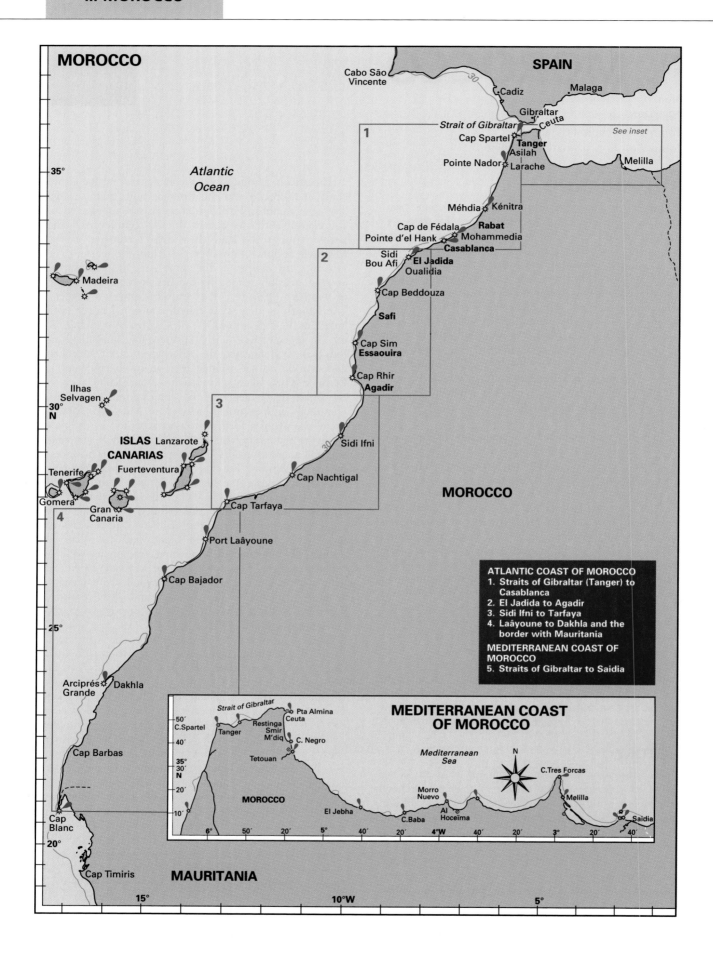

MOROCCO

Atlantic Ocean

35°

SPAIN

Cabo São Vincente

Cadiz

Malaga

Gibraltar
Ceuta

Strait of Gibraltar

See inset

1

Cap Spartel
Tanger
Asilah

Melilla

Pointe Nador
Larache

Méhdia
Kénitra

Cap de Fédala
Rabat
Pointe d'el Hank
Mohammedia
Casablanca

Sidi
Bou Afi
El Jadida
Oualidia

2

Cap Beddouza

Safi

Madeira

Cap Sim
Essaouira

Cap Rhir
Agadir

Ilhas
Selvagen

30°
N

3

ISLAS
CANARIAS
Lanzarote

Fuerteventura

Sidi Ifni

Cap Nachtigal

Tenerife

Gomera
Gran
Canaria

Cap Tarfaya

MOROCCO

4

Port Laâyoune

Cap Bajador

25°

ATLANTIC COAST OF MOROCCO
1. Straits of Gibraltar (Tanger) to Casablanca
2. El Jadida to Agadir
3. Sidi Ifni to Tarfaya
4. Laâyoune to Dakhla and the border with Mauritania

MEDITERRANEAN COAST OF MOROCCO
5. Straits of Gibraltar to Saidia

Arciprés
Grande
Dakhla

Strait of Gibraltar

50'

C.Spartel
Tanger

Restinga
Smir
M'diq

Pta Almina
Ceuta

MEDITERRANEAN COAST OF MOROCCO

40'

C. Negro

35°
30'
N

Tetouan

Mediterranean Sea

N

Cap Barbas

20'

C.Tres Forcas

10'

MOROCCO

Morro
Nuevo

Melilla

El Jebha

C.Baba

Al
Hoceïma

Saidia

Cap
Blanc

6°

50'

20'

5°

40'

20'

4°W

40'

20'

3°

20'

40'

20°

Cap Timiris

MAURITANIA

15°

10°W

5°

part of the Ottoman Empire. The most remarkable event of this period was the establishment of the pirate 'Republic of the Bou Regreg', on the Atlantic coast around Rabat, in the beginning of the 17th century. Spanish ships were the main target of their attacks but they strayed as far north as Ireland and traded weapons with the English and French. Towards the end of the 17th century the new dynasty of the Alaouites emerged from the south and during the 55 years of Sultan Moulay Ismail's reign, the entire country was subjugated again. Morocco enjoyed its last 'Golden Age' and Meknes became the new Imperial Capital. At his death in 1727 Ismail left a great empire and from his numerous sons, Sidi Mohammed emerged as the new sultan. Morocco continued to prosper but after Mohammed's death in 1790 the country fell back into a state of civil war. The 20th century is marked by a growing European influence and at the Treaty of Fes in 1912, Morocco was divided into French and Spanish Protectorates. Spain took the north where, since the 15th century, they occupied the enclaves of Ceuta and Melilla, and a strip of Sahara down to French Mauritania, and France controlled the area south of the Rif mountains. Spain showed little interest in developing their part of the Protectorate but under the inspired leadership of Marshal Lyautey, the French introduced their own administrative system alongside the Moroccan bureaucracy and built new French towns next to the Arab medinas, as well as new roads and irrigation systems to develop the country. Before the beginning of the Second World War, moderate nationalist feelings had surfaced, but during the war Moroccan forces fought alongside French troops. After the war this Moroccan loyalty was not rewarded and Istiqlal, the party for independence, grew stronger. When in 1953 Sultan (later King) Mohammed V openly supported the independence movement, he was exiled but this only increased his popularity. Under pressure from increased violence and unrest he was allowed to return to Morocco in 1955 and in 1956 France and Spain signed treaties with the King for the complete independence of Morocco.

Ancient castle formally protecting the Bay of Tanger
Graham Hutt

Recent history

Mohammed V, the grandfather of the present king, Mohammed VI, led the country to independence after French colonial rule ended in 1956. After the sudden death of his father, Hassan II, still in his early twenties, assumed control in 1961. Helped by the fact that he was a direct descendant of the Prophet and as such also the religious leader, he maintained control of his country through good leadership and shrewd political manoeuvring.

In July 1999, King Hassan II died and Mohammed VI inherited the throne at 36 years of age.

One of King Hassan II's remarkable initiatives was the Green March in 1975, when 350,000 unarmed Moroccans moved into the Western Sahara which until then had been a Spanish colony. Attention was deflected from internal problems and the population was united for the common cause of a Greater Morocco. This initiative brought its difficulties. Supported by Algeria, the population of the new territory started a war for independence and relations with Algeria were strained for many years, although they have recently improved. The Western Sahara issue is still not resolved, although renewed efforts by the UN are currently under way. Through a new Maghrebian unity, Morocco hopes to find new markets for its agricultural products and gain access to the rich oil and gas reserves of Algeria and Libya. Morocco is a large producer of phosphates but has no other significant natural resource. Phosphates and derivatives account for 60% of export earnings and agricultural exports, tourist revenues and remittances from Moroccans working abroad make up the rest. Morocco's export of agricultural products has been severely cut since the full integration of Spain and the rest of Europe into the EU.

Spain retains sovereignty of two small enclaves on the Moroccan coast: Ceuta and Melilla. These, along with two small islands are all that remain of the Spanish colonial rule.

With high unemployment and other internal problems, King Mohammed VI is determined to bring the country closer to Europe and into the 21st century, giving more freedom and education to his people.

Planning your cruise

Time zone

Morocco is on UT (GMT) all year round: 2 hours behind Southern Europe time in the summer.

Money

Morocco's currency unit is the Dirham (Dh) with an exchange rate of approximately Dh15=£1.00 and Dh9.5=$1.00. (2005). Moroccan traders often express prices in francs, where 100 francs equal 1Dh. In coastal towns in the north, euros can often be used.

Eurocheques, travellers' cheques and cash are accepted at banks and international giro cheques can be cashed at post offices. With an American Express credit card, travellers' cheques can be bought from the American Express representative, Voyage Schwarz, which has offices in Tanger, Casablanca, Rabat,

Typical souk in Morocco   *Graham Hutt*

Berber ladies at the market   *Graham Hutt*

Marrakech and Agadir. Using a Visa credit card, varying amounts up to Dh8,000 can be withdrawn at ATMs, depending on the bank. Many shops take Visa, including, surprisingly, many of the small shops in the souks and casbahs.

Taking Dirhams in or out of the country is not permitted, though small amounts do not seem to cause any concern. Changing left-over notes is possible when receipts have been kept but it is preferable not to draw more than is needed. Notes can also be changed in Gibraltar or Algeciras. The Spanish enclaves within Morocco: Ceuta and Melilla, use euros. Credit cards, Eurocheques and travellers' cheques are accepted and there are no exchange controls.

Health precautions

There are no mandatory inoculations except for yellow fever if coming from an infected area. Pharmacists are well trained but stock only a limited range of drugs. A good anti-diarrhoea drug should always be carried on board. Repatriation insurance in the case of major surgery is advisable. Many yacht insurance policies include this.

CRUISING GROUNDS

The N coast of Morocco borders the Atlantic for some 30M from Cap Spartel to Ceuta, from where the Mediterranean coast extends 165M to the Algerian border. Most of this coast is flanked by the inaccessible Rif Mountains, interrupted by beaches in the bay S of Ceuta, the Bay of Al Hoceïma and the coast E of Cabo Tres Forcas. Several strategically located rocks and islets off the coast are still in Spanish hands as well as the enclaves of Ceuta and Melilla. There are few anchorages with good shelter. Ceuta and Melilla are conveniently located to stock up on items not available in Morocco. Although Morocco is visited by the largest number of European tourists in the Maghreb, around 1.5 million a year, this is hardly noticeable along the coast. The ports offer a unique view of the traditional Moroccan lifestyle and yachts will find a friendly welcome everywhere.

The Atlantic coast, although not spectacular from seaward, offers a glimpse of the past in the form of many ancient cities and ports which, in some cases have been in use for thousands of years. It is possible and practical to visit the entire coast of Morocco without having to spend a night at sea.

Anchoring

Smuggling and illegal emigration are a constant problem to the Moroccan authorities. Even though there does not seem to be a law forbidding anchoring along the Moroccan coast, care must be exercised because of the kif (marijuana) trafficking mentioned below. Yachts close to the shore are sometimes checked by military boats to ensure they are engaged in legitimate activities. Thus, beware of lingering or anchoring near the shore without first informing the authorities that you wish to do so. Generally, local officials will not allow yachts to anchor in the vicinity of ports. Although much of the coast looks deserted, there are hidden military posts along the entire coastline at regular intervals and it will not be long before you will be made aware of this if you venture too close without first obtaining clearance. This is particularly true of the coastline between Melilla and Ceuta and in the Bay of Tanger. There are good fishing areas and lovely bays on the north coast which may be used if the nearest harbour authorities are informed in advance.

In case of an emergency or change of plan try to inform the authorities of your position by VHF on Ch 16. Never go ashore without authorisation in deserted parts of the coast or without first clearing customs, since you will almost certainly be arrested.

Marinas

The only two yacht marinas in Morocco are Marina Smir and Marina Kabila, both near the Spanish enclave of Sebta (Ceuta). Smir offers every facility a yacht requires and naturally has a daily rate. Kabila is currently closed to yachts because of silting. Several more marinas are planned elsewhere, but it is anyone's guess if and when they are completed. It should be noted that at present, these two little-used marinas, charge a rate higher than most in Europe and in contrast to marinas in Spain and Gibraltar, the price is not negotiable, except for long term stays of several months or more.

Good all-weather ports

Entry safe by day and night and in bad weather:
Mediterranean coast: Tanger, Ceuta and Melilla (not in strong easterlies). Gibraltar.
Atlantic coast: Mohammedia, Casablanca, Jorf Lasfar, Safi, Agadir.

Harbour entry

Generally, except in the large commercial ports, entry at night is not advisable. Most of the harbours are fishing ports, often with no specifically designated place for yachts. It is easier to see the best place to moor by daylight and to avoid the many lines crossing between the boats which also frequently cross the harbour entrance. Some of the harbours are difficult to navigate, with entrances prone to silting although, once inside, they are quite safe. Daylight is also generally considered to be more auspicious, especially if you are engaged in something as unusual as sailing a pleasure yacht! (I have frequently been asked, 'Why do you come by yacht, rather than by air, which is so much faster?') It should be appreciated that space is always made for a visiting yacht, but there may be only a single alongside berth available where two or three yachts can usually rack out if necessary. This is especially true along the Atlantic coast of Morocco, where cruising yachts are a new sight in most ports.

Harbour charges

Since most of the harbours in Morocco are fishing ports with no specific facilities or infrastructure to accommodate yachts, it has in the past been unusual for formal charges to be made, though often 'bakhshish' was asked for, usually only between 10 and 20 Dirhams per day (USD 1-2). Often a packet of cigarettes was sufficient. This is changing with the introduction of a tariff. The Ports Authorities have recently announced a

new directive to standardise charges for all vessels visiting ports called the ISPS fee, which applies commercial rates to all vessels. Some yachts have already been caught up in this directive, paying exorbitant rates and some harbourmasters have refused to implement the measure on pleasure craft. In May 2005 a directive was given that yachts are exempt from this charge.

The administration of port finance is also being re-organised. The raising of invoices was formerly the responsibility of ODEP, a government agency. In future, charges and invoices will be the responsibility of the port captain. A standard rate and official charges will be the result of these changes, but it is not known when these will be implemented, or how much charges will be. My guess is that apart from the two marinas, charges will remain very low, at between Dh10 to Dh100 per day. (USD 1 to 10).

Because of the fluidity of the situation, port charges are not listed except in Marina Smir, and for (Spanish) Ceuta and Melilla which have published prices.

Harbour security

There are no particular problems in any port in Morocco. The army and police have a discreet presence in every harbour. If the yacht is to be left for any length of time in a port, consider paying a guardian to keep an eye on it. There will be no shortage of volunteers; ask the harbourmaster for advice. Look on it as a harbour due. All fishing boats have guardians and it is a way of providing a little income for often poor families. When arranging a guardian keep in mind that a fisherman brings home between Dh 500–1000 (£35 to £70) per month. It is possible to employ a watchman for just a few dollars a day. Other security considerations are addressed in the main introduction.

The kif trade

The growing and processing of kif (marijuana, hashish), is an important economic activity in the Rif mountains on the north coast, with some communities totally sustained by it. This may be of little concern to a yachtsman, but it is important to avoid a misunderstanding about the purpose of your own visit. It is legal to grow and sell the drug, but illegal to buy or transport it. There are many smuggling routes to Europe and shipment by yacht is one, as witnessed by the numbers of yachts confiscated there and many more in Moroccan ports, with the crews in Tanger jail. Police often photograph yachts when cruising along the coast, which is regularly patrolled. Although the official attitude to kif is unambiguous, officials in some of the smaller ports seem happy to ignore or profit from it. It is by far the biggest source of income in the otherwise poor north and it is not uncommon to be asked, even by officials, to buy a few kilos. This may be done either to test the purpose of your visit or to propose a real transaction, though a serious attempt at a business deal will almost never be made directly. Providing you are aware that there is a traffic it is easy to avoid it. It should be noted that the dealers' profit is not only made by selling kif, but also by informing the police of his customers! He often gets the kif back in the end to re-sell, thus profiting three times from any sale!

Woman at the well: some water is further away in Morocco than a long hosepipe!   *Graham Hutt*

Availability of supplies

Fuel
Ceuta and Melilla have very cheap, good quality diesel. In Morocco it is more expensive but available from pumps in several ports and elsewhere it can be obtained in drums, which can be delivered for a small fee.

Water
Generally there is a sufficient supply of good quality water but it is not always a convenient hose pipe length away. Sometimes a small charge is made, especially if you require assistance carrying cans aboard.

Electricity
Nominal voltage is 220V, 60Hz. This is available in the marinas and it is often possible to arrange in other ports with a long lead, even if no specific provision is made, except in some of the very small harbours.

Provisions
Supermarkets exist only in the larger towns, but between the small shops and markets most requirements can be met. All fresh produce is seasonal and often grown locally. The quality is excellent and, due to less intensive farming techniques, fruit and vegetables generally are very good. Chicken and meat are not tampered with and because refrigeration is often not available, meat is freshly butchered; the heads of slaughtered animals are displayed by the butcher as proof of freshness.

Shopping at the markets is fun. After a round of all the stalls a bag full of good quality fruit and vegetables may cost no more than £2. Tanger has a particularly fascinating market and the small villages are rewarding, especially on the weekly souk (market) days. Farmers from the mountains bring their produce which varies from livestock such as chickens, rabbits or a goat, to fruit and vegetables. Donkeys get new shoes, saddles are repaired and at the end of the day the farmer leaves again with a new supply of staple articles.

Chickens in the small villages are delicious and can be bought alive; the merchant will be happy to dress them on the spot. Once used to these different customs it is difficult to revert to the plastic wrapped products from the European supermarket.

Locally produced bottled soft drinks are very good value for money, as is the local beer. Local wines are not on a par with European wines and are expensive. Canned food is not usually available. There are supermarkets and shops in the Spanish enclaves. Ceuta is a free port operating in competition with Gibraltar. Bonded supplies in Gibraltar are on the shelves in Ceuta at comparable prices without the hassle of customs formalities. Generally, prices in Ceuta and on the Spanish mainland are around 20% cheaper than in Gibraltar, but will vary with the exchange rate.

Repairs
Marina Smir has excellent haul-out facilities for any size of yacht and Kabila has a small travel-hoist. With Gibraltar and Puerto Sotogrande (10M NE of Gibraltar) nearby, both with large travel-hoists, the area is well served with repair facilities. Most diesel engines can be repaired or even completely overhauled at very low prices in almost any Moroccan port. Emergency repairs to other engines can be carried out anywhere. Fuel systems for any make of diesel engine can be repaired but it takes time to find the right workshop.

Entry formalities

Every port has its own variation of entry and exit procedure, but the formalities are no great problem, if sometimes lengthy. Officials will show up soon after arrival. Immigration police, or the gendarmerie in the small ports, will always visit to check passports, which they sometimes retain, together with the ship's papers. These are returned shortly before departure, so if planning an early start, allow time to get them back. Customs officers will visit along with the harbourmaster. Some of the smaller harbours are not official ports of entry, but this is not usually a problem unless you want to travel inland, in which case your passport may be retained and a shore pass issued.

Entry into the small ports is an interesting experience. The officials will probably all arrive together and the yacht may also be honoured by a visit from the caïd, equivalent to a French prefect or mayor, appointed by the government. Officials are friendly and speak French or Spanish and sometimes, a little English. Entry procedures are free of charge.

Tips, which might be considered as bribes, must be avoided, but the practice of bakhshish exists and it is not uncommon to be asked for cigarettes or whisky by the officials.

The main concern for customs officials boarding your yacht appears to be guns. If you have a weapon onboard, it must be declared and it will be bonded while in port. Note that this and other cargo and crew information is exchanged between the ports by fax. Alcoholic beverages on board for personal use are not of great concern but large quantities should be declared and may be sealed in a locker until your departure. Generally, a glimpse inside the boat will satisfy official curiosity. The capitainerie and marine marchande operate in all ports but generally are not interested in yachts staying only a short time.

When making a trip inland be sure to take passports or your shore pass if one is issued in lieu, as these are required by hotels.

Note Formalities and inspections in some harbours, particularly on the northern coast, have in the past been excessive. This has been the case at Al Hoceïma – where as many as 10 officers may board your vessel – Marina Smir and Kabila, where yachts have undergone a thorough searching taking an hour or more for no apparent reason, both on arrival and departure. However, things are changing with the recently declared policy of encouraging yachtsmen. Letting the harbour authorities know your next destination will greatly assist your passage through the formalities. Before exiting, officials will most probably again stamp passports out, even if you intend to visit another port.

Yachts are a rarity in Morocco at present, so many of the port authorities simply do not know how to handle them, especially in the context of a fishing harbour. No doubt as more sailors visit and as the authorities gain greater familiarity with the yachting community, they will learn to discriminate between pleasure sailors and those very few who are involved in other activities and the government will develop a more systematic and practical approach. Being friendly and retaining a sense of humour is essential.

Visas

Most Europeans, North American, Australian and New Zealand citizens do not need a visa to enter Morocco for visits up to 90 days. Citizens of Luxembourg and South Africa do require them and they are best obtained in their country of residence, normally taking 24hrs to process. There are Moroccan consulates in Málaga and Algeciras, Spain, but it takes longer to obtain visas there. Visitors with Israeli or South African stamps in their passports may be refused entry into Morocco although there does not seem to be a consistent policy. It is possible to renew or extend a visa. In practice, yachtsmen rarely have a problem, whatever their nationality and can usually obtain a shore pass even if a visa is theoretically required.

Embassies

UK 17 Blvd de la Tour Hassan, Rabat
☎ 07/720905-6/238600 www.britishembassy.gov.uk
41 Ave Mohammed V, Tanger 09/941557
Fax 09/942284 *Email* uktanger@mtds.com
Consulate 36 rue de la Loire – Polo, Casablanca
02/857400 *Fax* 02/834625/26

USA 2 Av. De Mohammed El Fassi, Rabat
☎ 07/762265/767939 *Fax* 07/765661
www.usembassy.ma
Consulate 8 Boulevard Moulay Yousef, Casablanca
☎ 02/264550 *Fax* 02/204127

Canada 13 Bis Rue Joafar Assadik, Agdal, Rabat
☎ 07/687400 *Fax* 07/687430
Email: rabat@dfait-maici.gc.ca

France 3 Rue Sahnoun, Agdal, Rabat
☎ 07/689700 *Fax* 07/689701
Consulate 49 Ave Allal Ben Abdallah, Rabat
☎ 07/268181 *Fax* 07/268171

www.consulfrance-rabat.org
2 Place de France, Tanger ☎ 09/932039/40
Fax 09/938984 www.ambafrance-ma.org

Netherlands 40 Rue de Tunis, Rabat
☎ 07/733512/726780 *Fax* 07/733335
Email nlgovrab@mtds.com
Consulate Immeuble Miramonte, 47 Av. Hassan II, Tanger ☎ 09/931245

Denmark 4 Rue de Khemisset, Boulte 203, Rabat
☎ 07/774205/32684/07/774125
Consulate 150 Meskini, Casablanca ☎ 02/314491

Sweden 159 Av. John Kennedy, Souissi, Rabat
☎ 07/756446/633210 *Fax* 07/633210
Email ambassaden.rabat@foreign.ministry.se
www.swedenabroad.com
Consulate 3 Rue du Lt. Sylvestre, Casablanca
☎ 02/304648

Norway 9 Rue de Khenfira, Agdal, Rabat
☎ 07/764088 *Email* emb.rabat@mfa.no
www.norvege.ma/info/embassy
Consulate 3 Rue Henri Regnault, Tanger
☎ 09 933633

Irish, Australian and New Zealand citizens are advised to use UK consular facilities while in Morocco.

Internet facilities

These are new to Morocco, but an amazing number of internet cafés have sprung up in the past year, giving easy and usually fast access to the internet in every town and city, usually within easy reach of harbours.

While logged on, check out the travels in Morocco of sailing yacht *Witte Raaf* who has been along the Atlantic coast visiting ports and taking fine pictures: www.witteraaf.info

Telephone

Overseas calls can be made at post offices but there are often queues. There are kiosks in most towns, selling telephone cards, which can be used on any public international phone. The larger hotels also have facilities, although very much more expensive and usually without STD dialling. The GSM mobile phone network is very well advanced and works in almost every town as well as several miles offshore along much of the coastline. Ensure the International Roaming facility is activated with your mobile telephone company before leaving Europe. The mobile GSM system is often cheaper than using the local public phone system.

Tourist information

The ONMT (l'Office National Marocain du Tourisme, also called Syndicat d'Initiative), has offices in all major cities in Morocco. Their London office is at 174 Regent Street ☎ 44 (0)171 437 0073/74. They have useful city plans and general information but for any serious information the travel guides listed under 'Books' in the Appendix are indispensable.

Tour guides

As with *bakhshish*, (see that section in the Introduction page 4) understanding this issue in advance can make the difference between having a relaxing time in Morocco and leaving the country exhausted by minor

II. MOROCCO

struggles with the ubiquitous 'volunteers' who intend to help you with the details of life for a small fee - whether you want it or not! This is particularly problematic in Tanger. Europeans are accustomed to deciding when they need assistance and so it can be disconcerting to find that payment is expected for services rendered without ever being consulted: a porter to help with bags, a tour guide, an attendant to wash and watch over your car, etc. Even when asked in advance, it may seem that declining is simply not an option. If you genuinely have no intention of accepting such offers/demands for payment, or if you are aggressively pestered as is common in Tanger and Tetouan, be sure not to engage in any conversation beyond a polite 'no thank you', for verbal engagement is taken as a sign of interest. 'No' is taken to mean 'perhaps'. However, do consider that it can be a tremendous relief to relinquish some of one's autonomy and simply permit people to help, whilst enjoying the luxury of highly personalised attention. Once you have chosen a particular person to help you with a task and settled on a price you both think is fair, you can rest assured that he will personally fend off all other contenders for the honour and usually do his job very attentively.

At times you may want a guide. In El Jadida, for example, a tour guide will willingly spend an entire day taking you round the extensive sights for some 50 Dirhams - just $5.00 (although more may be appropriate). Many guides, official or not, speak excellent French and English and know a good deal about the history of their towns. Spending several hours with an articulate guide now and then can teach you much about Morocco, its culture and history.

Many guides will have a personal agenda (e.g. taking you to visit 'my brother' the carpet merchant) so be sure to steer your own course through the *souk* without getting bamboozled into buying what you do not want. In Marina Smir, Kabila and M'diq there are usually taxi drivers who will take you to Tetouan, Chefchaouen, the Oued Laou market and the surrounding villages for a very reasonable fare. For a small extra charge they are often prepared to act as a tour guide, ensuring that you are not disturbed on your excursion. Insofar as you can anticipate them, it is wisest, financially, to outline all such desires in your initial negotiations.

In summary, rather than clinging to a 'do-it-yourself' approach in Morocco, it often makes more sense to think through your needs and wishes so that you can negotiate clearly when the opportunity arises, and then allow the abundant volunteers (who may desperately need a few extra Dirhams) to help you execute them. Rather than resist it, let this different system work for you from the start.

Note For any train or bus excursion, it is wise to know the schedule yourself. Tourists are occasionally followed onto trains and told that they must get off and change to another in some town or other, only to find that such route/schedule revisions were concocted to lure them into the shops of the family of the 'guide' who gave them this advice. In any case, if you want to make your own way around Moroccan cities, a general piece of advice is that you will be hassled much less if you at least look as if you know where you are going, even if you do not.

Photography

There is no particular problem, providing pictures are not taken of military objects which include naval patrol boats. When taking pictures of people keep in mind that there is an Islamic religious objection to making an image of a person, though, with modern publicity and television this is fading. Objections can usually be smoothed away with a small tip.

Business hours

Banks are normally open Mon–Fri 0830-1130 and 1500-1630.

Shops are normally open 7 days a week from early morning to late in the afternoon with a long lunch break. As everywhere, markets have the best assortment in the mornings.

Public Holidays

New Year's Day 1 January
Feast of the Throne 3 March
Labour Day 1 May
Green March 6 November
Independence Day 18 November
Islamic holidays are listed in the Introduction.

Tipping

Tipping follows the same rules as in Europe although it is not uncommon to have tips refused in the small villages along the coast. In European style restaurants and tourist areas, tipping is expected. It is useful to have European or American cigarettes on board as a gratuity for small services.

Overland travel

Like all of North Africa, Morocco has a good, cheap public transport infrastructure:

Trains The railway system covers most of the northern cities and is the most comfortable way to travel. It is worth paying the very small price difference to travel first class.

Buses and coaches There is a regular bus service connecting almost every town and village in Morocco. This is a slow method of travel, except for the inter-city CTM coaches, but interesting, since you will pass along minor roads and see the countryside. Most larger towns and cities are served by a coach service. Many of these are modern air-conditioned vehicles.

Taxis Inter-city service taxis will wait until full and then take passengers from one town to another and drop off along the way. The price for this is comparable to a bus service but very much quicker. Petit taxis operate within towns and cities and are very cheap, but since the meters rarely work, a price should be agreed in advance to avoid argument at your destination. Petit taxis will only carry a maximum of 3 passengers, whereas the more expensive Mercedes taxis will take more.

Donkey and cart Although most villages, towns and cities have taxis operating, you can always be sure to get a ride on a donkey/mule and cart. A rather bumpy, but delightful way to travel for short distances. Some railway stations outside the towns are served in this way to transfer passengers the short journey to the town centre. Some towns also have a regular horse and cart service for both sightseeing and as a regular taxi service.

Car hire This is available in the larger towns, but is very expensive compared with Europe or the USA. Typically 700 to 1,000 Dirhams ($70 to $100) per day for a small car for 3 days and cheaper for longer periods. If you do hire one, be careful when passing through towns and villages, where speed restrictions as low as 40 kilometres per hour are in effect but often not marked. With plenty of police available and an increasing use of radar in the country, you are sure to be stopped and fined if exceeding the limit, unless you are equipped with a good knowledge of Arabic to argue or joke your way out of it.

Own vehicle If you have a motorbike onboard, this can usually be used without any problem or paperwork. Short term insurance cover may be obtained at the Spanish border or in the ports if required. If you take in a car from Spain, formalities can be completed fairly quickly in Tanger or Ceuta. You will need your original registration document and the vehicle needs to be in the driver's name. Complications arise if you are using a friend's vehicle, unless you have a legal document giving authorisation. Most European insurance companies (with the exception of Spain) do not automatically include Morocco, but insurance agents are located in the ports to provide short term cover. Hire cars from Ceuta may be taken into Morocco by arrangement with the company, but not those hired in mainland Spain.

International travel

Air Tanger, Casablanca, Marrakech and Agadir all have airports operating international flights.

Sea Several ferries operate from Tanger and Ceuta to Algeciras. In summer a fast boat operates between Marina Smir and Benalmadena (near Málaga). A ferry operates from Melilla to Málaga and Almería.

ORDER OF MOROCCAN PORTS

Many yachts, probably the majority setting off for the Moroccan Atlantic coast, do so after first calling at Gibraltar. Gibraltar is therefore covered in the previous chapter. The route to the Canaries and Cap Verde Islands is very popular and increasingly so with the Atlantic Rally for Cruisers (ARC) taking some 200 or more yachts together across the Atlantic to the Caribbean every year.

The order for the Moroccan ports is

1. Atlantic coast of Morocco:
1. Straits of Gibraltar (Tanger) to Casablanca,
2. El Jadida to Agadir,
3. Sidi Ifni to Tarfaya,
4. Laâyoune to Dakhla and the border with Mauritania.

2. Mediterranean coast of Morocco:
5. Straits of Gibraltar to Saidia.

This section covers the ports from Ksar-es-Seghir and Ceuta in the Straits of Gibraltar, followed by Marina Smir and all ports going E to the Algerian border.

II. MOROCCO

ATLANTIC COAST OF MOROCCO

Introduction

As you contemplate visiting the Atlantic ports of Morocco, whether en route to the Canaries, or for tourism within the country, remember that some of the ports you are sailing into have been in use for thousands of years. You are sailing in the wake of Phoenicians, Carthaginians, Romans, Portuguese (all involved in the trans-Saharan slave and gold trades, with a stopover on their long voyage to the East Indies), Spanish (17th and 20th-century occupations) and many bands of pirates. These, along with sailors and sultans native to these parts, have all left their mark on this coastline. From these shores, Thor Heyerdahl set out in *Ra* to prove – successfully – that ancient seafarers, using boats constructed of reeds and bamboo, as used by the Ancient Egyptians, crossed the Atlantic long before Columbus.

Moreover, four of the five Atlantic ports which the Portuguese fortified in the 15th century, seen largely today as they were originally built, can be visited and are included in this book. These cities – Asilah, El Jadida, Safi and Essaouira – essentially retain their massive limestone ramparts and are some of the most gracious, clean and quiet of the Moroccan cities. The small port of Asilah, for example, has a history going back at least 3,600 years. Called Zilis by the Phoenicians, this was one of the most important trading cities of Tingitan Mauritania. The 15th-century fortifications which can be seen today, largely intact, are of Portuguese origin. Other ancient harbour towns are Azzemour, just north of El Jadida, a Carthaginian port built for ships trading between Portugal and Guinea; El Jadida, one of the most protected cities of its time, and still standing with its full ramparts intact; Safi and Essaouira; both pre-Roman. All these cities were fortified by the Portuguese and their limestone ramparts and elegant façades of houses within them, lend an unusual graciousness and grandeur, enhanced by the natural cleanliness brought about by the sheer impenetrable faces of limestone from which they were constructed. Many of the cities themselves are equally well preserved.

Unfortunately, new marinas planned for Asilah, Agadir, Casablanca and Mohammedia have been shelved, though work is still slowly underway in Casablanca. There is much to be said for visiting these places as they stand now, while sailing can be full of unexpected adventures and challenges! Sailing in Morocco is still in its infancy. One thing is certain: the spontaneity with which the locals will welcome yachtsman.

Weather and sailing conditions

Conditions are quite different from those in the Mediterranean. The Atlantic coast tends to have stable weather from June to October, with light winds from the SW or NW. Temperatures are usually lower than along the Spanish coast, although the humidity increases as you move south past Casablanca. If a strong westerly wind gets up while you are at sea, or a depression passes through, there is little you can do except keep well out to sea. Some ports can be entered in any conditions and these are listed. The swell several miles out is far less than that encountered close inshore. This is due to the steady shelving of the sandy bottom, which causes huge rollers to build and break near the shore, even in light winds. When entering rivers, keep a lookout astern for unexpected rollers sneaking up from behind. It is an alarming experience to have a succession of two-metre, steep-sided rollers hit your stern when the sea is otherwise flat and you are in a confined channel concentrating on transit lights ahead, as happened to me entering Oued Sebou on a calm moonlit night.

During winter, light NE or SW winds can be expected for much of the time. Fronts associated with fast moving depressions occasionally move NE from the Canaries, causing squalls and sometimes more prolonged periods of strong winds, particularly from November to April. Winter daytime temperatures are not normally less than 16°C.

A weatherfax is a great asset when sailing in the Atlantic and is a better longer range indicator of weather than in the Mediterranean. If you have a personal computer onboard, a weatherfax programme can be purchased quite cheaply and connected to your HF-SSB radio. This will enable you to see any depressions moving from the Canaries, where in stable conditions, a high or low pressure system usually sits, sometimes for weeks, giving a steady airflow and minimal swell. Using a GSM mobile phone connected to a laptop computer, forecasts can also be obtained via the Internet. It only takes a minute to download once the connection is established. GSM coverage along the Atlantic coast is excellent well out to sea.

The Atlantic swell is irksome at first, but in summer it is only about a metre in height, usually from the SW or NW. In winter it is frequently around 3 to 5m, even in light winds and sometimes much more. Exceptions are around Essaouira, where the swell is often 2m in summer, providing excellent surfing opportunities.

Most yachts travelling S to the Canaries with the intention of crossing the Atlantic, do so between October and December to catch the change in the trade winds and Gulf Stream, which are more favourable for the crossing in December and early January.

Tides

There is a 14-minute time difference between HW Gibraltar and HW Casablanca and little more as you move south. Gibraltar and Casablanca are standard ports and local tide tables can easily be obtained from either port. Most harbour authorities are happy to give a photocopy of their tables. Alternatively visit http://easytide.ukho.gov.uk

Current

Generally, a steady surface current of about half a knot, moving S, can be expected for most of the Atlantic coastline as far as Agadir.

1. Straits of Gibraltar (Tanger) to Casablanca

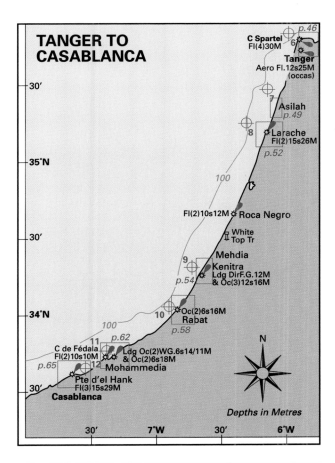

WAYPOINTS – MOROCCO ATLANTIC COAST

⊕6	35°50′N	6°00′W	Cap Spartel
⊕7	35°28′N	6°10′W	Asilah
⊕8	35°15′N	6°20′W	Larache
⊕9	34°18′N	6°45′W	Mehdia
⊕10	34°00′N	6°55′.W	Rabat
⊕11	33°45′N	7°23′W	Mohammedia
⊕12	33°38′.5N	7°33′.5W	Casablanca
⊕14	33°38′.5N	7°39′W	Pte d'el Hank

Important note on waypoints and co-ordinates

Please refer to the important note regarding waypoints in the Introduction (page 12).

MO 1 Tanger

Tucked into the NW of a bay at the entrance of the Straits of Gibraltar, protected from the Atlantic, this very ancient port is 31M W of Gibraltar and a port of entry.

Location
35°47′.6N 05°47′.5W

Distances
Cádiz 56M
Gibraltar 31M
Ceuta 27M

Tides

MHWS	MHWN	MLWN	MLWS
2.4m	1.9m	1.0m	0.6m

Charts

	Approach	Port
Admiralty	92, 142, 773, 3133	1912
French	1701, 7042	1701
Spanish		4461

Lights
Approach
1. **Cap Spartel** 35°47′.6N 05°55′.3W Fl(4)20s95m30M Dia(4)90s Yellow square stone tower
2. **Punta Malabata** 35°49′.1N 05°44′.8W Fl.5s77m22M White square tower on dwelling
3. **Monte Dirección** 35°46′.1N 05°47′.3W Oc(3)WRG.12s89m16-11M On terrace of white house 140°-G-174.5°-W-200°-R-225° F.R lights on radio mast 1.1M SW; on hospital 1.8M WNW and Grand Mosque 1.7M NW

Harbour
4. **Breakwater head** 35°47′.6N 05°47′.5W Fl(3)12s20m14M White tower
5. **S mole head** Oc(2)R.6s7m6M
6. **NW inner jetée** Iso.G.4s6m6M
7. **Entrance inner harbour N mole** F.G.4m6M
8. **Entrance inner harbour S mole** F.R.4m6M

Communications
VHF Ch 6, 14. 16

The port

The commercial port of Tanger (various spellings) is a practical harbour in which to make a first acquaintance with Morocco. The old fishing port, Port de Plaisance, was closed to yachts for almost a year for dredging and building works, but was reopened in late 2004. More work is due and depths have not been published. Two new pontoons have been installed for yachts, replacing others which sank and the work is continuing. This inner harbour is safe from most wind directions, though some swell does enter during strong E winds. Ferries from Algeciras arrive frequently and present a hazard to watch out for in the entrance. Security is excellent, with 'guardians' employed to watch the yacht quays.

PILOTAGE

By day

The harbour can be entered in any conditions though the approach between Tarifa and Punto de Malabata is very difficult in strong W winds. Approach from the W is assisted by the unmistakable sight of Cap Spartel (also known as Cabo Espartel and Cape Spartan) and its lighthouse. From the E, the steep headland of Punta de Malabata with its lighthouse provides a good landmark.

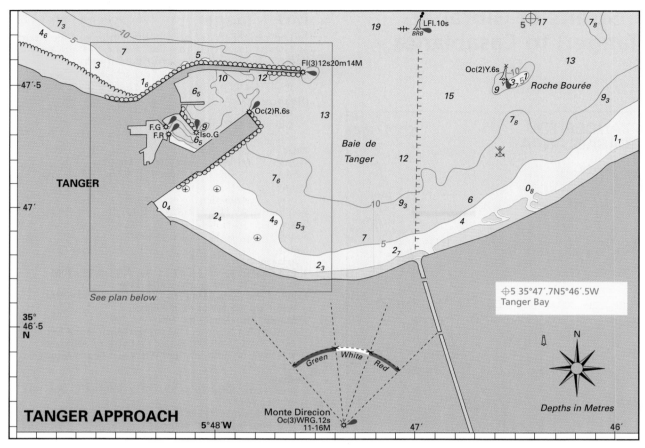

TANGER APPROACH

Within the approach chart:

TANGER

Baie de Tanger

Roche Bourée

Fl(3)12s20m14M

Oc(2)R.6s

Oc(2)Y.6s

F.G
F.R
Iso.G

LFl.10s
BRB

See plan below

⊕5 35°47′.7N5°46′.5W
Tanger Bay

Monte Direcion
Oc(3)WRG.12s
11-16M

Green White Red

Depths in Metres

5°48′W   47′   46′

35°
46′·5
N

47′·5
47′

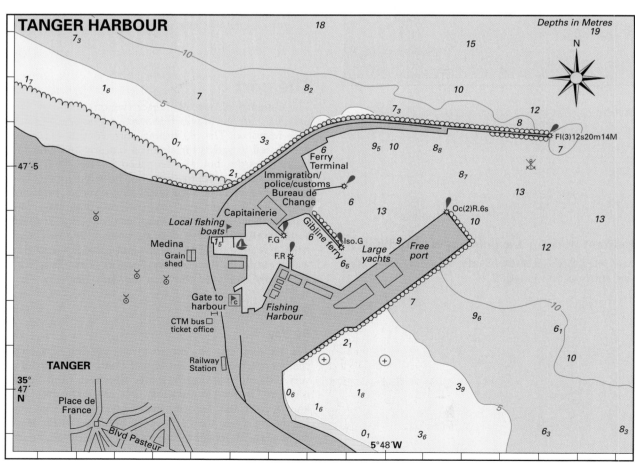

TANGER HARBOUR

Depths in Metres

Fl(3)12s20m14M

Ferry Terminal

Immigration/
police/customs

Bureau de
Change

Capitainerie

Local fishing
boats

Gibline ferry

Large
yachts

Free
port

Oc(2)R.6s

Iso.G

F.G
F.R

Medina

Grain
shed

Gate to
harbour

Fishing
Harbour

CTM bus
ticket office

Railway
Station

TANGER

Place de
France

Blvd Pasteur

35°
47′
N

47′·5

5°48′W

Tanger Harbour entrance viewed from W. Cathedral spire just visible to left of Grand Mosque, almost in transit
Graham Hutt

Closer to the port the white tower at the end of the N breakwater and the large cranes are visible from some distance off, as is the white minaret of the Grand mosque, with the Catholic church spire nearby. If arriving from the tideless Mediterranean, do not forget that currents and tides are an important consideration here. (See section Transiting the Straits page 33.) Strong currents and overfalls are present near the E entrance to the Bay of Tanger, especially around HW. Two buoys near the entrance mark a rock and Roche Bouree, a small sandbank.

By night

No problems with a night entry but keep well N of the sandbank mentioned above. Cap Spartel light has a 30M range and the harbour lights are easily located. Ferries will be seen entering and leaving until around midnight. Transits can be obtained from the buoy marking the rock NE of the entrance (Fl(2)15s) and the end of the N mole (Fl(3)12s) visible at 12M.

Berthing

Beware of ships entering and leaving, as well as ferries turning just inside the entrance. Proceed carefully into the fishing port. The yacht area was less than 2m at LWS in some parts but has recently been dredged. New

depths are unknown. Two new pontoons have been placed for the use of yachts and more are due to be added at a later date.

Formalities

Customs and immigration police are very efficient and come to the yacht. They will usually show up within minutes of your arrival. Since Tanger is a commercial 'free port', the police issue a *permis d'escale* in lieu of passports which are retained until departure. This card must be shown when passing the guarded harbour gate on re-entry.

Facilities

Water and *electricity* Available on the pontoons.
Fuel Diesel is available in drums.
Provisions A small *alimentation général* in the harbour sells a little of everything from bread to photocopies. The main markets in the Medina are a short walk from the port in Rue du Portugal and Rue de la Plage close to the Grand Socco square where there is abundant fresh produce at very reasonable prices. Between Ceuta, for canned and processed articles, and Tanger, for fresh and many dried products, a yacht can provision well for a long sea voyage. Tanger has a sizeable textile industry and it is worth shopping in the modern town around Rue Mexique.
Gas Bottles can be filled at the SGP plant outside Tanger near the intersection of road P38 to Tetouan and the railroad.
Showers The yacht club has showers and washboards for clothes washing and permission to use them when berthed in the fishing port is never refused. As an alternative it is worth exploring the douche public (*hammam*) in the Medina, 5 minutes walk from the port. Men and women can use it during the same hours.
Repairs Emergency engine repairs can be carried out.
Post office The main post office on Boulevard Mohammed V has a 24hr telephone service.
Tourist information On Boulevard Pasteur, 200m from Place de France in the new town.
Bank There are several banks in the port near the ferry terminal and there is a small change shop on the way out of the port. In the town most banks are found on Boulevard Mohammed V or Boulevard Pasteur.

ASHORE

History

Known in history as Tingi, Tanger was well known to Phoenicians and Carthaginians who used the port before setting off across the Atlantic or voyaging south. The Carthaginian navigator Hanno mentioned the city when he visited in 500BC on his way to Guinea. It was famous for its salted fish and anchovy sauce, which were held in huge vats at nearby Lixus and used to supply ships. Anchovy with garlic sauce is still a speciality of the area today. Tingi was later associated more with Mauritania than the Roman rulers of Carthage until around 50BC. In AD3, Tingi became the capital of Tingis Mauritania under the rule of Diocletian, retaining the Spanish connection. Vandals occupied Tingi in 429 under the rule of King Genseric, who also ruled Spain. Tingi became part of the Byzantine empire until Moussa ibn Nasser captured it in 705 during the Islamic conquest, which swept westwards from the Middle East. It was from here that a large Berber army was assembled

Tanger harbour viewed from N

under Tariq, which conquered Spain through Gibraltar giving his name to the Rock – Jebel Tariq. (Mountain of Tariq.)

Berber tribes of the Rif rebelled against the forced conversions to Islam, re-conquering Tingi for a short time in 739. During successive take-overs, the port flourished as a gateway trading post for ships en route through the Straits, as it does today.

Spanish, Portuguese and the English all occupied the town from 1471. The British withdrew after the dispute between Charles I and the British Parliament in 1679. By 1810, after a long period of decline, there were only 5,000 inhabitants left. Later in the 19th century, several European countries vied for control of Tanger, including France, Spain, Britain and Germany. In 1906 Tanger was given a special international status as a 'free port.' This lapsed when Morocco gained independence. Apart from Moroccans, the population at the time was a cosmopolitan mix of European and American writers, artists, bankers and entrepreneurs. In 1956, the international status ended and the banks and companies moved back to Europe but Tanger has still retained some of the cosmopolitan character from those days.

Sights locally

The ancient medina is close to the port, remaining much as it has for over a thousand years. Filled with small shops and bazaars, it is easy to get lost in its narrow winding streets. Although without the medieval feel of the medina in Fes or Marrakech, it gives a good idea of the lifestyle to the S of the Straits, which is so different from that of Europe. Tanger is the gateway to Morocco and in many ways is a microcosm of much that can be found in cities throughout the whole country, both good and bad.

The European town, kept separate from the old medina, is a pleasant ensemble of wide streets and green squares with restaurants, coffee bars and shops of all kinds.

Eating out

There is a wide range of restaurants ranging from the most simple eating houses in the Medina to good European style restaurants in the modern town. The Rough Guide has a good listing.

Transport

Train An excellent train service to Rabat, Casablanca, Meknes, Fes and along the coast to El Jadida. The railway station, which used to be immediately outside the harbour gate, has been relocated outside the town, a short taxi or bus ride away but a very long walk.
Buses Ticket offices for buses are at the harbour gate but the inter-town buses leave from the outskirts of Tanger.
Ferries Regular ferry services to Algeciras, Gibraltar and Sète.
Air The airport is 15km out of town.
Car rental All the big companies are to be found on Boulevard Pasteur or Boulevard Mohammed V.
Tanger offers excellent opportunities for trips inland.

Coastline from Tanger to Asilah

From Tanger, the spectacular Cap Spartel (Cabo de Espartel) can be seen immediately after leaving the bay. This area is often shrouded in mist, especially in the mornings and particularly during E winds. Rounding the promontory can be tricky if there has been a prolonged period of westerly wind, building up a standing surface current with tidal races from the Atlantic as well as a long heavy swell. East-going currents up to six knots can be experienced in the area immediately N of the cape, with high overfalls at HW, so it is important to make the exit from the Mediterranean with favourable tides if the wind is westerly. (See section: Transiting the Straits page 33 for more information on currents in the Straits.)

Once rounded, the high mountainous cape soon gives way to a flat landscape with miles of golden sand dunes, deserted beaches and a favourable current, leaving the 1,000ft high Cap Spartel looking like an island. Asilah is 20M from the cape. Once into the Atlantic, going S, there are virtually no safe anchorages or natural bays, only harbours. The heavy swell caused by the gradual shelving is more noticeable 2-3M from shore, so it is unwise to get too close except in settled weather. Look out for tuna nets, which can extend four miles out to sea (see Marine Life in the introduction). These are sometimes present around the entrance to Asilah.

Because of the difference between sea and land temperatures in summer, there is often a sea mist all along the Atlantic coast, reducing visibility to between two and four miles. Prevailing winds on this NW coast tend to be either NE, or SW, except when depressions are passing. The current follows the coastline south at a rate of about 0.5kt between Cap Spartel and Asilah.

MO 2 Asilah

Asilah is the first port on the Moroccan Atlantic coast, 25M S of Tanger. It should only be entered in calm weather and with care.

Location
35°28′N 06°02′W

Distances
Cap Spartel 20M
Tanger 25M
Larache 16M

Tides

MHWS	MHWN	MLWN	MLWS
2.8m	2.0m	1.4m	0.6m

Charts

	Approach	Port
Admiralty	3132	–
French	–	–
Spanish	447	4461

Lights
1. **Dique N Ldg Lts 140°** *Front* F.R.7m mounted on low concrete tower
2. **Dique S** *Rear* F.R.9m mounted on low concrete tower
   Cap Spartel (Cabo Espartel) 35° 47.6′N 05°55.3′W
   Fl(4)20s30M Dia(4)90s Tower 24m

Communications
VHF Ch 16

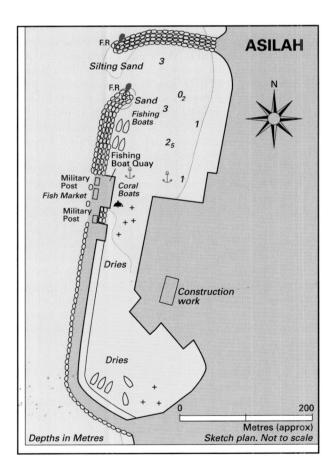

The harbour

This is a quiet clean harbour quite unlike any other in Morocco. Entry is not advisable in anything other than calm weather as depths are uncertain due to a sandbar across the entrance. The long Atlantic swell is deceptive, even in calm weather and depths are considerably reduced in the troughs.

The well advertised plans for a new marina here seem to have been shelved, along with the new Atlantic port to replace Tanger, between Asilah and Cap Spartel.

PILOTAGE

Entry into Asilah is straightforward, though dangerous in strong W winds. The harbour breakwater is clearly visible between the open beach to the N and the city walls to the S. Atlantic rollers enter the mouth of the harbour in westerlies, considerably reducing the depths, which used to be dredged to 5m. One yacht reported depths of less than 2.2m in the entrance in 2004 but this has not been confirmed. It is usual for these Atlantic ports exposed to the W to silt up during strong W gales and the local harbour authorities do not publish data on the entrance depths for this reason.

Turn sharply to starboard after rounding the entrance to avoid being lifted up by a roller and broached towards the shallows.

Berthing

Berth on the short W quay running parallel to the breakwater where depths at LWS are around 2.2m. Several large fishing vessels are usually anchored in the lee of the breakwater.

Depths once inside the harbour are 2.2 to 3m in the centre, but only as far as the southern end of the jetty wall. Beyond that, although boats are moored, the harbour dries out and there are projecting rocks which can be clearly seen at LW. In winter, beware of breast lines extending from the coral boats moored alongside, which are laid out across the harbour to pull them off the quay during strong easterly winds. These are not used in summer, when the weather is more settled and the boats go out every day.

Moor alongside the coral boats, or anchor in the lee of the breakwater south of the entrance in sand. The

Asilah viewed from the west

Asilah: the author's yacht alongside coral-fishing boats
Graham Hutt

Asilah medina. Wall murals are unique features of this
quiet town   *Graham Hutt*

harbour jetty is only 70m long and several vessels moor
alongside the high wall. Fishing boats moor at the N end
and coral boats to the S. With the larger boats inboard,
climbing the ladder up to the quay is made easier.
Locals are very friendly and always ready to assist. The
coral and fishing boats leave early in the morning every
day in summer except Fridays, but an attendant
fisherman will re-tie your mooring lines, avoiding the
necessity to get up early. If you do anchor out, fishermen
will offer to take you ashore in their small smacks for a
few Dirhams, avoiding the need to launch your tender
and then having to worry about it while ashore.

Formalities

Although not a port of entry, the officials and police are
very friendly and willing to give temporary visitors a
pass to stay by holding their passports without stamping
them until they are ready to depart. If you intend to stay

in Asilah and require an entry stamp for travel inland, it
is possible to obtain this by visiting Tanger port
overland, but it would be wiser to call in at a port of
entry beforehand, than rely on this unofficial
arrangement. Local police will visit the yacht by taxi and
take the captain to their nearby offices to complete
formalities.

Facilities

Water May be obtained in cans if necessary, but no hosepipe
facilities exist at present.

Electricity None on the quayside but the coral boats often
have generators running and can provide a mains power
point for a few hours if necessary.

Fuel This can be arranged by locals and brought to the yacht
in cans.

Provisions Local shops have all the usual items.

Gas Calor gas readily available and also the large old style
screw top bottles.

Post office and *banks* In the centre of town.

Repairs As in almost any port in Morocco, most types of
mechanical repairs can be undertaken in Asilah, but no
specific yacht facilities are available. A small slipway S of
the jetty hauls out fishing boats.

ASHORE

History

Asilah has been known by a number of names, all of
which derive from Zilis, the name it was given when
founded as a commercial port by the Phoenicians in the
second century BC. It has been occupied by the
Carthaginians, Byzantines, Romans and rebuilt in the
9th century AD by the first Moroccan dynasty, the
Idrissids.

The Normans then conquered it, followed by the
Omeyyad Caliph of al-Andalus in 966.

The inhabitants of Asilah became very wealthy,
educated and warlike, according to Leon el Africano, an
erudite and well-travelled fellow from Granada, who
wrote in the late 15th century. Though perhaps less
warlike now, these adjectives seem appropriate for this
gracious, cultured town today.

In 1471 30,000 Portuguese soldiers disembarked
from 500 boats at Asilah (an amazing fact considering
the tranquillity and size of the port today), took the city
and built the massive fortifications and sea wall which
still stand and define the medina today. Just over a
hundred years later, Portugal's King Sebastian, who
hoped to win Morocco for Christendom, landed in
Asilah en route to the fateful Battle of the Three Kings
at Ksar el Kebir, just SE of Larache. In this battle he and
two Moroccan kings lost their lives and, in its aftermath,
so many Portuguese nobility had to be ransomed, that
Portugal went bankrupt, losing all its Moroccan ports
which were subsequently absorbed by Spain.

In 1691, after a hundred years of Spanish
domination, Asilah reverted to Moroccan rule and
became famous for its pirates who roamed the area
working with bands from Sale until as late as 1910. Their
headquarters here provoked mid 19th-century
bombardment by both the Austrians and Spanish, as
well as by the famous bandit-turned-Regional Governor,

Moulay Ahmed Raisuli. His Hispanomuslim-style palace, built in the first decade of the twentieth century, looks out over the sea towards the far end of the medina and is well worth a visit for its spectacular architecture.

History was again repeated by the inclusion of Asilah in the Spanish Protectorate from 1911-1956.

Sights locally

This is a clean, quiet port and unlike any other in Morocco. The medina lies within the 15th-century Portuguese walls, just beyond the southern end of the harbour. Although small, it has unusually wide streets and is pleasant to shop in. One feels graciously invited to look around, rather than being intimidated, as in Tanger and other towns. Bargaining is a far less aggressive affair and 'guides' and touts do not bother you here.

Wonderful wall paintings and modern murals are to be seen within the medina and are a feature of the annual festival described below.

The long stretches of soft white sand on either side of the port, (especially to the N, where they stretch half way to Tanger) provide the opportunity for privacy, even in the tourist season. Here, as on many other Moroccan beaches, you can also hire a camel.

Local speciality

Asilah is most famous for its month-long cultural festival, which takes place every year in July or August. Visitors from every part of the globe come for this event, where arts, crafts, music and many other attractions are well organised and include artists and musicians from all over the world, including the USA and the Middle East. This is a time when you are particularly fortunate to be visiting Asilah by boat, for hotel rooms are always fully booked. Much of the town's fresh, modern appearance and the excellent restoration work that has been carried out, is attributable to the once Mayor of the city, Mohammed Benaissa, who was formerly Minister of Culture and is currently Minister of Foreign Affairs.

Eating out

Many good restaurants line the sea front just outside the harbour and uphill from the promenade, interspersed here and there in tree-lined streets. As with all coastal towns, fish is naturally the local speciality and, due to the Spanish influence, there is a predominance of Spanish cuisine. Restaurant Alcazaba, opposite the main gate to the medina is excellent, as are several of the eating houses along the promenade.

Coastline from Asilah to Larache

This 15 mile stretch of coastline is similar to that from Cap Spartel to Asilah, with long stretches of sandy beaches, except that the backdrop of mountains is more evident here through the haze, which is often present in summer. Beware of tuna nets laid out along this stretch of coast (see page 10).

Coastline from Larache to Oued Sebou

This 60 mile coastline from Larache to the river consists of white beaches, scrubland and low cliffs. White tombs can be seen just above the beach at Moulay Bousselham, some 20M south of Larache. Behind the beach dunes is a large lake, which is the habitat of several rare species of birds, well protected by wardens.

Keep well out to sea in the tuna fishing season as nets can extend at least four miles from the shore.

MO 3 Larache

A challenging port to enter, 16M S of Asilah, though once inside it is safe with interesting sights ashore nearby.

Location
  35°12'.3N 06°09'.5W

Distances
  Asilah 16M
  Mehdia 62M

Tides

	MHWS	MHWN
Range	3.6m	2.9m

Charts

	Approach	Port
Admiralty	3132	–
French	–	–
Spanish	447	4461

Lights
Entry signals
•/Red Lt – caution for entering.
Two • – port closed except for motor fishing vessels.
Blue flag with PC/2 Red Lts – port closed.
Approach
1. **Outer bar Ldg Lt 102°** *Front* Iso.2s4M White ▲ on red mast 6m 352°-vis-212°
   Rear 200m from front Iso.2s4M White ▼ on red mast 8m 352°-vis-212°
   Inner bar Ldg Lt 145°30′ *Front* F.R.19m2M White mast 12m 015.5°-vis-275°
   Rear 70m from front F.R.28m2M Church tower 19m 055.5°-vis-235.5°
   Training wall head F.G
   Entrance Iso.G.4s7M Green mast 4m
Harbour
2. **N breakwater head** Oc(4)15s15m17M Horn(4)60s White tower 7m
Communications
  VHF Ch 16

The harbour

Lying on the S side of the entrance to the river Oued Loukkos, Larache is well protected from the Atlantic, as the river curves sharply once inside the sandbars. Although deep-draught fishing vessels of over 50ft in length operate daily from the port, keeled yachts should only attempt entry in exceptionally settled weather as a strong current runs between two sandbanks and the entrance is prone to silting. Once inside it is spacious and safe. It is one of those harbours which is easy once done but also easy to misjudge at the first attempt.

II. MOROCCO

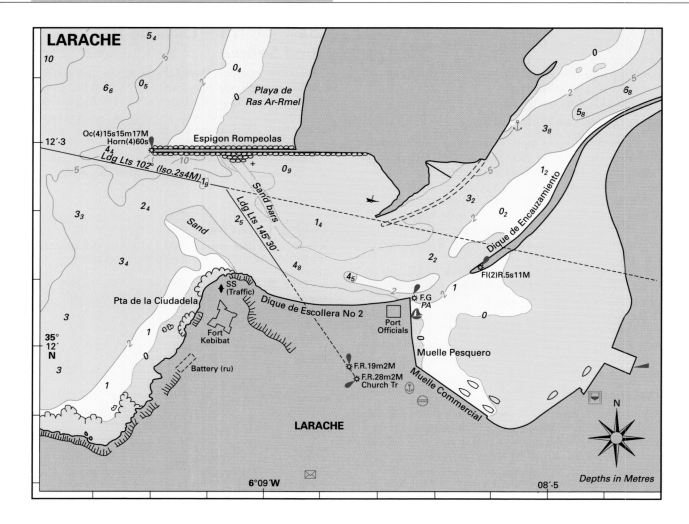

PILOTAGE

By day

Two sandbars stretch across the river near the entrance, with a distance of some 15m between them, forming a channel as shown on the plan. They lie barely submerged at LW, with strong overfalls caused by the fast running current. A channel with a minimum depth of 1.5m allows access between them to the port. Entry to the channel is via a gap between a NE and SW sandbank. After traversing SE and then E across the river, entry into the port from the channel is through another gap created by a NE running sandbank.

You would be strongly advised to wait for a fishing boat to guide you through this tricky river entrance as the strong current necessitates a fast passage between the sandbanks. At LW, current runs along the channel, but at HW, a cross current develops as sandbanks are submerged. Moroccan seafarers are always ready to act as pilot and take pride in doing so.

By night

Night entry not recommended.

Berthing

Depths of 3 to 4m at LW can be found once inside the harbour. Go alongside the W jetty just under the harbourmaster's office, where a police launch is usually moored. Stay as far N as possible as it is shallow S of the port building.

Formalities

Larache is a port of entry and officials will visit the boat. Customs and police are located within the port and are very friendly. Port authorities are willing to assist with entry along the transits if requested on VHF Ch 16.

Facilities

Water Is available from a tap on the jetty.
Fuel May be obtained in cans.
Provisions Local markets have a good selection of fresh food.
Gas Camping Gaz available in the town.
Post office and *banks etc.* In the Place de la Libération and Avenue Mohammed V, are banks, the PTT, a tourist office (Syndicat d'Initiative) and a (Spanish) Catholic church.
Repairs All types of mechanical repairs can be undertaken here.

Larache fortress: an imposing sight   Graham Hutt

Ancient Lixus. In Roman times anchovies were salted in these vats to supply ships   *Graham Hutt*

ASHORE

History

Larache was founded in the 7th century AD, when some of the Arabs who brought Islam to Morocco from the Middle East, settled across the river Oued Loukkos from Lixus, which by this time was in decline. Larache has been inhabited continuously since then.

In the late 15th century the threatening presence of the Portuguese in Tanger, Asilah, El Jadida and other towns along the coast, convinced the Sultan of Fes to establish a fort to defend the city of Larache and control the mouth of Oued Loukkos. Today, the ruins of this fort lie just outside the medina gate Bab el Kasbah. Larache became a pivotal port for the Muslims, and was successfully defended against Europeans for over a century. Although Larache fell to the Spaniards in 1610,

it was regained and repopulated in 1689 by the Alouite Sultan Moulay Ismail who also took Tanger, exercising power from 1672 until 1727 from Tanger to Senegal. Before its colonisation by Spain in 1911, Larache spent relatively little time under European control, which accounts for the Moroccan style of its medina, which contrasts sharply with that of El Jadida, for instance, and with the Andalucían style of the new town built after 1911.

Given its close proximity to Fes, Larache could have been as important a port as Tanger and Casablanca, were it not for its dangerous sandbars. Many of the ships used by the famous pirates of Sale and Rabat were built here.

Sights locally

Small fishing boats can be hired for a few Dirhams for trips across Oued Loukkos to one of Larache's principal attractions: an immense extension of tree and café-lined beaches, or to the ruins of ancient Lixus, some 3M inland on the river. (Cost 50-100 Dirhams.) Both Lixus and the beach can also be reached by taxi and the city buses. Lixus is the site of the mythological Gardens of Hesperides to which Hercules travelled in search of golden apples in his eleventh and penultimate labour. The megalithic stones in its Acropolis confirm its importance in prehistoric times, although its ruins are mostly Phoenician, Carthaginian and Roman. There are several temple sanctuaries from the various historical ages with confirmation of the Christian presence in Morocco in the years before the Islamic conquest. These can be seen in the ruins of a Christian basilica. From this Acropolis, there is a splendid view of Larache port and the town, and of the active salt pans below the ruins (see Local speciality). Between the hill and the main road can be seen the ancient vats used for storing anchovy sauce or garum used to sustain crews of ancient sailing ships.

Larache itself is less compelling than these peripheral attractions. Because it is on the main road from Tanger to Rabat, heavy trucks trundle through the centre, making it somewhat dusty. Nonetheless it is beautifully situated on a hill overlooking water on two sides, has a relaxed, friendly feel and an aura of faded elegance.

Local speciality

Apart from the fishing industry, Larache is the first of many towns on the Atlantic coast with an important salt-panning industry. Large areas between the main road and the beach are segmented and salt water is allowed to sit and evaporate for a year or more. The resulting salt surface is then raked off, heaped into stacks and sold when dry. Some of the lower ruins at the ancient city of Lixus, are those of first century (BC) salt factories, attesting to the antiquity of this specialised practice in the Larache area.

Eating out

The main road from Tanger to Rabat passes through the centre of town which is close to the port. Consequently, there are many small bars and restaurants lining the entire route. Spanish influence dominates the local cuisine.

MO 4 Mehdia and Kenitra

Two harbours lie in the river Oued Sebou: Mehdia, a small fishing and commercial port a mile from the entrance and Kenitra, 8M upriver. Large vessels transit the river under pilotage.

Location
34°16'.0N 06°41'.4W (W of entrance to Oued Sebou)

Distances
Larache 62M
Mohammedia 46M

Tides

	MHWS	MHWN
Range	3.6m	2.9m

Charts

	Approach	Port
Admiralty	856, 3132	1912
French	6145	7550
Spanish	215	–

Lights
River Oued Sebou – Entry signals
Flag S flown if bar practicable. R over G flag if bar is impassable.

Mehdia Approach
1. **Entrance Ldg Lts 102°30'** *Front* DirF.G.12M Green and white stripes on ▲, on black metal framework tower 10m
2. *Rear* 800m from front Oc(3)12s74m16M Red tower on white dwelling

Kenitra Approach
South bank fixed

Transit lights
1. **Leading (arc)** DirF.G.12M Green, white stripes, on ▲, on black metal framework tower 10m
2. *Rear* Oc(3)12s74m16M Red and white tower
3. **Ldg Lts 060°** *Front* F.R.2m7M Tide gauge
4. *Rear* 213m from front F.R.5m8M Black and white beacon

Harbour
5. **Jetée Nord head** Oc(2)R.6s17m5M Red and white tower
6. **Jetée Sud head** Iso.G.4s16m6M White tower 10m

Communications
VHF Ch 16

Coastline from Mehdia to Rabat

This 16-mile stretch is unremarkable: white sandy beaches and cliffs, until you approach the river Oued Bou Regreg, which splits in two the walled town on the northern bank, Sale, and its twin city Rabat, which extends to the south. High walls encircle Rabat on both the seaward and river sides.

Mehdia Port

The port of Mehdia (also spelled Mehdya and Mehdiya), built on the S bank of river Oued Sebou, 1.5M upstream, is easily accessed by precision navigation using transits along a narrow channel in the wide river. Large ships under pilotage navigate at HW to the port of Kenitra, 8M further on. The entrance is only safe in settled weather or with E winds.

The river is navigable up to Kenitra, some eight miles further upstream.

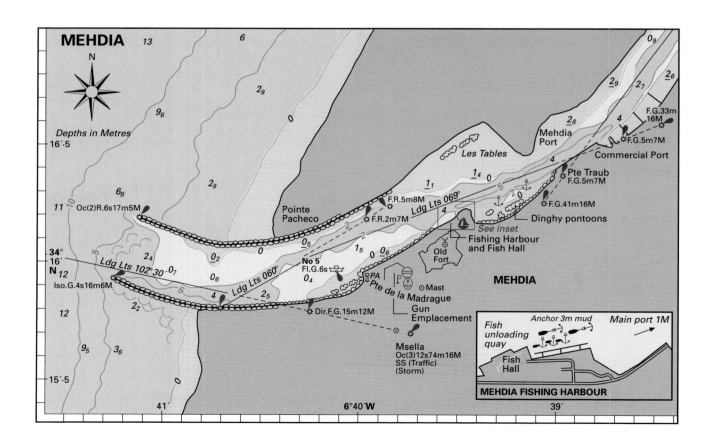

PILOTAGE

By day

River Oued Sebou entry signals:
Flag S flown if bar navigable. R over G flag if bar is impassable.

The entrance leading into the mouth of the river is formed by two breakwaters projecting half a mile out to sea. Large ships transit the river at high water as far as Kenitra, always with a pilot onboard. Several sand banks make it essential to pay great attention both to the chart and to the state of the tide. A fast-running current of 3 to 4kts out of the river is due to the 2 metre height difference upstream. This is enough to neutralise the neap flood current at HW and cause prolonged periods of slack water at springs. During the rainy season, the river floods its banks and is often one metre higher than charted.

Minimum depth at MLWS is around 2m in the channel between sandbanks. Keep well to starboard on entry to avoid the first sandbar, which lies mid-river and extends to the N bank. Head for the tower transits indicated on the chart on a course of 102°. Keep a good lookout astern, since huge rollers occasionally enter, even when the Atlantic is calm. Local fishermen wait at the entrance, watching the wave patterns before making a fast entry upstream. If in doubt, larger vessels anchor on the northern side of the entrance in 6-9m of coarse sand and wait for calmer waters and a high tide.

Once in the river, the fishing port, with its market and long buildings, will be seen 200m past an ancient circular gun emplacement on the S riverbank. Several fishing boats are usually moored either alongside the jetty, or anchored nearby.

By night

Although entry is not recommended at night, a transit can be identified between the southern breakwater light and a lit tower further upstream if the lights are working. The sets of transit lights are often reported to be out. Light buoys, positioned midstream, are not always in place and if there, are often unlit.

Note Due to shifting sands in the river, the use of transits between dredging as shown on the chart may be incorrect. The port pilot can be called on Ch 16 and he will give directions in French over the VHF. Alternatively, follow a vessel under pilotage, or a larger fishing boat.

Berthing

Yachts can berth alongside the fishing quay for entry formalities. A short distance further upriver is a pontoon for tenders, with steps leading up to the large car park. Depths by the pontoon, which is very close to the edge of the river, are very shallow at low water and yachts should not attempt to go alongside even if possible at HW. A short distance from the bank there are depths of over 3m with good holding in soft mud. Stern and bow anchors are needed to keep fore and aft of the fast-running current. Fishing boats use the bank opposite to careen.

Two miles further upstream is the larger freighter and tanker port of Mehdia with cranes looming on the quay. This part of the port is not recommended for yachts as it is an industrial zone with high-sided jetties, but no doubt it could be used for larger yachts, or if you are not confident about anchoring. There are many convenient places where a yacht may anchor in the river between the two port areas.

Formalities

Formalities can be carried out on the fishing quay or at the main harbour upstream. Mehdia is a port of entry, although, as the port is split between the fishing and commercial port, customs officials will probably come from the commercial port.

Facilities

Water Available in cans.
Fuel Available in cans or by bowser arranged with the port.
Provisions A small open market lies on the hill high above the road running past the port with fresh fruit, vegetables and meat. A more abundant supply is available a short taxi journey away in Kenitra.
Gas Obtainable in Kenitra.
Post office and *banks* In the centre of Kenitra.
Repairs Emergency repairs can be undertaken but there are no specific yacht repair facilities.

ASHORE

History

The port was founded in the 6th century BC as a Carthaginian trading post. The Almohads built naval shipyards here, and by the 16th century the port, then known as Al Mamoura and located just south of the Oued Sebou, was an active commercial port. Portuguese took the port in 1515 but were unable to hold it. It subsequently became another pirate base along with Sale and Algiers. The Spanish took Al Mamoura in 1614 and built the huge fortress high on the hill above the present port. This was seized by Sultan Moulay Ismail in 1689 and renamed El Mahdia, 'the citadel delivered'. In the late 19th century, the French used this kasbah as a

Mehdia dinghy pontoons looking NE towards the commercial port

Fish landing quay and moorings in Mehdia. Commercial port can be seen upriver   *Graham Hutt*

military base. It sustained extensive damage in their clashes with the American Expeditionary Force which landed at Kenitra in November of 1942. In 1947 the Americans returned to establish an important military base, now under Moroccan command.

Sights locally

The old town and kasbah are located directly across the road from the port on a hill with access via steep steps at the top of which is a shantytown. Wealthier residents live further SW, near the beach in the new town. The impressive 17th-century Spanish/Alouite fortress overlooks the harbour from the hilltop, commanding panoramic views of Oued Sebou the port and the town. The spectacular entrance, recently restored, gives access to the remains of the fort.

Mehdia's extensive beaches start on the southern breakwater where the new town begins. Plage Mehdia is the beach serving the inhabitants of Kenitra, an industrial city some 6M inland along the Oued Sebou, with miles of soft white sand and continuous rollers. Like much of the Moroccan coastline, this is a surfers' paradise and a sailor's nightmare with prevailing onshore winds.

The miles of flat, wet reedy marshland give protection for many species of wildlife, and there are protected areas nearby at Lac de Sidi Bourhaba, Merdja Zerga, where flamingos winter and Moulay Bousselham, another large area of flatland nature reserve around a lake. This is a popular place in summer and there is a small village to cater for the (almost exclusively Moroccan) tourists. Moulay Bousselham was an Egyptian to whom the conversion of the Atlantic coast of Morocco to Islam is attributed.

Eight miles N, off the main road to Tanger, lie the Roman ruins of Tamuzida. Meknes and Fes are directly inland and the ancient city of Rabat is 15M south. All are well worth a visit, although it may be more convenient and safer to leave the yacht in Mohammedia or Casablanca for this excursion.

Eating out

The nearest restaurant is a few minutes' walk W of the port gate. Known as 'Belle Vue Restaurant', it is perched on the hillside above the road with good views across the river. For a more lively scene, it would be worth making the trip into the new town, where cafés and restaurants on the seaward side of the road have inviting terraces overlooking the beach.

Kenitra port just ahead: large freighters are piloted the 8 miles up river   *Graham Hutt*

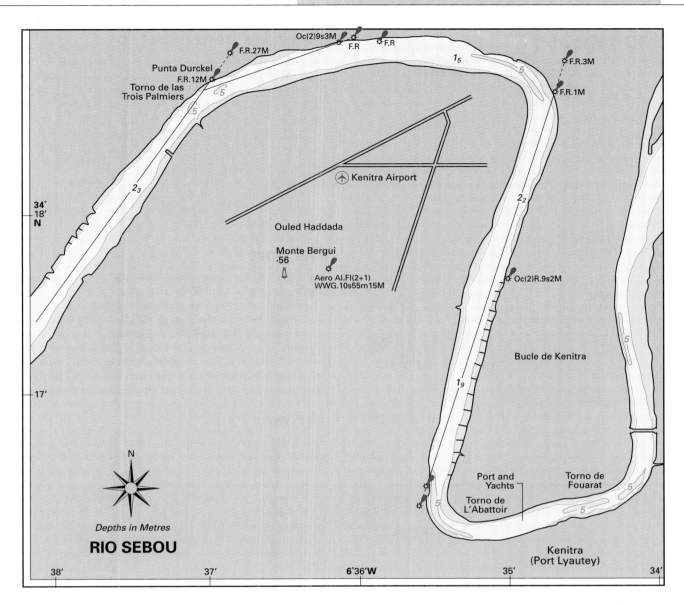

Oc(2)9s3M
F.R.27M
F.R
F.R
F.R.3M
F.R.1M
Punta Durckel
F.R.12M
Torno de las
Trois Palmiers
1₅
5
5
5
2₃
Kenitra Airport
34°
18'
N
Ouled Haddada
2₂
Monte Bergui
·56
Aero Al.Fl(2+1)
WWG.10s55m15M
Oc(2)R.9s2M
17'
Bucle de Kenitra
5
1₉
5
N
Port and
Yachts
Torno de
Fouarat
Torno de
L'Abattoir
5
Depths in Metres
5
5
RIO SEBOU
Kenitra
(Port Lyautey)
38'   37'   6°36'W   35'   34'

II. MOROCCO

Local transport

Taxis can always be found waiting in both the fishing and freighter ports. Buses also use this coast road, and stop at both port gates.

KENITRA

If you are interested in sailing up the Oued Sebou and mooring in the very safe harbour of Kenitra, this would be a superior base from which to make such excursions.

The river is navigable and large freighters are able to transit at high water following transits and buoyage. It is possible to moor alongside the main quay in Kenitra, since there are rarely more than two or three ships in the port. The quay is high, so look for a place where a ladder has been built into the wall. This port, obviously built with splendid facilities for many more ships than are now visiting, is consequently very quiet, safe and clean. Friendly police and customs officers are present and there is a very relaxed atmosphere.

The port gates open into the town which, although not attractive as a tourist destination, has many places to eat out as well as to purchase any supplies needed. All mechanical repair facilities are available here and a small boatyard is located at the end of the port.

History

This small industrial city of some 300,000 inhabitants is especially well known for its history as a military base. Its impressive port was originally developed by the French in 1913 to replace Larache, lost to the Spanish in 1911, and for a while it was known as Port Lyautey.

The town, like the port, has a forgotten air about it. This is commonly attributed to the fact that Kenitra was the base for a 1972 coup on the monarchy, which resulted in the withdrawal of financial support for the town. Kenitra is an interesting trip 8M further up the winding river Oued Sebou and is an excellent port to leave your yacht for excursions to Rabat, Fes, Meknes and Volubilis; the magnificent Roman ruins just north of Meknes. Good rail links to these cities are available from the station located a short distance from the port.

MO 5 Rabat

The capital of Morocco once had a fine harbour and ship building facilities. It is now almost impossible to navigate with a keeled yacht due to sandbanks which are left undredged.

Location
34°03′N 06°52′W

Distances
Mehdia 16M
Mohammedia 33M

Tides
Differences on Casablanca (standard port) – 5mins

MHWS	*MLWS*	*MHWN*	*MLWN*
+0.2m	0.3m	+0.1m	0.2m

Charts

	Approach	*Port*
Admiralty	856, 3132	–
French	6145	7551
Spanish	–	216

Lights
Entry signals
R flag at masthead of signal station – entrance prohibited.
R flag at half-mast – entrance dangerous for small boats.

Approach
1. **Rabat LtHo** 34°02′.1N 06°50′.8W Oc(2)6s31m16M Yellow tower black lantern 24m 290°-unintens-020° F.R on radio mast 12M NE Oc(2)R,6sm, F & G Lts 14M SW at Skhirat
2. **Rabat Salé** 34°03′N 06°46′W Aero Fl.10s on top of control tower

Coastline from Rabat to Mohammedia

This 33-mile stretch of coastline from Rabat consists of sandy beaches and rocky areas. Running parallel to the beach are two ranges of hills, the first a mile inland and the other 5M from the coast. Features of the coastline are the village of Temara, where the mosque minaret can be seen 7M S of Rabat, and the steel works of Skhirat, where a high mast is conspicuous, some 15M SW of Rabat. An islet, Sidi el Bou Derbala stands out at 33°50′N 07°09′W. Another minaret at Mansouria is conspicuous 9M SW of the islet. Current is half a knot running SW along the coast.

The port

Although once a large commercial harbour, few yachts today venture into Rabat due to the difficulty of negotiating the sandbar which now restricts entry to high water between shifting sandbanks. Even then, the estuary is only navigable with difficulty if any swell is present. Thus, Rabat is listed here with its history less for its attraction as a good harbour, but for its importance as a famous ancient port, now the capital of Morocco, which can be visited from adjacent ports.

PILOTAGE

Two breakwaters lead into the centre of the river and a shallow sandbar lies across its mouth, which, except in

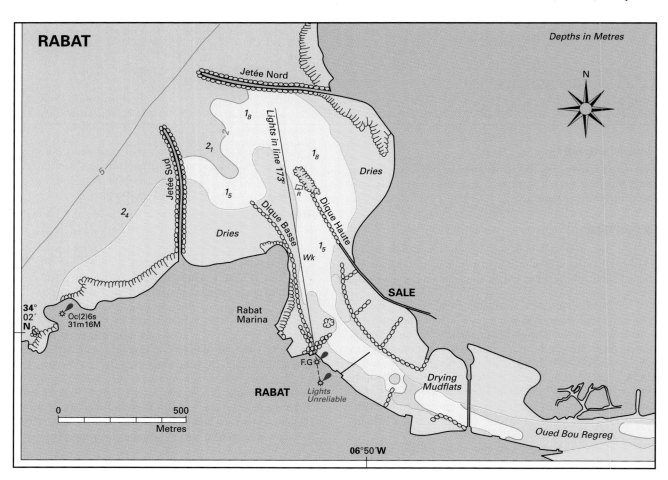

exceptionally settled weather, is clearly visible by the rollers breaking over it. Fishing boats can be seen waiting to ride the crest of rollers to clear the bar. Once over, there is a short span of deeper water before the bottom shelves to a drying sandbank either side of a narrow channel. The entry is well lit, but should never be attempted at night. Large areas of drying flats can be seen on either side of the river at LW. The flood tide has a maximum rate of 2kts and ebb of 4kts.

Berthing

Shallow draught yachts have been seen anchored well inside the river, parallel to the kasbah ramparts, where the sandy bottom dries out, and on the drying mudflats further E. It is possible to walk ashore at low water. It would be possible to anchor on the extensive drying mud flats either side of the river where, no doubt, a warm welcome would be received.

Formalities

Rabat is not a port of entry and there are no officials.

Facilities

Provisions Available in the town.
Post office and *banks* In the town on either side of the river.

ASHORE

History

The name Sale derives from Sala Colonia, the Phoenician and later Roman trading port, located on the silted south bank of Oued Bou Regreg in the area today known as Chellah. From the 8th century, Sala Colonia was occupied by Berbers who followed a form of government inspired by the Qu'ran but based on Berber custom known as Kharajite. Aggravated by the presence of such heretics, the conservative Zenata tribe built a *ribat* (fortified monastery) on the site of the present-day Kasbah des Oudaias, as a base from which to attack and convert them. Two centuries later, a second and far more extensive *ribat* was built by the Almohad Sultan Yacoub el Mansour 'the Victorious' (over the King of Castile in 1195). In time the south side of the river came to be known as Rabat.

Of the ports included in this guide, the history of Rabat and Sale is distinctive in that it is integrally linked with that of the Spanish Province of Andalucía. The immense 3-mile ring of walls around Rabat were specifically built to house and organise troops preparing to defend and extend the Muslim territories of the Almohad dynasty in Spain. Rabat was conceived on imperial proportions. Its Hassan Mosque, built but left incomplete in 1197, was to be the second largest in the Muslim world, with a capacity for 40,000. The cultural unity of Spain and Morocco at this time is evident in the striking correspondence between the minaret of this mosque (the Tower of Hassan), the Koutoubia in Marrakech and the Giralda of Seville: all designed by the same architect.

Sale became a thriving city. Its rich Merinid constructions attest to its vitality as the principal port of Morocco from the 13th to 16th centuries. Meanwhile, Rabat languished. When Leo Africanus (a Muslim from Granada) visited in 1500, he found no more than 100 houses and few shops.

After the conquest of Moors in Granada in 1492, the last Muslim kingdom in Spain, intolerance against even converted Muslims mounted until their final expulsion from Spain in 1611. At this time many thousands of Andalusian refugees came to settle in Sale and Rabat. Rabat's Almohad walls were so extensive that the newcomers constructed the Andalusian Wall (along what is now Blvd Hassan II) to define and protect a smaller city, the present medina, built in the style of the Andalusian cities from which they had come. To this day, the medinas of Rabat and Sale are renowned for preserving the architectural style, customs and music of medieval Andalusia.

Immediately upon arrival, many of the refugees began taking revenge on the Spanish and Christians in general, through piracy. Sale and Rabat were proclaimed the independent corsair Republic of Bou Regreg. Famous in fiction for selling Robinson Crusoe into slavery, and enormously successful between 1620-1630, when they took over 1,000 European ships from the Atlantic. They ranged as far as Plymouth and Ireland. The Pirates of Sale were renowned and feared by all seamen navigating the area. These famous 'Sallee Rovers', based in the kasbah of Rabat, were not subdued until Moulay Ismail incorporated them (and their revenues) into his state in the late 17th century. Piracy from bases along this coast continued to be a problem for shipping until 1910.

Today, as the capital of Morocco, Rabat has grown into an agglomeration of nearly 1.5 million inhabitants, extending far beyond the Almohad walls and encompassing the formerly distinct city of Sale.

Sights locally

Composed of sister cities – Rabat and Sale – flanking the mouth of Oued Bou Regreg, Rabat is a beautiful and photogenic city. The town is filled with superb historic monuments. Its extensive medinas are rich in Moroccan foods and merchandise. Unlike Marrakech and Fes, no guides are necessary in either Rabat or Sale. On the Rabat side, the old city stands in marked contrast to the new, providing a clear illustration of the concept of the first Resident-General under the French Protectorate, Marshal Lyautey, that the new French infrastructure and its physical manifestations should be kept distinct from, and conform to, traditional Moroccan forms of power and urban spaces. Thus the Ville Nouvelle was situated apart from the medina of Rabat, in a pattern which would be followed in other major Moroccan cities. Although this was a controversial urban planning policy at the time, the result seems well worth it, given the degree of preservation of old Moroccan medinas, unique in North Africa.

RABAT CITY

There is a lot to see in Rabat, which has some of the most outstanding city walls and gates in the world. Hassan Mosque was built in the 12th century, but was left incomplete at the death of Yacoub el Mansour in

Rabat ancient Medina walls   *Graham Hutt*

1199. The views across the old city and Sale from the minaret, which was intended to be 100ft higher, are spectacular. The mosque was destroyed in 1755 by an earthquake centred in Lisbon.

The mausoleum of King Mohammed V (grandfather of the present king) is built on the site where he gathered people in 1955 to thank God for Moroccan independence.

The Almohad walls at the Kasbah des Oudayas (Gate Almohad) were fortified by pirates in the 16th and 17th centuries, adding bastions such as the Tower of the Corsairs at the end of Calle Laalami. Within the kasbah's winding streets, is the 1150 Almohad mosque (oldest in Rabat) restored by renegade English architect, Ahmed el Inglesi in the 18th century (who also built Marine Gate at Essaouira).

In the Old Wool Market is the site where captives of the Pirates of the Republic of Bou Regreg were sold into

captivity in the 16th/17th centuries, just outside their kasbah. Along Rampe S. Maklouf (river road) are many antique shops.

The ruins of Chella, site of the port town Sala Colonia from Phoenician to Arab times is worth a visit.

The Merinid ruins are still in good enough condition to locate the mosque with its ablutions court and prayer hall, and the tomb and *zaouia* (place of religious retreat, a separate courtyard with minaret which housed up to 16 men in retreat) of Abu el Hassan who ruled a vast empire from Tunisia to Spain between 331–1351 and was known as the Black Sultan being the son of an Abyssinian mother.

The National Archaeological Museum (near Grand Mosque and the Royal Palace) houses remarkable treasures, including superb bronzes and mosaics of Volubilis, a nearby Roman city.

SALE

Sale can be reached by crossing main Hassan II bridge (especially if you travel by taxi) but also by small boats which constantly cross the Bou Regreg. You will immediately notice a change from Rabat to a far more conservative, Muslim, non-European style. The medina is very traditional, with wares grouped by trades/guilds. Following the Rue de la Grande Mosque, you arrive at the Great Mosque of Sale. Surrounded by active *zaouias* and the famous, now inactive, Abu Hassan Medersa, a 14th-century Merinid religious school. Built in Hispano-Muslim style (visitors to Granada's Alhambra will be struck by similarities), it is related to the great Bou Inania *medersa* in Fes and Meknes and is adorned with beautiful traditional decoration. It commands superb views over Sale, Bou Regreg, to Rabat.

Local specialities

Sale is well known for its ceramics. A complex of some 20 potteries lies upriver and can be reached by petit taxi from Rabat or after crossing to Sale by boat (ask for *al fajarrín* and point upriver!) The new Sale style of ceramics uses as principal motifs traditional Berber facial tattoos and the *fibula*, a triangular silver brooch used to fix both ends of a cloak around a woman's shoulders: a Roman practice continued in the traditional garb of Berber peoples across the Maghreb. In the contemporary urban Moroccan context, the *fibula* has recently become a symbol of the Berbers in their struggle for recognition.

In Rabat, there is a carpet market on Thursday mornings in Rue des Consuls (near the kasbah), to which people from surrounding mountain towns and dealers bring a diverse selection of carpets. A huge Thursday market, Suq El-Jamis, takes place near the national highway outside Sale, and gathers artisans from both Rabat and Sale.

Eating out

Restaurants of all classes and cultures are in Rabat: Lebanese, Chinese, Korean, Indian and even a McDonalds: all to be found along with traditional large and small eating houses.

One of the many ancient gateways to Rabat Medina
Graham Hutt

Sable D'Or

Originally hailed to be the foundations for one of the finest marinas in Morocco, located near the prestigious area of Temara, 8M S of Rabat, the marina breakwaters built in 1998 can be seen, but no infrastructure has yet been built. Plans for further development have, like others in Morocco, been shelved for now and the structure should not be approached.

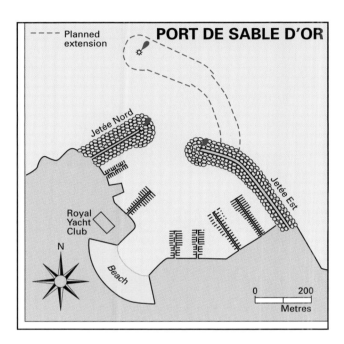

MO 6 Mohammedia

A large commercial port 13M N of Casablanca with a marina section always ready to accommodate visitors. A port of entry which can be used in any conditions.

Location
33°45′N 07°22′W

Distances
Mehdia 46M
Casablanca 13M

Tides

	MHWS	MHWN
Range	3.5m	2.7m

Charts

	Approach	Port
Admiralty	856, 860, 3132	861
French	6142	6142 (inset)
Spanish	527	5271

Lights
Approach
1. **Punta Almina** 35°54′N 05°16′.8W
   Fl(2)10s148m22M White tower on building
Harbour
2. **Entrance Ldg Lts 265°** 33°43′.0N 07°24′.1W
   Front DirOc(3)12s11m18M 262.5°-intens-267.5° White column, black bands 10m
3. *Rear* 110m from front DirOc(3)12s14m18M 262.5°-intens-267.5° White column, black bands 13m
4. **Jetée Nord head** Iso.WG.4s8m9/5M White tower, green tank 5m 191°-G-240°-W-191°
5. **Jetée Sud head** Oc(2)R.6s8m6M Red tower, red tank 6m
Communications
VHF Ch 16, 11, 13

The port

Mohammedia is one of Morocco's major commercial ports and contains the nearest there is to a marina on the Atlantic coast with its cosy yacht club. There were plans to develop the facilities into a full marina, though these have been shelved while Casablanca marina is being built. Mohammedia is taking the yachts normally moored in Casablanca, which is closed. Two pontoons currently serve members of the club nautique, whose staff are very friendly and helpful. Club facilities are situated across the harbour, separate from the fishing fleet.

PILOTAGE

By day

The port lies on the SW side of the bay of Fédala, with the Cap easily identified by the white oil storage tanks which can be seen from a distance of 20M. Ships are often moored 2M NE of the harbour entrance, where offshore oil pipeline berths are located. The N head jetty is marked by a white tower with green stripes, whilst the S head jetty has a white tower with red stripes. Two underwater obstructions N of the port will not worry yachtsmen, being 9m deep. Depths in the entry channel are in excess of 5m.

By night

A light on Cap de Fédala (Fl(2+1)) is visible for 20M.
The first leading light, (130° Oc(2)WG.6s) is on a black and white chequered pedestal. The harbour entrance is marked by lights atop two white towers with black stripes, both DirOc(3)12s.

Mohammedia moorings looking SE towards the clubhouse
Graham Hutt

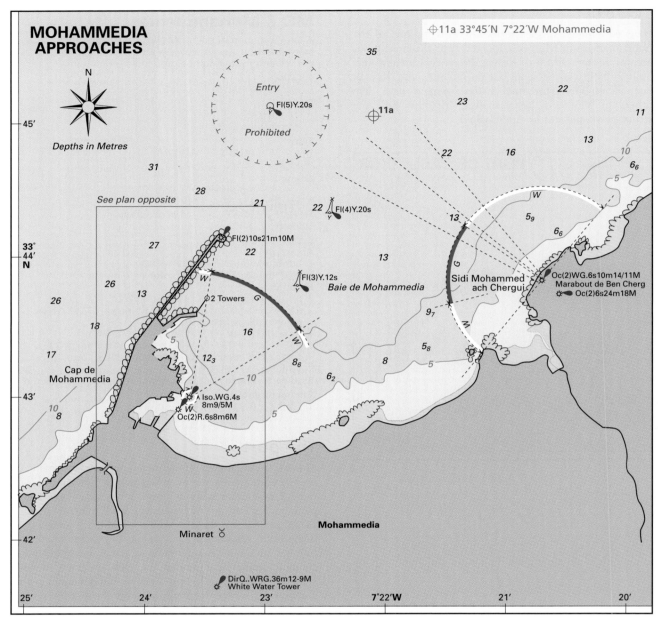

MOHAMMEDIA
APPROACHES

⊕11a 33°45'N 7°22'W Mohammedia

N

Depths in Metres

Entry
Fl(5)Y.20s
Prohibited

See plan opposite

Fl(2)10s21m10M

2 Towers

Fl(4)Y.20s
Fl(3)Y.12s
Baie de Mohammedia

Sidi Mohammed
ach Chergui

Oc(2)WG.6s10m14/11M
Marabout de Ben Cherg
Oc(2)6s24m18M

Cap de
Mohammedia

Iso.WG.4s
8m9/5M
Oc(2)R.6s8m6M

Minaret

Mohammedia

DirQ..WRG.36m12-9M
White Water Tower

Berthing

Minimum depths in the outer harbour are around 5m. Yachts should proceed SW, past the two outer moles, and then W into the inner harbour, where two pontoons will be seen on the NW side of the harbour. These are the club nautique berths and are always full, but the club manager will usually assist visiting yachts to anchor NE of the yachts on the pontoons, taking a line to one already moored. Alternatively, anchor W of the pontoons in depths of 3-5m.

At the end of 2004, visiting yachts were able to use the inside of the quay at the entrance to the fishing and yacht harbour (SW of Jetee Nord) near the pilot boats. The harbourmaster's office has moved to the head of Jetee Nord. This quay is well fendered, though there are no ladders to assist with the high-sided jetties at LW.

Formalities

Mohammedia is a port of entry and officials will visit your yacht.

Facilities

Water and *electricity* Available on the pontoons.

Fuel Available by arrangement with the yacht club.

Provisions The fish market is located close to the main gate, near the yacht club facilities. A large supermarket Marjame is as well stocked as those in Europe: 10 minute taxi ride from the port. There is an excellent hardware shop called Fast Ways (diagonally across from the Hotel Sabah), which is well stocked with tools and equipment. There are grocery shops along the Avenue des F.A.R. and at its end, off to the left of the kasbah on Boulevard Moulay Youssouf, lies the town's marketplace.

Gas Available by arrangement with the club nautique staff.

Post office and *banks* In the centre of town.

Repairs Emergency repairs can be undertaken. A 30-ton floating crane is available.

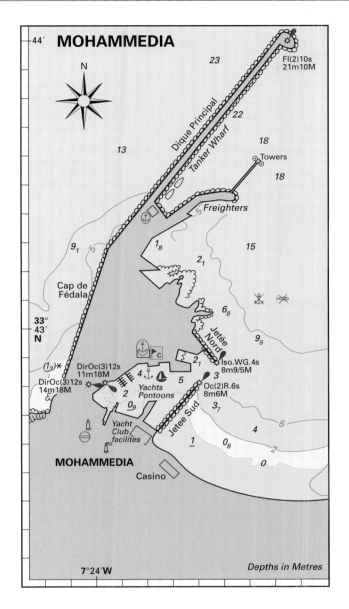

Yacht club facilities A very well-equipped exclusive yacht club complex is located on the south side of the harbour and is available to visiting yachtsmen at the discretion of the manager. As well as a swimming pool, the club has a sailing school to encourage the children of those who summer in Mohammedia (primarily families from Casablanca), to take up the sport.

ASHORE

History

The port of Mohammedia (formally known as Fédala) has been active since the 14th century, reaching a peak in the 17th and 18th centuries, when it engaged in horse trading with Europe. In 1960, a long period of decline was reversed by the inauguration of an important oil refinery by King Mohammed V. The town was renamed Mohammedia. This recent period of growth and prosperity has resulted in increased tourism and the construction of elegant hotels and a golf course nearby.

Sights locally

Emerging from the well-tended marina and port gardens heading E into town, the most direct route takes you past a series of warehouses on a dusty track for a hundred metres. This leads to the port entrance, (visible from your mooring) the fishing harbour and the yacht club, set in a large garden. On the far side of the breakwater is the site of a planned new marina, and beyond this, a long stretch of beach.

The town of Mohammedia spreads out SE of this point. Although there are no historical monuments to visit, aside from the kasbah which dates from 1773, it provides an excellent reminder that there is much more to Morocco than the richly-stocked souks and densely-packed old medinas you may have previously visited. This is a prosperous and elegant resort town with large trees and colourful shrubs along its residential streets.

Local specialities

Each July there is a popular festival in Mohammedia, consisting of cultural events, arts and crafts exhibitions, marathons, etc. For centuries Mohammedia has been a centre of horse breeding and training and a racecourse is located in the town.

Eating out

Mohammedia has some superb restaurants. Enquire at the tourist office (14 Rue al Jahid) or consult a recent guidebook for a current list of these. This is a town where it is worth the trouble to ask around and be selective!

Coastline from Mohammedia to Casablanca

From Mohammedia the coastline begins with long sandy beaches, giving way to rugged low lying cliffs.

Mohammedia yacht club facilities. Always a friendly welcome here
Graham Hutt

MO 7 Casablanca

This is the principal port of Morocco, 120M S of the Straits of Gibraltar. Currently the yacht harbour is closed while a new and larger facility is being built.

Location
33°37′.5N 07°34′.5W

Distances
Mohammedia 13M
El Jadida 50M

Tides
Standard Port

	MHWS	MHWN
Range	3.7m	2.9m

Charts

	Approach	Port
Admiralty	3132, 856, 860	861
French	6111	5697
Spanish	527	50

Lights
Approach
1. **Oukacha LtHo** 33°37′.1N 07°33′.9W VQ(2)2s29m18M
   110°-vis-255° White tower, red lantern
   Auxiliary F.R.12M 055°-vis-110°
2. **Roches Noires** Oc.WR.4s21m16/12M 090°-R-162°-W-090°
   White round tower, red lantern

Harbour
3. **Approach Ldg Lts 228° Muelle de Fosfatos**
   Front DirOc.4s30m18M 225.5°-intens-230.5° Red tower, white stripes
4. *Rear* 770m from front Oc(4)WR.12s48m16/12M shore-W-245°-R-285° 138°-obscd (silo)-153° Red grain silo
5. **Azemour** (cape light) 33°20′.6N 08°18′.3W
   Fl(2)WR.6s45m15/11M 075°-W-100°-R-245° White tower

Communications
VHF Port Ch 16, 12, 14, 24hrs.

The port

This huge principal commercial port of Morocco is also the home of the navy.

The yacht basin, at the far end of the port is very sheltered and safe. Since Dec 1998 it has been closed for dredging and new infrastructure in preparation for the inauguration of a new marina but this could take another two years beyond 2006 complete.

Another new commercial quay is being built between Jetée Transversale and Jetée Nouvelle. Visiting yachts entering the port are usually turned away while there is no marina, but it is possible to anchor E of Jetée Nouvelle.

Entry is safe and straightforward in all weathers although a considerable swell can be experienced with a NE wind.

PILOTAGE

Entry signals
Black ball over black cone/3G(vert) Lts.– dangerous swell, force 5 within next 24hrs
Black ball over 2 black cones/GRG(vert) Lts – very dangerous swell, force 6 or above within next 24hrs

By day

Some distance from the main mole, Jetty Moulay Youssef, on a transit of 228° are two buoys marking the mid-channel entrance. Large vessels are often anchored to the W of these buoys. By day and night the most conspicuous feature is the huge mosque to the W of the port. Depths in the entrance are substantial and do not become noticeably shallower until well inside the yacht basin.

By night

The mosque W of the port will be seen well before the lighthouse at night. The two entry buoys mentioned above (leading Fl.G.6s, followed by Fl.G.12s) mark the mid-channel approach.

Berthing

(In the marina): Follow the NW mole, Moulay Youssef, past the naval yard to the end of the port, where entry to the yacht harbour will be observed. Moorings exclusively for the use of military personnel are the first

apparent N of the marina and should not be approached despite its name (Bassin du Tourism).

The new marina will accommodate some 300 yachts with all modern facilities but there is no information or indication of when work will be completed. Further information will not be available until completion.

Until the marina opens an alternative is to anchor E of Nouvelle Transversale in 4-7m sand. This area is sheltered from the NW prevailing winds, though will be uncomfortable in the NE winds.

Formalities

Officials will visit the yacht and are very efficient and friendly. Immigration police can be contacted by phone on ☎ 317628 and will visit before you leave. If at anchor and not intending to go ashore, officials have not insisted on any formalities.

Facilities

Currently under construction July 2005.
Provisions Shops, supermarkets and fruit and vegetable markets abound in Casablanca.
Gas Available from many shops or ask the boat watchmen to arrange it for you.
Post office and *banks* In the centre of town.
Repairs All repairs can be undertaken here although at present there is no lift-out facility. Opposite the pontoon is a wall which dries out at LW. With a range of 2.9m most underwater jobs can be carried out.

ASHORE

History

There is evidence of Phoenician 7th-century BC and Roman occupation at Casablanca. The Almohads conquered the town in 1188 from the Berber tribe Barghawata, and developed it as a port. The Portuguese established a settlement here in the 14th century on the site of the village of Anfa, which soon became a centre for pirate activities. The Portuguese re-established themselves in the late 16th century, renaming the town Casa Blanca, (White house). In 1755 an earthquake destroyed the settlement. The town was rebuilt at the end of the 18th century by Sultan Mohammed Ibn

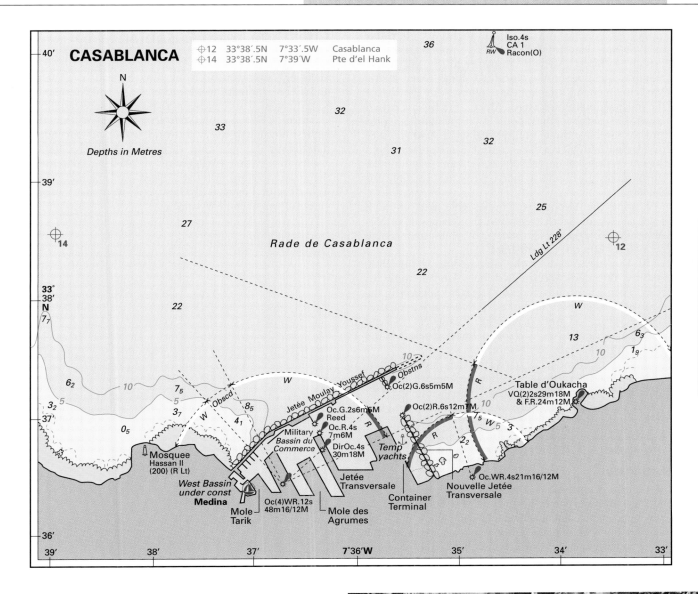

CASABLANCA

⊕12	33°38'.5N	7°33'.5W	Casablanca
⊕14	33°38'.5N	7°39'W	Pte d'el Hank

N

Depths in Metres

Iso.4s
CA 1
RW Racon(O)

Rade de Casablanca

Ldg Lt 228°

W

Table d'Oukacha
VQ(2)s29m18M
& F.R.24m12M

Obstns
Oc(2)G.6s5m5M

Jetée Moulay Youssef

Oc(2)R.6s12m7M

W Obscd

Oc.G.2s6m5M
Reed
Oc.R.4s
7m6M
DirOc.4s
30m18M

Military
*Bassin du
Commerce*

Mosquee
Hassan II
(200) (R Lt)

West Bassin
under const
Medina

Mole
Tarik

Oc(4)WR.12s
48m16/12M

Jetée
Transversale

Mole des
Agrumes

*Temp
yachts*

Container
Terminal

Oc.WR.4s21m16/12M
Nouvelle Jetée
Transversale

Abdellah, who constructed the spectacular Grand Mosque.

In the 20th century the French constructed an artificial harbour under the patronage of Sultan Abd al-Aziz, which marked the beginning of Casablanca's rapid expansion into a modern commercial capital. The medina, which was formally the Jewish quarter until the establishment of Israel, was extended during this period.

Casablanca is not an important city in terms of historic monuments or ambience, but it is the economic capital of Morocco. The port handles a vast range of traffic from European cruise liners to phosphates. Its population by the turn of the century had barely reached 20,000. Since then it has risen to be the main port and industrial powerhouse of Morocco, with a population estimated to be around 4 million people.

Sights locally

Casablanca is a huge sprawling city, a mixture of ancient and modern. Leaving the yacht basin via a gate shared with the naval yard takes you to the main road: left into town and right along the Corniche. This leads to the immense and stunning Hassan II Mosque. The mosque,

Casablanca Souk: an Aladdin's cave for locals and tourists
Minaret

given by the nation to King Hassan on his 60th birthday in 1989 was inaugurated in 1993. It was designed by French architect Michel Pinseau and is the tallest religious building in the world. At some times in the Moslem calendar, a laser beam shines from the top of the mosque, pointing towards Mecca, the holiest city of Islam. This is the furthest point W in the Muslim world and the largest mosque outside the Saudi Arabian cities of Medina and Mecca. The central courtyard can hold 20,000 people while 80,000 more can pray on the surrounding esplanade. Guided tours are available for Dh100.

Beyond the Mosque is a fashionable area of Saudi palaces, elegant beach clubs and the Marabout of Sidi Abderahmen: a picturesque cluster of white tombs rising on a rocky outcrop just offshore.

At the lower end of the old medina is the 18th-century Borj Sidi Mohammed ben Adullah, built to resist Portuguese raids and in its eastern section is the Grande Mosque, built in the late 18th century until after the recapture of Anfa from the Portuguese. Several nights a week there is a coloured-lights display at the fountain in the Place des Nations Unis.

Also recommended, is a visit to the church of Our Lady of Lourdes at the medina entrance, with its remarkable expanse of stained glass windows. The church was built in the 1950s and the windows designed by Gabriel Loire.

See MacLaughlan's list of *Historic Casablanca Architecture – a checklist* for more information.

Eating out

Within the yacht basin is a moderately priced restaurant with good atmosphere, Restaurant Port du Peche. This also acts as the club nautique meeting place until the new facilities are in place. Good fish restaurants are also to be found along the Corniche, at the far end of which is Ain Diab, where there are also some Japanese and Korean restaurants.

The best restaurant in Morocco is said to be Sijilmassa on Rue de Biarritz, a Moroccan-style restaurant complete with bellydancers (go armed with DH 10 notes!) Near the Boulevard Mohammed V are several other reasonably priced Moroccan-style restaurants – Ryad Zitoun (31 Bd Rachidi ☎ 223927) Ouarzazate (Rue Mohamed El Qorri) and the Bahj (Rue Colbert) – and the more expensive Al Mounia (Rue du Prince Moulay Abdallah).

Coastline from Casablanca to El Jadida

Heading southwards from Casablanca, the most impressive landmark in Morocco: the Grand Mosque of King Hassan II will be seen to port. (Described under Casablanca.) Even more spectacular by night, this, the highest mosque in the Arab world, stands out for miles, diminishing the lighthouse of Point d'Oukkacha. Rocks and tombs, with a background of low-lying hills, form the coastline from Point d'el Hank to El Jadida. Keep well clear of Pointe d'El Hank, 1M W of the mosque especially in strong SW winds.

2. El Jadida to Agadir

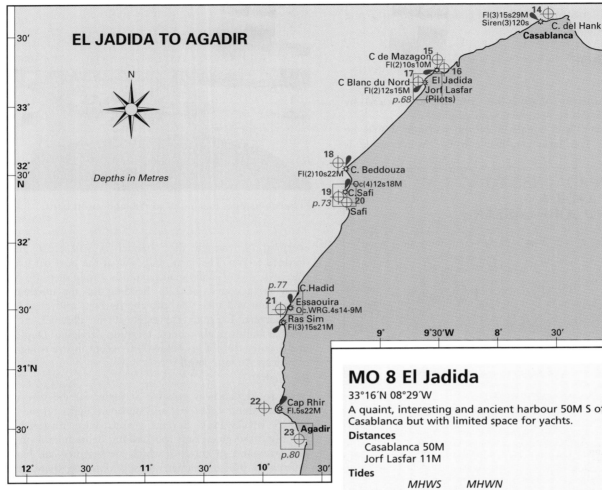

EL JADIDA TO AGADIR

N

Depths in Metres

FI(3)15s29M
Siren(3)120s
14
C. del Hank
Casablanca

C de Mazagon
15
FI(2)10s10M
17
16
C Blanc du Nord
FI(2)12s15M
p.68
El Jadida
Jorf Lasfar
(Pilots)

18
FI(2)10s22M
C. Beddouza

Oc(4)12s18M
19
C Safi
p.73
20
Safi

p.77
C.Hadid
21
Essaouira
Oc.WRG.4s14-9M
Ras Sim
FI(3)15s21M

22
Cap Rhir
FI.5s22M

23
Agadir
p.80

WAYPOINTS – MOROCCO ATLANTIC COAST

⊕14	33°38′.5N	7°39′W	C del Hank
⊕15	33°20′N	8°30′W	El Jadida
⊕16	33°16′N	8°29′W	El Jadida Port
⊕17	33°10′N	8°40′W	Jorf Lasfar
⊕18	32°35′N	9°20′W	Cap Beddouza
⊕19	32°20′N	9°20′W	Off Safi Port
⊕20	32°19′N	9°17′W	Safi Port
⊕21	31°31′N	9°48′W	Essaouira
⊕22	30°40′N	10°00′W	Cap Rhir
⊕23	30°25′N	9°41′W	Agadir
⊕24	29°22′N	10°13′W	Sidi Ifni
⊕25	28°50′N	11°10′W	Cap Nun

MO 8 El Jadida

33°16′N 08°29′W

A quaint, interesting and ancient harbour 50M S of Casablanca but with limited space for yachts.

Distances
Casablanca 50M
Jorf Lasfar 11M

Tides

	MHWS	MHWN
Range	3.6m	2.8m

Charts

	Approach	Port
Admiralty	3132, 862	–
French	6120	6119
Spanish	216	527

Lights
Approach
1. **Oukacha LtHo** 33°37′.1N 07°33′.9W VQ(2)2s29m18M
   110°-vis-255 White tower, red lantern
   Auxiliary F.R.12M 055°-vis-110°
Harbour
2. **Jetty Nord head** 33°15′.6N 08°29′.8W
   Iso.WG.4s7m13/9M 120°-G-235°-W-120° Square concrete
   tower, green band 5m
3. **Jetty Sud head** F.R.10m9m7M White column red top

Communications
VHF There is no night radio watch, although during the day channels 12 and 16 are supposed to be monitored, but it is unusual to get any response.

The harbour

This fishing harbour retains a relaxed atmosphere and a friendly welcome awaits yachtsmen, though space is limited to a place beneath the restaurant, built over the Association Nautique. This jetty belongs to the

II. MOROCCO

Association, which is a well-run sail training centre with dinghies and sailboards, used by the youngsters of the town. It can therefore get noisy during the afternoons, but discipline is very good and you will not experience any problems from the happy children swimming and sailing around.

PILOTAGE

By day

The sandbanks around the entrance are moved by Atlantic gales so approach with caution.

A wreck half a mile S of the harbour should be avoided. The large sandbank S of the entrance is

El Jadida harbour looking W to club and yachts berth
Minaret

creeping N, though the channel is still clear and dredged to 3m. The shoal reef NW of the port off Cap Mazagan is very shallow and extends a mile or more N. Entry on a course of 220° heading for the northern breakwater will take you into the harbour and clear of the dangers. Keep to the right of the channel, as a sandbar builds in the centre between dredging. Depths in the entry do not go below 3m, except in the troughs of a deep Atlantic swell.

By night

Entry to El Jadida is possible at night, but be sure to correctly identify the port and starboard lights on the N and S breakwaters. Several vessels have mistakenly identified the green and red flashing lights inland on a pharmacy and an antenna, which are brighter and have alarmingly similar characteristics. Confusing them will land you on the shallow coral reef off Cap de Mazagan mentioned above. The wreck S of the harbour is lit at night.

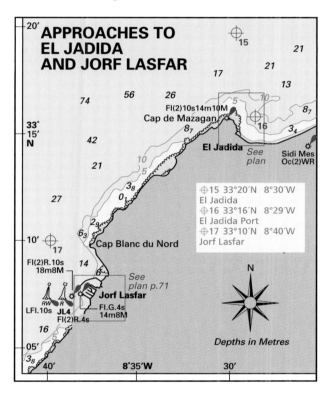

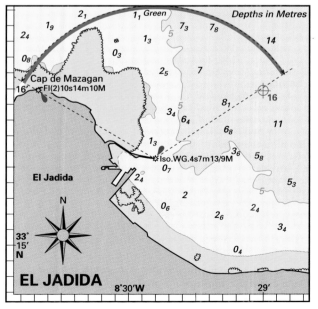

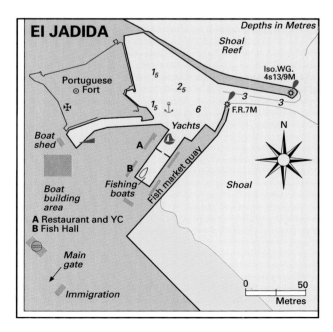

Berthing

Once inside, depths of 6m exist in the main channel of the harbour. Steer SW towards the short fishing harbour, heading for the restaurant and club nautique. Depths very quickly reduce to 1.5m beyond the restaurant and the far end dries out. Do not proceed beyond the restaurant, where a short wall leads to steps. Moor alongside, forward (NE) of the steps at the very end of the quay. Secure ropes to the railing beneath the restaurant and to the large bollard (formed by the buried muzzle from an ancient cannon) on the N corner of the jetty. A tidal range of 3m should be considered when mooring. Some surging can be expected here during W winds. Minimum depth alongside is 2.5m, though one yacht reported shallower depths in summer 2004. A below-water ledge extends beyond the steps further back towards the fishing quay. An alternative, if no room is available here, is to anchor in 2m sand NE of the club opposite the entrance. There are usually small fishing boats moored here who will not object, though due to silting, depths may be less than shown.

Formalities

El Jadida is a port of entry and the police, customs and immigration officials will come to the yacht to complete the paperwork. The officials are very friendly, although the customs officers here expect a 'gift' before completing their task and will return with their boss, who will also expect to be reimbursed for his effort. Keep the cigarettes or whisky handy. . .or just sit it out until they depart!

Facilities

Water Available from a tap on the jetty by permission of Association Nautique.

Electricity Not generally available, although it is possible to run a cable from the restaurant located next to the jetty by arrangement with the owner.

Fuel Available and may be brought to your yacht in cans, or fill up at the fishing quay, where a pump is located. (Taking into account depths and tide.)

Provisions Many shops are located just outside the port with a good range of items. Follow the old city wall to the right for the fish, meat and fruit markets. Also two supermarkets in town. One is a *hypermarché* with a very well-stocked liquor shop attached.

Gas Can easily be arranged with Ahmed, the gatekeeper.

Post office and *banks* Located just outside the main port gate in the centre of town. Several banks here have automatic cash facilities and up to Dh8,000 can be withdrawn on Visa cards. Diners Club cards are also accepted.

Repairs This is one of the best ports for engine repairs, which do not exist in the port itself, but mechanics and tradesmen will come to the boat. In the town are workshops catering for complete overhauls for any engine and the engineers, who may not be literate, are nevertheless as competent as those in Europe and very much cheaper. Arrange anything necessary with the guardian.

Note A small gate from the restaurant and club nautique leads into the main harbour. The gate has been manned for 30 years by Ahmed (soon to retire and give way to Rachid), a very friendly old fellow who can arrange anything for visiting yachts from tour guides to engine overhauls. He will appreciate 'a souvenir' in return. Ahmed or Rachid will happily look after your yacht and ensure its safety while you leave for excursions.

ASHORE

History

The name El Jadida derives from *Al Brija al Jadida*, which means 'the new little port.' The Portuguese began building this massive fort, then called *Mazagao*, to consolidate their Atlantic trade advantage in 1513 on the site of an abandoned Almohad fortress. Two hundred and fifty years later Mazagao was one of the last and best-situated Portuguese bastions along the Moroccan coast, only falling to Sidi Mohammed Ben Abdallah in 1769 after a prolonged siege. When the Portuguese finally sailed out they left the city partially burned and mined. After much loss of life, the triumphant Moroccans were forced to abandon it.

Forty five years later Mazagao was rebuilt, re-baptised *El Jadida* (the new), and resettled. The moats on two sides were filled in, connecting the formerly detached, impenetrable fortress with the land. Gradually Muslim inhabitants settled around it, while Europeans and Moroccan Jewish merchants, who were pivotal to trade with the interior, congregated within the walls of the old city. In 1912 the city, again called Mazagan, became an important regional administrative centre in the French Protectorate. The final reversion to the name El Jadida in 1956 marks the end of the assorted colonial intrusions into Morocco which began with the Portuguese five centuries ago.

Local specialities

Primarily a fishing town, because of the splendid beaches this is a popular tourist resort. The town is renowned for its beautiful women. Well worth a visit is the Hotel Palais Andalous. This splendid building in typical Hispano-muslim style, reflects in its spectacular ceramics and elaborate stucco work, many features of the Alhambra in Granada and the palace built by Muslim artisans in Seville and Reales Alcazares.

El Jadida yacht club gate looking NE from behind restaurant
Minaret

II. MOROCCO

El Jadida ancient Byzantine cystern discovered recently under a house *Graham Hutt*

Splendid Moroccan design and workmanship in the facade of this hotel in El Jadida: Hotel Anduluz *Graham Hutt*

Sights locally

Once outside the port, to your left will be seen the famous beach of Sidi Bouzid, with a long elegant corniche, where vacationers from all over Morocco promenade on summer evenings and socialise in cafés, bars and discotheques. Straight ahead lies the Place Mohammed V, the functional centre of El Jadida where you will find banks, PTT (post and telegraph), at the south end of the plaza, a helpful tourist office (NW corner of the plaza), photographic shops, traditional cafés, etc. And to the right, past a long block devoted on the seaward side to the city market, you will come upon the high walls of a wonderful old Portuguese fortress-city, well worth a visit.

Today, the *Cité Portugaise*, as this old fortress-city is known, is a beautiful, relaxed and interesting place to visit. From the ramparts one gets a sense of the original situation of the city, its moat (now limited to one side), and its harbour (now silted up). Descending into its immense cistern, one is stunned to silence by a vast shimmering space, its ribbed Gothic vaulting supported by 25 huge pillars. This cistern, featured in films such as *The Harem* and Orson Welles' *Othello*, seems secret and indeed it was completely forgotten after the 1769 fall of the city, only to be casually found by a shopkeeper in 1916 as he was increasing the size of his store.

Because El Jadida is a university town, it is possible to find especially well-versed and enthusiastic guides needing a few Dirhams to show you some of these sights in detail, but there is none of the confusion and 'volunteer' pressure of bigger cities, it is just as possible for you to explore them alone.

Eating out

The local marina restaurant serves a basic menu at a reasonable price. Since the town is a holiday resort, it is full of restaurants of every type and size.

Transport

Although the railway line passes through the town, it is now only used for freight. However, a good bus service operates and the station can be found at the far end of the ramparts of the *Cité Portugaise*. In the summer it would be wise to purchase bus tickets to Casablanca and Marrakech a day in advance of any excursion as it is a busy route. Taxis can also be found everywhere.

Because it is so quiet and safe, and your yacht will be well guarded, El Jadida is a particularly good port to use as a base for excursions. Marrakech, for instance, is 4 hours away by bus.

Note

Any assistance by way of woodworking tools, etc. for the repair of their equipment would be very much appreciated by the yacht club, which is run with almost no funding. It will greatly facilitate your stay.

Coastline from El Jadida to Jorf Lasfar

From El Jadida, this part of the coastline starts with the low-lying coral ledge surrounding Cap Mazagan. Keep at least 1.5M out from El Jadida before heading S. When leaving El Jadida and rounding the cape, Jorf Lasfar will be seen 10M to the S. The coastline rises into a rocky cliff 60m high on approaching the port.

MO 9 Jorf Lasfar

This large phosphate port for deep-draughted vessels, 70M S of Casablanca, is an excellent bolt-hole in bad weather. The port, though not interesting, has recently welcomed yachts and is a port of entry.

Location
33°07'N 08°38'.5W

Distances
El Jadida 11M
Safi 60M

Tides

	MHWS	MHWN
Range	3.6	2.8

Charts

	Approach	Port
Admiralty	3132, 862	862
French	6170	–
Spanish	216	216 (inset)

Lights
Approach
1. **Cap Bedouza** 32°32'.6N 09°17'.0W Fl(2)10s65m22M
   Turret on fort
Harbour
2. **Dique Principal head** Fl(2)R.10s18m8M
3. **Epi head** F.R.15m8M
4. **Contradique head** Fl.G.4s14m8M R light on tower 1M S

Communications
VHF Ch 12 and 16

Coastline from Jorf Lasfar to Safi

This coastline is rocky, with long stretches of low-lying cliffs and 50 foot sand dunes. A large inland lake and connecting lagoon lie behind dunes near Oualidia.

Nearing Cap Cantin (Beddouza), 7M to the north, the white mosque of Sidi Bou Seksou is conspicuous. Rocks extend about a mile from the cape, and the sea starts breaking much further out in the relatively shallow

5m depths. It is advisable to give the cape a clearance of at least 3M. Sardine nets are laid out from May to December in the area between Cap Cantin and Essaouira. A wreck lies four miles NE of Cap Safi.

The port

Although not recommended as a port worth visiting, Jorf Lasfar is nevertheless one of the largest and safest shelters to run to in bad weather, with easy access in any conditions. It is primarily intended for the export of phosphates which are mined in this area, mostly in Ganturs 100M away. Several yachts visited in 2004 and were made welcome.

PILOTAGE

By day

The port can be clearly identified from several miles away by the cranes and large ships moored inside. The entry channel is on the S side of the breakwater, with a high tower painted with red and white stripes on the clifftop above the entrance.

By night

Night entry presents no problems for any vessel. The port is well lit as is the entrance, as noted on the chart and there have been no reports of malfunctioning lights.

Berthing

Yachts are usually directed to the SW side of the Commercial quay. Tugboats and pilots use the adjoining service quay. Yachts would not normally wish to stay here, as there are no facilities or provisions.

Formalities

Port of entry, officials will visit the yacht.

Facilities

There are no facilities currently available for small vessels. There are no villages within walking distance, nor any supplies available in the immediate vicinity. However, El Jadida is 10M away and is served by the main coastal road which passes the port with a regular taxi and bus service.

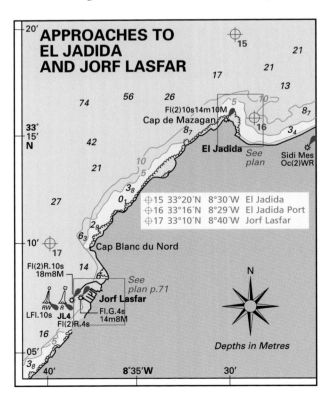

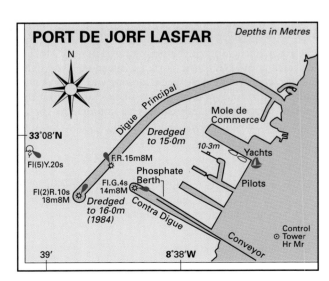

II. MOROCCO

Oualidia lagoon, once overlooked by the favourite palace of the King. Now too silted to be used as a good anchorage
Graham Hutt

Oualidia Lagoon

Sadly, this lagoon N of Safi, on the shores of what was formerly the King of Morocco's favourite palace, has become too silted for use by yachts and should not be considered except as an overland excursion.

Seaweed, which is exported to Japan, is an Industry around Jorf Lasfar
Graham Hutt

ASHORE

Morocco has the largest reserves of phosphates in the world, having been mined since Roman times. Jorf Lasfar was formerly a small fishing port where gambas (large prawns) were landed, but became the largest phosphate port in Morocco in 1997.

Sights locally

The ruins of the ancient Berber city of Tit, near Moulay Abdallah is 3M NE of the port. Tit (meaning 'eyes' – the watchtowers would have been looking out to sea) was built as a fortified monastery, one of several built on the Atlantic coast in the 12th century to counter the threat of Norman invasion.

MO 10 Safi Port

A large and very busy fishing and commercial port 60M S of Jorf Lasfar. Facilities for yachts are few, but this is a good place to visit and a port of entry.

Location
32°19´N 09°15´.5W

Distances
Jorf Lasfar 60M
Essaouira 56M

Tides

	MHWS	MHWS
Range	3.4m	2.7m

Charts

	Approach	Port
Admiralty	3132	862
French	6169	6103
Spanish	529	254

Lights
Approach
1. **Ldg Lt 150°** *Front* Q.11m12M 060°-vis-240° Red and white mast
2. *Rear* 150m from front Q.14m12M 060°-vis-240° Red and white tower

3. **Pointe de la Tour** 32°20´.0N 09°16´.8W Oc(4)12s90m18M 302°-vis-164° Yellow tower
4. DirFl(2)WRG.6s11m14/13M 085°-G-097°-W-103°-R-113°
5. **Spur W of entrance** F.G.10m6M
Harbour
6. **Grande jetée head** Iso.G.4s12m8M White and green tower F.G 400m and 800m SE
7. **Elbow** F.G.6m3M 133°-vis-335° White and green pedestal
8. **Jetée Transvaal Nord** Oc.R.4s7m6M Grey and red hut
9. **Mole de phosphates head** F.R.8m7M
Communications
Port VHF Ch 16, 9, 10, 11, 12 24hrs.

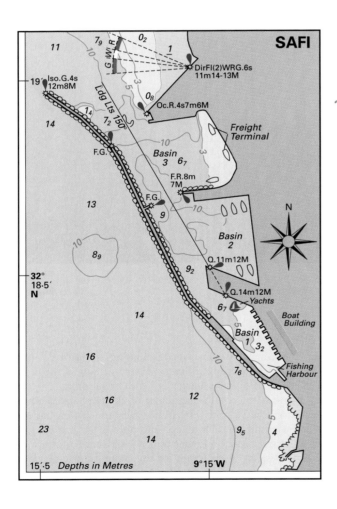

SAFI

The port

Safi is a very busy fishing port with a large area to the S of the harbour dedicated to boatbuilding. The centre and N end of the port is used for commercial shipping with cement and phosphate loading facilities. Several changes have taken place here recently. The fishing fleet has been moved out of basin no 2 to the S end of the port, where they are tightly packed and racked-out 7 deep. The old fishing basin is now used for commercial vessels, whilst the N basin is used for bulk carriers to load phosphates.

It is well sheltered from most wind directions, although a swell does enter the port during strong NW winds. The prevailing wind from N–NNE is usual in the months between April and October, getting up before midday, often reaching 30kts in mid-afternoon and dropping at night. Winter winds are more moderate and prevail from the SW–NW with occasional storms.

The port lies just outside the NW corner of the city walls, which were built by the Almohads in the 12th century.

PILOTAGE

By day

Sea mist is often encountered along this part of the coast in summer.

A large silo nearly 70m high, can be clearly seen at the southern end of the harbour. A long mole projecting NW leads into the port. The channel is dredged to a depth of at least 7m. Large freighters enter the port.

By night

The end of the mole is well lit (Grande jetée head Iso.G.4s12m8M) and leading lights S of the harbour guide into the channel as shown on the chart.

Note Lights are frequently reported to be dysfunctional.

II. MOROCCO

Berthing

Berthing is restricted due to limited space and there is no consistent berthing arrangement for yachts. They are currently directed to the quay NW of the fishing port. This is alongside the coastguard cutter at the S end of the port near the fishing fleet. Depths here are around 6m. Some visitors are directed to either side of the Quay de Phosphates, the NE corner of which has been dredged.

Formalities

Safi is an efficient port of entry and officials will arrive at your yacht.

Facilities

Water Is available from large hose connections.
Fuel Can be delivered to your boat by bowser or in cans.
Provisions Most supplies are available from the well-stocked shops just outside the port.
Gas Camping Gaz and propane/butane refills are available from local hardware shops.
Post office and *banks* In the centre of town.
Repairs No yacht repair facilities are available in the port, but as in most Moroccan towns, engineers can easily be arranged in the town and any supplies can be purchased there.

ASHORE

History

Safi, dating from Phoenician times, was first intensively developed by the Almohads during the 12th to 13th century. At that time Asfi, as the city was known, was renowned as a religious and intellectual centre in an occidental Muslim world which stretched well up into Spain. The Portuguese conquered it in 1508.

Safi's present concentration on phosphates dates from the French colonial years of last century. After independence, Maroc-Chimie built the huge processing plant which lies along the coast just south of the city. This has made Safi one of the key ports of Morocco.

It was from Safi that the Norwegian explorer Thor Heyerdahl sailed his papyrus, bamboo and reed-built boat, in an attempt to prove that the ancient Egyptians could have crossed the Atlantic to found the Inca and Aztec civilisations, accounting for the many similarities between the two ancient civilisations. These similarities have remained a mystery to ethnologists, because they have not accepted that the Atlantic could have been crossed before Columbus. Heyerdahl succeeded on his second attempt in 1970, reaching Barbados after 57 days.

Sights locally

The fish-market on the quay is one of the most fascinating in Morocco. All types of fish can be seen and purchased, including very long conger eels, caught nearby. Due to the cold currents which bring sardines close to shore just to the north, Safi has been one of the most important sardine fishing ports in the world for centuries. Boat building is a family business here, with the designs being carried in the minds of those families for centuries, without reference to printed plans. Each boat carries a distinctive traditional family characteristic.

Safi port: a very tight squeeze for yachts in summer
Minaret

Safi fishing harbour: an even tighter squeeze for the fishermen! *Minaret*

Local specialities

In addition to viewing its fascinating traditional boat building, the ceramic home industry in Safi is huge. A visit to the Potters' Quarter is highly rewarding.

Safi has one of the principal urban popular ceramic traditions in Morocco. Its pots, vases and plates can be purchased all over Morocco (and abroad), but there are distinctive colours and patterns which mark traditional Safi wares, just as there are for the ceramics of cities like Fes, Meknes and Sale. Unlike the hand-coiled, unglazed wares made at home by women in rural areas of Morocco, urban ceramics are made by men in *ateliers* in the Potters' Quarter, concentrated just outside the city walls, as was customary in medieval Europe. This is due to the smoke and fire hazard posed by the kilns and to the need for access to water and the constant delivery of clay and wood. The techniques in use at Safi are very

Safi famous for its pottery, the ancient kilns are in everyday use
Minaret

ancient, as pots are thrown on sunken kick wheels and are fired in specially-shaped two-tiered, wood-burning kilns. Safi pots are still painted by hand. It is possible to observe all phases of the manufacturing process, from a lump of clay to the fired, painted product. Considering all the time and effort evident in the Potters' Quarter, you will find prices for these wonderful ceramics extraordinarily cheap.

Eating out

As usual, the medina contains many places where one can eat well and inexpensively. There are several nicer restaurants around Place de l'Independence near the Wafa Bank. North of the city on Route Sidi Bouzid, are magnificent views of Safi, leading up to the restaurants Le Refuge (French and seafood) and La Corniche

Artist at work in Safi. Note the hands stencilled with henna
Graham Hutt

(Moroccan and seafood). Take a petit taxi for this excursion.

Transport

Safi is a safe place to leave your yacht for excursions inland. Europcar rental has an office located in Place Ibnou Sina. The train and bus stations are located some 1500m S of Place de l'Independence, on the extension of Rue de R'bat and Avenue du President Kennedy, respectively. A railway line connects Safi with all the coastal towns to the north, as far as Tanger, but recent information suggests that this coastal line is now only used for freight once south of Casablanca. The line running inland to Marrakech, Meknes and Fes still carries passengers.

Coastline from Safi to Essaouira

This stretch, 56M from Safi changes from rocky cliffs to desert. Features along the coast include: a tower 80m high, 3M SW of Sidi Rhouzia (32°15´N 09°16´W) and, 4M further south, a red cliff, Jorf el Houdi, distinctive in its sugar-loaf shape. Another similarly shaped cliff lies 7M further SW.

A distinctive change begins here as farmland gives way to desert conditions. This brings with it a change in wind direction and general weather conditions: warmer and more humid.

The NW swell along this part of the coast is rarely less than 2m for most of the year, though current is negligible. Winds are generally from the SW, except for strong northerly winds which often occur from April to August. From August to November, winds are usually light. Winter storms usually begin in December, bringing strong SW gales until March, with a swell of around 5m.

A mile N of Oued Tensift River, 3M south of Soueira Kedima, the ruins of an old Portuguese fort can be seen. The wide Oued Tensift looks inviting, but has a shallow sand-bar, making entry impossible. Ten miles further SW, the tomb of Sidi Yssahak is conspicuous. Several more white-painted tombs can be seen between Sidi Yssahak and Cap Hadid,(31°42´N, 09°41´W). This cape should be given a clearance of 3M, as submerged rocks extend well offshore. Jebel Hadid, a mountain range a short distance inland extending from Oued Tensift to Cap Hadid, can be clearly seen from several miles offshore. 10M north of Essaouira, the tomb of Moulay Bouzerktoun can be seen. Sandy beaches are the main feature approaching Essaouira, with the snow-capped Atlas mountains visible in the background.

II. MOROCCO

MO 11 Essaouira

A very pleasant fishing harbour, and interesting town. Port of entry/departure with dangers around the entrance.

Location
31°30′.5N 09°47′W (Between Ile D'Essaouira and the port)

Distances
Safi 56M
Agadir 75M

Tides

	MHWS	MHWN
Range	3.6m	2.8m

Charts

	Approach	Port
Admiralty	3133, 863	863 (inset)
French	6206	6204
Spanish	529	254

Lights
Approach
1. **Sidi Mogul** 31°29′.6N 09°45′.9W Oc.WRG.4s18m14-9M 034°-G-124°-W-136°-R-214°-W-260°-W(unintens)-350°-W-034° Tower

Harbour
2. **Jetty head** 31°30′.5N 09°46′.6W Q.8m12M Horn 60s 208°-vis-108° Column
3. **Spur** Oc(2)R.6s2m6M Red pedestal Obscd seaward
4. **E Mole head** Fl.G.4s2m5M Pedestal

Communications
VHF Ch 16, 9.

Coastline from Essaouira to Agadir

With a backdrop of the snow-capped Atlas Mountains well inland, this shoreline consists of rocky cliffs, mountains, long beaches and desert scrubland. Cap Sim is formed by a cliff 100m high with a rocky reef extending 1 mile W of the cape. The lighthouse is a large tower with black and white bands, with four smaller towers surrounding it. A 3M clearance should be given to the cape. A conspicuous tower (31°10′N 09°40′W) 10M ENE of Cap Tafelney, stands on Jebel Amsittene, which is 1,000m high. A reef extends 3.5M from Cap Tafelney. From Cap Tafelney to Cap Rhir (30°38′N 09°53′W) the coastline is mountainous. This promontory is 360m high and the lighthouse can be clearly seen. Agadir lies 18M S of the cape. Currents along the coast are S around 0.5kts.

Brief squalls can be experienced at any time in this area, especially around the capes, caused by the extreme differences of temperature between the high snowy mountain tops of the Atlas range and the nearby hot desert sands. Generally during summer, periods of calms can be expected, with land and sea breezes alternating from the W to E. In winter, Atlantic depressions sweeping through the Canaries give rise to a very heavy and dangerous swell, reaching 12m. Fog is frequent from June to October.

The port

This is a fascinating and very ancient harbour though with the hazard of high winds blowing most of the time and a normal swell of around 2m. There is a large rocky patch to the W of the entrance. Once inside it is welcoming and very pleasant. The harbour gives good protection in all weather conditions, although a breeze funnels through the entrance. Agadir, 65M further on, is easier to navigate as a final departure point for the Canaries, though not as interesting as Essaouira. There are plans to develop the port to the S.

PILOTAGE

By day

A rocky reef extends W of the harbour and an island to the S. Entry should be made between the eastern dique and the island Isle de Mogador, on a course of 128° heading for the lighthouse Phare de Mogdoul. Enter once the breakwater is 10° abaft the beam, where minimum depths of 2.5m will be found in mid-channel.

By night

Night entry not recommended especially in strong W winds, when a high sea gets up between the island to the S and the harbour entrance. Though the harbour diques are well lit, lines are often stretched across the harbour entrance after dusk and fishing nets laid. Note the lighthouse on Sidi Mogdoul dune is narrowly sectored red, green with a white to assist with navigation. Using this and the light on the end of the S mole, night entry is possible.

Berthing

Minimum depths of 3m are to be found in mid-harbour though some silting does take place. Although mooring rings can be seen on the jetty just inside the entrance to the E, do not approach this section of the wall, as a shallow rocky ledge extends from it. Moor alongside the pontoon lying off the jetty next to Chez Sam restaurant, just inside the harbour entrance near the harbourmaster's office. This is where the coastguard and police launch are berthed. There is only room for one yacht here, though racking out three or four deep is possible.

Formalities

Essaouira is a port of entry and officials will come to the yacht. The port authorities are very friendly, if quite inquisitive. Expect an invitation to an official's home for cous cous!

Facilities

Water On the quay by arrangement with the restaurant Chez Sam.

Fuel Can be brought to the boat

Provisions Local shops and the market are near to the port and can supply most provisions. See 'Sites locally' for more information.

Gas Camping Gaz readily available.

Post office and *banks* In the centre of town.

Repairs Most repairs can be undertaken locally. A slipway at the N end of the port can facilitate haul-out of vessels. Although unaccustomed to keel yachts, these small

boatyards are generally well able to cope with unusual situations and any hull shapes, using various wedges and blocks providing the depths are sufficient.

ASHORE

History

Essaouira was visited from at least the seventh century BC by the Phoenicians, but its first prominence in the ancient world dates from the first century AD, when it was known in Rome as the source of imperial purple dyes and fine marquetry woodwork. For a short time after 533 Essaouira was occupied by the Byzantines, who reinstated Christianity in Morocco after the Vandal depredations which had led to the sack of Rome, but when the first wave of Arabs spreading Islam swept across North Africa in the late 7th century, they found avid converts in Moroccan Berbers. By the 10th century the town, already an important port which transmitted all goods from southern Morocco, was known as Amogdul (the well-guarded), after the Berber Muslim patron saint of the city, Sidi Mogdul, who is buried 3km away.

The Portuguese, who distorted 'Amogdul' into 'Mogdura' were forced to abandon Mogdura along with Safi and Agadir in 1541.

In 1764, the Alaouite Sultan Sidi Mohammed Ben Abdellah (1757-90) decided to make this a key military and commercial port and the town was renamed Essaouira, Arabic for 'fortified place'. Well fortified it was: the immense artillery platform of La Skala defended the city from sea attacks, while city walls repelled insurgent tribes on land. In the 19th century Essaouira was the only Moroccan port south of Tanger

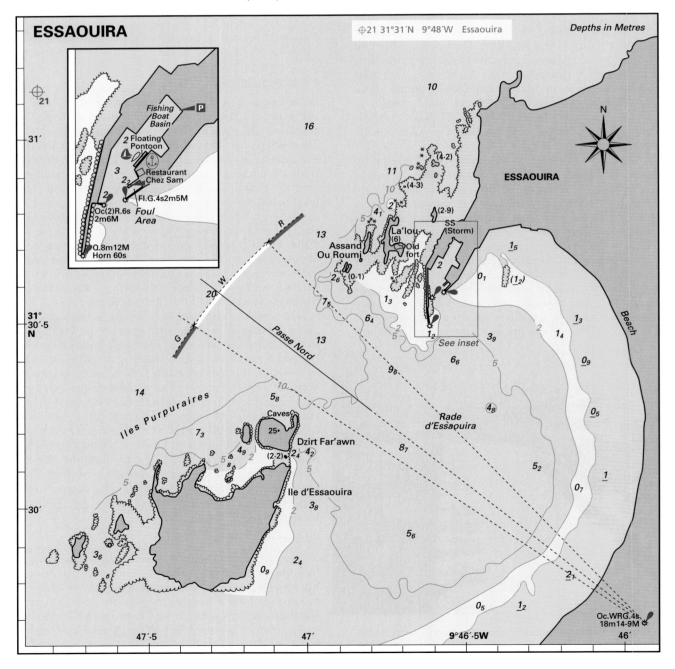

ESSAOUIRA

⊕21 31°31′N 9°48′W Essaouira   *Depths in Metres*

open to European trade. By the mid-19th century, Jews comprised one third of the population of the town – some 4,000 people. But by the late 1960s, prompted by changes in attitude relating to Moroccan independence and fear of reprisal for aggressive Israeli military actions, most of them had left.

Under the French Protectorate this cosmopolitan city entered a severe decline due to the promotion of the ports of Casablanca and Agadir and, in the late 1950s, to the exodus of the Jews. Although it was popular in the 1960s and '70s with occasional hippies such as Jimi Hendrix, Essaouira has only recently recovered its balance as a small-scale but thriving fishing and market town and tourist destination. It is home to many famous artists.

Sights locally

After the busy port of Safi, Essaouira is a pleasant, unhurried town and the port reflects the more desert-like life here. Passing through the gate in the harbour wall takes you to Place Moulay el Hassan. In addition to a Tourist Office; banks, cafés and some fine restaurants are located in this plaza. Jack's Kiosk is an important landmark where every essential can be found, from newspapers, magazines and second-hand books in diverse languages, to international telephone services and fax facilities and assistance with travel arrangements.

Darb Laalouj is a cross-street on the general north-south axis which houses many woodworkers as well as the excellent Museum of Sidi Mohammed Ibn Abdellah, once the home of the Pasha. It contains carpets, traditional weapons and musical instruments with superb marquetry inlay, objects showing the long history of the tradition of thuya marquetry and woodworking in Essaouira, displays which suggest the meaning of Berber symbols found on diverse art forms, etc.

Near the western end of Darb Laalouj lies the entrance to the Skala de la Ville. Impressive European cannons line these great sea ramparts and from their North Bastion, one can get an overview of the Medina.

Essaouira: the small boats used to harvest seaweed are towed by fishing boats   *Minaret*

Local specialities

According to Cicero, the magnificent marquetry tables, still made in Essaouira, were highly prized in Rome. To this day, the quality of woodworking here is as breathtaking as the wood principally used for its execution: thuya. A beautiful walnut-like wood derived from a coniferous tree rare elsewhere, grows abundantly around Essaouira. It is used extensively in the production of ornamental objects: bowls, boxes, candlesticks, lamp-holders, carvings and desktop items, both for everyday use by Moroccans and for the tourist trade. Thuya is a very brittle decorative wood, not ideal for construction. The root is very hard and has the same characteristics as burr walnut. Fine banding and cross banding are used to create decorative effects similar to the characteristic found on Sheraton furniture.

The woodworkers' *souk* runs along the rampart walls along the Rue de la Skala, and on streets perpendicular to it. Essaouira is unusual in that there seems to be no pressure to purchase and on the base of most items can be found the price, or at least the starting point for negotiations. A reduction of about 30% can be expected after haggling. As in Safi, you will also be invited to see the craftsmen at work producing these beautiful handmade items. Note particularly the exact fitting lids and the very high quality of finish on almost everything. Many of the abstract forms made from the natural twisting roots are truly spectacular and very cheap. For some contemporary pieces which play upon these natural abstractions, visit the Galerie d'Art Frederic Damgaard (Av. Oqba Ibn Nafia).

Eating out

Unlike Safi, where the police exclude all casual visitors from the port, here the public are encouraged to mingle with the fishermen and to eat in one of the restaurants inside the port. There are two kinds: open air with tantalising aromas where fresh fish are grilled by several independent fisherman-chefs along the quayside, and a

Essaouira looking S through harbour entrance, yacht masts just visible top left   *Minaret*

more traditional restaurant at the end of the port (Chez Sam). At the open air grills you choose your fish, negotiate the price per kilo and see it cooked to perfection in front of your eyes. Chez Sam has excellent seafood, atmosphere and service. The Chalet de la Plage on the corniche is slightly more expensive, but its lovely terrace bar and the quality of its food make it well worth it. For superb Moroccan food in a truly Moroccan setting, dine at the small Hotel Villa Maroc (10 Rue Abdellah Ben Yassin, just behind the clocktower).

The Isles Purpuraires were renowned in Roman times as the source of dyes for the imperial robes of the Caesars. King Juba II (to whom Caesar Augustus had granted the Kingdom of Mauritania Tingitana circa 25BC), established factories here for the extraction of drops of colour from a certain type of mussel for making dyes. Nowadays these islands are renowned for another rarity, their birds, especially the Eleanora's Falcon, and visiting is restricted. Permission can be obtained to visit the islands by boat, as explained in the Tourist Office in Place Prince Moulay el Hassan.

The climate is semi-tropical in Essaouira. With a constant high Atlantic swell and a breeze for most of the year, this is an ideal location for surfing. Surfers head south of town (off the road to Agadir) to the extensive sandy beaches known as the plages sauvages.

Transport

An early morning bus leaves for Marrakech from the Hotel des Isles, just S of the port overlooking the beach. This bus is timed to link up with trains from Marrakech to Rabat and Casablanca. Otherwise, the new bus station is unfortunately some 2km east of the north gate of town (Bab Doukkala), and due both to its distance and to the unsavoury nature of the 'suburbs' and Quartier Industrielle en route, taking a taxi there is advised. (There is a petit taxi rank by the clock tower near Place Prince Moulay el Hassan.) Grand taxis and buses for all other destinations leave from this new bus station. Note that on the return trip, however, grand taxis are usually willing to let you off at Bab Doukkala or the clock tower.

English made cannons look W on a typical salt-laden windy day in Essaouira   *Graham Hutt*

MO 12 Agadir and Anza

The last port offering shelter going S, 220 miles from the Canaries. The port is very dirty and with few facilities.

Location
30°24′.8N 09°38′W (S of Grand Jetée)

Distances
Essaouira 75M
Lanzarote 212M

Tides

	MHWS	MHWN
Range	3.7m	2.8m

Charts

	Approach	Port
Admiralty	3133	863
French	6178	5955
Spanish	217, 530	181

Lights
Approach
1. **Cap Sim** 31°23′.9N 09°49′.9W Fl(3)15s104m21M Turret on fort black/white bands
2. **Cap Ghir** 30°38′.1N 09°53′.1W Fl.5s85m22M White tower
Harbour
3. **Grande Jetée** Oc(2)R.6s8m8M Horn(2)30s Red and white tower
4. **E breakwater** Fl(2)G.6s5m4M White tower, green top
Port d'Anza
5. **W mole** Fl.R.4s.5M White and red tower
6. **E mole** Fl.G.4s.5M White and green tower

Communications
VHF Ch 16, 12, 24hrs.

The port

Agadir is the most important of the southern Moroccan ports and the last to offer good all round shelter. For some yachtsmen this will be the preferred departure point for the Canary Islands and Atlantic crossing, being 220M from Lanzarote, though note that this puts you on a tight reach to the Canaries with the prevailing wind. Another consideration is that the harbour is now very polluted with plastic, sewage and rotting fish and room is tight despite all the extension work in Anza.

The Moroccan Saharan coastline continues S for another 600M to Mauritania. Agadir is a new town and the harbour is artificial, although sheltered by Pointe Arhesdis. The harbour is busy and a swell caused by the traffic in and out is noticeable.

A new commercial port, Port d'Anza, adjoins Agadir to the NW. Plans were in hand to move commercial activities to Anza and develop the old port into a major marina to compete with the Canaries. This, like plans elsewhere for marinas in Morocco, seems to have been shelved along with finishing the new port. The yacht club section of Agadir is fast falling into decay and may become unusable unless a major renovation is undertaken.

PILOTAGE

By day

Although entry is difficult in strong westerlies, this is a well protected harbour which can be entered in most conditions. Beware of tunny nets laid out from April to September, which can extend 4M from the shore. The very large grain silo built on the W mole of Port d'Anza will be seen from afar.

Three buoys form a transit with the inner W mole giving entry from the S into the harbour, following the Grande Jetée.

Depths in the entrance are in excess of 7m, though silting occurs. Just S of the harbour entrance, a NE current of 2kts has been reported. Once round the E breakwater, head E past the ferry terminal on the right and the Moroccan Navy berths left, and continue to the eastern end of the harbour.

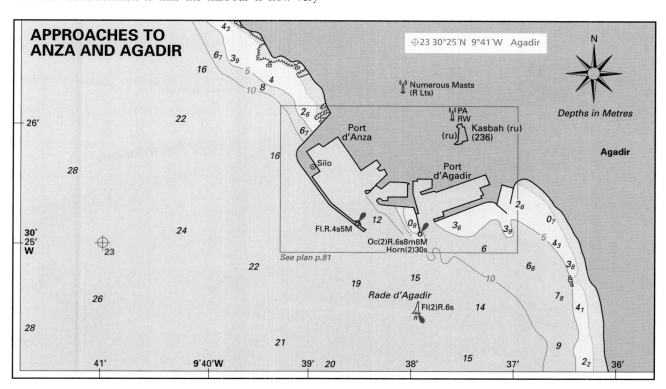

Agadir old port and the new port of Anza while still under construction

By night

The jetty head lights (Grande Jetée Oc(2)R.6s8m8M and E breakwater Fl(2)G.6s5m4M) have been reported dysfunctional on several occasions, though the port is generally well lit, as is the Kasbah N of the port.

Berthing

Since the completion of Port d'Anza pressure is off the old harbour, even though plans to develop both basins have not yet materialised. Some moorings are available in Grand Bassin, but they are usually occupied by local boats. Anchor in 4 to 5m as close to the yacht moorings as is practical. It may be possible to anchor stern or bows to the pontoon, if there is a space. It is often possible to moor alongside another yacht if the harbour area is too crowded to anchor.

Formalities

Agadir is a port of entry and the port officials are very friendly and relaxed. The harbour authorities do not come to the yacht: head for the yacht club office and you will be directed to the customs and police offices.

Facilities

Water Available on the quay from one long hose.
Electricity No supply available.
Fuel Can be supplied in cans, or from the fishing harbour.
Provisions Local shops very close to the port have all the usual commodities. A small shop selling drinks and bread is located within the port. A very large hypermarket Marjane has opened in the S of the town.
Gas Camping Gaz available in the town along with the larger old style bottles.
Post office and *banks* In the centre of town.

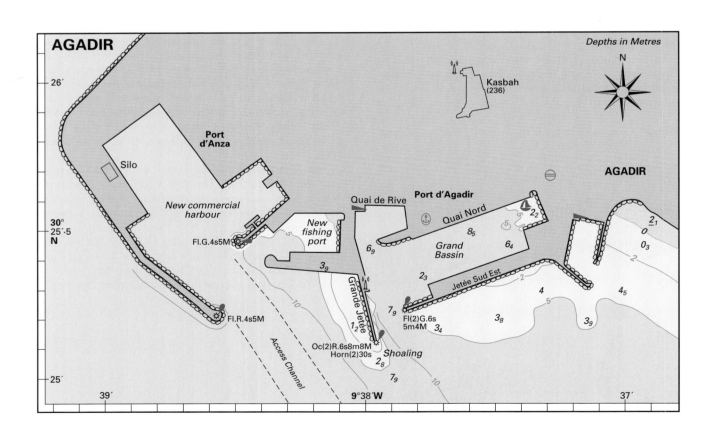

Agadir's ailing yacht basin, well overdue for an overhaul

Taroudannt: an oasis in the desert near Agadir   *Minaret*

Repairs There is a slipway for emergencies in the fishing harbour. All the usual Moroccan chandlery items are available here, including polypropylene rope, galvanised rigging screws and other fittings.

ASHORE

History

Agadir is a new town and all that remains of the old city, destroyed in an earthquake in 1960, is the restored kasbah. These ruins are worth a visit and are a solemn reminder of the incredible forces of nature which we are powerless to subdue.

Sites locally

This is a modern tourist town, complete with a casino. Tourism is the largest industry here, with a local airport serving the town with international flights, mostly via Marrakech and Casablanca. Nearby is the oasis of

Agadir: a very modern town and crowded beaches *Minaret*

Taroudannt, well worth a visit for its beauty and tranquillity.

Eating out

Many superb local and tourist type restaurants are in the town. Inevitably, fish is the main local dish. As you travel south on this Atlantic coast, the fish get bigger and better.

Note on the coastline S of Agadir

Further S, facilities are sparse, but the following are briefly mentioned because of their location as landmarks along hundreds of miles of deserted beaches. Most began as long jetties stretching out from the shore but offering no shelter. There are plans to develop some of these into enclosed harbours along the lines of Jorf Lasfar, and some have begun to evolve, but like most plans for improvements to facilities, things move slowly here!

The coastline is mainly desert, with 500M of sand and spectacular dunes. The area is very exposed with no bays or safe anchorages for protection in poor weather. Many wrecks can be seen on the beaches between Agadir and Dakhla.

A light, Cala Nun (Cap Drâa) Fl(2)25M (28°40´.5N 11°07´.5W) lies on the beach five miles S of Cala Nun between Sidi Ifni and Tan Tan. It does not relate to either port but is a coastal marker between the two at the the entrance of an unnamed river.

3. Sidi Ifni to Tarfaya

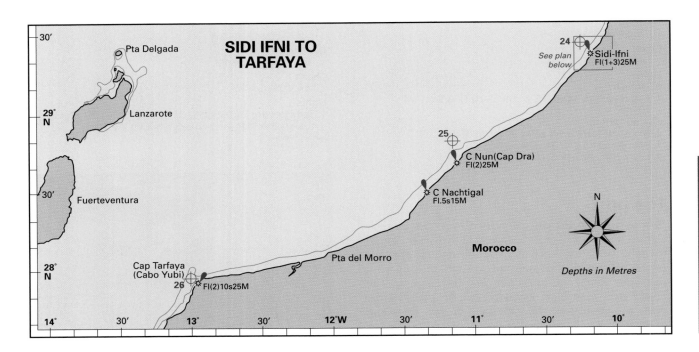

SIDI IFNI TO TARFAYA

Pta Delgada

Lanzarote

29° N

30′

Fuerteventura

24
See plan below ⊕ ☼ Sidi-Ifni Fl(1+3)25M

25 ⊕
☼ C Nun(Cap Dra) Fl(2)25M

☼ C Nachtigal Fl.5s15M

Morocco

N

Depths in Metres

28° N

Cap Tarfaya (Cabo Yubi) 26 ⊕ ☼ Fl(2)10s25M

Pta del Morro

14° 30′ **13°** 30′ **12°W** 30′ **11°** 30′ **10°**

WAYPOINTS – MOROCCO ATLANTIC COAST
⊕24 29°22′N 10°13′W Sidi Ifni
⊕25 28°50′N 11°10′W Cap Nun
⊕26 28°00′N 13°00′W Cap Tarfaya
⊕27 27°05′N 13°29′W Laâyoune

MO 13 Sidi Ifni

A double fingered jetty, with good anchoring on the S side in settled weather.

Location
  29°21′.5N 10°12′.5W

Tides
  Tidal range here reduces to 1.9m MHWS and a mean range of 1.6m.

Chart
  Admiralty *3133, 863*

Lights
Approach
1. **LtHo NE of the jetée** Fl(1+3)30s57m25M F.R 80m on 4 radio masts 2.2M ENE

Harbour
2. **Jetty head** Iso.R.4s11m5M Fl.R.3s marks inner jetty head
3. **Overhead transporter** Fl.4s10m5M

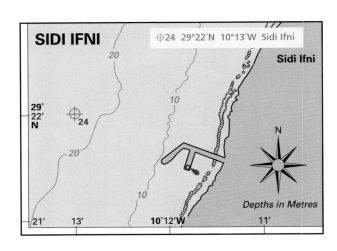

SIDI IFNI

⊕24 29°22′N 10°13′W Sidi Ifni

Sidi Ifni

29° 22′ N ⊕ 24

N

Depths in Metres

21′ 13′ **10°12′W** 11′

Anchorage

Anchor in 2.5m of sand in the SE lee of the inner jetty. Although not a port of entry, there are shops nearby which can be visited with the permission of local police.

MO 14 Tan Tan

A large and still developing port about which little is known, close to Cap Nachtigal.

Location
28°29′N 11°20′W

Chart
Admiralty *3133*

Lights
Approach
1. **Cap Nachtigal LtHo** (NE of the port) Fl.5s35m15M Tower.
Fishing Harbour
2. **Main SW Jetty head** F.13m Black pedestal
3. **Spur head** F.R 11m Red pedestal
4. **Cross Jetty head** F.G.11m Green pedestal

The port

This port has in the past been used by yachts on their way to the Cape Verde Islands and has been found friendly. Work has been in progress on the port for several years with the government wanting to increase the commercial infrastructure of the region. The breakwaters have been extended but no plans of the port are available. Information of its size and orientation can be gleaned from the aerial photograph taken in 1999.

MO 15 Tarfaya

A small port on the point of C Juby (also called Capo Yubi and Cap Tarfaya), still incomplete.

Location
27°53′.1N 12°57′.2W

Distances
Fuerteventura 54M

Charts
BA *1870, 3133*

Lights
1. **Tarfaya LtHo** Fl(2)10s25M 27°55′.3N 12°56′.3W Masonry tower 13m 3F.R(vert) on radio mast 1.6M NNE

Tarfaya: another recent development in the Sahara

Tan Tan, deep in the desert; this developing port is now in use

4. Laâyoune to Dakhla

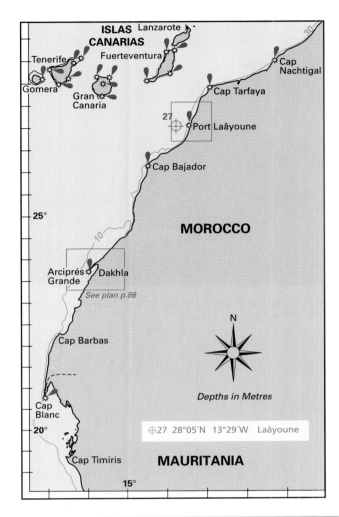

MO 16 Laâyoune

The facility consists of a very long jetty projecting out into the sea, and a small fishing harbour to the N. Anchoring is possible between the two.

Location
27°05′.5N 13°27′W (Fishing harbour)
27°04′N 13°28′.5W (Muelle de Forbucraa – long mole)

Distance
Fuerteventura 74M

Charts
Admiralty *3133, 863*

Lights
1. **Fishing Mole** Fl(2)4s
2. **Barge berth head** WR.11m18MW7M/R5M. 010°-W-070°-070°-R-010°.
3. **Muelle de Forbucraa** 27°03′.9N 13°27′.7W Fl.5s 48m18M Horn Mo(U)120s
4. **North end** F.G.17m3M White and green post.
5. **South end** F.R.17m3M White and red post

The harbour

Facilities consist of a small fishing harbour to the N, and a mile SW, a very long pier extending towards a disused phosphate berth, now used mainly as a fuelling jetty and for landing provisions for this isolated town. A cargo jetty is located half way along the S side of the pier.

The harbour provides limited shelter for the local fishing fleet. Anchorage is possible inside the south-going mole of the fishing Muelle de Forbucraa head (27°03′.9N 13°27′.7W) Fl.5s18M. Light (on end of barge berth jetée) WR.18M. Lights at 30m intervals along jetty.

Note From Laâyoune S lies a very politically sensitive area with a high degree of surveillance due to the ongoing dispute over the Spanish Sahara.

Laâyoune: a very long jetty, not easily missed

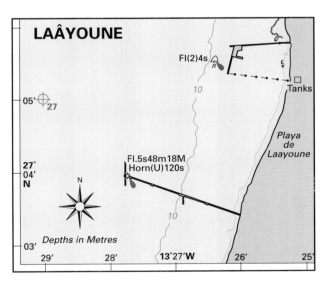

MO 17 Dakhla

The last port of Morocco on the Tropic of Cancer, 180M
from the border with Mauritania.

Location
23°41′.8N 15°55′.1W

Chart
BA *1690*

Light
Muelle Transversal No 3 Head Fl(2)10s8m8M Grey
truncated conical tower 5m. Obstruction light on radio
mast 0.7M WNW, on TV mast 0.6M WNW

The port

A huge natural south-going protective finger provides
shelter from the W, but is open to the S. A long dique
extends to offer deep water facilities for commercial
shipping. Resolving the political issue of this area makes
it expedient to develop the facilities here and the
government is keen to include the area in its plan and
make it an important addition to the maritime
infrastructure. Phosphates and other minerals abound in
the region and the fishing grounds are amongst the best
in the world. A similar though larger projecting pier has

been recently built 2.5M further SW but there are no
details available and it has not yet been named.

Anchoring is possible where depths permit, between
the peninsula and the drying bajo de al Galeota Grande,
but beware of shifting sands and inaccurate depths
towards the sides of the Canal Principal.

Dakhla: on the Tropic of Cancer, only 180M to the border
with Mauritania

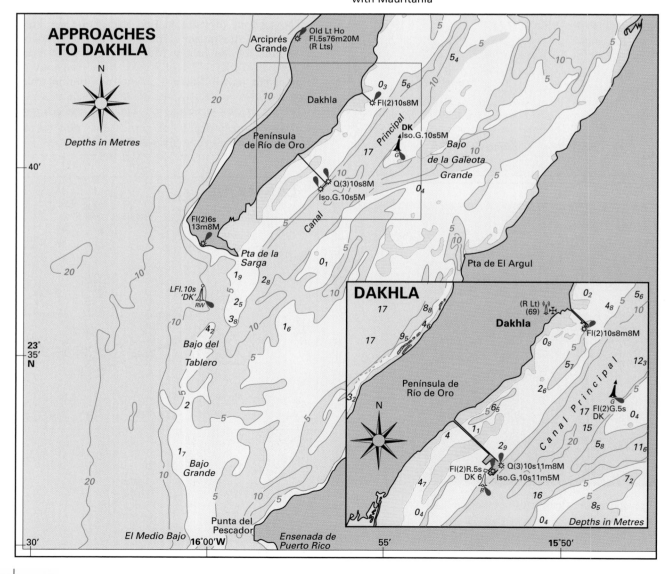

MEDITERRANEAN COAST OF MOROCCO
5. Straits of Gibraltar (Ksar-es-Seghir) to Saidia

This section covers the Western Straits into the Mediterranean from Ksar-es-Seghir to the Algerian border, including the Spanish enclaves and islands.

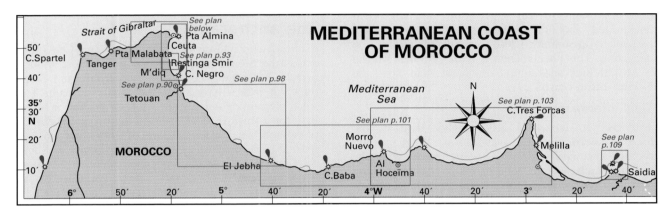

II. MOROCCO

Introduction

Weather and sailing

Once into the Mediterranean and heading E, weather and sea conditions are very different from the Atlantic and Straits, becoming increasingly difficult to predict. A full gale can be blowing in Tarifa, while a short distance away E of the Straits, winds are light. There is almost always some wind in the Straits and E or W most of the time.

The general summer wind pattern is light overnight, rising to F3 to F4 during the afternoons and going down at sunset.

The certainty of a strong E (Levanter) wind blowing in 2–3 days time is indicated by long smooth cigar shaped clouds or 'saucer' clouds as noted under Gibraltar page 23.

In winter, lighter winds usually prevail except when depressions move N along the Moroccan Atlantic coast from the Canaries bringing gales and rain to the Straits and into the Mediterranean. With high pressure in winter, the wind is often NE, bringing sunny but cold

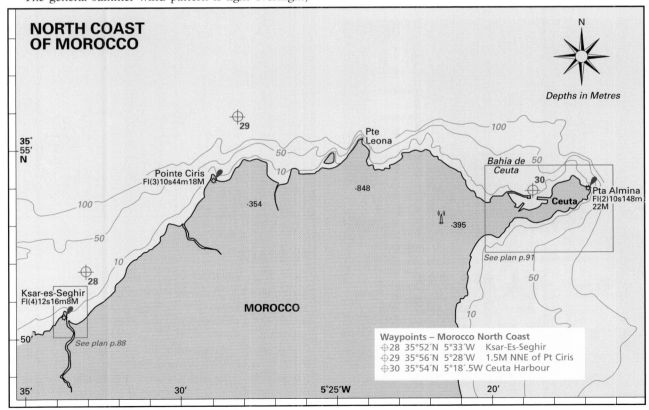

Waypoints – Morocco North Coast
⊕28 35°52′N 5°33′W   Ksar-Es-Seghir
⊕29 35°56′N 5°28′W   1.5M NNE of Pt Ciris
⊕30 35°54′N 5°18′.5W Ceuta Harbour

settled weather lasting for several days.

Sea conditions change once into the Mediterranean, from the long Atlantic swell which most yachts are able to ride out whatever the wind strength, to a much shorter swell in winds up to F5. In stronger wind conditions a very steep sided and uncomfortable swell is produced against which it is difficult to make progress.

Conditions in the Mediterranean can change rapidly from flat calm to 2m seas within minutes when unexpected and unexplained squalls pass through, particularly in summer. Close to headlands this can be dangerous. This phenomenon is more prevalent on the N Spanish side and around headlands than along the North African coast.

Tidal information

Sea level at Tanger is 2–3m higher than in the Mediterranean due to evaporation. When sailing through the Strait into the Mediterranean with the predominantly westerly wind behind, a feeling of going 'downhill' is reinforced by the fast E-going currents, even when the tide is going W. Many yachts call in at Gibraltar or begin their journey to Morocco from there, hence Gibraltar is covered in the previous section. See Transiting the Straits, page 33 for more information.

The constant flow of water from the cold Atlantic into warm waters of the Mediterranean gives rise to an abundant fish life in the Straits. Many pods of dolphins and different species of whales invariably accompany yachts for parts of the journey and it is common to see different types of shark, tuna and swordfish or marlin. Beware of heavy overfalls and currents in the areas E of Tanger bay, Tarifa Point and E of Ceuta.

In the mountains above Ksar-El-Seghir, a pleasant place to worship   *Graham Hutt*

MO 18 Ksar-es-Seghir

This small bay with a jetty, within sight of Gibraltar between Tanger and Ceuta, provides a useful anchorage in settled weather when waiting for the tide to turn in the Straits.
Location
   35°51′N 05°33′.5W (Pierhead light)
Lights
   Fl(4)12s16m8M Column on metal framework tower 11m

The anchorage

Ksar-es-Seghir, midway between Tanger and Ceuta and across the Straits from Gibraltar, is a remote though useful anchorage when contrary current and wind direction makes passage in the Straits difficult. The small pier jutting out E from Punta de Alcazar is home base for a small fleet of open fishing boats. Landing is prohibited: this is not a port of entry and has no facilities. The small village is on a route known as Routa de Contrabandistas: the smugglers route, which runs between Ceuta (Sebta) and Tanger. For this reason, there is a heavy police and military presence in the hills above. However, yachts have been allowed to anchor in the bay to await the tide change.

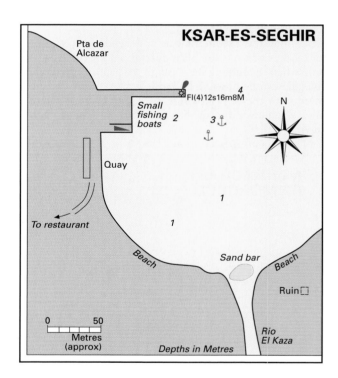

PILOTAGE

The village of Ksar-es-Segir will be seen above the anchorage. The Punta de Alcazar light, mounted on the pier head of Ksar (Fl(4)12s16m8M), has been destroyed several times in storms and its current characteristics are uncertain.

Anchor SE of the end of the jetty but keep an eye on the echo sounder as depths decrease to less than 2m towards the quay and S towards the beach. The spring range is about 1.5m. Protection from the W is reasonable but swell from the NW may roll around the pier and to the E it is quite open.

ASHORE

On the S side of the bay is a river which can be explored by dinghy. There is a restaurant and bar a short distance from the landing up on the hill and some basic provisions are obtainable – if you can negotiate your way ashore with the local police.

Note

A new commercial harbour is being constructed 6M E of Ksar-es-Segir to take traffic from Tanger. Works are not expected to be completed until 2007.

The bay and pier of Ksar-es-Seghir looking N   *Graham Hutt*

MO 19 Ceuta (Sebta)

A marina in the Spanish enclave of Ceuta, 13M due S of Europa Point, (Gibraltar) and 27M E of Tanger. Tetouan is nearby across the land border.

Location
35°54'.0N 05°18'.6W

Distances
Tanger 27M
Gibraltar 13M
M'Diq 16M

Tides
MHWS	MHWN	MLWN	MLWS
1m	0.8m	0.4m	0.2m

Charts
	Approach	Port
Admiralty	92, 142, 773, 3578	2742
French	7042, 7300	7503
Spanish	44C, 105, 445, 451	4511

Lights
Approach
1. **Punta Almina** 35°54'N 05°16'.8W Fl(2)10s148m22M White tower on building

Harbour
2. **Dique de Poniente** Fl.G.5s13m10M Siren 15s Conical concrete tower F.R on Tank Farm 1.3m W
3. **Dique de Levante** Fl.R.5s13m5M Conical concrete tower
4. **Spur E corner** Fl(2)G.8s7m1M Green post
5. **Muelle de Espana head W corner** Fl(2+1)R.12s7m1M Red post green band
6. **Nuevo Porto Deportivo breakwater head** Fl(4)R.11s8m1M Red round mast
7. **Breakwater** Fl(4)G.11s6m1M Green metal post
8. **Head** Fl(4)G.11s5m1M Green round metal mast
9. **Muelle de Ribera W** Oc.G.4s8m1M Green round metal mast
10. **E end** Fl(2+1)G.21s7m1M Green round metal mast, red band.

Communications
Marina Office ☎ 908 502274
Port Authority ☎ 956 502274.
VHF Ch 16, 9, 12, 13, 14, 15 (24hrs)

The marina

In the past Ceuta had a reputation of being a smuggling base with no secure place for yachts. This has changed and it now has a splendid marina away from the main harbour. This is fenced in around its entire perimeter, offering security. An enormous amount of money has been spent on developing the marina and the area around it. The road reconstruction is now almost finished and the noise and dust has subsided.

Because of its small size and excellent facilities it is almost always full, though room can usually be found along the N wall if not on a pontoon. It is an excellent place to stock up: probably the best and cheapest in the western Mediterranean and a rival to Gibraltar. There are now no reported problems with thieving drug addicts, as used to be the case. The authorities have invoked a limit on the number of times a yacht can visit. See under Formalities. Road works near the marina have been underway for two years or more and are still in progress. (Jan 2005).

II. MOROCCO

PILOTAGE

By day

The hills on the W side of Ceuta are high (850m) and very steep. To the E is a conspicuous lighthouse on the S face of Punta Almina. Ceuta town itself is low-lying though the harbour is easily seen. There are low-lying rocks to the E of the entrance, N of Monte Hacho. The final approach has to be made from the N quadrant so care must be taken with the set and tide in the Straits, especially in strong westerly winds. Ferries and hydrofoils from Algeciras will be seen entering and leaving the harbour throughout the day and until around midnight.

Once through the outer moles, continue SW where a large futuristic glass tower situated on the outer end of the harbour's central mole will be observed. An ancient limestone observation tower will also be seen on the SE mole. Rounding this to port enters the marina.

By night

The port is well lit and lights reliable. The lighthouse NE of the port on Punta Almina is the most conspicuous light, followed by the entry lights (Fl.G.5s and Fl.R.5s). The marina entry light (Fl(4)R) is sited on the old round tower protecting the marina to the N.

Berthing

Minimum depths in the entrance of the marina are 5m, with around 2.5m once inside. Finger pontoons will be seen once round the breakwater with moorings available for up to 200 boats.

The outer pontoons nearest the tower have depths of around 4m and the E end is principally for visitors. When full, some yachts have been directed to use the N wall, where bollards and services are also located.

If there is no room in the marina, an alternative, especially for larger yachts, is alongside on the W side of the central jetty of the main harbour or further in behind the short mole running SE. This area is usually oily and uncomfortable because of the ferries arriving and turning in the port. Anchoring is usually prohibited anywhere in the harbour.

Charges for a 12m yacht.

Marina charges are complicated to calculate but cheap in Ceuta. 'Lights dues' for 20% of a year is charged on entry and covers two months stay. Add to the daily rate, calculated on the mx2 rate. The day is calculated from midnight to midnight. There is a different rate charged for the pontoon, and alongside the wall. In practice, the result is a charge of around 12 Euros per day for a 12m yacht.

Formalities

As in Spain, there are technically no formalities required for a yacht coming from Spain or Gibraltar, though customs and immigration authorities may call at the yacht and check that papers are in order. More checks are done here than in most Spanish ports because of the incidence of smuggling drugs and illegal immigrants.

In 2004, marina administration was transferred to the Ministerio de Formento. This has resulted in better security and more efficient coordination with port

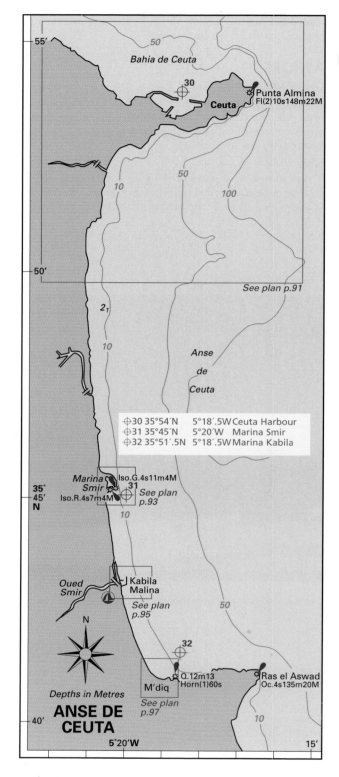

⊕30	35°54′N	5°18′.5W	Ceuta Harbour
⊕31	35°45′N	5°20′W	Marina Smir
⊕32	35°51′.5N	5°18′.5W	Marina Kabila

authorities.

A 'permisio' is now required and is obtained on entry which allows up to six visits per year to the marina, to reduce congestion. There is confusion over this which has not been applied to sailing schools who frequent Ceuta on a regular basis.

Facilities

Water and *electricity* At each berth on the quay.
Fuel There is now a fuel station in the marina itself, located

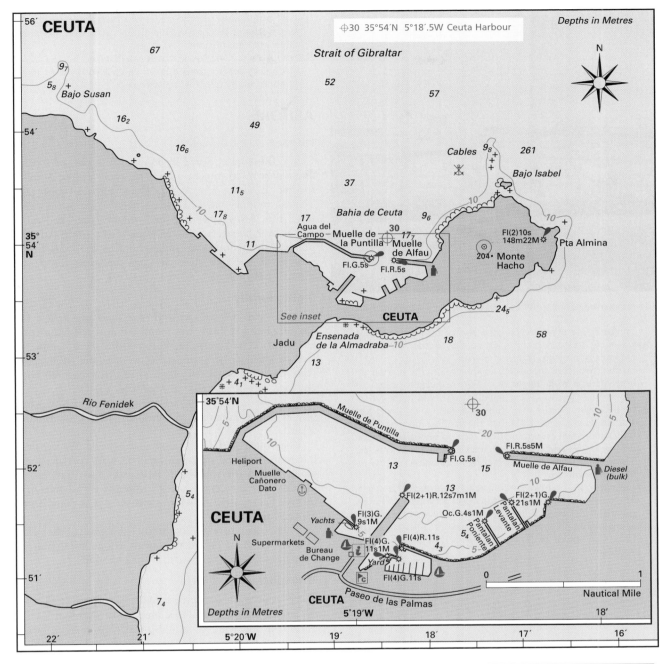

56′ **CEUTA** Depths in Metres

⊕30 35°54′N 5°18′.5W Ceuta Harbour

67

Strait of Gibraltar

9_7

5_8 Bajo Susan

52

57

16_2

49

16_6

N

Cables 9_8 261

11_5 Bajo Isabel

54′

37

17_8

10

Bahia de Ceuta 9_6 10

10

17 Agua del Campo

30

17_7

Muelle de la Puntilla

Muelle de Alfau

Fl(2)10s 148m22M

Pta Almina

35° 54′ N

11

Fl.G.5s

Fl.R.5s

204• Monte Hacho

24_5

See inset

CEUTA

Jadu

Ensenada de la Almadraba 10

18

58

13

4_1

35°54′N

Muelle de Puntilla

30

Rio Fenidek

5

20

10

5

52′

Heliport

Muelle Cañonero Dato

13

Fl.G.5s

15

Fl.R.5s5M

Muelle de Alfau

Diesel (bulk)

10

CEUTA

13

Fl(2+1)R.12s7m1M

N

Supermarkets

Yachts

Fl(3)G. 9s1M

Oc.G.4s1M

5_4

Fl(2+1)G. 21s1M

Pantalan Levante

Pantalan Poniente

5_4

4_3

5

10

Bureau de Change

Fl(4)G. 11s1M

Fl(4)R.11s

Yard

Fl(4)G.11s

0

1

Nautical Mile

CEUTA

Paseo de las Palmas

Depths in Metres

5°19′W

18′

22′

21′

5°20′W

19′

18′

17′

16′

7_4

51′

5_4

53′

Ceuta viewed from ENE with Morocco directly behind and
Marina Smir just off the left-hand edge of the picture

II. MOROCCO

Ceuta marina: usually full to capacity   *Graham Hutt*

on the S side of the rectangular end of the marina mole.

Showers and *toilets* A security key to the pontoons and toilet facilities is available from the marina office.

Provisions Two large supermarkets are close to the marina and both have a wide range of articles especially suited for provisioning yachts. These include powdered milk, canned butter, meat, dried hams, fruits and vegetables, beer, wine and spirits at lower prices than the Spanish hipermercados. Other shops sell everything from food to diving equipment, fishing tackle, portable radios, television sets, cameras, etc. These are very much cheaper than in Gibraltar and on the Spanish mainland.

Gas Available in the town or by arrangement with the marina office. If you have an odd fitting, ask a taxi driver for the gas plant, Butano SA. You can wait while your bottles are being filled. All types of bottles can be filled including Calor Gas butane bottles with snap-on fittings and propane bottles.

Tetouan. Traders selling Safi ceramics on the road between Ceuta and Tetouan   *Graham Hutt*

Post office and *banks* In the centre of town. There are change shops around the ferry terminal but check their exchange rates and commissions.

Repairs A light hoist (8-tons) is located in the marina. Most emergency repairs can be taken care of and a wide range of nautical chandlery is available here.

ASHORE

History

Ceuta, (known as Sebta in Morocco) is one of several anomalies in Morocco: a Spanish enclave, like Melilla, further E along the coast. Both remain important Spanish military bases. This has been a Spanish enclave since the 16th century. Spain formally controlled most of the northern coast of Morocco and some Atlantic ports. After Moroccan independence in 1956 Spain retained it because of its strategic location across the Straits of Gibraltar.

Sights locally

Ceuta is a duty-free port and is a shopping centre for Spanish families from the mainland and for Moroccan guest workers returning home from their work in Europe during the summer, as well as for Moroccans who daily cross the border to purchase commodities cheaper, or not available in Morocco.

It is also a town with easy access to the Moroccan border for excursions to Tetouan, Tanger or further inland.

The tourist office, located just outside the marina, has more detailed information. The walk to the centre along the palm tree-lined Paseo de las Palmeras is pleasant but the centre is very crowded with banks and shops. There are fine views across to Gibraltar from Monte Hacho.

There are several museums illustrating the rich history of Ceuta. The fortifications, which are mainly of Portuguese origin, are worth a walk around.

Transport

The border with Morocco is 3km away: a short taxi ride, or a regular bus service operates from the town to the border. If you want to visit Morocco from here, buses and taxis await on the Moroccan side. Tetouan is half an hour from the border and the two modern marinas of Kabila and Marina Smir are ten minutes away by taxi.

A daily ferry service operates to Algeciras.

Eating out

There are many restaurants of all categories in the centre of town and two in the marina.

MO 20 Restinga (Marina) Smir

26 miles from Gibraltar and close to Ceuta, this is without doubt the finest and safest yacht facility in Morocco for visiting inland, wintering and as a port of entry.

Location
35°45′N 05°20′.1W

Distances
Gibraltar 26M
Ceuta 12M
M'Diq 4M

Tides

MHWS	MHWN	MLWN	MLWS
1.0m	0.8m	0.4m	0.2m

Charts

	Approach	Port
Admiralty	773, 142	–
French	7042	–
Spanish	445, 451	–

Lights
Harbour
1. **N mole** Iso.G.4s11m4M
2. **S mole** Iso.R.4s7m4M

Communications
Port ☎ 977126
VHF Ch 9

The marina

The first marina to be built on the Mediterranean coast of Morocco, Marina Smir was constructed on a deserted beach 1 mile S of Point Restinga, between Ceuta and M'Diq. Once inside, this is a superb marina and very safe in all weather conditions. A secure place to leave your yacht for inland excursions or for wintering. It is part of a holiday resort with apartments, restaurants and boutiques and is very clean.

The port facilities are owned by the Spanish Marina Marbella and it is run on Spanish lines. Unfortunately it is expensive for Morocco and is usually empty, although berths for over 300 yachts are available. It has never overcome its reputation as a smugglers' haven where normal visitors are harassed by officials, and its very high prices.

PILOTAGE

By day

Approach to the port from Ceuta is straightforward by identifying Jebel Zem Zem, marked on the charts, and heading towards the S slope of the mountain. 2M N of the marina is a large white hotel complex: Club Mediterranée and immediately behind the marina is another white hotel. The breakwater is difficult to see until about two miles off despite its height, as it blends into the surrounding beach dunes. However, there are no other constructions nearby and the large travel-hoist at the N end will be seen first.

The entry channel is regularly dredged to around 5m and buoys are usually placed when depths are restricted by silting.

Beware of tunny nets laid out 4M NE of the port on a direct line with Ceuta. A small boat with a stub mast usually marks the end of the nets, but an additional large yellow buoy has recently been added. This marker is often not lit at night.

Entry is difficult in strong E winds due to the swell that builds up around the entrance. Keep to stb rounding the breakwater then move to mid-channel.

By night

Cabo Negro light (Oc.4s) has a range of 20M. The marina entry lights are usually reliable.

Berthing

On rounding the E breakwater head for the control tower and fuelling jetty, where customs and other port officials will be waiting. A mooring will be allocated once formalities have been completed, with a marinero to assist.

The author's Hartley Fijian yacht in Marina Smir. An excellent and spacious marina, usually empty
Graham Hutt

II. MOROCCO

Near Marina Smir: one of the best Moroccan restaurants
Graham Hutt

Charges for a 12m yacht

High season June–Oct
   Day Dh 189.00
Mid season Mar–June
   Day Dh 153.00
Low season Nov–Feb
   Day Dh 85.00
The following discounts apply for longer stays:
   1 month 10%, 3 months 15%, 6 months 20%.
Annual rate Dh 33,306+20% tax.
The annual rate includes one free lift out and return to water.
Multihulls 1.5x monohull rate.
Charges include electricity and water.
Add 20% tax to all prices.

Formalities

Smir is a port of entry and immigration officials, customs and local police are all conveniently located on the entry pier and are very efficient. There is an extensive police and military presence in the port and security is assured.

Note The port gained a very bad reputation in the 1990s from which it has not recovered. It was common for police and customs officials to carry out extensive and indiscriminate searches of yachts on arrival and departure and to demand 'bakhshish' in the form of whisky and cigarettes to avoid this procedure. No incidents have been reported recently.

Facilities

Water and *electricity* On the quay at every berth.
Fuel Available from pumps at the control tower jetty.
Shower and *toilet facilities* By arrangement with the tower who issue a key. Very clean.
Provisions A local shop selling fresh provisions is located just outside the port. M'diq is a short distance by taxi and is a small town with most items available.

Gas Available from nearby M'Diq.
Post office and *banks* In M'Diq town and in Tetouan.
Telephone Located in the marina office block. All connections are manual via an operator.
Repairs Facilities for haul out are excellent, with a 200-ton travel-hoist and very clean conditions. Mechanics and other workers can be arranged with the marina.

ASHORE

Although there is nothing to see in the immediate vicinity, Marina Smir is an excellent place to leave your yacht for excursions inland. Nearby are the towns of M'Diq, Tetouan, Chefchaoun and Ouad Laou, where a typical Berber market is well worth a day's visit. Superb beaches are on either side of the marina.

Local specialities

Along the road outside the port leading to M'Diq and Tetouan are several stalls selling ceramic pots, cous-cous, cooking ware, plates and ornaments. Local Berber markets can be found in the surrounding villages.

Eating out

Several restaurants are located within the port complex, including Chinese, Lebanese and high-class Moroccan restaurants and a pizzeria. These are expensive (apart from the pizzeria near the harbour office, which is very affordable and only open in summer and at weekends in winter). Consider a short excursion to M'Diq, where many open-air or more up-market fish restaurants can be found either along the seafront or on a parallel street. Aladdin's Lamp: a restaurant with several distinctive Persian style round towers, will be found four miles from M'Diq on the road to Tetouan and provides excellent typically Moroccan dishes at very reasonable prices in an extraordinary building. Well worth the taxi fare.

MO 21 Marina Kabila

This marina is a cheaper alternative to Marina Smir, though currently (Jan 2005) the entrance is silted and unusable except by small power boats.

Location
35°43′.3N 05°20′.08W

Distances
Marina Smir 2M
M'Diq 4M

Tides

MHWS	MHWN	MLWN	MLWS
1.0m	0.8m	0.4m	0.2m

Charts

	Approach	Port
Admiralty	773, 142	–
French	7042	–
Spanish	445, 451	–

Lights
1. **E pier head** Fl.10s
2. **Entrance E spur** Fl.R.5s
3. **Entrance W breakwater** Fl.G.5s

Communications
Port ☎ 975005/975264

The marina

Kabila Marina, lying 2M E of Marina Smir is another holiday complex, with the smaller marina well laid out with a capacity for 150 yachts.

Like Smir, it is hardly used except in summer, but it is much quieter than Smir in July and August where the local disco can be heard throughout the night.

The strange design of the marina – with a river flowing through it – ensures regular silting both from the river sand flowing downstream, and in the very narrow entrance from the E gales. It began silting as soon as it was completed in the mid 1980's and is impossible to enter at present (Jan 2005) except by small shallow draught boats and even these are discouraged by the officials. Infrastructure in the marina is very dilapidated.

Kabila Marina with the Rif mountains in the background
Graham Hutt

PILOTAGE

Use Marina Smir as a reference point. From the Straits of Gibraltar, head for the S slope of Jebel Zem Zem. Marina Smir will be seen with its travel-hoist. Kabila is difficult to identify until very close, when the white three-storey control tower will first appear, located 2M S of Marina Smir. Current and tide is negligible in this area. Entry is not recommended in strong easterly winds. Beware of tunny nets located E of Marina Smir.

The entry silts frequently, but minimum depths of 2.5m are usually found on the left side of the channel. Keep well over towards the outer breakwater on rounding the light. Depths increase once round the breakwater. Head for the visitors' quay, 30m directly ahead, below the control tower.

Berthing

You will be directed to a berth once formalities have been completed. Depths around the visitors' berth to the first pontoons are usually around 3m. Further in, depths shelve. There is little room for large yachts to turn because of the silting.

Charges

There seems to be no intention currently to re-open the marina entrance. No prices are available.

Formalities

Customs, police and immigration authorities are located in a separate building next to the tower. Entry and exit formalities here have in the past been protracted.

Facilities

Water and *electricity* At each berth.
Fuel Available from the visitors berth by arrangement with the marina office.
Provisions A local shop is located within the tourist complex next to the marina. M'Diq is nearby and can provide most essential supplies.
Gas Available in M'Diq.
Post office and *banks* In the centre of M'Diq and in Tetouan.
Repairs Engineers can be arranged with the marina staff and a small hoist is available up to 15-tons.

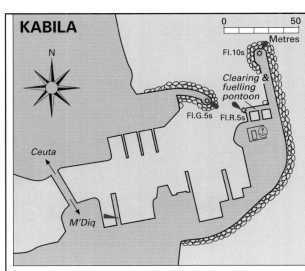

Kabila visitors' quay and harbourmaster's office, looking SSW from entrance *Graham Hutt*

ASHORE

As for Marina Smir, an excellent place from which to visit locally.

Eating out

As for Marina Smir and with the addition of several bars, open in the complex adjoining the marina in summer.

Between Jebha and M'Diq is this Rif mountain village and weekly market *Graham Hutt*

MO 22 M'Diq

A very picturesque and busy fishing harbour, under spectacular red cliffs in the lee of Capo de Negro (Ras el Aswad) a short distance from Marina Smir, but inadvisable for yachts.

Location
  35°41′N 05°18′.5W

Distances
  Kabila 4M
  Ceuta 16M
  El Jebha 42M

Tides

MHWS	MHWN	MLWN	MLWS
1.0m	0.8m	0.4m	0.2m

Charts

	Approach	Port
Admiralty	*773, 142*	–
French	*7042*	–
Spanish	*451*	

Lights
Approach
1. **Cabo Negro** 35°41′.2N 05°16′.4W Oc.4s135m20M White tower

Harbour
2. **E pier head** Q.12m13M Horn 60s 090°-vis-270°White tower, black lanterns
3. **Entrance W pier head** F.G
4. **Entrance E pier head of spur** F.R

Communications
  VHF Ch 16

The harbour

This was the only harbour in the bay of Ceuta until the two marinas were built. Yachts are no longer encouraged to use M'Diq and the harbour is officially closed to pleasure boats which are directed to Marina Smir. However, some yachts still venture in unhindered. Fishing boats fill the harbour, which is exposed to the SE. Their lines trail everywhere and the bottom is foul with ropes, anchors, fishing tackle and rubbish.

Inside is a Royal Moroccan Yacht Club, catering mainly for the needs of its own members, most of whom have now moved their boats to Marina Kabila or Smir.

PILOTAGE

By day

In good weather, there are no particular problems. The entrance is not easily visible until fairly close, but is identified by the red cliffs above and the striking Cabo de Negro, to the E. The port lies just E of the low-lying village and new apartments are scattered around the hills behind it. Once in the entrance, proceed carefully as there is not much room to manoeuvre and there are numerous semi-submerged mooring lines. Entry in strong E winds is not advisable because of the swell in the entrance.

By night

A night entry is not recommended because of the number of partially submerged lines around and nets which are spread across the entrance at sunset.

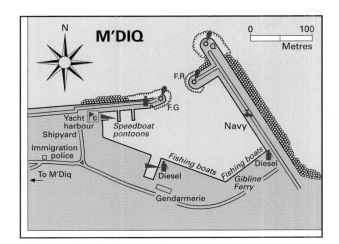

Fishing port of M'Diq. Officially closed to yachts, but some
still visit   *Graham Hutt*

II. MOROCCO

Berthing

Small yachts might find room in the yacht club but normally the place for visitors is along the crowded E pier which has some room for yachts lying to their own anchors bows or stern-to. These are currently occupied by fishing boats. The yacht club charges minimal harbour dues and the public quay is free of charge.

Formalities

All officials in the port which is a port of entry.

Fishing in the area is rewarding, with many large fish around Cabo Negro. Hammerhead and other types of shark, swordfish, tuna and other large fish are regularly caught in the area. Permission needs to be obtained from the authorities to anchor in the area and it should be obtained in writing, as you will almost certainly be paid a visit by the coastguards.

Facilities

Water and *electricity* Water is available from a tap on the E pier and electricity with a long lead. The yacht club has several water taps and electricity sockets.

Fuel Diesel available from a pump between the fish market and slip and petrol from a pump at the yacht club.

Provisions Good provisions can be found in several small shops in the village about 20 minutes walk from the port. The craft shop on the left-hand side, at the beginning of the main street, has a good assortment of leather clothing with very reasonable fixed prices (uncommon in Morocco).

Showers If berthed at the yacht club, their showers may be used.

Post office, telephone and *bank* In the village.

Repairs Local craftsmen work on the boats in the yacht club and there is a small shipyard for wooden fishing boats. It may be possible to get simple repairs done.

ASHORE

The beaches north of M'Diq are popular among Moroccan holidaymakers and in the summer there may even be a few European tourists. The fairly nondescript though pleasant village is a short walk from the port and aside from several restaurants and a good craft shop it has no particular attraction. Tetouan, 16km from M'Diq, is a striking town and well worth a visit. It is situated in a wide valley on the northern edge of the Rif mountains and, when the Oued Martin was still navigable, small boats sailed up to it. During the time of the Spanish Protectorate it was the capital of Northern Morocco and some of the architecture is reminiscent of the Moorish buildings in Andalucía. Spill-over tourism from the Costa del Sol has left its traces and Tetouan's attraction is slightly overshadowed by the problem of dealing with the many young guides, but do not let this stop you from visiting. There are frequent buses between M'Diq and Tetouan.

Eating out

Several eating houses and simple restaurants are located in the village. In summer time the restaurant in the yacht club is open and serves spectacular fish dishes. See as for Marina Smir.

The fishing port of M'Diq in quieter times, from the overlooking cliff

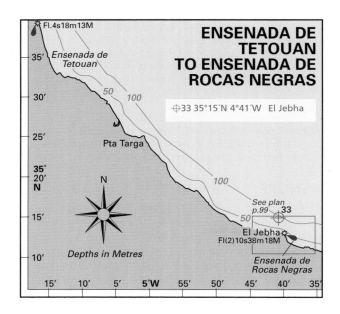

ENSENADA DE
TETOUAN
TO ENSENADA DE
ROCAS NEGRAS

⊕33 35°15′N 4°41′W El Jebha

Fl.4s18m13M
Ensenada de Tetouan
Pta Targa
N
See plan p.99 33
El Jebha
Fl(2)10s38m18M
Ensenada de Rocas Negras
Depths in Metres

MO 23 El Jebha

An ancient town, 42M from M'Diq, this is an ideal place for a relaxed visit, very remote from modernity.

Location
35°13′N 04°40′.8W

Distances
M'Diq 42M
Peñón de Véléz 20M
Al Hoceïma 40M

Tides

MHWS	MHWN	MLWN	MLWS
0.9m	0.7m	0.4m	0.2m

Charts

	Port
Admiralty	77
French	1711

Lights
Approach
1. **Punta de Pescadores** 35°13′.2N 04°40′.7W
   Fl(2)10s38m18M 090°-vis-270° Black lantern on white hut
Harbour
2. **Port de Pêche S jetty** Iso.G.4s8M

The harbour

The changing world of the past 100 years seems to have passed El Jebha by. Just 80M south of Marbella, and only recently connected to the mains electricity grid, this is the place to chill out.

The small port does not get many visitors but yachts can always find room and a friendly welcome between the fishing boats and the Moroccan Royal Navy gunboat. They deftly move and re-tie your lines when they leave early in the morning, without any disturbance whatsoever. Overall protection is good.

PILOTAGE

By day

El Jebha is situated 0.3M SW of Punta de Pescadores which is rocky with an islet close by. It is not as high as the surrounding coast and on its summit is a rock resembling a tower. The entrance to Cala Congrejo, E of Punta de Pescadores, is not clearly visible from seaward. There are no particular hazards around the entrance, though a swell builds in strong W winds.

By night

The light on Pta de Pescadores is low and not visible unless coming from the E. The harbour lights are not always reliable, so proceed with caution.

Berthing

If there is room, go alongside the N quay. The sunken wreck which lay on the N quay for many years is gone, but another (perhaps the same vessel) is now lying on the S side and is not suitable for going alongside. There are plans to build a quay in the S part of the port which will create more room for visiting yachts.

Anchoring

It is possible to anchor in the middle of the port but there is not much room to swing and care must be taken to avoid mooring lines. In good weather, yachts can anchor very quietly in Cala Congrejo but be sure to inform the authorities beforehand.

Returning from market the easy way   *Graham Hutt*

El Jebha harbour entrance with Rif mountains in the background

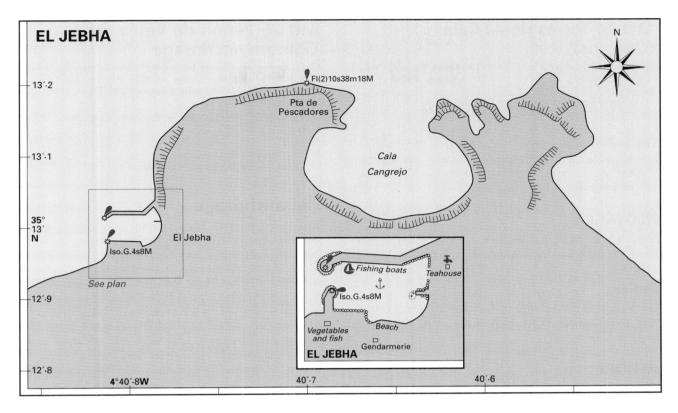

Formalities

Although entry into Morocco is possible here, it is not officially a port of entry. Entering here may give rise to suspicions that you have come to Morocco to buy kif (hashish). Therefore El Jebha is best visited after first clearing in Marina Smir or Al Hoceïma, and having informed the authorities of your intention to visit. Most likely the caïd, marine marchande and gendarmerie will all arrive at the same time. The port authorities offices are on the opposite side of the harbour. Officials are very friendly here and very pleasant to deal with, often inviting crew to their houses.

Facilities

Water and *electricity* It may be possible to fill water containers in one of the tea houses around the port. There is no electricity on the quay.

Fuel In containers from the village but at times in short supply.

Provisions Only very basic provisions are available from a small market near the SW corner of the port and several little shops in the village. Meat is not always available and chickens may have to be bought off the street. The best supplies can be bought on Tuesday at the weekly souk. Fresh bread is always available.

Post office Letters can be sent from the village but there is no post office.

ASHORE

Jebha is beautifully situated in an isolated, mountainous part of the coast where the cultivation of kif is the major activity. W of the port are deserted beaches and the rocks towards Cala Congrejo are good for snorkelling. This is the place to stay for a couple of days to get away from it all. If possible be there for the Tuesday souk when the village comes to life. The streets are filled with the donkeys of the mountain people from the Rif and small boats come and go to pick up families living in isolated parts along the coast. Few places in Morocco offer such an interesting insight into the old ways of life, and its accompanying hospitality, though nearby Ouad Laou comes close.

Eating out

There are some very simple eating houses in the village at exceptionally cheap prices.

El Jebha harbour entrance *Graham Hutt*

MO 24 Torres de Al Cala (Cala Iris)

A new small fishing harbour a short distance W of Isla Iris, recently opened.

Location
35°10′N 04°19′W (approx)

This harbour was opened in 2004 and no information has been released regarding coordinates or depths. Visiting yachts have been made very welcome. No official information is yet available.

PILOTAGE

The entrance is W, parallel to the beach, close to Isla Iris. One light has been installed, Fl.R.3s. Depths are unknown.

Berthing

Lay alongside the SE side of the quay by arrangement with the fishermen. There was plenty of room here in summer 2004.

ASHORE

There is nothing apart from a small tea house. The town is 4km E of the harbour.

The Spanish rock of Véléz de la Gomera, Spanish flag atop, viewed from NW

MO 25 Peñón de Vélez de la Gomera anchorage

Once a good anchorage for breaking the journey from Jebha to Al Hoceïma, but the political situation has now made this a prohibited area. (Summer 2004).

Location
35°11′N 04°17′.5W (Lighthouse Peñón de Vélez de la Gomera)

Light
Peñón de Vélez de la Gomera
Fl(3)20s47m12M Grey tower and dwelling

The anchorage

This has in the past been a useful anchorage in good weather, lying off the beach between Peñón de Vélez and Cabo Baba and a convenient stop to cut the stretch from Jebha to Al Hoceïma into two day-trips. However, the political fallout from another disputed rock further W, held by the Spanish, has caused problems for visiting yachtsmen here. The steep rock is still Spanish territory and was an island until silting connected it to the Moroccan shore by a narrow strip of sand. The Moroccans now want to take the rock back. The remote setting resembles a miniature Gibraltar. Yachts are usually approached by a RIB either from the Spanish Navy or the Moroccan Royal Navy, and told not to approach. Larger Moroccan military boats also patrol the area and warn yachts away if close inshore.

The surroundings are beautiful with steep barren mountains but it is completely open to the N and protection from the swell is poor.

Should the political situation improve and it is possible once again to do so, anchor in 8m or more, although holding is poor amongst gravel and rocks.

Formalities

See situation described above. Be sure to inform the authorities at the previous port if planning to spend a night here. There is a Moroccan police post among the scattered houses in the valley; they probably will not bother a yacht stopping for the night but do not land. You can be sure to be under surveillance.

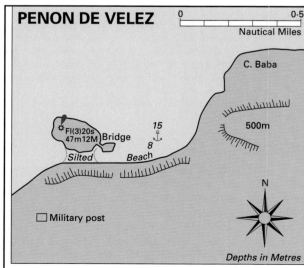

PENON DE VELEZ

0   0·5
Nautical Miles

C. Baba

Fl(3)20s 47m12M
Bridge
15
8
Silted   Beach
500m

Military post

N

Depths in Metres

MO 26 Al Hoceïma
(formerly Villa Sanjurjo)

75 miles SE of the Straits, a port of entry currently offering very poor facilities for yachts and protracted clearance procedures. Things are due to improve.

Location
35°14´.9N 03°55´W

Distances
El Jebha 40M
Melilla 60M

Tides

MHWS	MHWN	MLWN	MLWS
0.6m	0.5m	0.3m	0.2m

Charts

	Approach	Port
Admiralty	773	580
French	6570	5864
Spanish	431	431 (inset)

Lights
Approach
1. **Cabo Morro Nuevo, Pta de los Frailes** 35°15´.7N 03°55´.7W Fl(2)10s151m20M 082°-vis-275° White support, black lantern
Harbour
2. **Dique de Abrigo** Iso.G.4s14m4M White tower, green top
3. **Dique de Los Islotes** Iso.R.4s15m5M White tower, red top. Functioning of the leading lights is doubtful and therefore details are omitted.

Communications
VHF Ch 16

A medium-sized fishing and naval port in a beautiful setting, situated in the W corner of the Bay of Al Hoceïma. The port is enclosed by steep hills and protected from the S by a breakwater which connects the rocks of Los Islotes with the shore. This is another harbour in Morocco undergoing radical changes. So far, the improvements have involved the creation of a new ferry terminal but have not benefited visiting yachts. A road and steps lead up to the village of Al Hoceïma on top of the hill. The beach in the bay is popular. This is one of the only ports in Morocco where yachts have never been welcome, though this is offset by the fact that it is a good haven between the Straits of Gibraltar and Melilla.

PILOTAGE

By day

The headland of Cabo Morro Nuevo with the light of Punta de los Frailes is prominent and from the N, the port is not visible until well around the cape. A fairly strong westerly current (1–2kts) is common along this part of the coast and between Cabo Morro Nuevo and Punta Bocic it sets towards the coast. One large and two smaller fuel tanks on Los Islotes are conspicuous when approaching the port.

By night

Entry after dark can be hazardous because of the number of fishing boats using bright floodlights. Trawlers, drifters and line fishermen all operate in the area. The light on Cabo Morro Nuevo, Pta de los Frailes (35°15´.7N 03°55´.7W Fl(2)10s151m) has a range of 20M. Port entry lights have recently been moved, with the extension of the breakwaters, with the same characteristics as the main light. The old lights were very unreliable though it is not known if the replacements are any better.

Berthing

The usual place where yachts are directed is the inner harbour on the N side of Escollera, where the fishing boats and smaller pleasure boats lie alongside. It is very awkward and uncomfortable here, often racked out several boats-deep. However, in late 2004 yachts were being berthed on the S side of the Los Isolotes promontory towards the E end of the widened Escolera del Sur or opposite on NE end of ferry terminal berth.

Harbour dues are charged on an irregular basis and seem to be expensive for the facilities offered. The new regulations governing charges mentioned in the introduction will standardise the situation once agreed by the authorities.

As stated above, things are changing here. Work is still in progress, berthing arrangements change from one week to another and can be expected to vary until completion, sometime during 2005.

Note There is a submerged wreck just opposite the fish hall.

Formalities

A port of entry. Formalities are taken very seriously here and have in the past been the most unpleasant anywhere in Morocco. Besides the usual officials, naval personnel

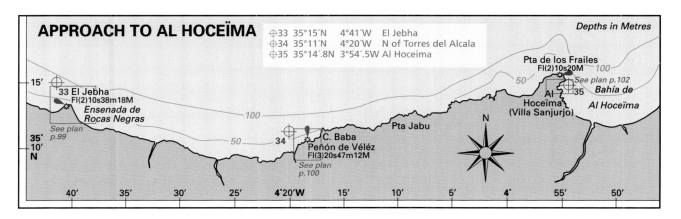

APPROACH TO AL HOCEÏMA

⊕33	35°15´N	4°41´W	El Jebha
⊕34	35°11´N	4°20´W	N of Torres del Alcala
⊕35	35°14´.8N	3°54´.5W	Al Hoceima

Depths in Metres

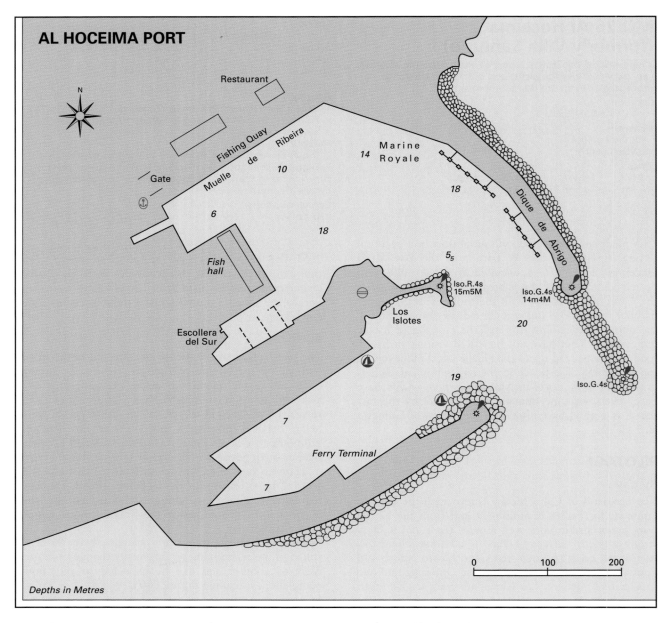

AL HOCEIMA PORT

Restaurant

Fishing Quay

Muelle de Ribeira

Gate

N

Marine Royale

14

10

18

6

Dique de Abrigo

18

Fish hall

5₅

Iso.R.4s
15m5M

Los Islotes

Iso.G.4s
14m4M

Escollera
del Sur

20

19

Iso.G.4s

7

Ferry Terminal

7

0   100   200

Depths in Metres

---

may also visit. It is not uncommon for up to ten officials to come aboard, all with their heavy boots on! Each seems to want to look around and fill in endless forms. It is similar to the situation in Algeria, though why here, is a mystery. Very late reports at the end of 2004 indicate things may be improving.

Facilities

Water and *electricity* Recently laid on the jetty at Los Islotes, but unavailable to yachts.

Fuel Can be delivered in drums, although pumps are expected to be installed.

Provisions Bread can be bought in the tea house near the fish hall. A large supermarket has opened S of the harbour. For other supplies climb up to the village or take a taxi. At the end of the road leading from the Muelle de Ribera up to the village is an alimentation général and butcher. Alternatively take the steps behind Hotel Quemado which lead to the centre of town where there are several small shops. The market is on the other side of town.

Post office In the centre of the village.

Telephone In the post office or local hotels.

Bank Several banks in the village and money can be exchanged in hotels.

Repairs The coral diving boats employ good mechanics who will be able to take care of most engine problems.

History

Both the English and French occupied the small islands in the southern part of the Bay of Al Hoceïma before the Spanish took over and, in 1673, changed Peñón de Alhucemas into a fortress. It was from this island that the Spanish General Sanjurjo invaded the mainland in 1926. Following the invasion the new town of Alhucemas was built in the barren hills and it retains a definite Andalucían atmosphere.

ASHORE

Although a pleasant place, the most interesting things to do are outside of Al Hoceïma. The fascinating city of Fes is only a day trip by bus. The road leads up to the highest parts of the Rif mountains with splendid views

Al Hoceïma in December 2004. Many improvements are
taking place here   *Hiria*

and declared Chefchaouen a sacred city. Until the
arrival of Spanish troops in 1920, it had been visited by
just four Europeans. As the Rough Guide puts it, 'There
are few journeys in Morocco as spectacular as that from
Al Hoceïma to Chefchaouen'.

Eating out

Several fish restaurants in the port along Muelle de
Ribera. The restaurants in the village seem to cater more
for tourists.

Transport

Buses from Al Hoceïma are convenient and cheap but
its location is isolated and a journey in any direction will
take several hours on scenic but narrow winding roads
through the Rif mountains.

over wide valleys on one side and the Mediterranean on
the other. During the various stops, one gets a good
impression of life in the small mountain villages, rarely
visited by foreigners. Of all the cities in North Africa,
Fes is the one where traditional life has survived with
the least compromise. Walking through the narrow
streets, being pushed aside by loaded donkeys, there is a
truly biblical atmosphere. Many of the craftsmen who
renovated the old Islamic monuments and who built the
spectacular mausoleum for Mohammed V in Rabat
came from Fes. Another interesting excursion is to
Chefchaouen, a formidably remote town in the Rif
mountains. The Moors (the mix of Arabs and Berbers
that conquered Spain), who were pushed out of
Andalucía after the fall of Granada in 1492, built
mosques, baths and tiled courtyards, planted fruit trees

Berber traders in the Rif Mountains near Al Hoceïma
                                         Graham Hutt

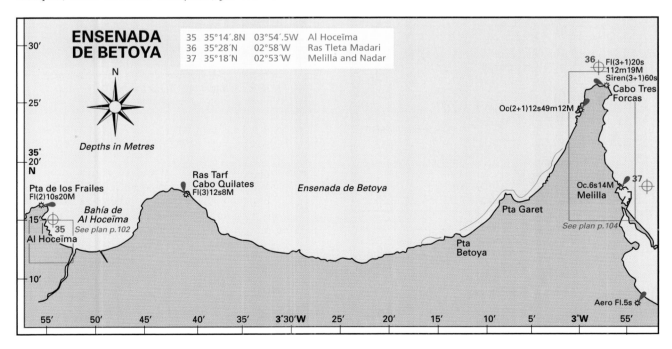

35	35°14′.8N	03°54′.5W	Al Hoceïma
36	35°28′N	02°58′W	Ras Tleta Madari
37	35°18′N	02°53′W	Melilla and Nadar

MO 27 Cala Tramontana anchorage

A quiet anchorage in a bay between Al Hoceïma and Melilla offering shelter from the NE to S but exposed to the W.

Location
35°23′.8N 03°00′.5W

Light
Ras Baraket on the N side of the entrance to Cala Tramontana 35°24′.1N 03°00.6W Oc(2+1)12s49m9M White round tower

Anchorage

A good anchorage on the W side of Ras Tleta Madari (formerly Cabo Tres Forcas) and a useful stop between Al Hoceïma and Melilla. Protection in the horseshoe-shaped bay, surrounded by the hills of the Tleta Madari headland, is excellent from NE to S. The only signs of civilisation, on this otherwise deserted part of the coast, are a few boats from the small fishing community near the beach. Conical hills on the N side at Ras Baraket and on the S side make the entrance well visible from seaward. Depths are around 5m over a sandy bottom, shoaling towards the shore. Depths in the bay vary depending on W gales.

Formalities

As with all anchorages in Morocco, it is important to first clear customs in a port of entry and to inform the officials of your intention to anchor.

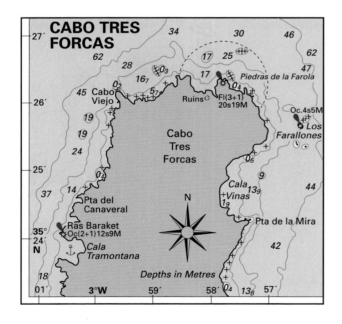

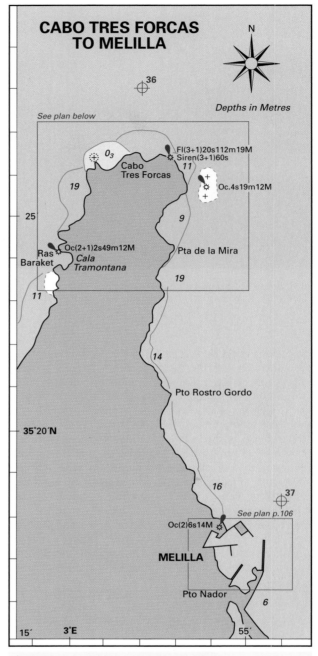

⊕36 35°28′N 2°58′W   Ras Tleta Madari
⊕37 35°18′N 2°53′W   Melilla and Nador

MO 28 Melilla

A Spanish enclave 36M from the Algerian border, excellent yacht facilities in a safe marina and port of entry for Spain.

Location
35°17′.4N 02°55′.5W

Distances
Al Hoceïma 60M
Ras el Ma 26M

Tides

MHWS	MHWN	MLWN	MLWS
0.6m	0.5m	0.3m	0.2m

Charts

	Approach	Port
Admiralty	773, 2437	580
French	6570	5864
Spanish	432	4331

Lights
Approach
1. **Cabo Tres Forcas** 35°26′.3N 02°57′.8W
   Fl(3+1)20s112m19M Siren(3+1)60s 083°-vis-307° (224°)
   Grey square tower and dwelling plus White bracket on metal hut
2. **Los Farallones** 35°25′.7N 02°56′.4W
   Oc.4s21m5M White and grey tower
3. **Melilla LtHo** 35°17′.7N 02°56′.1W
   Oc(2)6s40m14M Brown tower with aluminium dome

Harbour
4. **Main entrance Dique Nordeste** Fl.G.4s32m7M
5. **Head W** Fl.G.4s7m5M
6. **Pier No.1 elbow** Fl(2)G.7s7m3M
7. **Muelle de Ribera** Fl(2+1)12s7m3M
8. **Fishing basin E pier head** Fl(4)G.11s6m1M
9. **W pier head** Fl(4)R.11s8m1M
10. **Interior basin jetties** Fl.G/Fl.R
11. **Ore loading pier head** Fl(2+1)R.12s8m3M
12. **Minor embarkation dock breakwater head** Fl.R.5s4m5M
13. **Corner** Q(3)10s4m3M
14. **Pier head** Fl.G.4s3m1M

Communications
VHF Ch 9

The port

Another of the peculiar Spanish possessions on the Moroccan coast, Melilla used to be of commercial importance during the time of the Spanish Protectorate but declined after Moroccan independence. The main outer entrance is shared with the Moroccan port of Nador which has taken over the mineral trade. The ferry terminal is the most important activity today along with fishing and, to a lesser extent than in the past, smuggling.

The new and well protected marina built on the south side of the old jetty, Cargedero de Minerales, has only recently been completed and facilities installed. A friendly yacht club is located in the S corner of the Darsena Pesquero basin.

Security was a problem in the past, but this new facility seems to have solved this.

Melilla is quite useful as a base from which to explore Northern Morocco and now a safe place to leave a yacht.

PILOTAGE

By day

The headland of Cabo Tres Forcas is an unmistakable landmark and makes the approach to Melilla easy from any direction. The starboard entrance pier is Spanish and the port side is part of the Moroccan port of Nador, hence the unique peculiarity of the entrance.

Minimum depths of over 7m are found in the outer basin and the new marina entrance has been dredged to 9m.

By night

Cabo Tres Forcas light (35°26′.3N 02°57′.8W Fl(3+1)20s112m19M) is usually reliable and the best landfall. It is seen at a distance of around 15M. Closer in, both the Spanish and Moroccan harbours are equipped with the usual lights for night entry, but these are obscured by the bright lights on the quays until quite close.

Note The Nador red light is rarely functioning.

Berthing

Once inside the outer basin, head W to the outer mole of the new marina. Depths inside the marina are from 3.3m near the entrance to 2.1m at the end of the quays. Marineros are in attendance 24hrs a day and visitors are often directed to the main quay, rather than the projecting pontoons, except for longer stays. There is less security here, but the area is patrolled.

Harbour charges for a 12m yacht

A new scale of charges is being prepared but is currently unavailable. Until now, rates have been based on m x 2 x €0.19. This results in a comfortable €10 per day or less for a 12m yacht.

Formalities

Formalities are now more relaxed than previously. If coming from Spain, no formalities are technically necessary, but a visit to the capitainaria is advisable and officials may want to check papers. A new building housing the port officials is located at the S end of the marina mole.

Facilities

Water and *electricity* Laid at each berth on the pontoons.
Fuel From a pump on the S mole, at very cheap prices. (0.44 Euros per litre Nov 2004)
Provisions By Moroccan standards supplies are abundant, but they pale in comparison to Ceuta. There is a good mercado (covered market) with fresh produce. It is 200m past the end of the main street, Avenida del Generalisimo, about 20 minutes walk from the port. Just before the market there is a small but well stocked Moroccan-owned supermercado, Hakin with staple articles, beer, wine and spirits. Moroccans also operate many of the stands at the market. All shops sell duty-free electronic equipment, cheap alcoholic beverages and cigarettes. A new supermarket has opened 200m S of the marina, with another large one

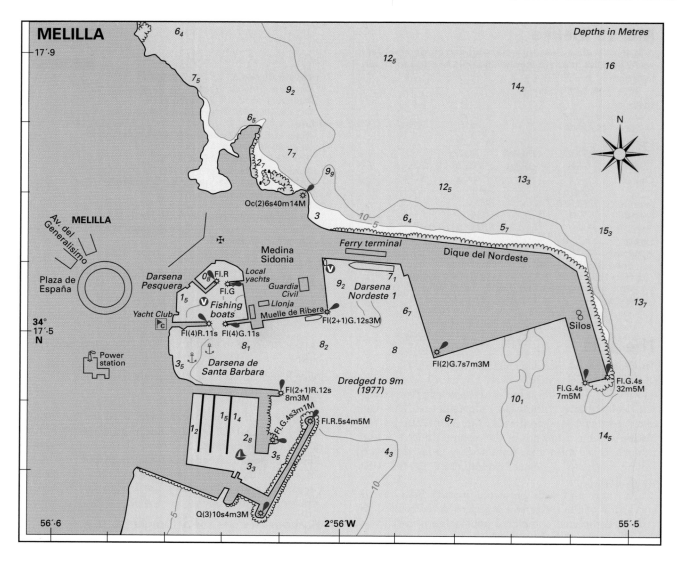

further S.

Showers New excellent facilities near the pontoons. (A long walk if on the quay)

Post office and *telephone* Off the N side of the Avenida del Generalisimo.

Bank In the ferry terminal and on the main street. Many money changers on the street corners but be careful of their rates and commission.

Repairs Most engine repairs can be carried out.

Lift out A 65-ton travel-hoist is now in place.

Chandleries There are now two in the harbour.

Internet café Several opened in the town, near the tourist office and near Darsena Pesquera.

ASHORE

The old fortified town, Medina Sidonia, is worth a visit. In the beginning of the century this was all there was of Melilla. It was built around 1497 after the Moors were defeated in Granada. There is a small museum and several buildings have been well restored. The main business activity in Melilla centres around the ferry terminal and duty-free shopping for mainland Spaniards and Moroccans, who cross the border daily. A separate and observable activity is smuggling. At night, a sizeable fleet of small overpowered motorboats, unlit and fully loaded, leaves the port to drop their cargo in Morocco. The Spanish customs ask no questions and the Moroccan operators obviously have the right contacts to go undisturbed about their business there. A reminder of how Gibraltar was, until recently.

Eating out

Not as many restaurants as one might expect in a city of this size. Some nice bars and restaurants have recently opened in the marina complex. Good tapas (typically Spanish hors d'oeuvre with several courses) available at the yacht club bar.

Transport

In summer, daily ferries to Málaga, Benalmadena and Almería. Out of season services reduce to 3 times per week. Buses to the border with Morocco, about 3km away, leave from Plaza de España.

MO 29 Nador

Just S and adjoining Melilla to the S, this commercial port is another world away when compared with the facilities in Melilla.

Location
35°17´.2N 02°55´.1W

The port

Nador is the Moroccan commercial and fishing port which shares the entrance with Melilla. The fishing port is crowded and the only place for a yacht is alongside a fishing boat where it may easily be damaged. The port is very oily, there are no shops or facilities in the immediate vicinity and there is little reason to visit Nador.

MO 30 Ras el Ma (Ras Kebdana)

A small, peaceful and very friendly fishing port due S of Islas Chafarinas, 10M from the Algerian border.

Location
35°08´.8N 02°25´.3W

Distances
Melilla 26M
Ghazaouet 27M

Tides

MHWS	MHWN	MLWN	MLWS
0.4m	0.3m	0.2m	0.1m

Charts

	Approach	Port
Admiralty	2437	–
French	6570, 6011	5864
Spanish	434	–

Lights
Approach
1. **Cabo del Agua** 35°08´.8N 02°25´.3W Fl(2)6s42m8M White tower on 8-sided dwelling
2. **Isla Congreso S point** 35°10´.5N 02°26´.1W Fl.R.4s36m5M Grey rounded tower Obscd when bearing less than 110°
3. **Isla Isabel II NW point** 35°11´N 02°25´.7W Fl.7s52m8M White tower and dwelling 045°-obscd-080° by Isla Congreso Harbour
4. **Ras Kebdana N breakwater head** Iso.G.6s12m10M White tower
5. **East breakwater head** Iso.R.6s13m10M White tower

The harbour

Ras el Ma is the ultimate sleepy fishing port on the North coast of Morocco. Built by the Romanians in exchange for phosphates in 1985 it escaped the attention of the chart makers until very recently but does now appear on British chart 2437. The port is situated on the E side of Pointe de Ras-Kebdana (Cabo del Agua in Spanish), S of the Spanish Chafarinas Islands. It offers good protection and the fishermen as well as the authorities are friendly.

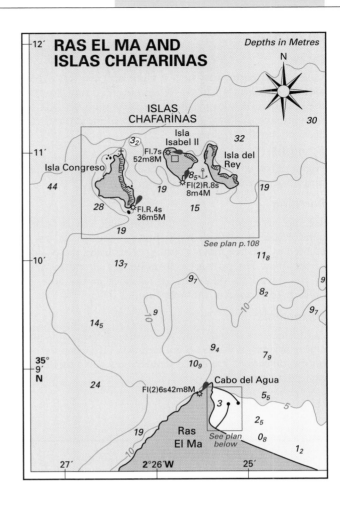

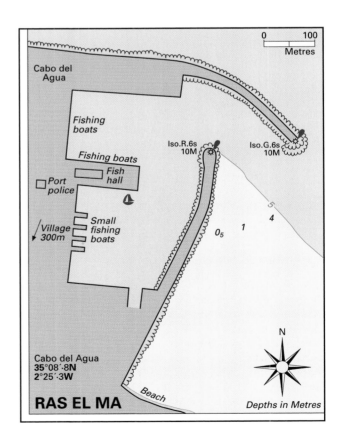

PILOTAGE

By day

In season, fishermen lay nets at night between Ras el Ma and the Chafarinas Islands. When entering, stay close to the starboard breakwater head, because the port side of the entrance shallows abruptly due to silting around the head of the SE breakwater.

By night

Night entry is not recommended as the nets laid as described above are very poorly lit, if at all.

Berthing

Tie up alongside, S of the fish hall. It is more comfortable if you can moor bows-E because of swell created by the fast moving fishing boats using the N side of the quay. The port is far from being full and in view of the dwindling quantities of sardines in the area, is unlikely to change in the near future.

Formalities

Authorities are friendly and yachts are a novelty. It is not a port of entry and has no immigration officials present, but no objections are raised if yachts do make this their first port of call.

Facilities

Water Use a long hose from the quay opposite the fish hall, mornings only.
Electricity None.
Fuel In containers from the village.
Provisions A good assortment of cheap fresh produce and soft drinks. If en route to Algeria one can stock up reasonably well here (by Moroccan standards).
Post office A short walk outside the village opposite the police station.
Bank One bank on the main street.
Repairs More likely you will be asked to lend a hand on a fishing boat with its own troubles. There is a new slipway to haul large fishing boats.

ASHORE

The rocky coast W of the port makes for good snorkelling and aside from the fishing boats the port is visited regularly by a seal who lives in the area.

In July and August, Moroccan tourists camp out on the beautiful beaches that stretch for miles towards the Algerian border.

The village is a short walk from the port and consists of no more than a dusty main street with tea houses and small shops.

Early morning buses leave daily to Berkane and Oujda. Berkane is amidst an extensively irrigated wine growing area and has a good market. Oujda is the

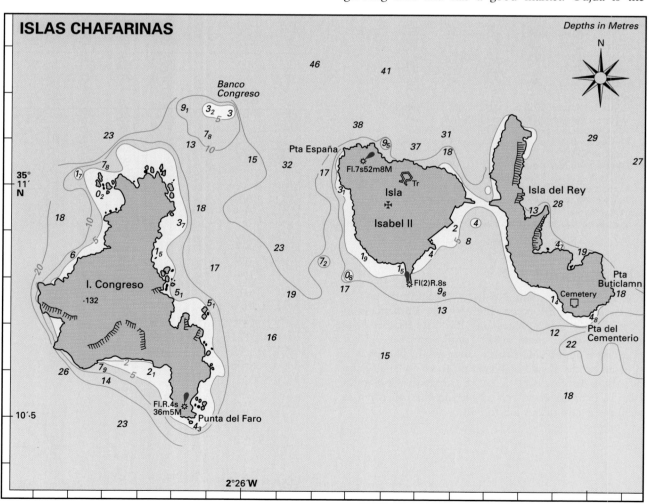

provincial capital with a dusty but lively daily market. Both towns can easily be visited in a day trip.

Under normal circumstances it is possible to obtain visas in Oujda to visit Algeria from the Algerian Consulate. The border was re-opened for a while in 2004, but is currently closed again.

Eating out

It is possible to dine well for virtually nothing in the most basic of eating houses to be found in Morocco. In the summer several 'tent restaurants' are installed on the beach, as in Spain. Several small eating houses around the market in Oujda serve sheep's head which seems to be a speciality. If this is unacceptable, try some other less exotic but well spiced dish from a stall around the market.

MO 31 Islas Chafarinas

A group of 3 small Spanish islands 2M N of Ras el Ma. Formerly having one useful anchorage, but due to political difficulties with the islands further W, approach is now prohibited.

Location
    35°10´.6N 02°26´W

Distances
    Ras el Ma 2M

Charts

	Approach	Port
Admiralty	580	–
French	5864, 6011	–
Spanish	4341	

Lights
1. **Isla Congreso S Point** 35°10´.5N 02°26´.1W Fl.R.4s36m5M Grey round tower Obscured when bearing less than 110°
2. **Isla Isabel II NW Point** Fl.7s52m8M White tower and dwelling 045°-obscd-080° by Isla Congreso
3. **Isla Isabel, S Point** Fl(2)R.8s8m4M Square truncated pyramidal metal tower

The islands

The most eastern island, Isla del Rey, and the middle island, Isla Isabel II, are joined by a partially destroyed pier. The bay to the S is the only natural anchorage suitable in N winds along the Mediterranean coast of Morocco. However, the area is a Spanish military zone and the authorities do not allow yachts to anchor in the vicinity of the islands, which are rich in fish. An unmarked fish farm has been placed on the S side of Isla Isabela which extends more than 300m S.

MO 32 Saidia

Another new development in Morocco currently on hold long before completion, a short distance from the Algerian border.

Location
    35°07´N 02°11´W (approx)

Distances
    Ras el Ma 2M

Charts

	Approach	Port
Admiralty	580	–
French	5864, 6011	–
Spanish	4341	

Lights
    Information unavailable

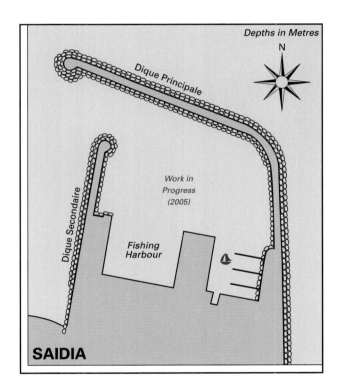

SAIDIA

The marina

The development of this new pleasure complex located E of Ras el Ma, 11M from Cabo de Agua (Ras Kebadana, 35°08´.8N 02°25´.3W) is near the village of Saidia and includes a marina. Work began in late 1998 but was soon suspended. The proposed marina will accommodate 180 yachts with a separate fishing harbour. This promises to be a quiet and safe marina with every facility for the yachting community, when (and if) completed.

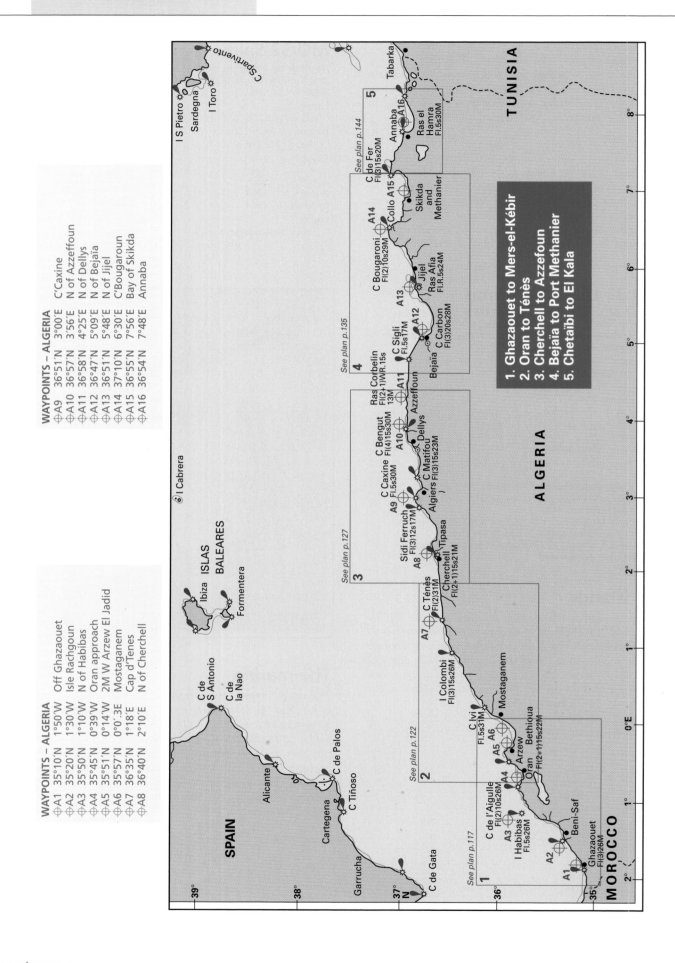

WAYPOINTS – ALGERIA

A1	35°10′N	1°50′W	Off Ghazaouet
A2	35°20′N	1°30′W	Isle Rachgoun
A3	35°50′N	1°10′W	N of Habibas
A4	35°45′N	0°39′W	Oran approach
A5	35°51′N	0°14′W	2M W Arzew El Jadid
A6	35°57′N	0°0′.3E	Mostaganem
A7	36°35′N	1°18′E	Cap d'Tenes
A8	36°40′N	2°10′E	N of Cherchell

WAYPOINTS – ALGERIA

A9	36°51′N	3°00′E	C'Caxine
A10	36°57′N	3°56′E	N of Azzeffoun
A11	36°58′N	4°25′E	N of Dellys
A12	36°47′N	5°09′E	N of Bejaïa
A13	36°51′N	5°48′E	N of Jijel
A14	37°10′N	6°30′E	C'Bougaroun
A15	36°55′N	7°56′E	Bay of Skikda
A16	36°54′N	7°48′E	Annaba

1. Ghazaouet to Mers-el-Kébir
2. Oran to Ténès
3. Cherchell to Azzefoun
4. Bejaïa to Port Methanier
5. Chetaïbi to El Kala

III. ALGERIA

Capital Algiers
Population Approximately 25 million

Preliminary note on Algeria

The inclusion of Algeria when current advice is to avoid visiting the country may appear contradictory. There are good reasons for its inclusion.

1. This book is designed not only for planned visits, but for emergencies in the event of breakdown or severe weather: the latter becoming a more common occurrence in the Mediterranean, even in summer. Algeria has a long coastline providing the most direct route from the Straits of Gibraltar to many destinations in the Mediterranean. No publication on North Africa would be complete without this stretch being covered. Even with the long bureaucratic clearing procedures, a visit may be preferable to staying at sea in some circumstances.
2. Algeria offers some of the most beautiful anchorages and interesting places to visit. It is hoped that the political situation will change, even within the lifetime of this pilot, and that Algeria will again be opened up for the yachting community in much the same way as Turkey was suddenly opened up in the early 1980's following a political change from military rule.

Please see warning note on page 112 for more information on visiting.

Introduction

Algeria is the second largest country in Africa and half the size of Europe. 85% of its territory lies in the Sahara Desert and the majority of its population lives in the green and fertile land bordering the Mediterranean. Two mountain ranges run parallel to the coast: the Tell Atlas which is a continuation of the Moroccan Middle Atlas and the Sahara Atlas which marks the transition into desert. Before the recent civil war, Algeria had the highest per capita income of all the Maghreb countries. Although the Algerian Mediterranean coastline holds great potential for tourism, it remains undeveloped, apart from a very small number of coastal towns which were once frequented by French Society tourists.

The current troubles, a result of an experiment in democratisation, mean that at present (Summer 2004) Algeria is difficult, though not impossible, to visit.

A BRIEF HISTORY

Algeria, with its present borders, scarcely appears in European history books until the 16th century. Earlier history is shared with its more powerful neighbours to the E and the W. The Phoenicians were the first to set up trading posts to barter with the Berbers – the original inhabitants of the area. In Roman times it was a province called Numidia. After the Arab invasions it became part of the Almoravid and Almohad dynasties from Morocco and in the 13th century Algeria was ruled by the Hafsids from Tunisia. At this time Western Algeria flourished under the influence of Hispano-Moorish culture. After the fall of Granada in 1492, Spain started to occupy ports on the North African coast. Its authority never extended much beyond garrison towns such as Melilla and Oran, the latter remaining in Spanish hands from 1509 until 1794. With Turkish support and the help of the Barbarossa brothers, (converted Muslim corsairs from Greece based in Jerba), the Spanish were driven out of Algiers by 1529 and it became a province of the Ottoman Empire, ruled by a succession of Deys and Beys. For more than two centuries it became home port to a notorious pirate fleet.

In 1710 the Dey of Algiers broke with Turkey and for the first time Algeria became independent. It did not last long. A famous incident formed the prelude to French intervention. During a discussion about a loan, the Algerian Dey struck the French ambassador in the face with a fly swat. This provided the excuse for the French to intervene and their forces landed in Sidi Fredj (now also called Sidi Ferruch) in 1830. Seventeen years of fighting followed before the major parts of the country were under French control but it took until 1871 to pacify the Kabylie region which has always been (and still is) a Berber stronghold. There followed a large influx of French settlers and Algeria was incorporated into metropolitan France. The country was reshaped into a beautiful Southern 'département.' Large ports were constructed and French architects converted Oran, Algiers, Bejaïa and Annaba into beautiful cities; nowhere in the Maghreb is the French influence as obvious as in Algeria. Agriculture was developed and Algerian grapes were used to improve the quality of French wines.

Recent history

The Algerians themselves benefited little from the prosperity brought by the French occupation and eventually this led to rebellion. In 1954 the Front de

Algeria cannot produce sufficient food products for the growing population. In Jijel Italian semolina is discharged

Libération Nationale launched a war for independence which was ruthlessly opposed. As fighting continued over the years the French Government under General de Gaulle was willing to compromise but under pressure from the Algerian French, who were defending the country that their fathers had built, the war continued. By 1961 serious negotiations had begun, leading to Algerian independence in 1962 but by that time more than one million Algerian lives had been lost in the long and bloody struggle.

Independent Algeria opted for a socialist government under a single party, the FLN, led by Ahmed Ben Bella, which nationalized all French property. Locally, reconciliation was impossible. Although the rights of the French settlers were guaranteed, practically all of them left. This sudden departure, coupled with damage caused by seven years of civil war, left the country in disarray. In 1965, Colonel Houari Boumédienne overthrew Ben Bella in a military coup, to be succeeded after his death in 1978 by Colonel Chadli Bendjedid. The basic policy of socialism, industrialisation and an anti-western foreign policy was continued. Despite this and antipathy to the French, France continued to be Algeria's major trading partner.

Algeria did well as large oil, natural gas and phosphate reserves were discovered in the Sahara. Ambitious plans were made for industrial development and housing projects to accommodate the rapidly increasing population and large agricultural cooperatives were set up to utilize the relatively small area of tillable land. With its sizable export earnings, it could afford large projects and food imports compensated for what the inefficient cooperatives could not produce. When oil prices slumped in 1985–86, plans had to be adjusted and food imports were reduced resulting in increasing unrest among the population culminating in the food riots of September 1988. Other factors behind this large uprising, in which many civilians were killed, were the lack of political and economic freedom under the FLN. Reforms have been instituted and in recent years foreign policy has become more moderate. In 1985 Chadli Bendjedid was the first Algerian president to visit the United States, where he subsequently came under pressure to institute democratic reforms.

Situation from 1990s

In 1992, under international pressure, democratic elections were held. This resulted in an overwhelming victory for the fundamentalist Islamic party, the FIS. Being unwilling to allow an Islamic republic to emerge, the ruling party, with the support of the USA overturned the election results and enforced military rule. This has resulted in a bloody civil war which has cost the lives of over a hundred thousand Algerians, foreigners and several nationalised Catholic priests. It is uncertain who the perpetrators were for most of the massacres, but the victims have usually been villagers not involved in any political issues.

Within the Maghreb, Algerian and Moroccan relations have been strained for many years because of border disputes and because of Algeria's support for the Polisario Front which opposes Moroccan control of the Western Sahara. Further deterioration of relations resulted from suspicions in Algeria that arms were being smuggled in from Morocco to support the terrorist groups carrying out the massacres. Likewise, the Moroccan Government blamed Algeria for the murder of two Spanish holidaymakers in 1996, which had a serious effect on tourism. The land border with Morocco has been closed for several years. Although very tense, the border with Tunisia is now open. (Summer 2004.)

Warning note

It must be appreciated that there is a civil war ongoing in Algeria. Entry procedures, always long and tedious, if courteous, must be viewed in this context. Visiting foreigners create a considerable amount of work and tension for the authorities.

It is possible to obtain a visa with difficulty and all nationalities now need one, including French, who were exempt for many years. These have to be obtained in your country of residence. In 2004 for reasons unknown, many visas were refused, even when all conditions for their issue appeared to be in order. Often an address in Algeria, or an invitation is required: something yachtsmen do not find easy to supply. (For further details see Visa section on page 115.) Many formalities seemed designed to discourage visitors.

On entry it is usual, once port formalities have been completed, to be given an armed guard for all trips ashore, including a visit to the local market. This guard usually consists of three uniformed officers all equipped with sub-machine guns. They are very friendly and polite but never relax. This role seems to be by government order for the safety and protection of foreigners.

As one Colonel said: 'Many Algerians have been killed and it is of no consequence to the outside world. However, if a foreigner is killed or taken hostage, it is an international incident: I lose my job and the world hears about it to the embarrassment of my country.' In the current circumstances, although seemingly excessive, it does provide security. Yachts will usually be allocated a place right outside the police post in the port and given a 24 hour armed guard. Many ports are now closed to yachts and considered military zones. Going ashore at night is usually prohibited. If no visa has been obtained by the crew, it is likely they will be confined to the port, or even to the yacht during a stay. Any necessary provisions can be ordered and will be brought to the yacht.

Given the above, it seems safe to visit, if tedious and inadvisable. Several French yachts and at least three Canadian yachts visited in the summer of 2004. All experienced long hard searches of the yacht by customs and police, sometimes carried out several times in the same port, with armed guards everywhere.

Entry formalities can take many hours: typically, as in Mostaganem, around five hours. All port officials, often as many as nine officers, board the vessel and each takes a turn filling in a pile of forms and then looking around the yacht, seemingly checking each others' inspection.

The only reasonable advice currently is to avoid visiting if at all possible.

General information

Socio-cultural guidelines

Photography

The attitude towards visitors taking photographs has relaxed, but photographing ports or industrial sites may cause difficulties and photographing military objects will certainly do so. As most Algerian ports are in bigger cities, objections on religious grounds to taking pictures of people in the vicinity is not as common as it is in the country.

Security

The Algerians are more conservative than their neighbours. Perhaps this is due to the years of war, first against French domination and then the internal strife that has wrecked the country for many years. Much of the bureaucracy originates from the time of French rule and French is the main language spoken in the larger towns and cities. Algeria is broadly split between Arabs and Kabyles, the latter being Berber descendants of the original inhabitants of the land from before the Islamic conquest in C7th. The Kabylies retain their own identity and language that distinguishes them from Arab Algerians. Despite attempts over many years to integrate them, they remain defiantly independent. The ports of Bejaïa and Annaba are in the Kabylie regions.

Inviting Algerian friends on board

One of the pleasant aspects of cruising in Algeria is that it is easy to meet very friendly Algerians who may go far out of their way to please the visitor. Returning the favour by inviting them on board may cause problems with the authorities, as Algerians are officially not allowed on board a foreign yacht. This rule is interpreted with varying stringency and it is best to check with the local police before making an invitation. This rule applies throughout North Africa.

Planning your cruise

Time zone

Algeria follows Central European Time, i.e. UT+1hr without Daylight Saving Time in the summer.

Money

Travellers' cheques and cash are acceptable but credit card and Eurocheques facilities are rare.

The real value of the Algerian Dinar (DA) is roughly a quarter of the official rate which is one reason why the cost of living is high for foreign visitors. Prices quoted are based on an official exchange rate of DA 57 = $1.00.

Changing money on the thriving black market gives a much better rate and even officials will offer to oblige. Do not be tempted; the risks are not worth it.

The Dinar may not be imported or exported and can only be exchanged legally within Algeria; it is not listed in the international market. Permission to change back left-over notes on leaving Algeria is not always given.

Declaration of Gold and Foreign Currencies

All foreign currencies, travellers' cheques and valuables (which includes weapons), on board at the time of entry into Algeria can be taken in or out of the country without paying any taxes but they have to be declared on the 'Declaration of Holdings of Gold and Foreign Currencies.' Failure to do so or making a false declaration can result in confiscation of all money plus heavy fines and even a prison sentence. All currency exchanges should be done officially at banks or hotels and the amount exchanged will be marked on this paper. Bank slips and forms should be kept as they may be checked on departure although in practice this is rare. Officially a minimum of DA 1000 has to be charged for every person on board but in practice this is often not enforced on yachtsmen. Start out changing what you think you will need and take things from there. If the amount seems reasonable in view of the length of the visit, there should not be any difficulty.

Health advice

Medical facilities in Algeria are elementary, drugs are scarce and basic commodities such as lavatory paper and tampons are unavailable. Have a good first aid kit. It is essential to have good medical insurance including repatriation as any serious accident or illness will have to be treated in Europe. Except for yellow fever if coming from an infected area, vaccinations are not required but consult your doctor.

CRUISING GROUNDS

The Algerian coast stretches for 570 nautical miles from Morocco in the west to Tunisia in the east. As far as Oran the sparsely populated coast is made up of steep hills with the Habibas Islands and several uninhabited islets a short distance offshore. From Oran to Algiers green wooded low hills slope gently towards the shore and several villages line the coast, although not many with a port. From Algiers eastward towards the beautiful Bay of Bejaïa the coast becomes increasingly mountainous, but this landscape terminates abruptly at Annaba where it becomes low until the Medjerda mountain range which forms the border with Tunisia. With the exception of the industrial areas around Arzew and to a lesser extent Skikda, the coast is unspoilt with some beautiful, deserted beaches often backed by steep mountains.

There are some anchorages which provide good shelter from either the W or E but good all round shelter is only found in the ports. The coast between Ziama Mansouriah in the Gulf of Bejaïa and Jijel and the coast from Collo to Skikda in particular, offer several beautiful anchorages in good weather.

The commercial ports of Arzew, Algiers and Annaba are among the largest on the North African coast and as such not particularly interesting. Entry into the port of Algiers has been forbidden to yachts for many years and this prohibition has been extended to several other ports, all noted in this pilot. Visiting yachts will find a better welcome in the smaller commercial and fishing ports where they will generally find friendly people. Although day hopping from port to port is possible, lengthy formalities have to be carried out in every port. Apart from the marina in Sidi Ferruch (also called Sidi Fredj), there are yacht clubs in the commercial ports of Oran and Annaba, though these are closed at present. There are also seven fishing ports, six ports which combine commerce and fishing, and a several good weather anchorages.

As the Algerian coast is on the shortest route from Gibraltar to the Eastern Mediterranean, there is heavy traffic in the sea lanes between 10 and 15 miles off shore.

The country has never exploited its tourist potential which lies mainly in the beautiful and varied landscape. Visiting yachts are rare, though much appreciated by the locals. Like most Arabs, the Algerians are genuinely friendly if somewhat reserved.

Anchoring

Under normal circumstances yachts can anchor along the Algerian coast. It offers some of the most beautiful anchorages anywhere in the Mediterranean. Fish is abundant and there are hundreds of peaceful and sheltered coves to explore. The authorities are not used to yachts, however, and are always suspicious. A patrol boat will almost certainly visit and ensure that you have cleared customs and received permission to anchor. Never take a dinghy ashore without permission. Always inform the authorities of your itinerary. This may seem intrusive, but it is for your protection. Information is passed from port to port and the officials will be waiting for your visit.

Good all-weather ports

Entry safe by day and night and in bad weather: Ghazaouet, Oran, Mostaganem, Ténès, Bejaïa, Jijel, Skikda (not in a strong northerly) and Annaba.

Harbour charges

These are not mentioned in the text, since in fishing harbours and commercial ports formal charges are not levied. Sidi Ferruch marina does charge at an unrealistically high rate.

Availability of supplies

Fuel

Good quality diesel and engine oil is available in many of the ports. Prices are basically the same everywhere and the lowest in the Mediterranean, even at the official exchange rate. Due to the restrictions. one has to pay in Algerian Dinars.

Water

Water is available in most ports though scarcer west of Ténès. Quality is generally good, except in Oran. With some improvisation, hoses can be hooked up in several ports but supply is variable. Elsewhere containers are necessary. Water is usually free of charge but it is a precious commodity in most ports. Deck washing is unacceptable for instance, except in Sidi Ferruch and Cherchell.

Electricity

Nominal voltage is 220v, 60Hz. With the exception of Oran, Sidi Ferruch and Annaba electricity is not available in the ports.

Provisions

Basics such as bread, vegetables, fruit, milk, meat, etc. are usually available though often not all together at the same time of the day. Except for subsidised products such as bread and milk, some food prices equate to UK prices but are more often higher. Bring all staple foodstuffs. Butter, cheese, cream, tea, coffee, soft drinks, mineral water, canned products, oil, pork, toilet paper, wine, beer and liquor are usually unavailable or of poor quality.

Repairs

Emergency engine repairs can be carried out in the major cities if the engine is common in Algeria. As a rule spare parts are not available but, as in all of North Africa, the Algerians are masters at repairs and improvisation. In Sidi Fredj and Oran, where there are a few local pleasure craft, simple yacht repairs can be carried out.

Official ports of entry

Ghazaouet, Beni Saf, Oran, Mostaganem, Ténès, Cherchell, Sidi Ferruch, Dellys, Bejaïa, Djen Djen, Skikda, and Annaba.

It is best to avoid entering at the commercial ports of Ghazaouet and Annaba and to go to Beni Saf, Oran, Mostaganem, Bejaïa, Jijel, Skikda or one of the fishing ports; nevertheless, the ease with which clearance is obtained varies and depends largely upon the attitude of local officials towards the yacht and her crew.

Entry formalities

Yachts are a rarity and entry procedures are geared to merchantmen. This results in much tedious form filling which must be borne patiently. It is important to fly an Algerian courtesy flag. Officials are correct but unsure and this is sometimes covered up by formal or authoritative behaviour and a yacht, as an unusual visitor, is often suspect. Be open and friendly. It is a good idea to announce your arrival by VHF.

Bakhshish is not generally necessary and offering it may be interpreted as a bribe (see note on page 4 of the Introduction).

Merchant ships have sometimes found the authorities sensitive about detail: for instance inspecting medicines in life rafts or fining them for failing to lower their flag at sundown. Yachts generally escape such attention.

Yacht papers required are ownership papers and radio licences.

A current Crew List will also need to be produced and an inventory of all boat equipment with serial numbers of electronics and another list with boat data. (See appendix for guidelines regarding these forms. It will speed up formalities.

Crew members need valid passports and all nationalities now need visas. As a rule passports stay with the PAF (Police au Frontière, see below) and are collected immediately before departure. Technically, the crew of a vessel is not required to have visas as long as individuals stay in the port area, but without them it is difficult to obtain a permis d'escale, the permission to leave the port, which is issued in all commercial ports. Crew without a visa will usually be confined to the yacht. (See also Visas in general introduction on page 16.)

When entering the ports there is no need to seek out officials; they will be waiting. In the bigger ports the PAF, customs and the coast guard will always show up and sometimes the port captain visits. Generally in the smaller ports, only the PAF is interested, unless the stay is longer than a few days; then the others may become involved. Officials usually behave correctly and courteously and only a few are officious. The best way to deal with any akward questions is to remain friendly and maintain innocence, while keeping a low profile.

Upon departure, yachts are considered to leave Algeria even though they stay in territorial waters on the way to the next port and customs clearance has to be repeated. After a few ports, customs may give up searching the boat, but paperwork for all will still have to be dealt with.

The authorities encountered will be:

The PAF (Police au Frontière) – border police in civilian clothes or blue uniform. Checks passports and visas of all crew and oddly they sometimes ask for the value of the boat; curiosity seems to be the reason for this question, as for many of the others.

Customs – almost always wear uniform and come on board with a minimum of two persons. Besides their usual functions, they enforce the strict currency regulations. In the first port a thorough inspection can be expected. It is illegal to bring drugs or pornographic material into the country and there are very heavy penalties for those breaking the law. All weapons (particularly important), valuables, alcohol and currency have to be declared. Weapons will be impounded during the stay and large quantities of liquor will be sealed on board. A visiting yacht does not have to pay duty on these articles.

The coastguard – mostly young servicemen, always in uniform. A branch of the Algerian navy operating coastal patrol boats. Their list of questions varies from port to port but it is always long and is mainly concerned with the boat, safety and radio equipment. Often the coast guard personnel are brash because of their youth. In case of an emergency at sea they provide assistance free of charge

The capitainerie (harbourmaster) – in the commercial ports.

The gendarmerie – only on rare occasions (chiefly out of curiosity).

Visas

Currently all nationalities need a visa which is only obtainable from the Algerian Consulate in the country of residence. Check for details with an Algerian consulate beforehand, as this changes from time to time. Some travel agents in the country of residence will obtain a visa for a fee.

In Tunisia, the most logical place to apply for a visa is at the Algerian Embassy in Tunis at 136 Avenue de la Liberté, half a block from the US Embassy, but this was refusing to accept applications from non-residents of all nationalities in Summer 2004. The procedure requires four passport size photos and the cost depends on nationality. It can take from 24hrs to several weeks to obtain it. Applicants with stamps from Israel, South Africa, South Korea, Taiwan or Malawi in their passports will be refused visas.

In the past, vessels calling in at Algerian ports could obtain an *escala technique*, a document that enabled them to be treated as a yacht in transit with crew members being allowed ashore for a limited period. An inland pass was also obtainable. This facility is still technically possible, but not implemented because of the security situation. Travel inland is not recommended in any case under the present circumstances.

Typical souk street: few visitors   *Graham Hutt*

III. ALGERIA

Embassies

United Kingdom 7th Floor, Hotel Hilton,
  International. Alger. Pins Maritimes Palais des
  Expositions, El Mohammadia, Algiers
  ☎ (212) 2123 0068.

United States 4 Chemin Cheikh Bachir Ibrahimini El
  Biar, Algiers, ☎ (213) (2) 691255x7019 *Fax* 693979

France: 25 Chemin Abdelkader Gadouche 16035
  Algiers ☎ (213) (0) 21692488
  www.ambafrance-dz.org

Germany: 165 Chemin Sfindja (Ex Laperlier) B.P. 664
  Algiers ☎ 021/741956/741289 afternoons re visas.
  Email zreg@algi.diplo.de

All embassies: www.embassyworld.com/embassy

Tourist information

Information on Algeria is hard to come by. The ONAT
(Office National Algérien du Tourism) has offices in the
big cities in Algeria but their information is limited and
their desire to impart it even more so. The best sources
are the travel guides listed under 'Books.'

Business hours

Algeria follows the Islamic week; banks and offices are
closed on Thursday afternoons and Fridays.

Opening times vary but most shops and offices open
between 0800 and 0900. The afternoon break is from
1200 to 1500 and closing times are between 1700 and
1900. Small shops and markets are often open seven
days a week.

Public holidays

New Year's Day	1 January
Labour Day	1 May
Anniversary of the overthrow of ex-President Ben Bella	19 June
Independence Day	5 July
Anniversary of the Revolution	1 November

Tipping

For a visiting yachtsman in Algeria there may be few
occasions to tip but one may wish to be able to repay
some of the hospitality or friendliness that will be
encountered. Practically any clothing item can serve this
purpose as well as American or European cigarettes.

Telephone

International calls are best made from a post office.
They are all routed through Algiers and consequently
may take some time when made from another city.
Many local phone boxes prove to be defective. The
GSM mobile phone system operates throughout the
country, but not all European companies have roaming
agreements with Algeria.

Overland travel

At present (Summer 2004) it is very dangerous for
foreigners to move around in Algeria without an armed
military escort. There is little to stop you doing so if you
have a visa. Without a visa it is most probable that you
will be confined to the port, or even the yacht. However,
under normal circumstances the following applies: Buses
are the best way to get around as the railway system is
not well developed. Taxis and louages (see under
'Overland Travel' Tunisia on page 156 for more
information on these) are more expensive but very
efficient for town-to-town visiting. Car rental is
expensive as it must be paid with officially exchanged
money. Hitching is commonplace for men though never
for women.

International travel

Algiers: Regular flights to several European capitals.
Flights from Oran.

Several ports have a regular ferry service to France.
Check out the current situation on the internet, as it
changes according to need but regular ferries operate
from several ports to Marseille and Sète as well as to
Alicante. http://www.cemar.it/dest/ferries algeria.htm

Tidal information

Tides along the entire Algerian coast are around 0.5
metres or less and are therefore not mentioned.
Additional information relating to local currents is
included where necessary.

Note on night entry

A separate night entry heading is not included in this
section because insufficient information is available on
the reliability of lights upon which night entry depends.
Information is provided where appropriate and where
special navigational information is considered helpful.

Most Algerian ports are large and deep, posing few
navigational problems by day or night.

Order of Algerian ports

The port order is from the Moroccan border heading E
to Tunisia.

Important note on waypoints and co-ordinates

Please refer to the important note regarding waypoints
in the Introduction on page 12.

Revised port information

The revision of information was made possible by
information obtained from visiting yachtsmen, including
myself, in summer 2004. Due to the problems in the
country and the utmost suspicion of our intentions, it
was impossible to get detailed information or modified
port plans from the authorities. However, it is apparent
that little has changed over the years and updates have
been made and charts updated from new British
Admiralty charts where necessary. Port information is
provided even where ports are currently prohibited areas
for yachts.

1. Ghazaouet to Mers-el-Kébir

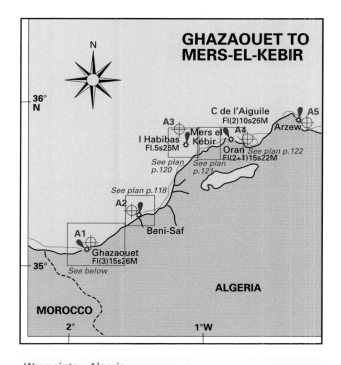

See plan p.122
See plan p.120
See plan p.121
See plan p.118
See below

Waypoints – Algeria
⊕A1 35°10′N 1°50′W Off Ghazaouet
⊕A2 35°20′N 1°30′W Isle Rachgoun
⊕A3 35°50′N 1°10′W N of Habibas
⊕A4 35°45′N 0°39′W Oran approach
⊕A5 35°51′N 0°14′W 2M W Arzew El Jadid

A1 Ghazaouet

A large commercial port of entry close to the Moroccan border, sheltered from the E by Plateau de Touent.

Location
   35°06′.3N 01°52′.2W (100m N of Les Deux Frères light)

Distances
   Ras el Ma 27M
   Beni-Saf 28M

Charts

	Approach	Port
Admiralty	2437	178
French	6011	5873

Lights
Approach
1. **Main light** 35°05′.9N 01°52′.3W Fl(3)15s92m26M Tower on dwelling 058°-vis-248° obscd by Plateau de Touent when bearing more than 237°
Harbour
2. **Jetée Nord head** Oc.R.4s17m8M
3. **Rocher Les Deux Frères** Fl(2)G.6s26m5M
4. **Inside of N jetée** F.R.8m6M
5. **S Mole** F.G.8m5M

Communications
   VHF Ch 16

The port

Ghazaouet is a large commercial port protected from the E by the Plateau de Touent which towers above the village and from the N by a long breakwater extending from the plateau. A small bank surmounted by the rocks of Les Deux Frères forms the SW extremity of the port

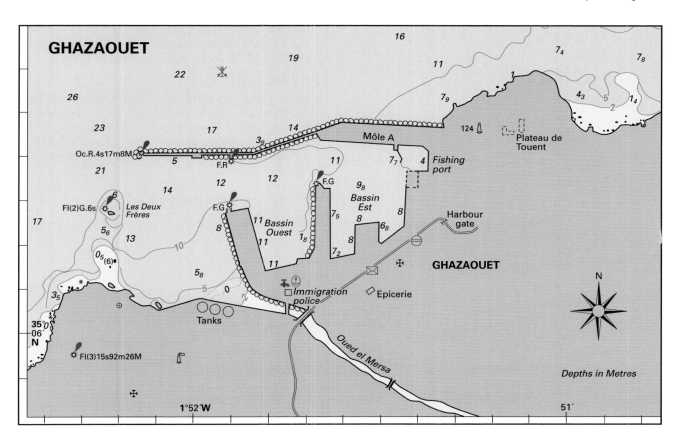

entrance. The setting of the harbour and village is very attractive. The port was once important for the export of minerals from Morocco (which does not have any large commercial ports on the Mediterranean coast) but after border disputes, Morocco pulled out. Today's main activities are fishing and repair/refitting work.

Berthing

As directed on entry.

Formalities

Officials will turn up as described in the introduction.

Facilities

Water Containers can be filled at a tap near the police office in the SW corner of the port.
Fuel Available in the port.
Provisions There is a small grocery shop outside the harbour gate behind the police office and further supplies are obtainable in the village.
Post office and *bank* In the village.

A2 Beni Saf

A large commercial port with one of the largest fishing fleets in the Mediterranean, 54M W of Oran and a Port of Entry. Difficult to enter in N and NW winds.

Location
35°18´.5N 01°23´.3W (Light on S mole)

Distances
Ras el Ma 54M,
Ghazaouet 28M
Oran 54M

Charts

	Approach	Port
Admiralty	2437	178
French	5940	5876

Lights
Approach
1. **Ile Rachgoun** 35°19´.5N 01°28´.7W Fl(2)R.10s81m16M Yellow square tower on hut
Harbour
2. **Jetée Nord head** Iso.G.4s11m7M 072°-vis-342° Black column on hut
3. **Jetée Est head** Oc(2)R.6s9m8M Red column

Communications
VHF Ch 16

The port

Beni Saf is the most active fishing port on the Algerian coast and possibly in this entire part of the Mediterranean. The friendly town, up in the hills overlooking the port, is spread out across a valley which descends down to the harbour. Initially constructed in French colonial times for shipping iron ore from mines in the vicinity, fishing became the main activity after the mining company left in 1977.

PILOTAGE

From the head of the N breakwater a bank extends 300m in an ENE direction. Entry can be difficult in fresh N and NW winds and dangerous in gales.

Berthing

This medium sized port is filled by its large fishing fleet. Fishermen may invite yachts to come alongside but most likely you will be directed to the short quay in the SE corner next to the patrol boat of the Coastguard. This is more convenient for clearing customs. There is no room to anchor.

Beni Saf fishing harbour viewed from the N

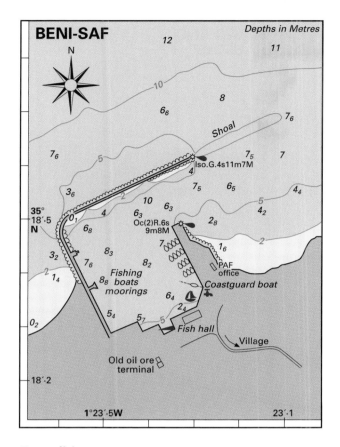

```
BENI-SAF                    Depths in Metres
        N              12              11
                        10
                6₆          8
                        Shoal           7₆
                                7₅      7
  7₆                        Iso.G.4s11m7M
    3₆                    4    7₅    6₅      4₄
35°              2    10  6₃        5    4₂
18'·5        0₁  4    6₃
N            6₈    Oc(2)R.6s  2₈      2
                    9m8M              1₆
  3₂    7₆  8₃    8₂   7              PAF
    2   1₄ 8₈  Fishing  6₄  Coastguard boat  office
            boats
0₂          moorings  5₄  2₄
        5₄      5₇  5  Fish hall
                        Village
        Old oil ore
        terminal
18'·2
        1°23'·5W              23'·1
```

Formalities

Port of entry. Officials are friendly but security is high. Armed guards are placed on the jetty during a stay and crew are not allowed into town. (Summer 2004.) Passports stay with the PAF and have to be picked up shortly before departure.

Facilities

Water From a tap on the quay. Patience is required since most of the time pressure is low. Alternatively carry containers from the fish market.

Provisions Bread from a small shop just outside the port and fresh fish around the fish market. More shops and a well stocked market (by Algerian standards) in the village. In the covered market hall one is 'allowed' to buy oil, a sack of flour or a TV antenna from disinterested government employees.

Showers There is a *hammam* in the village. (See Introduction on page 4 re Hammams.)

Post office Next to the covered market.

Bank In the village.

ASHORE

Sites locally

From Beni Saf it is easy to visit Tlemcen, a city rich in history, located 800m high in the Tell Atlas mountains. In the 15th century it was an important trading centre between Europe and Africa. Although much has been demolished over the years, the remaining monuments, built Hispano-Moorish style and the beautiful setting in the mountains, make Tlemcen well worth a visit.

Eating out

A few simple eating houses around the port.

A3 Bou-Zadjar

A small fishing harbour 8M S of Iles Habibas, 1.5M E of Cap Figalo. A useful stop from Beni Saf to Iles Habibas.

Location
35°35'0N 01°9'.5W

Charts
Admiralty 822

Communications
VHF Ch 16

The anchorage

An interesting little bay surrounded by steep hills on a thinly populated part of the coast and a useful stop en route from Beni Saf to Oran or the Habibas Islands. It is shown without name on British Admiralty charts, though now charted by SHOM on 5886. Good protection can be found from NE through S to SW. When entering in the middle of the bay, which is only 300m wide, beware of the submerged rocks on the W side. The bottom shoals gradually towards the head of the bay. Anchor in the middle, sand, 5–7m.

A4 Mersa Ali Bou Nouar

A picturesque bay with good protection from NE through S to SW, 6M SW of Iles Habibas.

Location
35°38'N 01°04'W

Distances
Cap Falcon 15M
Iles Habibas 6M

Charts
French 5886

Communications
VHF Ch 16

The harbour

A fishing harbour in the SW corner of Mersa Bou Zadjar bay (also spelled Mersa Buzudjar), 1.5M E of Cap Figalo. It is a useful place for yachts to stop in order to make a daytime approach to Iles Habibas. There is nothing in the harbour and the village of Bou Zadjar is some distance away on the other side of the bay. There are no customs officials and it is not a port of entry. There is an alternative good weather anchorage between moored fishing boats in front of the village on the other side of the bay.

A5 Iles Habibas

Two islands and numerous islets and rocks 9M NNE of Cap Figalo. Two anchorages offer good protection in prevailing winds but only approach in good conditions and by day.

Location
    35°43´.3N 01°08´W (Lighthouse on island)

Distances
    Beni-Saf 28M
    Oran 27M

Charts

	Approach	Anchorage
Admiralty	2437	822
French	5940, 5948	5886

Lights
Approach
1. **Iles Habibas** 35°43´.0N 01°07´.2E Fl.5s112m26M Red square tower on dwelling

The islands

The Iles Habibas, situated 9M NNE of Cap Figalo, are made up of two islands and numerous islets and rocks. They are uninhabited except for the lighthouse keeper and a couple of military guards. Two anchorages offer good protection in the prevailing winds. For those who like an untouched, splendid, natural setting, this is among one of the most attractive places to visit on the entire North African coast. Be sure to bring snorkel/diving gear to explore the unpolluted

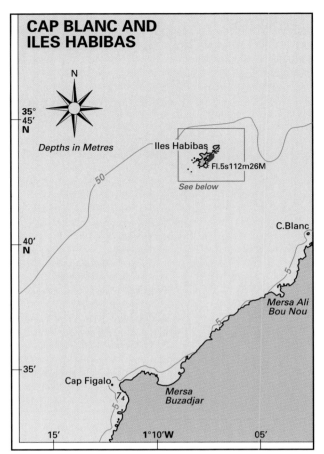

CAP BLANC AND ILES HABIBAS

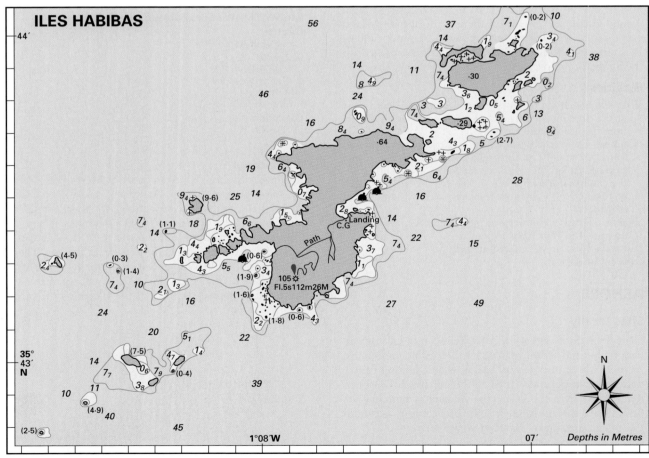

ILES HABIBAS

underwater world. A good path leads up to the lighthouse which offers a spectacular view of the islands and the coast. The visitors' book in the lighthouse was started in 1879 and it is closer to a museum piece than anything one will ever find in a real museum in Algeria. The first entries are from French survey lieutenants, followed by naturalists, divers and a few visiting yachts. The bay on the SW side at the foot of the lighthouse offers good protection from N and E winds and is a good base for diving or fishing expeditions. There is a large mooring buoy which can be used but make use of a kedge. Holding is not good but with enough scope the anchor will eventually set somewhere behind a rock. In 2004 the two mooring buoys on the E side of the island were missing. The Coastguard may recommend a little quay in the narrow inlet; it has only 1.5m alongside and is amongst rocks.

PILOTAGE

Only by day in good weather. The SW bay can be entered from the S by keeping midway between the SW extremity of the island and 0.4M SW of the lighthouse. With the lighthouse bearing about 070° steer for the big white mooring buoy. This route has depths of 4m or more but keep a good lookout on the bow for rocks.

Formalities

The Coastguard has three young men on station, who have no boat. They may arrange to visit by fishing boat and have been known to swim back ashore with notes above their heads! This is obviously not a port of entry.

Facilities

None and more likely the Coastguard will ask you for something because they are dropped there for a two week stay with less than abundant provisions.

A6 Mers-el-Kébir

A large naval and commercial port 3M W of Oran, currently closed to yachts.

Location
  35°43′.5N 0°37′.0W

Distances
Oran 1M

Charts

	Approach	Port
Admiralty	2437, 1909	812

Communications
  VHF Ch 16

The port

A large naval, military and commercial port 1M W of Oran.

Easy and safe to enter in any weather, but entry by yacht is currently forbidden.

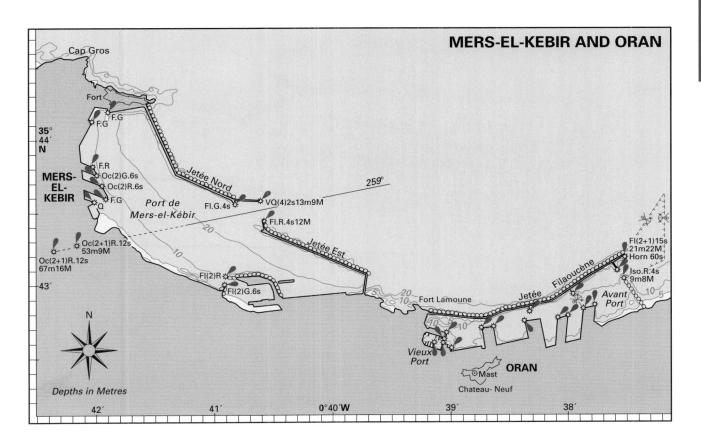

MERS-EL-KEBIR AND ORAN

2. Oran to Ténès

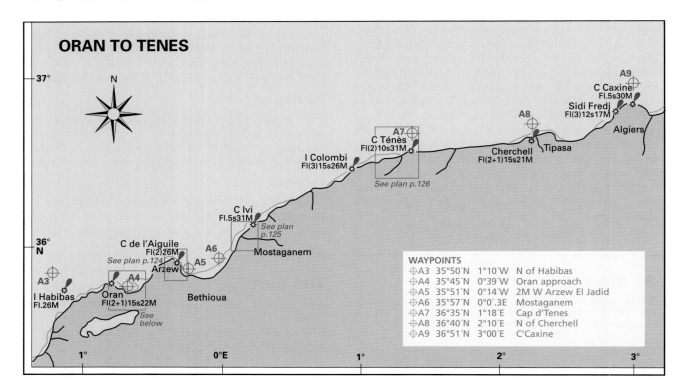

ORAN TO TENES

37°

N

A9
C Caxine
Fl.5s30M

Sidi Fredj
Fl(3)12s17M

A8

Algiers

A7

C Ténès
Fl(2)10s31M

Cherchell
Fl(2+1)15s21M

Tipasa

See plan p.126

I Colombi
Fl(3)15s26M

C Ivi
Fl.5s31M

See plan p.125

36°
N

C de l'Aiguile
Fl(2)26M

See plan p.124

A6

A5

Arzew

Mostaganem

A3

I Habibas
Fl.26M

A4

Oran
Fl(2+1)15s22M

See below

Bethioua

WAYPOINTS			
⊕A3	35°50′N	1°10′W	N of Habibas
⊕A4	35°45′N	0°39′W	Oran approach
⊕A5	35°51′N	0°14′W	2M W Arzew El Jadid
⊕A6	35°57′N	0°0′.3E	Mostaganem
⊕A7	36°35′N	1°18′E	Cap d'Tenes
⊕A8	36°40′N	2°10′E	N of Cherchell
⊕A9	36°51′N	3°00′E	C'Caxine

1°   0°E   1°   2°   3°

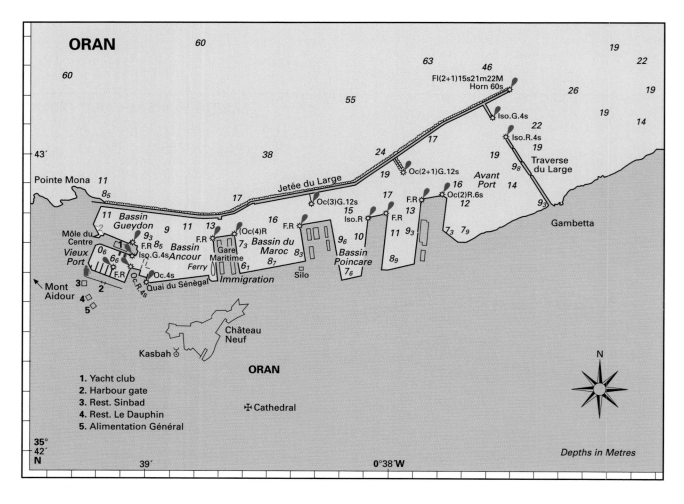

ORAN

60

60

63

19

22

46

Fl(2+1)15s21m22M
Horn 60s

55

26

19

Iso.G.4s

19

17

22

19

43′

38

24

Iso.R.4s

19

Traverse
du Large

Pointe Mona 11

19

Oc(2+1)G.12s

Avant
Port

9_8

8_5

17

Oc(3)G.12s

16

17

F.R

Oc(2)R.6s

14

9_3

11

Bassin
Gueydon

9

11

13

(Oc(4)R

16

15

Iso.R

13

12

7_3 7_9

Gambetta

Môle du
Centre

9_3

F.R

Bassin
Ancour

F.R

7_3

Bassin du
Maroc

F.R

9_6

10

11

9_3

Vieux
Port

0_6

8_5

Iso.G.4s

Gare
Maritime

Bassin
Poincare

8_9

6_6

6_1

8_7

8_3

Ferry

Oc.4s

Immigration

Silo

7_6

Mont
Aidour

3

F.R

Oc.R.4s

Quai du Sénègal

2

4

5

Château
Neuf

Kasbah

ORAN

1. Yacht club
2. Harbour gate
3. Rest. Sinbad
4. Rest. Le Dauphin
5. Alimentation Général

✠ Cathedral

N

35°
42′
N

39′   0°38′W

Depths in Metres

A7 Oran

A large commercial port in Oran, the second largest city in Algeria 42M W of Mostaganem. A port of entry.

Location
35°43′.2N 0°37′.5W

Distances
Beni-Saf 54M
Iles Habibas 27M
Mostaganem 42M

Charts

	Approach	Port
Admiralty	2437, 1909	812
French	5948	5673

Lights
Approach
1. **Jetée du Large head** 35°43′.2N 0°37′.5W
   Fl(2+1)15s21m22M Horn 60s White metal framework tower
Harbour
2. **Epi du Large** 35°43′.1N 0°37′.6W Iso.G.4s8m7M Black column
3. **Traverse du Large** 35°43′.0N 0°37′.5W Iso.R.4s9m8M Red column check
4. **N side Vieux Port, Mole du Centre SE corner** Iso.G.4s9m6M
5. **N side Vieux Port, Mole du Centre NE corner** F.R.9m7M
6. **S side Vieux Port, Mole St Marie E corner** Oc.R.4s9m7M
7. **S side Vieux Port, Mole St Marie E jetty head** F.R.6m7M

Communications
VHF Ch 16

The port

Oran is the second largest city of Algeria with around 650,000 inhabitants. The large commercial harbour has seven basins and yachts can usually stay in the W basin, Vieux Port. A small yacht club with floating pontoons is located on the N side of Vieux Port. Currently this is used by fishing boats. Opposite the yacht club are quays for an active fishing fleet. The club is friendly but has no facilities to offer.

PILOTAGE

Tunny nets may be laid between March and November in the area of Baie des Aiguades, SE of Cap Falcon. Entry into the port of Oran is easy in good weather. Fort Santa Cruz (at an elevation of 352m on Jebel Murdjadjo E of the port between Mers-el-Kébir and Oran) is a good landmark. In a rare W gale, a current sets S across the entrance.

Berthing

As directed on entry but head for the Vieux Port. The bottom between the pontoons of the old yacht club is fouled with moorings and cables.

Formalities

Customs will search your boat whether or not she has been examined in other ports. The PAF will ask the skipper to call at their office (a long walk from the yacht club on the other side of the port, near the ferry terminal) and will keep passports there. The yacht club charges approx Dn 30 per day regardless of size. If you are allowed into town alone in the evening, ensure there is somebody to open the gate when returning.

Facilities

Water A trickle of water in the daytime from several taps on the pontoons. Usually there is more pressure in the evening.
Electricity Can be arranged at the yacht club.
Fuel In the port.
Provisions Aside from an alimentation général and a fishmonger outside the harbour gate (Oran is one of the few ports where good size swordfish are brought in daily) there are no shops near the port. There are more shops in the former Jewish quarter in the city which can best be reached by bus.
Showers Run down facilities in the yacht club.
Post office and *bank* In the city.

ASHORE

History

In 1791 Oran, then a Spanish city, was largely destroyed by an earthquake which killed half of the population. The Spanish king left the ruins to the Turks who settled a Jewish community there. When the French arrived in 1831 the city had 4000 inhabitants. Oran prospered under French rule and grew to the present size and the large commercial port was constructed. After independence the growing population made further expansion of the city necessary and the government decided to build a new, truly Algerian city. In the Eastern part of Oran these ambitious plans have been largely realised but the western part, near the Vieux Port, has not been developed.

Sites locally

A walk from the port to the Château Neuf park leads through the former Spanish and Jewish quarters, though little remains of them. There is a good view of the city and port from this well-kept park; the impressive Château Neuf was the seat of the Spanish governor until 1701 and today is used by the military. It is not open to the public. Alternatively there is a 4km walk to the Spanish Santa Cruz castle, 350m high on Jebel Murdjadjo (or Mount Aidour by the old name). Most people prefer to take a taxi. The summer heat should not be under-estimated. Either way, the view from Santa Cruz is equally rewarding.

Eating out

A small restaurant next to the yacht club and two upmarket restaurants near the fish quay. Outside the gate, opposite the petrol station, you will find Sindbad and further along the road another 100m, Le Dauphin.

A8 Arzew

A large port easy to enter in any conditions but with limited facilities for yachts. A Port of Entry.

Location
35°51′.0N 0°17′.0W

Distances
Oran 20M
Mostaganem 19M

Charts

	Approach	Port
Admiralty	837	838

Lights
Jetée Est Q(4)6s15m12M
Jetée Abri Oc.G.4s10m9M
Jetée Secondaire Fl.R.4s6m2M
Approach buoys N F.G.
SW Fl.G.

Communications
VHF Ch 16

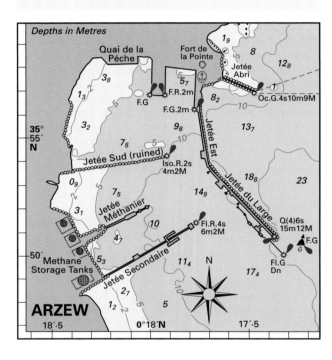

The port

Arzew is a small village where one of the biggest commercial harbours of Algeria was built for the exportation of liquified gas and oil. A new port complex, Port D'Arzew El Jadid, is now completed 2 miles ESE of the port.

There is nothing of interest for a yacht, but it offers a safe and easy to enter harbour in any conditions.

PILOTAGE

From the NE, a long deep water jetty will be seen 2 miles from Arzew constructed parallel to the open beach. From Cap Carbon from the N, a fortress will be seen on the hill above the port. Several lit buoys are marked on chart 838.

Berthing

Berth as directed by the officials.

Formalities

Port of entry with the usual officials in attendance.

Facilities

Water Containers can be filled and a there is a hose in the fish port.
Fuel Diesel in the port.
Provisions Shops a short walk into town.
Post office and *bank* In the town.
Weather forecast Available from the Harbourmaster's office.

A9 Port d'Arzew El Jadid

A huge new complex for supertankers 2M SE of the old commercial port described above. A Port of Entry but not recommended except in an emergency, when it can be entered in any weather.

Location
35°51.0′N 0°18′.0W

Distances
D'Arzew 2M

Charts

	Approach	Port
Admiralty	837	838

Lights
Est approach buoy Fl(3)G.10s
Est Jetée Fl.R.2s
Port de Servitude E breakwater Fl(2)R.6s
W breakwater Fl(2)G.6s
West Jetée Fl.G.2s
Approach buoy W Fl.R.4s

Communications
VHF Ch 16

The port

This is a large new complex built for supertankers 2 miles SE of the old port. No facilities exist for yachts but it may be possible to shelter here in an emergency. Entry possible in any weather.

PILOTAGE

The outer breakwater is over a mile long running parallel to the beach, lit at both ends.

Several lit buoys for tanker discharge are marked on chart 838, W of the port.

Berthing

As directed by officials.

Formalities

Port of entry, but not advised for yachts.

Facilities

Water Not known.
Fuel Not known
Provisions Very small but developing village nearby. Shops at Arzew.
Post office and *bank* In Arzew.

A10 Mostaganem

A commercial port in the Bay of Arzew. A Port of Entry but in 2004 yachtsmen were not permitted to venture ashore beyond the port gates.

Location
35°56′N 0°04′.2E

Distances
Oran 40M
Ténès 75M
Arzew 19M

Charts

	Approach	Port
Admiralty	1909	178, 837
French	5951	–

Lights
Harbour
1. **Jetée du Large** Fl(4)WR.12s17m13/10M 197°-R-234°-W-197° White tower, red top
2. **Mole Sud Ouest head** Oc(2)G.6s13m5M 248°-vis-073° White column, green top
3. **Inside of Jetée du Large** Oc(2)R.6s11m7M
4. **Mole d'Indépendence head** Fl.G.4s11m6M 351.5°-vis-261.5° White hut, green top

Communications
VHF Ch 16

The port

A medium-sized commercial port situated in an agricultural area in the NE corner of the Bay of Arzew. The dusty port is situated on the northern edge of the town and in the summer heat, walking to the centre is tedious. The rather non-descript surroundings of the practically empty port are offset by the friendly officials. Visiting yachts in 2004 experienced a long though courteous reception but were not allowed outside the port, even with the armed guards.

PILOTAGE

By day

Aero RC and radiobeacon on the entrance pier.

By night

At night the lights are obscured by street lights until fairly close.

Berthing

Plenty of room. Moor as directed – usually alongside the NE Quay at the end of the port near the tugboat berth and officials, after clearing customs (see below).

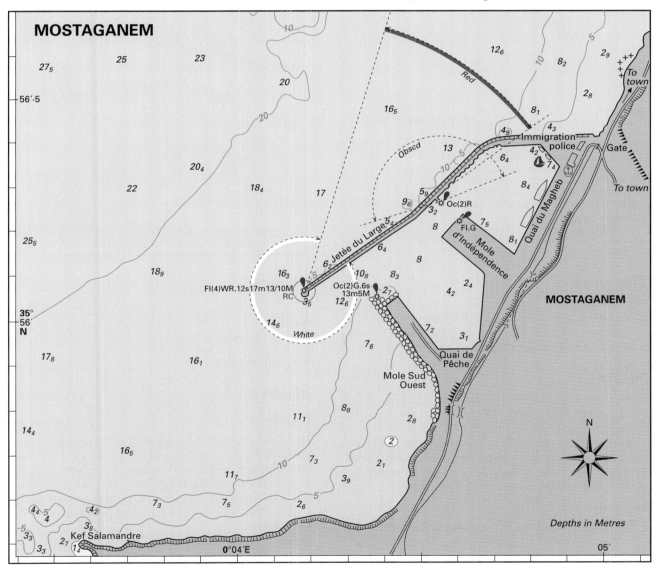

III. ALGERIA

Formalities

Port of entry. Formalities are usually carried out on the Quai de Pesche, SW of the entrance. Yachts are then directed to the NE corner of the port. A permis d'escale is issued to leave the port area. (when this is permissible). Entry formalities, always long in Algeria, took over five hours to complete in summer 2004 and one hour for departure.

Facilities

Water Containers can be filled.
Fuel No diesel in the port.
Provisions From small shops a short walk into town.
Post office and *bank* In the town.
Weather forecast Available from the harbourmaster's office.

ASHORE

At one time Mostaganem was important for exporting wine and cereals but its main activities are now fishing and importing potatoes, sugar and timber. It is a modern, European-style city with around 300,000 inhabitants.

Eating out

Coffee bar at the harbour gate.

A11 Ténès

A commercial port 43M W of Cherchell and a Port of Entry.

Location
36°31′.7N 01°18′.9E

Distances
Mostaganem 75M
Cherchell 43M

Charts

	Approach	Port
Admiralty	1909	178
French	3234	5708

Lights
Approach
1. **Cap Ténès** 36°33′.1N 01°20′.6E Fl(2)10s89m31M White square tower on dwelling
Harbour
2. **Detached breakwater W head** Q.10m10M
3. **Detached breakwater E Head** Iso.G.4s10m6M
4. **Jetée NW head** Oc(2)G.6s10m7M
5. **Jetée NE head** Oc(2)R.6s10m8M
Lights are reported to be unreliable.

Communications
VHF Ch 16

The port

A medium-sized commercial port similar to Mostaganem, with a detached mole. Commercial traffic has declined since the civil war and today's main activity is fishing, leaving plenty of room in the port.

PILOTAGE

Yachts can enter either end of the detached mole, though in strong winds the W end should not be used, to avoid being set down on to the SW jetty.

Both ends of the mole are lit. Note that the port entrance lights are obscured by the detached mole until rounding the mole, enhancing a night approach by giving a light sector as indicated on the chart.

Berthing

Follow instructions from the harbour authorities.

Formalities

Port of entry.

Facilities

Water On the SW quay.
Provisions In the village 1.5km from the port.
Post office and *bank* In the village.

ASHORE

Sites locally

The small village of Ténès, with 15,000 inhabitants, lies 1.5km from the port on a hill. The site of Ténès has Phoenician and Roman origins but there are no monuments remaining from those eras. The old Berber village of Vieux Ténès, 2km S of the new town, is worth a visit if this becomes possible. Just N of the port is a good beach.

3. Cherchell to Azzefoun

A12 Cherchell

One of the most attractive harbours on the Algerian coastline, 34M W of Sidi Ferruch. A Port of Entry.

Location
36°36´.8N 02°11´.5E

Distances
Ténès 45M
Sidi Ferruch 34M

Charts

	Approach	Port
Admiralty	1909, 1910	1710
French	3202	5699

Lights
Approach
1. **Forte Joinville** 36°36´.7N 02°11´.4E Fl(2+1)15s37m21M
   White tower, black lantern
2. **Ecueil du Grand Hammam** 36°36´.9N 02°11´.7E
   Q.13m7M ⚓ card BY
3. **Jetée Joinville head** 36°36´.8N 02°11´.5E Iso.G.4s10m7M
   White tower
Harbour
4. **Quai Nord E end** F.G.7m5M
5. **Quai Est N end** F.R.7m5M

Communications
VHF Ch 16

The port

A very attractive and peaceful harbour. The small town of Cherchell is set amidst green hills and the fishing port is constructed in a natural setting between the coast and an off-lying rock. There is an active fishing fleet operating in the port and the prawn fishermen seem to be prosperous.

PILOTAGE

A submerged wall extends S from Ecueil du Grande Hammam. When entering, round the head of Jetée Joinville at a short distance but keep well clear of Ecueil du Grande Hammam. The small craft harbour S of the port entrance is very shallow. The entrance to the fishing port is narrow with a lively traffic of fishing boats in the early morning and late afternoon. In bad weather the entrance is very dangerous and should not be attempted. The anchorage off Cherchell is very poor; it is entirely exposed and even moderate breezes raise a heavy sea.

Berthing

There is not much room and several fishing boats are moored in the middle. Moor as directed.

Formalities

Port of entry.

Facilities

Water Taps all around the port with plenty of good water which is only turned on in the morning.
Fuel Available only from bowser.
Provisions A good assortment of fresh produce can be found at the market and several small shops around it in the pleasant village, a short walk from the port.
Post office and *bank* In the village.

ASHORE

Sites locally

The history of Cherchell goes back to the Phoenician trading post of Iol which enjoyed great prosperity. Evidence of this period is found in two small museums and some Roman ruins around the town:

The Numidian King Juba II ruled Iol (the old name for Cherchell) with Roman protection from 25BC to AD25. In honour of the Roman emperor he renamed the town Caesarea. Juba was educated in Hellenistic style in Rome and being married to the daughter of the Egyptian Queen Cleopatra, he developed a broad interest in the arts of different civilizations. Consequently, he enriched Caesarea with a large art collection from Mediterranean countries. Even though many of these were copies of classic masterpieces, the importance is significant today because much of the original work has been lost. Some of the best examples are on display in the Louvre in Paris and a mosaic,

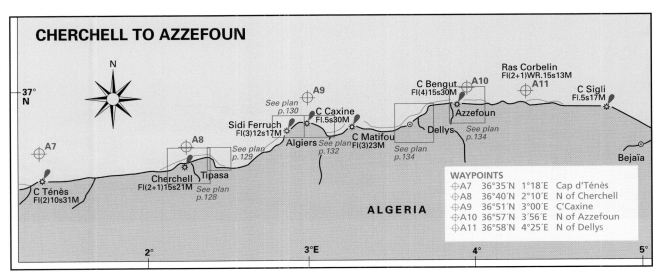

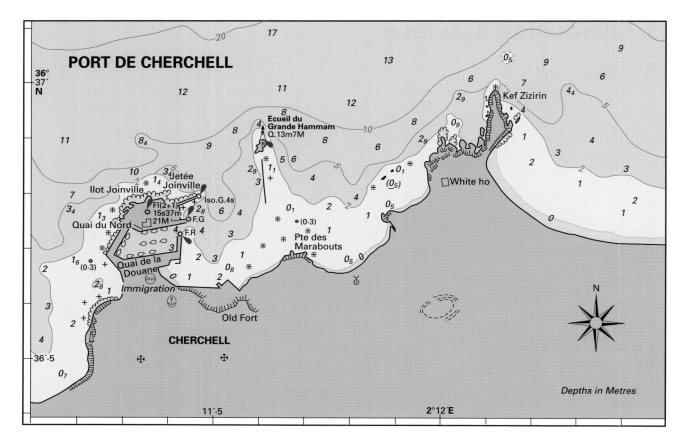

picturing a race horse, decorates the El Djezaïr Hotel in Algiers. Among the collection in the museum of Cherchell are statues of Apollo and the Emperor Augustus. Mosaics are found in the tranquil outdoor museum. Both can easily be visited in one day. Compared to the museums, the Roman ruins are relatively insignificant although they make for a pleasant walk.

Cherchell and the beaches around it are a popular resort area and in summertime Algerian holidaymakers liven up the streets in the village.

Nearby, Tipasa is a modern summer resort in an idyllic setting with unique remains of the Roman era. If the weather makes anchoring there unsafe, Cherchell is a good base for a visit.

Eating out

A seafood restaurant near the port and several eating places in the village.

Cherchell fishing harbour. The basin in the foreground is shallow

A13 Tipasa

A pleasant anchorage in a bay between Ras El Kaliea in the W and the Islets of Sidid Said to the E. The anchorage offers some protection from the W but is exposed from NW to E. In 2004 yachts were turned away.

Location
36°35′.6N 02°27′.1E

Distances
Sidi Ferruch 22M
Algiers 35M

Charts

	Approach	Port
Admiralty	–	178
French	5699	–

Lights
Ras el Kalia Oc.4s32m12M

The anchorage

Tipasa has two ports located either side of a N going mole, both too small and shallow for a yacht but the bay is a pleasant good weather anchorage. It lies between Ras el Kalia in the W and the islets of Sidi Saïd to the E and offers some protection from the W, but is exposed from NW to E. Anchor in 3.6m. Even light onshore breezes can make landing with the dinghy difficult.

Currently it is not possible to use the anchorage facilities (summer 2004).

ASHORE

It is near the interesting ruins of an old Phoenician and Roman trading post which can be visited in the Parc Archéologique. Even though it has been developed on a small scale for tourism, the site amidst the thickly wooded coast is very attractive. The 'Travel Survival Kit' has a good description of its history and archaeology.

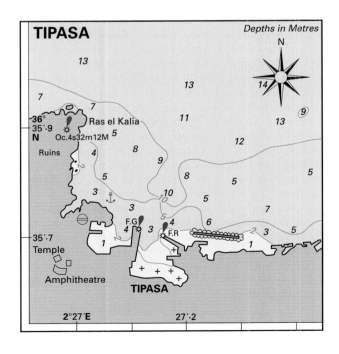

A14 Bou Aroun

A tiny fishing harbour, probably too shallow for most yachts 10M E of Tipasa.

Distances
Tipasa 10M

Location
36°37′.6N 02°39′.5E

Charts
Admiralty 1910
French 3030

The harbour

A very small fishing harbour approximately 10M E of Tipasa. The entrance has depths of around 4m or more, but the port itself is too shallow for most yachts. There are plans to develop this harbour.

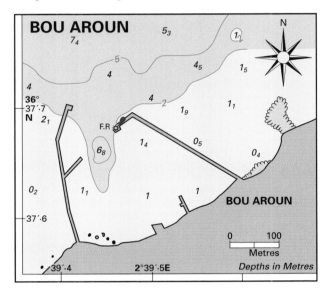

A15 Chiffalo

A very small shallow harbour 1M E of Bou Aroun.

Location
36°38′.4N 02°40′.4E

Distances
Sidi Ferruch 10M

Charts
French 3030

The harbour

A tiny harbour 1M NE of Bou Aroun. The depth outside the port is about 2m and inside the depth is around half a metre deep. There are plans to dredge a channel and develop this harbour.

III. ALGERIA

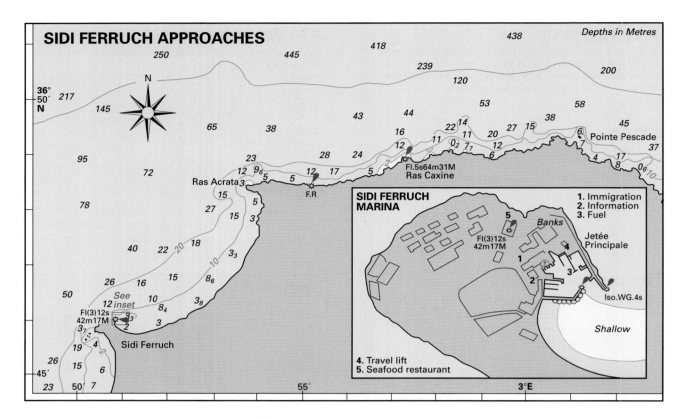

SIDI FERRUCH APPROACHES

Depths in Metres

SIDI FERRUCH MARINA

1. Immigration
2. Information
3. Fuel
4. Travel lift
5. Seafood restaurant

A16 Sidi Ferruch (Sidi Fredj)

The only marina in Algeria and a port of entry. Dilapidated and left undredged it is situated in a large holiday resort 55M W of Dellys on the W side of Cap Caxine.

Location
36°46′N 02°51′E (Light on Jetée Principale)

Distances
Cherchell 34M
Dellys 55M

Charts

	Approach	Port
Admiralty	1910	–
French	3030	–

Lights
Approach
1. **Ras Caxine** 36°48′.8N 02°57′.4E Fl.5s64m31M
075°-vis-300° Yellow square tower, green top
2. **Sidi Fredj Marina** 36°46′N 02°50′.9E Fl(3)12s42m17M
Low tower on hotel
Harbour
3. **Jetée Principale head** Iso.WG.4s14m11/8M
190°-W-129°-G-190°
4. **Marina entrance starboard side** F.G
5. **Marina entrance port side** F.R

Communications
VHF Ch 16

The marina

Sidi Ferruch, (or Sidi Fredj), is a large holiday resort and tourist complex for rich Algerians and Algiers based diplomats, with the only marina in Algeria. It now lacks the facilities normally associated with a marina, having fallen into a state of disrepair. The artificial surroundings of smart restaurants, apartments and hotels give a very distorted view of the country. On the other hand, authorities are used to yachts and it is the port nearest to Algiers, where yachts are unwelcome. Besides beaches there are no particular points of interest and the nearest village, Stauoéli, is 5km away. Most of the yachts in the harbour belong to French and other expatriate diplomats based in Algiers.

PILOTAGE

The peninsula of Sidi Ferruch on the W side of Cap Caxine, is low and unremarkable except for the buildings around the port. When coming from the NW and rounding the marina complex, beware of shoals extending 50-100m offshore. One shoal at the root of Jetée Principale is almost totally submerged. The port side of the entrance has been silted up for several years leaving a channel with depths of less than 2m. Any attempt at entry should be made well to starboard, though silting also occurs around the stb light.

In NE winds of force 5 or more entry should not be attempted, as waves break on the banks around the entrance. Entry in summer 2004 indicated depths of around 1.8m in the entrance and little more on the fuelling jetty with lesser depths elsewhere.

The best way to enter, bearing in mind the shifting sands at the entrance, is to anchor 100M E of the entrance and first check the channel by dinghy to ascertain the route it takes and depths. Local storms are frequent and each one moves the sandbank. This marina is rarely dredged.

Night entry should not be attempted as the harbour lights are unreliable and there are only a few street lights working in the port.

Berthing

Space is severely limited, but with so few visitors, the fuelling jetty is made available. This is the deepest part of the harbour, with depths of around 3m. Officials will be sure to meet and direct you from this jetty. Harbour charges for visitors are high compared with the services available but the first forty eight hours are free of charge. The few visitors' berths available lack any privacy, with hoards of holidaymakers promenading along the quay and speedboats whizzing in and out unrestricted.

Formalities

Port of entry; the authorities are friendly here and used to yachts.

Facilities

Water and *electricity* The water taps on Jetée Principale are broken and only a few electric sockets function. Water is available on the opposite quay and some visitors had submerged hoses to taps there.

Fuel Diesel, petrol and engine oil at the fuel quay. Good quality and very cheap.

Provisions A very limited supply from a so-called supermarket in the harbour. No fresh vegetables, milk, meat or chicken. Reasonable supplies in Staouéli.

Showers Warm showers available near the Harbourmaster's office.

Post office In Staouéli.

Telephone In the hotels.

Foreign Exchange In the hotels at bank rates.

Repairs A 16-ton travel-lift. Emergency repairs can be carried out, providing you can supply any spare parts needed.

ASHORE

Sites locally

The main reason for visiting Sidi Ferruch is its proximity to the beautiful capital of Algeria. Algiers is built like an amphitheatre in green hills which rise steeply from the port and compared with the other big cities in the Maghreb it is the most cosmopolitan. Many prominent buildings from French colonial times have been well maintained and the Arabic character is still found in the ancient kasbah. There are several good museums, mosques and an extraordinarily pretty post office. A tour of the city can best be planned with the tourist information office, when functioning.

Sidi Ferruch was designed by a well-known French architect Fernand Pouillon, an enthusiastic sailor who spent the last years of his life on board his boat there. After his death in France, his boat was set up as a monument in the port.

Eating out

Several very expensive restaurants around the port and a good French-style seafood restaurant at the end of the small channel which cuts across the peninsula.

Transport

Buses every 30 minutes to Algiers. Bus stop outside the harbour and the ride takes about 45 minutes. Trips with excursion buses to Algiers can be arranged at the hotels.

A17 Algiers

A large commercial and military port in the capital, situated in the Bay of Algiers. Yachts are only permitted entry in an emergency and not without authority.

Location
36°46′.5N 03°05′E

Distances
Sidi Ferruch 12M
Dellys 42M

Charts

	Approach	Port
Admiralty	1910, 855	2555
French	3043	5638

Lights
Approach
1. **Roche M'Tahen** 36°47′.8N 03°04′.1E Q(3)10s12m8M ♦ card BYB
2. **Port d'Alger Jetée Kheireddine head** 36°46′.7N 03°04′.8E Fl(2)3s23m16M Horn Mo(N)30s Metal tower 154°-vis-055° RC F.R lights on radio masts 2.6M NW

Harbour
3. **Jetée Kheireddine spur** Fl.G.4s10m11M
4. **Jetée du Vieux Port N end** Fl.R.4s10m12M
4. **Jetée de Mustapha spur** Iso.G.4s12m12M 295°-vis-104° White tower, green top
5. **Passe Sud Brise-lames Est head** Oc.R.4s12m13M 005°-vis-312° White tower, red top 5F.R(vert) on each of 2 radio masts 1.07M SSW Fl.R(by day F.R) on Memorial des martyrs 1M SSW

Communications
VHF Ch 16

The port

Algiers is a very large and busy port with commercial, military and fishing harbours. Yachts have always been redirected to Sidi Ferruch, even when it is impossible to enter that marina. Protests regarding depths and room there usually fall on deaf ears.

Entry into Algiers port can be granted in an emergency which must be approved through communications with the harbour authorities on VHF Ch 16.

PILOTAGE

Entry to the port is very straightforward with no off-lying dangers once round Cap Caxine or coming from the E.

Berthing

The port may only be entered by yachts in an emergency. If entry is necessary, ask permission by VHF on Ch 16. If granted permission to enter, yachts are usually berthed on mole El Djezair S of the fishing area.

Formalities

Very strict officious formalities, but done with courtesy and efficiency. Yachts are simply not welcome here and never have been.

Facilities

None except local shopping. The local bakeries produce some of the finest bread in the Maghreb.

III. ALGERIA

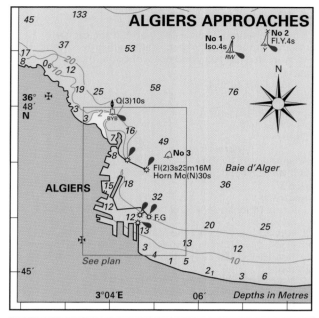

ALGIERS APPROACHES
Baie d'Alger
See plan
Depths in Metres

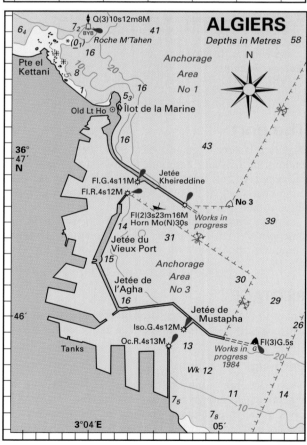

ALGIERS
Depths in Metres
Roche M'Tahen
Pte el Kettani
Anchorage Area No 1
Old Lt Ho
Îlot de la Marine
Jetée Kheireddine
Fl.G.4s11M
Fl.R.4s12M
Fl(2)3s23m16M Horn Mo(N)30s
Works in progress
Jetée du Vieux Port
Jetée de l'Agha
Anchorage Area No 3
Jetée de Mustapha
Iso.G.4s12M
Oc.R.4s13M
Tanks
Works in progress 1984
Wk 12

ASHORE

The capital of Algeria with nearly 4 million inhabitants is a spectacular city. The ancient souk has been the site of uprisings against the government and retains a medieval atmosphere. The people are very conservative but typically inquisitive and hospitable. (Apart from officials in the port!)

A18 La Pérouse

A scenic anchorage on the E side of the Bay of Algiers near Cap Matifou, sheltered from the E and N with good holding.

Location
36°48′.3N 03°14′.0E

Distances
Algiers 8M

Charts
Admiralty 855

Lights
1. **Pier head** F.R.10m7M White column, red top, on hut
   Obscd by Cap Matifou when bearing more than 145°
2. The existence of **Ras Matifou buoy** (Iso.R.4s) is uncertain.

PILOTAGE

Coming from the E, keep well clear of Cap Matifou. The islands on the NE end of the cape have rocks around them and overfalls extend half a mile off the cape.

The anchorage

This anchorage in the NE corner of the Bay of Algiers, just S of Cap Matifou, offers good holding and excellent protection from easterlies. A pier juts out SSW from the headland; anchor behind it between local boats or take a vacant mooring if available. The 'harbour' is well silted A good stop-over between Sidi Ferruch and Dellys. Officials are friendly but not accustomed to visiting yachts and they may insist that you row ashore with them to do the routine paperwork. Ensure the authorities in your previous port of call are informed of your visit beforehand.

ASHORE

Sites locally

To the S is the small beach resort, Alger Plage, and the ruins of the old Phoenician and Roman city, Rusguniae.

Eating out

There is a restaurant in the village and traditional tea houses.

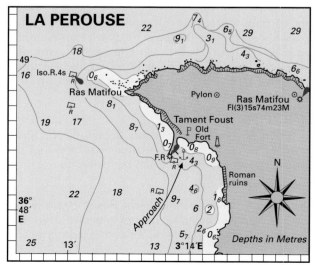

LA PEROUSE
Iso.R.4s
Ras Matifou
Pylon
Ras Matifou Fl(3)15s74m23M
Tament Foust
Old Fort
F.R
Roman ruins
Approach
Depths in Metres

A19 Zemmouri Bahar (formerly Courbet Marine)

A small, shallow harbour between Cap Matifou and Dellys.

Location
36°48′.3N 03°33′.6E

Distances
Dellys 18M

Charts
Admiralty 1910

Lights
Jetée Nord head 36°48′.3N 03°33′.6E Q.12m10M White tower red top
NW pier 36°48′.3N 03°33′.6E Fl.G.5s17m7M

The harbour

A small harbour between Cap Matifou and Dellys. Depth in the entrance is 4–5m but shoals to less than 1.5m towards the west breakwater and the beach in the SE corner of the harbour. Silting occurs and the approach should be made with care. This is not a port of entry.

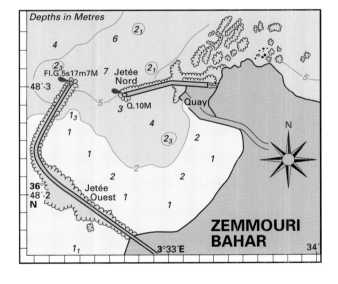

A20 Dellys

A small commercial and fishing port and port of entry on the E side of Cap Bengut.

Location
36°54′.8N 03°55′.2E

Distances
Sidi Ferruch 55M
Bejaïa 60M

Charts
BA 1910, 1710

Lights
Approach
1. **Cap Bengut** 36°55′.4N 03°53′.7E Fl(4)15s63m30M 079°-vis-287° Obscd by Pointe de Dellys when bearing less than 270° White square tower green top
2. **Pointe de Dellys** 36°55′.4N 03°55′.4E F.R.41m15M 066°-vis-336° obscd by Cap Bengut when bearing less than 094° Yellow tower, red lantern
Harbour
3. **Jetée head** Oc.4s12m9M Obscd by Point de Dellys when bearing less than 193° White tower, green top
4. **Quay Sud SE corner** Oc.R.4s8m5M Obscd by Point de Dellys when bearing less than 203° White tower, red top.

Communications
VHF Ch 16

The port

A small commercial and fishing port although, as with many of the smaller commercial ports in Algeria, not much frequented in recent years by merchantmen. There is an active fleet of fishing boats which produce considerable wash in the port and if tied up alongside one of them, good fenders are needed. Protection is mediocre and northerly winds set up a considerable swell. There is not much room for yachts but it may be possible to anchor in the port or temporarily pick up a vacant mooring.

PILOTAGE

By day

From Pointe de Dellys a shallow spit extends 0.3M NE and the remains of a small jetty extends to the SE of the point. Keep well clear of the point which has a rocky ledge extending NE. A west-setting counter current

Dellys harbour viewed from the SE

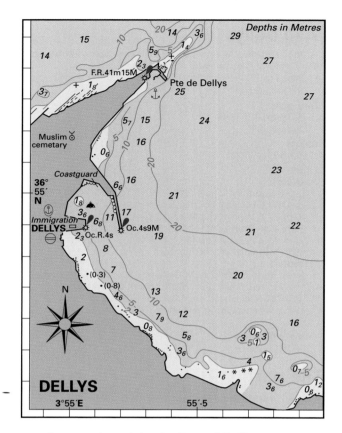

DELLYS

3°55'E   55'.5

may be experienced in the Bay of Dellys, turning N close to the port entrance and bending NE off Pointe de Dellys to join the main E current along the coast.

The harbour lights often do not function, though entry by night would be straightforward.

Berthing

As directed. Beware of the wake from passing fishing boats, which can be dangerous when tied up alongside the W quay. It is preferable to go further inside the port near the coastguard boat if the officials allow. Alternatively one may find a free mooring or room to anchor in the port (with tripping line). Holding is not very good; the best place may be SSE of Pointe de Dellys in sand 15–25m deep. Close to the point the bottom is rocky.

Formalities

Port of entry and the officials are pleasant to deal with.

Facilities

Water Only near the coastguard boat in the N corner.
Provisions A reasonable assortment of fresh produce in the village.
Post office and *bank* In the village.

ASHORE

Dellys is a pleasant and lively village set against green wooded hills and is one of the more attractive places along the Algerian coast.

Eating out

A few eating houses in the village.

A21 Azzefoun (formerly Port Gueydon)

A small harbour consisting of a single pier SW of Cap Corbelin, offering little protection.

Location
36°54.2'N 04°25'.3E

Distances
Bejaïa 35M
Dellys 25M

Charts
Admiralty 1910

Lights
Jetty head Oc(2)R.6s6m4M Obscd by Cap Corbelin White pedestal, red head on jetty head

The harbour

Azzefoun is a small town S of Cap Corbelin with a harbour consisting of a single pier extending SW. A new harbour is being built, which was begun several years ago and which is still incomplete. Little protection is offered.

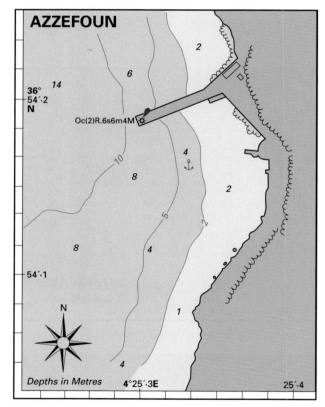

4. Bejaïa to Port Methanier

A22 Bejaïa

A large commercial port situated in spectacular surroundings S of Cap Carbon, 64M E of Dellys. It is very sheltered and with plenty of room and a port of entry.

Location
36°45′.2N 05°06′.1E

Distances
Dellys 64M
Jijel 34M

Charts

	Approach	Port
Admiralty	1910, 252	1710
French	3029	5641

Lights
Approach
1. **Ras Carbon** 36°46′.6N 05°06′.3E Fl(3)15s220m28M Obscd by Cap Noir when bearing more than 333° White round tower on house
Auxiliary Fl.WR.1.5s32m10/7M 094°-W-114°-R (obscd by coast)-126°-W-295°-W (obscd by coast)-316° White round tower, square dwelling
Harbour
2. **Jetée Est head** 36°45′.2N 05°06′.2E Oc.4s16m12M Obscd by Cap Bouak when bearing less than 205°
3. **Jetée Sud head** 36°45′.2N 05°06′.0E Oc(2)R.6s11m10M
4. **Vieux Port entrance N side** F.G
5. **Vieux Port entrance S side** F.R

Communications
VHF Ch 16

The port

The commercial port of Bejaïa is large and dusty but the town and beautiful surrounding mountains make up for it. If one can put up with the discomforts of the port, Bejaïa tops the list of interesting places to visit on the Algerian coast. There is plenty of room in the Vieux Port and it is secure in all weather.

PILOTAGE

Straightforward with no off-lying dangers. Jebel Arbalou 1317m high, about 10M W of Bejaïa, is visible from over 50M in clear weather. Ras Carbon is easy to make out

Bejaïa commercial port and fishing harbour

with the lighthouse on top and the remarkable gate at the foot. From the North, Bejaïa is not visible until well around Ras Carbon.

Berthing

As directed. Yachts are usually accommodated in the W corner of the Vieux Port, close to the harbour gate leading into town. Announce your arrival by VHF Ch 16 and a pilot boat will probably accompany you to a berth.

Formalities

Port of Entry. PAF found at the ferry terminal and are friendly. This is one of the best places in Algeria to carry out the formalities, which only take 2 to 3 hours: half the usual time!

Facilities

Water Available at a tap 25m from the harbour gate.

See plan p.136
See plan p.138
See plan p.143

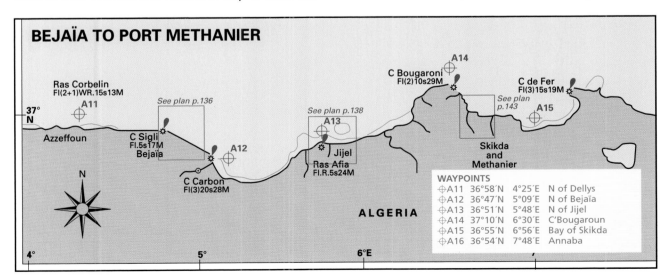

BEJAÏA TO PORT METHANIER

Ras Corbelin
Fl(2+1)WR.15s13M
A11
37°N
Azzeffoun
C Sigli
Fl.5s17M
Bejaïa
A12
C Carbon
Fl(3)20s28M
N
A13
Jijel
Ras Afia
Fl.R.5s24M
A14
C Bougaroni
Fl(2)10s29M
C de Fer
Fl(3)15s19M
A15
Skikda
and
Methanier
ALGERIA
4°
5°
6°E

WAYPOINTS			
⊕A11	36°58′N	4°25′E	N of Dellys
⊕A12	36°47′N	5°09′E	N of Bejaïa
⊕A13	36°51′N	5°48′E	N of Jijel
⊕A14	37°10′N	6°30′E	C'Bougaroun
⊕A15	36°55′N	6°56′E	Bay of Skikda
⊕A16	36°54′N	7°48′E	Annaba

III. ALGERIA

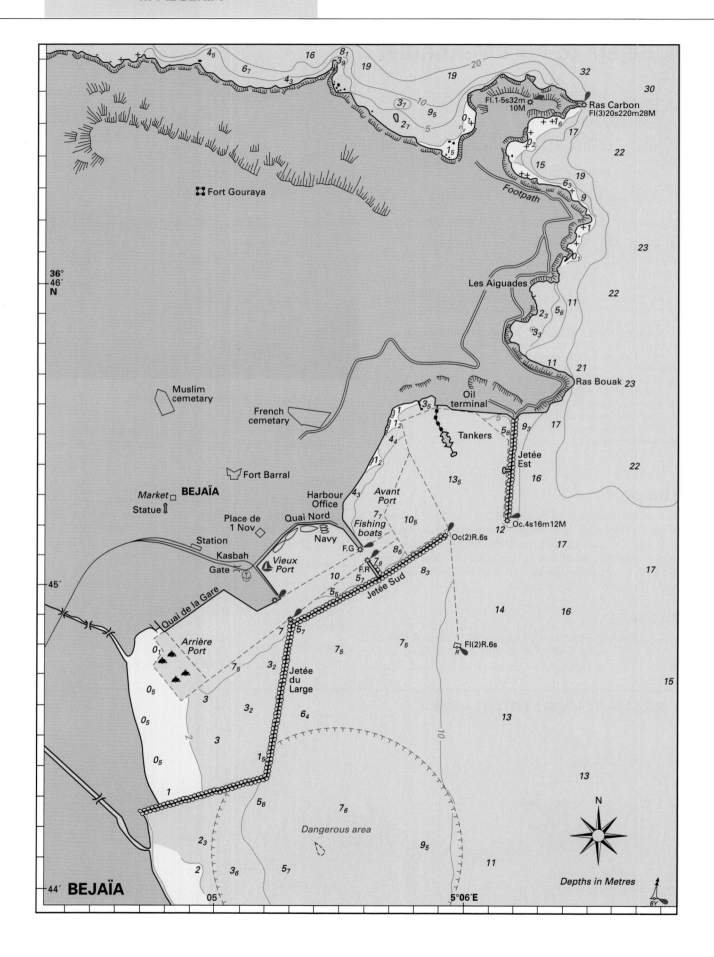

Fort Gouraya

Ras Carbon
Fl.1·5s32m 10M
Fl(3)20s220m28M

Footpath

Les Aiguades

Ras Bouak

Oil terminal

Tankers

Jetée Est

Oc.4s16m12M

Muslim cemetary

French cemetary

Fort Barral

BEJAÏA

Market
Statue

Place de 1 Nov

Station

Kasbah
Gate

Harbour Office

Quai Nord

Navy
F.G

Vieux Port

Avant Port

Fishing boats

F.R

Jetée Sud

Oc(2)R.6s

Fl(2)R.6s

Quai de la Gare

Arrière Port

Jetée du Large

Dangerous area

N

Depths in Metres

BY

BEJAÏA

Cap Carbon N of Bejaïa port

Fuel Diesel available in the port.

Provisions A few small shops and good market not far from the port. Once outside the harbour gate walk along the street parallel to the train tracks in the shade of the trees and turn right at the statue at the end. The market is 50m from the statue.

Post office and *bank* In the centre of town.

Note The banks in town did not have any cash in summer 2004. Only the bank in the port would change money as required for official purchases.

ASHORE

Sites locally

It is a short walk from the port into the lively town and to a well stocked market. Although many buildings have been neglected since independence, the evidence of prosperity under French rule is apparent, from pleasant squares and stylish architecture throughout the town. From Place de Novembre 1 in the town centre, there is a beautiful view of the harbour and the Bay of Bejaïa which, without exaggeration, is one of the prettiest on the North African coast. Once outside the town, a path cut out of the rocks leads to the cape via Les Aiguades, which has a small cosy restaurant where wine and beer are served. Views from the path over the Bay of Bejaïa are splendid and even in mid-summer it is cool and quiet.

The coast north of the port is rough with mountains dropping steeply into the sea and a visit to Bejaïa is not complete without walking up to the lighthouse on Ras Carbon, one of the highest in the Mediterranean. The surrounding shoreline is rich in fish and excellent for snorkelling.

There are Roman ruins at Djemila.

Other worthwhile excursions a little further away, requiring a taxi, are to Pic des Singes with its wild monkeys and to Fort Gouraya with splendid views across to the high peaks of the Djurdjura Massif. Alternatively, it is worthwhile hiring a car to go further inland and explore the mountainous Kabylie region. There is a small museum in Bejaïa at Place de Novembre 1 with paintings of landscapes of the Kabylie and its friendly people, the original inhabitants of Algeria from pre-Islamic times.

Eating out

Several restaurants in town.

Transport

Regular ferry service to Marseille and other Algerian ports. Train and air service to Algiers.

Always work for fishermen – at sea and in harbour
Graham Hutt

A23 Jijel

A commercial and fishing port, 34M E of Bejaïa and Port of Entry.
Now declared a military zone.

Location
36°49'.5N 05°47'E

Distances
Bejaïa 34M
Collo 48M

Charts

	Approach	Port
Admiralty	252	1712
French	3029, 3023	–

Lights
Approach
1. **Ras el Afia** 36°49'.2N 05°41'.5E Fl.R.5s43m24M 027°-vis-255° Obscd by Cap Cavallo when bearing less than 064° Yellow 8-sided tower, red top.

Harbour
2. **Jetée Nord** Oc(1+2)WR.12s19m12/9M Yellow square tower, black top 096°-R-101°-W-096° Obscd by the heights of Picouleau when bearing less than 094° F.R lights on masts 4.4M ESE
3. **Jetée Nord head** Iso.G.4s9m6M Black column
4. **Nouveau mole** Fl.R.4s
5. **Jetée Sud head** F.R.7m3M Red column
6. **Inner harbour entrance** F.R/F.G

Communications
VHF Ch 16

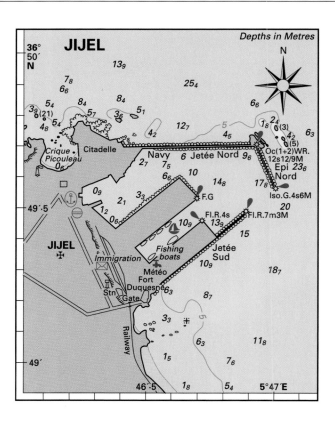

The port

This commercial port is used by a small fishing fleet, and freighters regularly call at the SE basin. The port entry layout has been modified recently (Dec 2004) but no revised plans are available.

The NW corner of the port along Jetée Nord is used by the Algerian navy

Note: The harbour was considered a military zone in 2004. Yachts were told to anchor by day south of the mole outside the port, but to enter at night for police protection.

PILOTAGE

Beware of rocks 300m NE of the islet in Jetée Nord. Particular care should be taken at night since they are only covered by a narrow red sector of the approach light on the islet.

Berthing

During strong summer easterlies a considerable swell enters the port. Berth as directed or anchor in 6 to 8m of coarse sand due south of the SW mole. Rocks line the corner of the anchorage but are clearly visible by day.

Formalities

Port of entry.

Facilities

Water In the S corner of Quai Sud.
Provisions A good assortment from several shops and a market in the village.
Post office and *bank* Along the main street in the village.

Weather forecast Can be requested from the Météo office on the way out of the port.

ASHORE

The coast around Jijel is less spectacular than that to the West or East and the town is flat without any grandeur, but not unpleasant and the many tea houses remind one more of Morocco than Algeria. People are friendly. A good assortment of fresh produce can be found in several shops and the market, not far from the port. The long beaches east of Jijel are popular but not overcrowded with holidaymakers.

Eating out

Some simple eating houses in the village.

A24 Djen Djen

A large new commercial port 3M E of Jijel with no facilities for yachts.

Location
36°49′N 05°51′E

The port

A large container and mineral port, 5 miles East of Jijel. The ambitious plans for this port included a new railroad to be built. No place for yachts and no information available on the port.

A25 Mersa Zeitoun

An anchorage with good protection from the E, on the W side of Cap Bougaroun, 25M E of Jilel.

Location
36°57′N 06°16′E

Distances
Jilel 25M
Collo 20M

Charts
Admiralty 252

The anchorage

An excellent anchorage in E winds in a cove between a shoal spit and an islet with two conical summits at the S entrance point.

A26 Casabianca

An anchorage well sheltered from the N and E 1M N of Mersa Zeitoun.

Location
36°58′.2N 06°15′.3E

Distances
Mersa Zeitoun 1M

Charts
Admiralty 252

The anchorage

Anchorage with shelter from N and E winds 1M North of Mersa Zeitoun. Anchor in sand 10–12m deep off the beach near the house with a red roof. Yachts anchoring here in 2004 reported no problems and were made welcome.

A27 Collo

A scenic bay and one of the best open anchorages in Algeria, 48M E of Jijel , providing excellent shelter from the W and N. Amazingly, also a port of entry.

Location
37°00′.3N 06°34′.5E

Distances
Jijel 48M
Stora 19M

Charts

	Approach	Port
Admiralty	252	1712
French	3023	–

Lights
Approach
1. **Cap Collo** 37°01.0N 06°35′.1E Fl.G.5s26m12M 146°-vis-323° White 8-sided tower, green lantern.
Harbour
2. **Jetée head** F.G Obscd when bearing less than 221° White column, black lantern

Communications
VHF Ch 16

The anchorage and harbour

The scenic Bay of Collo is one of the best open anchorages in Algeria with excellent shelter from W and N winds. It is reasonably comfortable in light E winds, but becomes untenable if they reach gale force.

One breakwater with a single quay forms the port which is crowded with a small fishing fleet. Occasionally cork is exported from the port which is loaded by freighter from small barges.

PILOTAGE

Straightforward by day. The light at the end of the breakwater frequently does not work and night entry is not recommended. The quay is crowded and fishing boats are moored all around it.

Berthing

In summer 2004 yachts were directed to moor alongside the pilot boat on the mole, although the anchorage SW

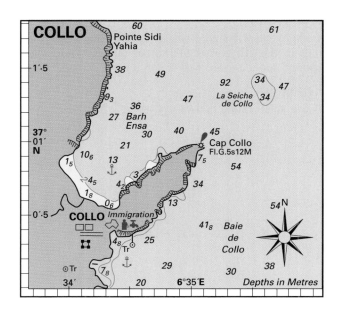

III. ALGERIA

Bay of Collo: anchorage of the fishing quay viewed from the S

of the mole was also available.

Anchor 200m SW of the quay in sand about 6m deep. Watch out for the mooring lines from boats anchored in the bay and stern lines from fishing boats at the quay. Alternatively one may anchor in Barh Ensa, in the cove N of Collo after formalities are complete.

Formalities

Port of Entry; the authorities are relaxed. It is best to take paperwork along when going ashore. The capitain du port (Toutaoui Belkacem) is very friendly and helpful.

Facilities

Water From a tap in the middle of the quay.
Fuel Diesel pump on the quay but some fishing boats would have to be moved.
Provisions Reasonable supply of fresh produce in the village.
Post office and *bank* In the village.

ASHORE

Sites locally

Collo, a small friendly village nestling amongst green hills in the NE corner of the bay and the untouched country around it are well worth a visit.

Eating out

A few small eating houses nearby.

A28 Pointe Esrah

A beautiful good weather anchorage on the E side of Pt Esra, 5M NW of Skikda, ideal for snorkelling.

Location
36°57′.4N 06°50′.9E

Distances
Skikda 5M
Collo 13M

Charts
Admiralty 855

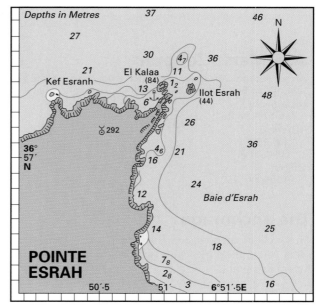

The anchorage

One of the several beautiful, peaceful anchorages along this part of the coast. Not very well protected but there is no problem in good weather and it is a paradise for snorkelling. Anchor SW of El Kalaa islet in clearly visible sand patches between the rocks, all in depths of 6–8m. (Admiralty charts are not detailed enough to show depths properly.) A few fishermen passing by from Stora will probably be the only company.

ASHORE

The Bay of Esrah, SE of the anchorage, has a beautiful beach and the area has been destined for future tourist development.

A29 Stora

A small fishing harbour S of Ile Srigina, 1M N of Skikda, with reasonable protection in bad weather. In summer 2004 it was prohibited to yachts.

Location
36°54´.1N 06°52´.9E

Distances
Jijel 62M
Collo 19M
Skikda 1M
Chetaïbi 31M
Annaba 55M

Charts

	Approach	Port
Admiralty	252, 855	–
French	3061	–

Lights
Approach
1. **Ile Srigina** 36°56´.3N 06°53´.3E Fl.R.5s54m13M Obscd by Pte Esrah when bearing less than 122° White square tower, red top.
2. **Ilot des Singes** 36°54´.4N 06°53´.1E F.WG.17m10/6M 193.5°-G-216°-W-023°-G-080°. White square tower, green lantern.
Harbour
3. **E Mole head** F.G White tower, green top
4. **Jetée head** F.R Pylon, red top

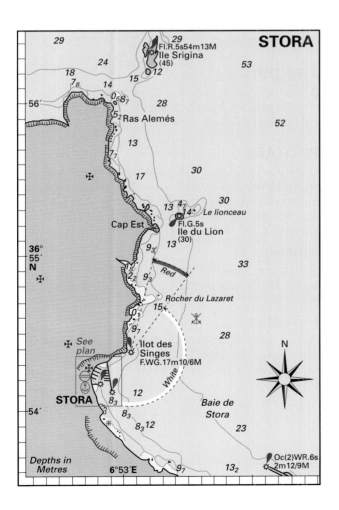

The harbour

Currently (summer 2004), entry to the harbour is prohibited. Yachts were directed to Skikda. However, the following notes are still valid.

A tiny fishing harbour on the W side of the Bay of Skikda with a small section reserved for Algerian pleasure boats. The village of Stora, with its steep streets rising directly from the waterfront, is untidy but pretty. The people are very friendly and it is a much more pleasant port than Skikda itself. The harbour offers reasonable protection but in bad weather, due to the surge and swell, the larger fishing boats move to Skikda, which is better protected. In strong N winds heavy seas roll into the Bay of Skikda; entry into both Stora and Skikda is dangerous under such conditions when a considerable swell enters the harbour.

PILOTAGE

When entering the Bay of Skikda from NW the commercial port of Skikda and the petrochemical port with refineries to the E are easily recognised, but Stora will not be visible until S of Ilot des Singes. The gas flares from the refinery behind Port Methanier are visible from over 20M when in operation. Local fishing boats do not use running lights at night.

Berthing

Tie up on one of the finger piers or alongside a fishing boat. Beware of warps crossing the finger berths when bad weather is expected.

Formalities

Friendly authorities, including Customs, are to be found at the port. A second visit from the Skikda Customs can be expected.

Facilities

Water Containers can be filled in a coffee bar at the port or at the fishmongers along the N quay.

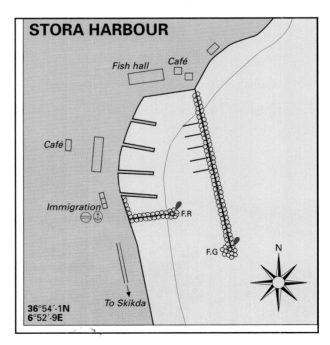

III. ALGERIA

Fuel Available at the end of the first fishing quay.

Provisions Limited supply of fresh produce from inconspicuous small shops, otherwise an exceptionally good market and good general shopping is found in nearby Skikda.

Post office 50m from the port.

Transport Regular buses from the port to the centre of Skikda. Car hire in Skikda.

Weather forecast From the capitainerie in Skikda or on request via VHF.

ASHORE

Sites locally

The modern town of Skikda with its important commercial and petrochemical ports is only a short bus ride from Stora. It is hard to see the attraction of Skikda but it is interesting to see what the socialist system has done for this city. When the French started construction of Skikda in 1838 all the ruins of the original Roman city of Rusicade were unfortunately destroyed. A more worthwhile trip is to Constantine, 90km inland. Built in a unique and strategic location on a high plateau cut out by the Rhumel River, Constantine has always played an important role in history. It is an easy journey from Skikda by train or bus. More information can be provided by the tourist information office in Skikda near the port.

Eating out

There is a good sea-food restaurant in the port even though it looks unpretentious from the outside. Other restaurants on the road to Skikda. Coffee bars in the NE corner of the port and along the path to Ilot des Singes.

Fishing harbour of Stora with Skikda left in the background

A30 Skikda (formerly Philippeville)

A large commercial port 30M W of Chetaibi and a port of entry; generally sheltered but uncomfortable in strong N winds due to heavy surge, when entry is hazardous.

Location
36°53′.6N 06°54′E

Distances
Jijel 63M
Stora 1M
Chetaïbi 30
Annaba 54M

Charts

	Approach	Port
Admiralty	252	855, 1720
French	3061	5787

Lights
Approach
1. **Ile Srigina** 36°56′.3N 06°53′.3E Fl.R.5s54m13M Obscd by Pte Esrah when bearing less than 122° White square tower, red top
2. **Jetée Nord head** 36°53′.6N 06°54′.2E Oc(2)WR.6s21m12/9M 160°-W-288°-R-160° White tower, red top

Harbour
3. **Jetée Nord Traverse Nord** 36°53′.5N 06°54′.3E F.R.10m6M 296°-vis-126° White tower, red top F.R.4M marks oil berth 750m ESE
4. **Jetée Sud (château vert)** 36°53′.4N 06°54′.3E F.G.10m5M 109°-vis-011° White tower, green top

Communications
VHF Ch 16

The port

A large and active commercial port which once had its own yacht basin. Port Methanier is located 2M E of the old commercial port.

PILOTAGE

Gas flares from the refinery behind the Port Methanier are visible from over 20M when lit. Local fishing boats use no running lights at night. In strong N winds heavy seas roll into the Bay of Skikda and entry is difficult and dangerous.

Berthing

Surge enters even the inner part of the port in strong N winds. Berthing is directed to Quai Sud, alongside the police post.

Formalities

Port of entry. Customs are friendly but business-like. Gate passes are issued for every crew member wishing to visit the town and foreign currency is usually checked.

A31 Port Methanier

A large new oil terminal port 2M E of Skikda only of interest in an emergency. Open to the E but good protection from the W and with easy entry. A port of entry.

Location
36°53´.8N 06°57´E

Distances
Skikda 2M

Charts

	Approach	Port
Admiralty	252	855
French	3061	5787

Lights
N Jetée head Fl.G.4s16m 10M
S Jetée head Oc.R.4s10m7M
Buoy N of entry Fl(2)R.6s
Transit lights Ldg Oc.5s *Rear* Oc.5s

Communications
VHF Ch 16

The port

A large new oil terminal port located 2M E of Skikda.

Of no interest to yachts, but offering easy entry and protection from the W in the event of an emergency or storms from the west. Open to the E.

PILOTAGE

Gas flares S of the refinery behind the port are visible from over 20M when in operation. Large tankers moor just E of the port.

Berthing

Berth as directed, but most likely you will be asked to go to Skikda.

Formalities

Port of entry.

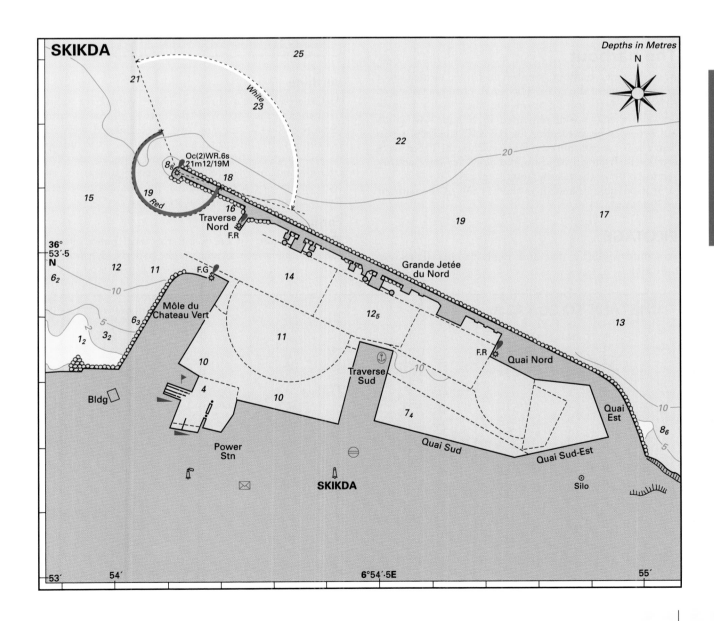

5. Chetaïbi to El Kala

A32 Chetaïbi (Mersa Takouch)

A small harbour in beautiful surroundings 22M W of Annaba, well protected from the N and NW.

Location
37°04′N 07°23′.5E

Distances
Stora 31M
Annaba 22M

Charts

	Approach	Port
Admiralty	2121, 252	1712
French	3024	–

Lights
Approach
1. **Cap Takouch** 37°04′.7N 07°23′.5E Oc.WR.4s128m8/5M
140°-W-278°-R (over Roche Akcine)-290°-W-320°
Harbour
2. **Jetée Est head** F.G.9m2M White column
3. **Jetée Ouest head** F.R.8m White column

Communications
VHF Ch 16

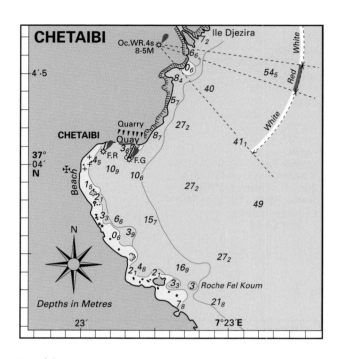

The harbour

Another open harbour, similar to Collo, nestled in a beautiful part of the coast. This small port, consisting of three jetties projecting from the shore with a quay between them, is well protected in N and NW winds but provides no protection in NE and E winds, when heavy seas can roll into the Bay of Takouch. There are a few small fishing boats moored and the only activity seems to be at the nearby granite quarry.

It is possible to anchor in the bay SW of the harbour in 10m sand.

PILOTAGE

Straightforward by day and night though lights are unreliable.

Berthing

As directed by the authorities. There is space for yachts to anchor in the bay SW of the port in 10 metres sand. (Summer 2004.) Shopping trips are arranged with the police by VHF and a three man armed escort is prompt in pre-arranged timing. The local people are very friendly and many invitations are received here to visit their homes for a meal. Under present circumstances this is unfortunately impossible.

Formalities

This not a port of entry, but the local police do not seem to mind yachts calling. Take paperwork ashore.

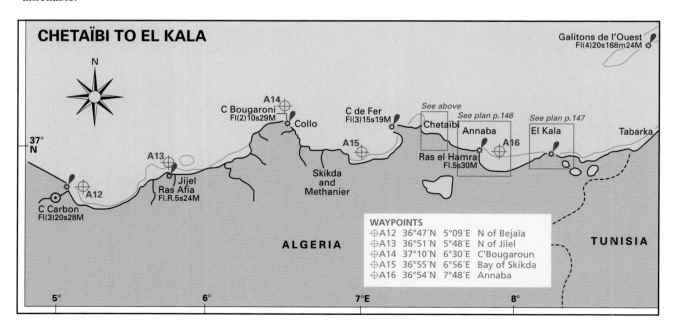

Facilities

Water No water in the port.
Provisions A few provisions can be found in the village a short walk up the hill.

ASHORE

The village and its location, tucked in the corner of the Takouch peninsula, is pretty. A charming place to stay in good weather to do some snorkelling.

Anchorage between the two jetties of Chetaïbi

A33 Annaba (formerly Bône)

One of the best protected commercial ports in Algeria, 49M W of Tabarka and a good fuel stop if en route to Tunisia. A port of entry.

Location
   36°54′.2N 07°47′.9E (50m E of entrance)

Distances
   Stora 55M
   Chetaïbi 27M
   El Kala 33M
   Tabarka 49M

Charts

	Approach	Port
Admiralty	2121	1567
French	4314, 3024	5669

Lights
Approach
1. **Cap de Garde** 36°58′.1N 07°47′.1E Fl.5s143m30M Grey square tower, white dwelling
2. **Fort Génois** 36°57′N 07°46′.6E Oc(2)6s61m10M 240°-obscd-263° within 0.5M White tower on building

Harbour
3. **Jetée du Lion head** 36°54′.3N 07°47′.1E Oc(3)G.12s16m9M White tower
4. **Quai Sud head** 36°54′.2N 07°46′.9E Oc(2)R.6s16m10M White tower
5. **Quai Sud N corner** 36°54′.2N 07°46′.8E F.R
6. **Mole head N side of fishing port (La Grenouillère)** F.G.3m2M
7. **Mole head S side of fishing port (La Grenouillère)** F.R.3m2M

Communications
   VHF Ch 16

The port

The large and active commercial port of Annaba is one of the best protected in Algeria.

If en-route to Tunisia, Annaba is a good port to fill up with diesel which is very cheap and good quality. Available in the fishing port, if the authorities allow you there to refuel.

Expect an armed guard to accompany any shopping trips (see Introduction page 112).

PILOTAGE

Straightforward but keep well to starboard at the entrance as Avant Port Freighters use tugboats to leave the port and need a large turning circle.

Berthing

The port has several basins but yachts are now directed to the inner SW corner alongside the police building in 'Petite Darse', not as previously to La Grenouillere. The latter fishing port in the NE end of the port is currently a prohibited area for yachts (summer 2004).

Formalities

Port of entry. Authorities are not particularly friendly.

Facilities

Water Available in cans.
Electricity Not available.
Fuel In the fishing port, (if they allow you in).
Provisions Not very convenient. Bread may be found in two small shops in the kasbah not far from the port but for

III. ALGERIA

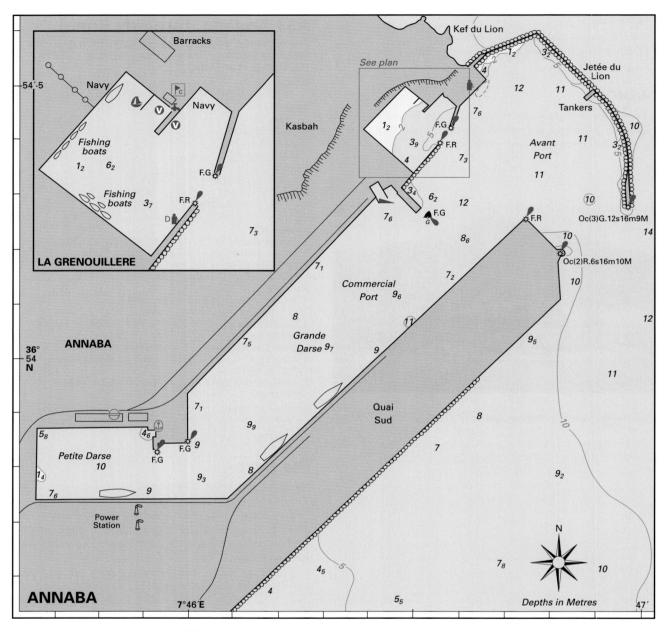

ANNABA

7°46'E

major provisioning take a taxi (about 15 minutes) to the new town.

Post office and *bank* In the centre of town.

ASHORE

The centre of Annaba is quite pleasant but it is a long walk through a shabby part of the harbour to reach it.

Sites locally

Not recommended and probably not allowed at present. Only 2km South of Annaba are the remains of the Roman city Hippo Regius with an interesting museum. In Annaba itself no monuments have been left from its long history.

Eating out

Nothing near the port but several eating places in the centre of town. Tea in the clubhouse.

A34 El Kala (formerly La Calle)

A small fishing harbour 9M W of the Tunisian border, prone to silting.

Location
36°54′.2N 08°26′.5E

Distances
Annaba 34M
Tabarka 15M

Charts

	Approach	Port
Admiralty	2121	1712
French	4314, 3424	–

Lights
Harbour
Entrance E side 36°54′N 08°26′.5E F.R.17m9M

Communications
VHF Ch 16

The harbour

This small fishing harbour is formed by an islet, Ilôt de France, which has been connected to the shore. A breakwater protects the entrance but the harbour is still poorly protected from strong NW winds.

PILOTAGE

Approach on a course due S midway between Ilôt de France and the breakwater and enter the port in the middle between the islet and the shore. The end of the breakwater was partially washed away in a NW storm some years ago and some big blocks still lie sunk off the E side. Rocks extend NW of the entry peninsular. The port is dredged but proceed with care as depths vary due to silting during storms. In NW winds a swell breaks over the reefs on either side of the entrance, making entry dangerous.

Berthing

Yachts are directed to tie alongside the quay in the NE corner as shown on the chart. Depths in the other parts of the port are uncertain.

Formalities

Port of entry.

Facilities

Water There are taps in the NE corner but no water.
Fuel Available in the port.
Provisions, post office and *bank* A short walk away in the village.

ASHORE

Sites locally

Until independence, the island was inhabited by Italian fishermen and the Arab town was on the shore. Unfortunately, the old Mediterranean style houses on Ilôt de France were destroyed in 1985 to make room for a hotel development but the small village has retained a pleasant character and is set in a very wild and secluded part of the coast.

III. ALGERIA

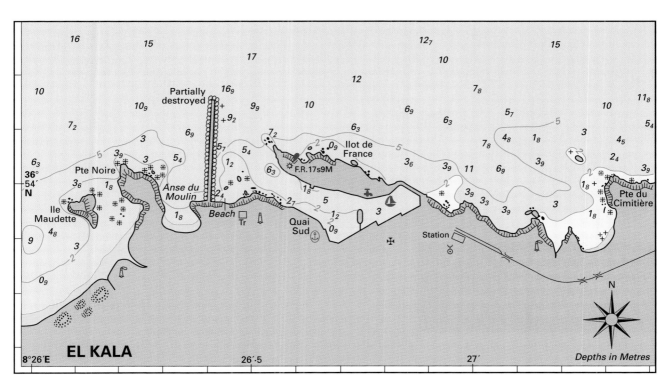

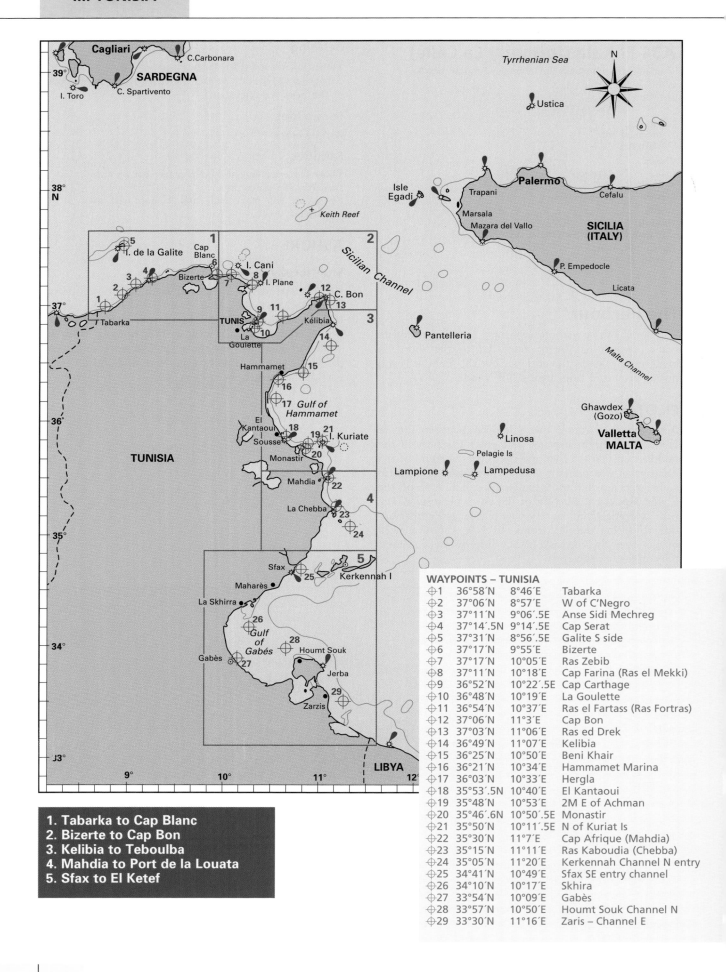

1. Tabarka to Cap Blanc
2. Bizerte to Cap Bon
3. Kelibia to Teboulba
4. Mahdia to Port de la Louata
5. Sfax to El Ketef

WAYPOINTS – TUNISIA

No.	Lat	Lon	Name
1	36°58′N	8°46′E	Tabarka
2	37°06′N	8°57′E	W of C'Negro
3	37°11′N	9°06′.5E	Anse Sidi Mechreg
4	37°14′.5N	9°14′.5E	Cap Serat
5	37°31′N	8°56′.5E	Galite S side
6	37°17′N	9°55′E	Bizerte
7	37°17′N	10°05′E	Ras Zebib
8	37°11′N	10°18′E	Cap Farina (Ras el Mekki)
9	36°52′N	10°22′.5E	Cap Carthage
10	36°48′N	10°19′E	La Goulette
11	36°54′N	10°37′E	Ras el Fartass (Ras Fortras)
12	37°06′N	11°3′E	Cap Bon
13	37°03′N	11°06′E	Ras ed Drek
14	36°49′N	11°07′E	Kelibia
15	36°25′N	10°50′E	Beni Khair
16	36°21′N	10°34′E	Hammamet Marina
17	36°03′N	10°33′E	Hergla
18	35°53′.5N	10°40′E	El Kantaoui
19	35°48′N	10°53′E	2M E of Achman
20	35°46′.6N	10°50′.5E	Monastir
21	35°50′N	10°11′.5E	N of Kuriat Is
22	35°30′N	11°7′E	Cap Afrique (Mahdia)
23	35°15′N	11°11′E	Ras Kaboudia (Chebba)
24	35°05′N	11°20′E	Kerkennah Channel N entry
25	34°41′N	10°49′E	Sfax SE entry channel
26	34°10′N	10°17′E	Skhira
27	33°54′N	10°09′E	Gabès
28	33°57′N	10°50′E	Houmt Souk Channel N
29	33°30′N	11°16′E	Zaris – Channel E

IV. TUNISIA

Capital Tunis
Population Approx 8 million

Introduction

Tunisia is the Maghreb's smallest country but is the one most visited. It has a varied landscape from mountains with cork forests and wild boar in the north, fertile farmland in the rolling hills of the Tell region, market gardens in the Cap Bon peninsula to desert with isolated oases under date palms in the south. Olive groves line the coast all the way from Cap Bon to Jerba. An enlightened agricultural policy has enabled the country to be practically self sufficient in feeding its increasing population of about 8 million. With a warm climate and miles of wide sandy beaches, it has been a popular holiday destination since the 1950's. There are extensive Punic and Roman ruins all over the country, even in the most isolated corners, and Berber dwellings in the desert.

The country can be divided into four regions. The green, mountainous north from the Algerian border to the Cap Bon peninsula has a sparsely populated coast, apart from near the major cities, which is lined by long stretches of empty beaches. In the centre of the country is the fertile Tell region. The densely populated and essentially flat Sahel coast stretches from Cap Bon to the Kerkennah Islands off Sfax. It is a low coast with long fine beaches backed by farmland and extensive olive groves with tourist centres at Hammamet, Sousse and Monastir. Finally, there is the Chott country south of the Tell and the Sahara regions bordering Algeria and Libya. Chott are large depressions, partly below sea level, covered with a thick layer of salt crystals. The oasis-like island of Jerba close to the Libyan border is an important tourist centre.

The country is rich in phosphates and some small oil reserves which contribute to overseas earnings, along with tourism, textile manufacturing and remittances from workers abroad. The European Community, mainly France and Germany, is the most important trading partner, although its rich neighbour Libya has been growing in importance since the border was reopened in 1988. Although there is a deep suspicion between the two countries, links here are bound to increase with the opening up of Libya to the West.

A BRIEF HISTORY

Recorded history begins with accounts of the seafaring Phoenicians trading with the indigenous Berbers, followed by the Carthaginian or Punic era which ended, after earlier Greek assaults, with the destruction of Carthage by the Romans in 146BC. The stability of the Roman Empire resulted in great economic development; the Maghreb supplied two thirds of Rome's grain requirement as well as olive oil, coral,

wood and pottery. Tunisia became the centre of Christian learning and leadership from the third to the sixth century with the spread of Christianity, giving rise to renowned theologians and debaters, including Tetulian and St Augustine. This was a turbulent time and eventually the 'Roman' Africans revolted, aided by the Vandals. Following the second fall of Carthage in 439AD, a new, chaotic, era began under Vandal and later Byzantine rulers, followed by Arab conquest after 670AD. Tunisia was then ruled from Damascus and Baghdad for 150 years until Ibn Aghlab established a dynasty and an active Islamic culture which made the country prosperous. The Aghlabites were overthrown by the Fatimids (descendants of Fatima, daughter of Mohammed) who established a Shi'ite regime rivaling the orthodox Sunni in Baghdad. Fatimid interest in Tunisia declined in favour of Cairo and rule was left to Berber governors. When one rejected Shi'ite for Sunni, the caliph of Cairo banished his troublesome tribes into Tunisia and for two centuries there was anarchy. In the 12th century, the increasing threat from the Normans in Sicily caused the Tunisians to seek help from the Moroccan Almohad dynasty resulting in the founding of the Hafsid dynasty which lasted until the 16th century. Commerce and arts were encouraged, enlivened by Andalucían Muslims expelled from Spain, but control of the country, never firm, slipped and in 1534 Turkish pirates drove out the last Hafsid prince. There followed a turbulent period, warding off Spanish attacks and a struggle between the seafarers and the army for control; this was the notorious period of piracy. Eventually, in 1705, one of the Beys, an army chief, founded the Hosainid dynasty and introduced some order. Efforts to control the country, together with courtly extravagance put the regime in debt to Europe and in 1881 the French moved in with the immediate aim of ensuring the security of their Algerian border, pre-empting Italian ambitions and protecting their investment.

Recent history

The people were unhappy under French rule and resentment grew during the depression of the 1920s. In 1934 the Neo-Destour party was founded by Habib Bourguiba and became the centre of opposition. After the Second World War the French showed little intention of making radical change and in 1956 in the face of growing resistance led by Bourguiba and international pressure, they agreed to independence. Nevertheless the French retained Bizerte as a naval port and following a short and unnecessary struggle in which 1300 Tunisian lives were lost, the last French left in 1963. The fight for independence was not as violent as in Algeria, partly through Bourguiba's moderation and partly because the French presence was not so firmly rooted.

Bourguiba set the country towards socialism, but in 1969 moved to the right. In 1987 he was replaced in a nonviolent coup by the present president, Zine El Abidine Ben Ali. Tunisia today has the most liberal laws in the Arab world regarding religion and women's rights. Although formally a democracy, politics are dominated by one party, the Rassemblement Constitutional Democratique. Within the Arab world, Tunisia has often played a mediating role and it maintains good relations with all Arab nations.

General information

THE TUNISIAN COASTLINE

The Tunisian coast extends 160M eastward from the Algerian border to Cap Bon, where it turns S for 330M to the border with Libya. The N coast as far as Cap Bon is for the most part mountainous, interrupted by quiet beaches around Tabarka and the Cap Farina headland, with a few off-lying islands and islets. The area is green and fertile; the Cap Bon peninsula in particular has extensive market gardens, fruit orchards and vineyards. Ras ed Drek just S of Cap Bon marks an abrupt change to the more flat and low coast of the Gulf of Hammamet. On the N coast is the marina of Sidi Bou Saïd, 4M N of Tunis, yacht clubs in Bizerte and La Goulette, the combined fishing port and marina of Tabarka, three fishing ports and several anchorages.

The 90 miles of coast from Cap Bon to Monastir becomes increasingly low with long beaches and hills further inland. The major tourist centres of Tunisia are found along this stretch. There are plenty of ports to choose from as you journey S. These include Kelibia, which is a port of entry, the marinas of El Kantaoui, the new Marina Jasmine, Monastir and the small fishing ports of Beni Khiar and Hergla.

A peculiar feature of the Tunisian coast S of Cap Bon is the abundant growth of thick, tough seaweed. During strong winds in the winter this seaweed is torn loose from the bottom and tends to clog the entrance of the smaller fishing ports, which consequently have to be dredged regularly to remain in service.

From Monastir onwards, 230M to the Libyan border, the coast becomes even lower with extensive sandy shallows. The tidal range increases to reach a maximum of 1.8m in Gabès. S of Sfax the coast becomes increasingly arid although it is still amazingly green in March with olive groves all the way to Zarzis. A short distance inland the true desert takes over and in Gabès the large oasis of Chenini comes right up to the coast. This area provides a quite different and interesting cruising ground which is worth exploring, especially with a shallow draught yacht, although there are several deep ports as well. Except for the island of Jerba, tourism is not obvious and yachts will generally find a warm welcome in some 15 ports. Mahdia and La Chebba are friendly fishing ports and Mahdia is a good and useful port of entry as well.

The Kerkennah Islands are an interesting cruising ground in themselves and with careful navigation even yachts drawing over 2m can explore some of the ports.

Tabarka fortress N of the port   *Graham Hutt*

With the gently sloping sea bottom and the calming effect of the seaweed, rough seas do not occur and consequently there are a surprising number of places to anchor in and around the banks. Sfax is a large commercial and busy fishing port and the other main ports are Gabès, Houmt Souk on the island of Jerba and Zarzis almost on the border with Libya. The mild winter is a good time to visit this area. With a draught of 1.5m several of the smaller fishing ports from which lateen rigged fishing boats still work the grounds can be visited.

In recent years Tunisia has built many new fishing ports and existing ports have been enlarged in order to exploit its relatively rich fishing grounds. Today almost every village has its own fishing port, some of them not more than 10 miles apart. These ports generally welcome yachts but entry depends on draught. Many of the smaller ports tend to silt up and are not dredged as

Tunisian market: note prices always displayed *Graham Hutt*

long as local boats, which often draw less than a metre, can get in and out. Entrance can also be complicated by excessive growth of seaweed, particularly S of Cap Bon. It is easy to run aground in Tunisia but as the bottom is almost always sand, soft mud or seaweed, the grounding event is seldom serious. Fishermen will usually help for a small reward.

Maritime Information

Weather

Tunisian weather is moderate compared with Italy and Sardinia. Summer cruising is usually accompanied by W, NW or E winds, keeping temperatures down. The Bay of Tunis usually experiences a brief spell of hot humid weather in late July and early August. Winter cruising can be very pleasant in the south, where temperatures remain considerably higher than in Tunis. The storms resulting from depressions sweeping through the Mediterranean tend to stay further north, up in the Golfe du Lion and northern Italy. Their effects do not normally reach the east coast with such severity. For 5 day synoptic charts see
http://meteonet.nl/aktueel/brackall.htm
or www.bbc.co.uk/weather/coast/pressure/

Good all-weather ports

Tabarka, Bizerte (commercial and fishing port), La Goulette, Hammamet (Marina Jasmine), Kelibia, Monastir (marina and fishing port), Mahdia, Sfax, Gabès and Zarzis.

Note on Tides

Tides are negligible along the N coast of Tunisia and along much of the E coast going S from Cap Bon. The springs range is less than half a metre. They become significant around Sfax and from there S are mentioned under each port.
http://easytide.ukho.gov.uk gives tidal information which is especially helpful around the Kerkennah Islands.

Marine life

Whilst much of the Mediterranean is dead, Tunisia remains rich in fish stocks. The fishing fleet is huge and tuna nets stretch for miles off many of the harbours. Shark, marlin, tuna, grouper and mackerel are all caught. The N coast is rich in coral and a tourist industry has built up in Bizerte and Tabarka to cater for scuba divers who spend a few hours visiting the reefs of coral and sponge, which are as magnificent and colourful as those of the Red Sea. This is a timely new development as the authorities seek to make conservation a priority in view of what has happened in the rest of the Mediterranean.

Tourism and conservation

Tourism is a big industry and a large foreign currency earner in Tunisia. Conservation to protect this, has become a big issue in recent years. Several coastal areas have been declared fishing free zones and coral fishing is very strictly controlled and licensed to a very few

Sea life is spectacular in the crystal clear waters
TNTO

people. A fleet of military vessels is tasked to patrol the coasts checking up on every kind of vessel. One of the most spectacular results of this policy is the development of the many scuba diving schools which use the protected areas to visit wrecks and coral reefs. The abundance of fish in these conservation zones and the spectacular and colourful coral reefs are testimony to the success of this approach. Though coral can be found in shops, it is used to draw tourists to visit the live coral reefs.

Planning your cruise

Time zone

UT+1 Summer and winter.

Money

The Tunisian Dinar (TD) can only be changed in Tunisia and importing or exporting Tunisian currency is forbidden. The Dinar is divided into 1000 millimes and most prices are expressed in millimes, often written as TD 2200 meaning 2200 millimes = 2.20 Dinars.

Travellers' cheques are accepted at all banks.

Credit cards are accepted in the larger towns and tourist centres and ATMs are widespread in most areas. Cash can be withdrawn on Visa universally, MasterCard often and others rarely. The Societe Tunisienne de Banque (STB) will advance cash against Visa and Mastercard. It can be difficult to get cash in some places against a non-Tunisian card, though not in the tourist areas.

There is no limit to the amount of foreign currency that can be taken in or out of Tunisia but keep all exchange receipts as they are needed for changing cash back into hard currency when leaving or when applying for a visa. Only 30% of the original amount, to a maximum of TD 100, can be reconverted. The Dinar is

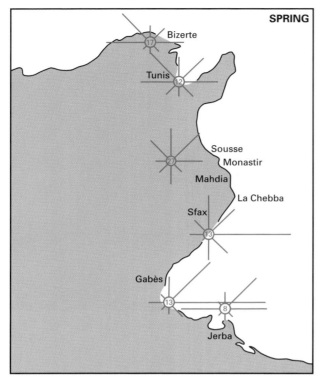

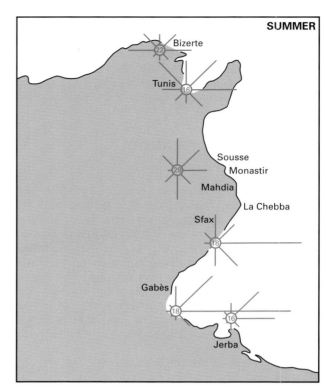

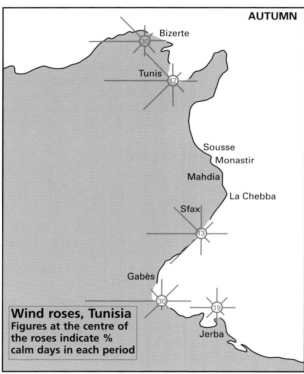

Wind roses, Tunisia
Figures at the centre of the roses indicate % calm days in each period

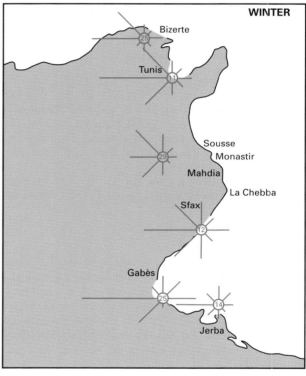

relatively stable and prices quoted in this pilot are based on an exchange rate of TD 1.5 = € 1. TD 1.2 = 1 US Dollar. TD 2.5 = £1.00 (2004 rates).

CRUISING IN TUNISIA

An increasing number of yachtsmen are discovering the delights of cruising the coasts of Tunisia, which welcomes visitors. It is particularly popular for Italian,

French and German yachtsmen. In Bizerte during summer 2004, in a six day period over fifty French and Italian yachts transited the visitors' pontoon on their way to or from the east Tunisian cruising grounds. Most marinas and fishing ports were quite full with transiting yachtsmen, but room is always found for another and more are being built. The fishing fleets are usually obliging and even the military vessels sometimes make way for visiting yachts.

It should be appreciated that summer gales, once a very unlikely event, have become normal over the past few years and most harbours offer protection from these.

Several new marinas are planned and surveys have already been completed, with construction underway. The new 'Marina Jasmine' at Hammamet has set the pace for new developments, which are due to be located near Sidi Bou Said, Tunis, Hergla, Skanes and Jebha.

Now that Malta and Cyprus have joined the EC, wintering facilities in Tunisia have become very attractive for the many yachtsmen who need a VAT exempt port. This includes yachts registered outside of the EC, as well as European yachts on which VAT has not been paid.

Anchoring

Anchoring is permitted in all but military zones provided the authorities are advised in advance. The number of restricted areas is increasing and the authorities appear more sensitive to their zones than they used to be. There is not usually a problem during daylight, but military boats patrol the coast at night and you may be asked to present ships' papers or to move into a port, even in bad weather. This is especially true in the northern regions of Bizerte and Tunis. The military areas in harbours are now well protected and often cordoned off: an unfortunate sign of the times

Harbour charges

Harbour charges vary depending on the type of port and facilities offered, from small fishing harbours with no charge to marinas which have standard price lists. In the fishing harbours where a charge is levied, it is very low and should be based on a government set rate of TD 1.00 per gross ton per week, payable at the CGP (Commissariat Général de la Pêche). Keep the receipt as remaining days can be used in other fishing ports when visited within the week paid for. Marina fees at the marinas of Sidi Bou Saïd, Al Kantaoui and Monastir are very reasonable. For long stays, prices can be negotiated. Marina Hammamet is more expensive than the others.

Prices for a 12m yacht in summer 2004 are included where known. Where not mentioned, charges can be expected to be low. In all cases, prices are far cheaper than in Europe.

Many harbours and all the marinas have web sites that can be used to check for latest information.

Security

No problem in most ports, though there have been some recent incidents of bike thefts in Tabarka. Tunisia is possibly one of the safest places in the Mediterranean for a yacht and her crew. However, do not leave valuable articles like shoes within easy reach on deck along public quays. Increased tourism has left its mark in Tunisia and pick-pocketing does occur in the tourist areas but not on the scale of Europe. In over thirty years of sailing this coast I have never experienced any problems from locals. Any that have occurred have been traced to other yachtsmen.

Drugs

The discovery of illegal drugs onboard, even in small quantities, carries a high penalty and can lead to imprisonment and almost certain confiscation of the yacht. (The water pipes 'hubble-bubbles' often seen in the cafés are smoked with a special kind of Egyptian mild tobacco called maassal and not with hashish. It is common to see large sociable groups gathered in the evening sharing a maassal pipe).

Health advice

Cholera and yellow fever inoculations are required if coming from an infected area. Basic health care is of a reasonable standard; most doctors have been trained in France. The best medical care is available in the private rather than public hospitals and prices are roughly the same as in Europe. It is a good precaution to have insurance covering repatriation to Europe in the case of major surgery. In the marinas of El Kantaoui and Monastir doctors are available in the port.

Animals

Cats and dogs on board need a certificate of good health and valid anti-rabies vaccination papers, though these are rarely asked for.

Availability of supplies

Fuel

Tunisian diesel has a high sulphur content but causes no problems in yacht engines. When cruising on Tunisian diesel it is advisable to change the engine oil more often as sulphur increases the acid level in the oil. Diesel (*Mazoot* in Arabic) is available in almost every fishing port. Easy places for filling are Sidi Bou Saïd, Kelibia, Al Kantaoui, Monastir and Bizerte.

Kerosene/Paraffin is called *petrolio blu* (Italian pronunciation) and is available from fuel stations

Water

Good quality water is in abundant supply along the entire Tunisian coast and is quite drinkable, often better tasting than bottled water. In some fishing ports containers may be necessary, as it is often not possible to hook up to a tap: have a long hose and a variety of fittings and hose clips on board. In fishing ports water is charged at 1TD per 1000 litres. Tanks can easily be filled in Tabarka, Bizerte, Sidi Bou Saïd, La Goulette, Kelibia, Hammamet, Al Kantaoui, Monastir and Mahdia. Ice is available in practically every fishing port and in some of the marinas the harbour attendants will deliver it.

Gas

Gas refills can normally be arranged with the port captains.

Electricity

Nominal voltage is 220V, but it can vary considerably. In Sidi Bou Saïd, for instance, 240V is the norm most of the time, which can result in overcharged batteries if cheap car-type chargers are used. In the four marinas 380/220V is available. With some improvisation electricity can be arranged in several fishing ports but S of La Chebba this will be rare.

IV. TUNISIA

Provisions

The best place to buy fresh produce is at the markets which are found even in the smallest villages. Modern storing techniques are rarely used and imported food products are not common, even in the supermarkets, except for the large European facilities found in some towns. Consequently supply is largely seasonal, with the best choice in winter, spring and early summer. Prices on the open market are usually well marked: a government requirement. Generally, the quality of fresh produce is excellent and prices are low. The supermarket chains, Monoprix and Magasin Général, are found all over the country, and now Carrefour has opened a huge store in Tunis. Wine, beer and hard liquor are normally sold only in these supermarkets with foreign and local brands available. Yachtsmen visiting or wintering in Tunisia often prefer to stock up with Italian wine in Lampedusa or Pantelleria, the Italian Islands between Tunisia and Malta. Customs authorities are not concerned about large quantities of wine, but are inquisitive and may be difficult about an excess of spirits, which are exorbitantly expensive in Tunisia. All glass bottles carry a deposit which is marked on the label. Canned products are not common and the choice is limited except in the large hypermarkets. Dairy products are of good quality. UHT milk is readily available, fresh milk from vats in the dairies at the market (take your own containers), French and Tunisian butter, and a limited choice of bland cheeses. Meat is always fresh but not hung and difficult to get in familiar cuts unless the butcher is shown how. Pork or wild boar can only be found in the capital and other areas where there is a concentration of Europeans. Turkey, chicken and rabbit are of good quality and widely available. Goods like cosmetics, paper towels, toilet paper, etc. are available in the supermarkets and pharmacies and often at the markets as well. Coffee (beans and instant) and tea available in most supermarkets.

Some Tunisian Wines

Priced at around TD 3-5
Red Wines
Magon, excellent
Pinot, excellent
Chateau Mornay, above average
Rosé wines
Koudiat, adequate
Chateau Mornag, adequate
White wines
Muscat de Kelibia, good if you like muscat grapes
Blanc Crystal, adequate

Repairs and chandlery

Most mechanical repairs and routine maintenance can be carried out in the marinas. Various specialists can be arranged at most ports. Hauling out is possible in almost all ports, but the marinas Monastir, Sidi Bou Saïd, El Kantaoui and Hammamet are more used to dealing with pleasure and keeled yachts. Alternatively, yachts can be hauled in the large travel-lifts intended for fishing boats in Tabarka, Bizerte, Kelibia, Monastir, Teboulba, Sfax and Mahdia. Here, prices are cheaper and controlled by the government. This is set at ten TDs per ton for haul-out and return to the water. The lift-out

facilities are the responsibility of the port authorities, whereas the propping and work is usually negotiated with private contractors found around the ports.

High pressure cleaning facilities are available in most ports, though not currently in Kelibia. Generally it is advisable to supervise the work yourself since most of the labourers are hard working but have more good will than craftsmanship. The availability of specialised yacht spares such as stainless steel hardware, rigging material, sail cloth, etc. has been very limited in the past, but see below. Galvanized materials, nylon rope, paints, antifouling, etc. as used by fishermen are available in the bigger ports like Bizerte, La Goulette, Sousse and Gabès and are very cheap, being manufactured in Tunisia. The quality can vary. Paint and antifouling are particularly inexpensive and also effective (Trans-Ocean antifouling is manufactured under licence) but it may take some time to find out where to buy these products. Engine spares are hard to come by although there are agents for well known brands like Perkins and Yamaha in Tunis. Duty-free import of spares for a 'Yacht in Transit' does not exist, although duty free import of personal belongings for yachts wintering in Monastir is possible. For the procedure check with the port captain in advance. Small parts of little value (as judged by customs) can be sent by mail. Other spares or new equipment are best imported as personal luggage; customs at airports rarely cause Europeans difficulties over such imports. As yachting develops over the years it can be expected that facilities will improve further.

Sailmakers and sail repair facilities

A company offering a service covering the whole of Tunisia has been established in Sousse: 'Seamtech'. Whilst principally a manufacturing base for sails, awnings, spray hoods etc., which are exported to Europe, it also has excellent sail repair facilities with a collection and delivery service throughout Tunisia. The work is overseen by experienced French management and can undertake any sail repair, as well as manufacture to order. The factory, currently 2500m² is expanding its facilities. A huge range of sail cloth is held in stock.

The same company is also agent for Profurl, International Paints, Plastimo (along with a licensed liferaft checking workshop), Soromap rigging and Lancelin ropes. Anything from these manufacturers' catalogues can be ordered.

Contact: Emmanuel on ☎ 98456 549 or
Raphael on ☎ 22 861 125.
Factory in Sousse ☎ 73 588 555 *Fax* 73 588545
Email manu@seam-tech.com

Laundry

Laundry service is available in the marinas of Sidi Bou Saïd, El Kantaoui and Monastir and soon in Marina Jasmine. Further details listed under each port.

Entry formalities

Yachts can make their first entry into Tunisia at any of the following ports: Tabarka, Bizerte, Sidi Bou Saïd, La Goulette, Marina Jasmine, Kelibia, El Kantaoui, Sousse, Monastir, Mahdia, Sfax, Gabès and Houmt-Souk. Papers required are:

Official ownership papers issued in the country of registration. On rare occasions the police may want to keep the ships' papers until departure.

Passports with any necessary visas. Visitors with Israeli or South African stamps in their passports may be refused entry. Passports normally stay on board. Please refer to the Visa section in this introduction for further details.

An insurance policy number is sometimes asked for on the entry form, though insurance is not required by law in Tunisia. Third party insurance is in any case all that is required and is usually inexpensive.

Crew lists and changes See Sample Crew List and Boating Terms section in the appendix for suggested format. Notify the port police of any crew changes. Difficulties will occur with immigration authorities when you want to depart from a port with new crew if they have not been informed beforehand. If you invite any Tunisian friends on board or plan to take Tunisian or European friends out for a day trip, police and customs have to be informed, with a complete crew list.

Clearance has to be obtained once only, at the port of entry, and it should be sufficient elsewhere merely to show the papers, which are usually photocopied in each port. If leaving Tunisia, allow enough time to notify the police and customs; they like to know where you are going and it is for your safety.

Harbour officials

Various authorities will have to be dealt with but the police and customs are the most important. Often the officials will be waiting on the quay and it is useful to have the paperwork ready before entering port.

Police (immigration police in grey uniform) check all passports and visas of those crew members who need them.

Douane (customs in brown uniform) will normally only make a quick check inside the boat on first entry. Officially all equipment on board has to be declared but in practice the important items as far as customs are concerned are firearms, and large quantities of liquor. Firearms will be taken into custody. Beer and wine are of no great concern but quantities of spirits, say more than a couple of bottles, will probably be sealed with enough left out for daily use. Electronic equipment, especially radio transmitters, is of particular interest to the customs and it will save time to make a list of these before arrival for transfer to the form provided.

Finally, customs will write out a *Demande de Permis de Circulation*, also called the *Triptique*, for the temporary import of the boat in Tunisia (see below).

The *Garde National* are the military police in green uniforms. They operate on land and at sea. Their role is supplementary to the clearance procedure and they are rarely involved. In the marinas of Al Kantaoui and Monastir they are kept informed by the capitainerie and

if they appear in other ports they may take details of the yacht data: insurance and equipment, especially radio transmitters.

Harbour authorities may be represented by the harbour master in the marinas, by a representative from APIP (*Agence des Ports et des Installations*) in the fishing ports or occasionally by the *marine marchande*.

The *Triptique* or *Permis de Circulation*

The *Triptique* is the permit allowing a foreign yacht to remain in Tunisian waters for one year from the date of entry. Within this year the yacht may cruise Tunisian waters for 6 months. When not sailing the yacht can be put under plombage (seal) by leaving the *Triptique* with the customs. The time the yacht remains under plombage is not counted as cruising time. When entering the country the customs officer will usually write out a *Triptique* valid for 3 months. An extension can be arranged with a customs office in any port and after it has been extended up to the maximum period of one year a new *Triptique* can be issued. The reason for limiting the *Triptique* is to keep a check on the papers of the crew. One copy of the *Triptique* is for the customs officer who writes it out and two remain with the skipper. When leaving Tunisia both copies are submitted to customs.

Visas

The following is a guide to the situation which has changed little over the years: it is wise to check with a Tunisian embassy and, if necessary, arrange a visa before departure from your base.

German and USA citizens may stay up to four months without a visa and citizens of Canada and all other European countries except the Benelux countries, three months.

Dutch, Belgian, Luxembourg, New Zealand and Australian citizens need visas to enter. If not obtained beforehand, the police at the port of entry can issue a 7 day transit visa and for a longer stay a proper visa may be obtained at the Commissariat de Police in Bizerte, Tunis, Nabeul, Sousse, Monastir, Sfax or Gabès. An extension to a transit visa is normally only for a month. New Zealanders and Australians have, for some reason, sometimes experienced problems getting transit visas extended. Extensions to regular visas and for non-visa nationals to stay beyond three or four months, have to be arranged at the same offices. Take two black and white passport photos, exchange receipts from the bank, Permis de Circulation and if relevant, a note or wintering contract from the port captain. Check beforehand with the local police for any changes in the procedure. Be prepared for delays as the procedure is rarely without complications (though not insurmountable) especially if staying longer than six months.

Embassies

UK Rue de Lac Windemere, Tunis
☎ 108700 www.british.intl.tn/
USA 144 Avenue de la Liberté, Tunis ☎ 282566
Fax 789719

Germany 1 Rue el Hamra Mutuellevi le, Tunis
☎ 786455 *Fax* 358191
French Place d'Independence, Tunis. Ave Habib,
Bourguiba ☎ 245700\358111
Italian 3 Rue de Russie, Tunis ☎ 341811 *Fax* 324155
Email AMBITALIA.TUN@Email.ati.tn

WINTERING IN TUNISIA

Monastir and El Kantaoui have been the most popular wintering marinas for some years. In 2003/4 Monastir was very full. The price and facilities at both marinas are similar and well below European prices. Both are secure places to leave a boat unattended, although the quality of care and supervision cannot be relied upon, especially in Monastir. A few yachts winter each year in Tabarka, Sidi Bou Said, La Goulette, Bizerte and Kelibia. Facilities have drastically improved at the new fishing port at Monastir, which welcomes yachts either on the hard or afloat. This is a good alternative to the overstretched main marina and cheaper.

Early booking for winter is essential at Monastir and El Kantaoui.

The new marina in Hammamet: 'Marina Jasmine', offers another large and safe place both for wintering afloat or ashore. The marina is fully functional although local facilities: shops, restaurants and recreational areas will not be completed before 2005.

The marinas at Sidi Bou Saïd, Hammamet, El Kantaoui and Monastir are suitable for laying up under plombage and it is also possible to winter afloat under this scheme but watch visa dates. A person wintering on his yacht in Tunisia is entitled to a visa for as long as he stays in the winter port but the complications of getting it vary between the marinas. In Sidi Bou Saïd and El Kantaoui yachtsmen do it themselves with varying degrees of success. In Monastir the port captain assists, which makes the procedure run more smoothly. One way around the difficulty is for the individual to temporarily leave Tunisia, as on re-entering, the clock is restarted. There is a residence tax for yachtsmen who stay uninterruptedly in Tunisia for longer than six months. A tax stamp costing TD 45 per person and available from the Recette de Finance, has to be presented upon departure. Obtaining this has the advantage of cheaper travel out of Tunisia. Tickets are double the price for non-residents. See below under 'International travel.'

Internet facilities

There are internet facilities in all towns, known as 'Publinet'. Connections are often slow, but at around 2 or 3 TD for an hour on-line, speed is not important.

Telephone

Public phones are located in Specialist shops known as 'Taxiphones'. They usually have photocopy and fax facilities. Taxiphones are very common, but because they are manned only in office hours, making calls at night can be a problem. The tariff on calls to UK is approx. 1.2 TD per minute.

GSM – Tunisia has a roaming agreement with many European networks and the system works throught the country. For some reason though, it cannot be used for data communications (connection to the internet via a computer) in some areas.

Mail

Postal services are reliable. Letters to or from Europe rarely take more than a week, and two weeks from the USA.

Tourist information

Tourist information offices are found in almost every town. Well produced brochures are available free, usually in several languages. They are a good source of information but for serious exploring, the travel guides listed in the appendix will be more helpful.

Business hours

Banks Mon–Fri 0800–1100 (summer) and additionally 1400–1600 in winter.

Supermarkets Mon–Sat 0830–1200 and 1600–2000.

Markets Open every day 0800–1200 and 1600–2000.

Public holidays

New Year's Day	1 January
Anniversary of the Revolution	18 January
Independence Day	20 March
Martyrs' Day	9 April
Labour Day	1 May
Victory Day	1 June
Republic Day	25 July
Women's Day	13 August
Anniversary of the PSD	3 September
Evacuation of Bizerte	15 October
New Era Day	7 November

Islamic holidays are listed in the Introduction.

Photography

In general, the Islamic rule of not taking pictures of people should be respected, although many do not mind. Just ask first or do not make it obvious. Do not take pictures of military camps, patrol boats and armed policemen on guard at government buildings and presidential palaces. Even in the centre of Tunis the police get very nervous if pictures are taken of the guards in front of the Ministry of the Interior.

Tipping

In everyday life tipping follows the same rules as in Europe although it is not uncommon to have tips refused. In European-style restaurants and tourist areas tipping is expected. It is useful to have some packets of European or American cigarettes onboard as an appreciation of small services. If offering a beer, European beer is very much appreciated, but not the local canned brew. (The latter though, is very much better than most European lager, to my taste.)

Overland travel

Tunisia has an excellent public transport infrastructure, though without the precise timing of Europe. Trains

El Kantaoui Marina   *Graham Hutt*

between the major cities are reasonably comfortable and reliable. Local buses are frequent and cheap. Taxis are yellow and everywhere. Prices are low. e.g. the fare (per taxi) from Sidi Bou Saïd to the centre of Tunis, a ride of about 30 minutes, is about TD 6. The start-up charge is TD 0.360, more if ordered by phone. Drivers are always fair, go by the meter and do not start to haggle once at the destination, as in many countries. Often the price asked is rounded down from the metered price, rather than up. There are also louages, usually Peugeot estate cars and minibuses which provide regional transportation for roughly the same price as the buses. Louages depart from central points in every town as soon as they are full, usually every few minutes. In rural areas they may well carry furniture in the back and live stock on the roof. Car hire is more expensive than in Europe but out of season it is possible to negotiate special prices even with companies like Hertz, Avis or Europcar.

International travel

Air There is a two tier price system for flights from Tunisia. Non-residents pay double fare. Yachtsmen are considered residents if they have a contract with a marina at the time of the flight, but most travel agents do not know about or accept this, or will feign ignorance and try to charge double. Often a letter obtained from the marina to verify your stay is sufficient to obtain the residents' rate.

The travel agency Sahlina Tours (Mlle. Tajouri Ryma) 49 Ave. de la Republique, Sousse, ☎ 03 211576 *Fax* 03 211577 are used to dealing with yachtsmen, and immediately treat them as residents.

Scheduled flights leave from Tunis to all major European cities. Most of the charter flights go to Monastir and Jerba. There are no direct flights to the US

and the best option is to fly via London. Tunisavia flies three times a week to Malta in summer. A new airport has opened in Tabarka (September 2004). Flight listings on the internet indicate that this is a charter destination from northern Europe, though currently internet bookings have proved impossible.

Ferry services

A regular service to Genoa operates from Tunis during the summer months and less frequently in winter. Weekly service to Trapani, Sicily which continues on to Cagliari, Sardinia. Weekly car ferry service to Catania, Sicily via Malta. Regular service to Marseille in summer and less often in winter. All Tunis ferries leave from La Goulette.

Twice weekly hydrofoil service from Kelibia to Trapani via Pantelleria from May 1 to October 31 when weather permits.

Order of Tunisian ports

The order given is as follows:
1. Tabarka to Cap Serrat and La Galite – E from the border of Algeria towards Bizerte, covering Iles Galite.
2. Bizerte to Cap Bon – Bay of Tunis and E to ports and anchorages around Cap Bon.
3. Kelibia to Telboulba – S along the E coast to Mahdia.
4. Mahdia to Port de la Louata – S in the shallows to Sfax.
5. Sfax to El Ketef – S and E including Jerba and the Kerkennah Islands to the Libyan border.

Important note on waypoints and co-ordinates

Please refer to the important note regarding waypoints in the Introduction page 12.

1. Tabarka to Cap Serrat and La Galite

T1 Tabarka

This is the first port in Tunisia sailing from the W, close to the Algerian border, and a port of entry with facilities to accommodate yachts up to 40 metres.

Location
36°57′.2N 08°46′E

Distances
Algerian border 6M
Galite 35M
Bizerte 65M

Charts
Admiralty *2121 1712*
French Approach *4219*, Port *4087*

Lights
Approach
1. **Ile de Tabarka** 36°57′.8N 08°45′.5E Fl2.5s72m17M White tower, black bands on castle
Harbour
2. **Fishing harbour Digue Nord head** Fl.G.4s10m6M Tower
3. **Digue Est elbow** Fl.R.5s
4. **Digue Interior** Fl.R.5s

Communications
Harbourmaster ☎ 78 670 599
VHF Ch 16. also 8, 10 and 14

The port

Tabarka is set amongst green mountains in the fertile valley of the Oued Kébir. The offshore rock crowned with the Genoese castle made a natural location for a harbour. Around the yacht basin there is the harbourmaster's office with showers and toilets, apartments and restaurants and the police and customs. The port lies E of the causeway connecting the rock with the mainland and the old port (now silted up) lies to the W.

PILOTAGE

By day

Approach from the N is straightforward with no off-lying dangers other than the rocks close to shore indicated on the chart. W of Tabarka the coast is made up of steep cliffs and to the E are beaches with mountains further inland. Tabarka Island with the Genoese castle and light tower on top provides a good landmark by day and night. Watch out for floating nets S of the entrance towards the beach. In order to avoid them, round the N breakwater fairly close.

By night

The port is well lit and the lights reliable. The hilltop fortress N of the port with a light near the point to the NE of the port is clearly visible from all directions.

Berthing

At the southern end of the port there is a section reserved for visiting yachts, but this has been taken over by local coral diving boats. Lay alongside the

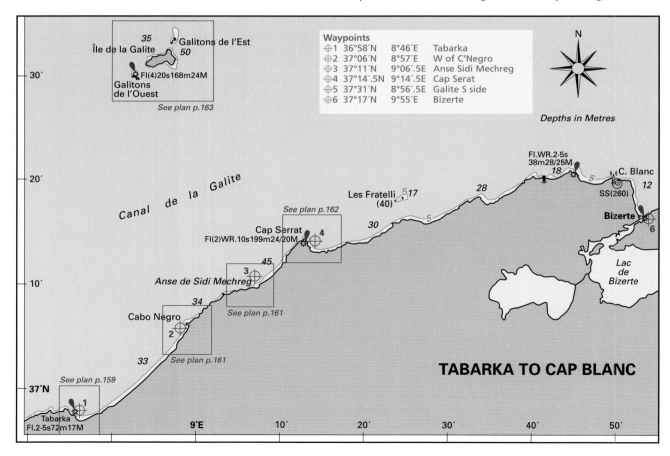

capitainerie or use a kedge to go stern/bows to, depending on what other yachts have done. Usually the police and port 'guardian' are around to assist with mooring. Beware protruding rings on quay.

Anchoring E or W of the island in sand is possible, but with the predominant NW wind little protection is found and care should be taken to avoid the fishing nets.

Charges for a 12m yacht
May–Oct
  Day TD13.5000
  Week TD65.000
  Month TD195.000
Oct–April
  Day TD 10.2000
  Week TD 45.000
  Month TD 135.000

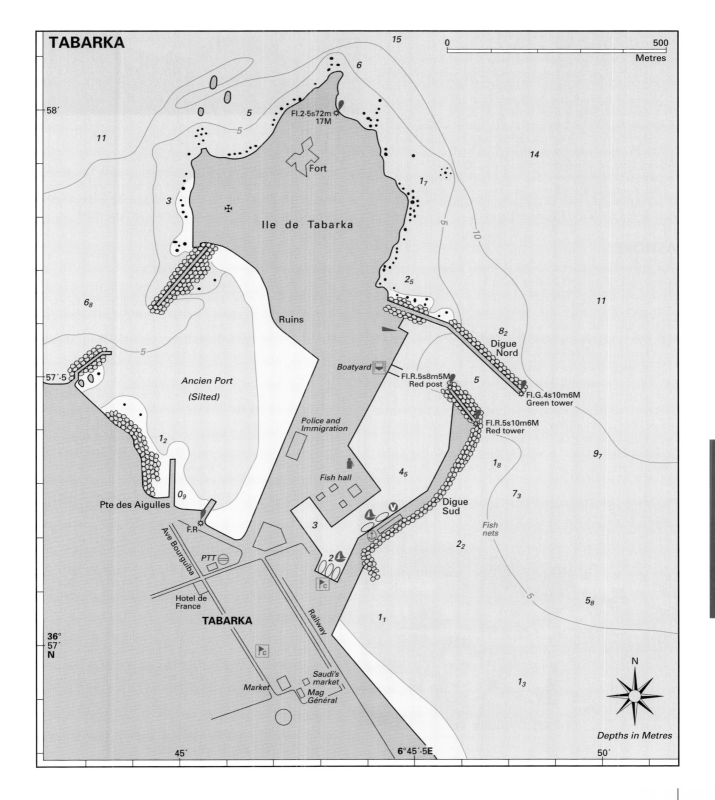

Formalities

Garde National, police and customs are located in the port. The capitainerie is in the SE corner of the port.

Facilities

Water and *electricity* Available by connecting to dilapidated spur boxes on the jetty.

Showers In the harbourmaster's building: 6 showers and 6 WCs.

Fuel Diesel available from a pump near the fish hall and petrol from gas station in the town.

Provisions Many small grocery shops nearby in the town. Wine, beer and the best assortment of cheese in the Magasin Général (wine from the back door). Shops in the simple village are a short walk away.

Good fresh produce available from street stalls and a small covered market near the Magasin Général. Every Friday there is a big souk, on the Bizerte road just out of town.

Post office and *bank* A short walk in the town.

Telephone In the post office and local Telenet office.

Internet (Publinet) One located just outside marina and the other a short walk into town.

Repairs There is an engine repair shop on the street facing the port. The fishing port has a slip and 250-ton travel-lift. Arrangements for slipping and repairs are made through the APIP in the port, who run the boatyard.

Laundry In the town, 50m from the port.

ASHORE

The spectacular Roman ruins at Bulla Regia are about 60km from Tabarka. To visit them it is best to gather a group and arrange a louage for the day. A winding road takes you into the cool mountains to Aïn Draham, 1000m up, with spectacular views of the Oued Kébir valley. From there the road descends into the valley of the Oued Ghezala towards Bulla Regia.

Although there may not be many yachtsmen who combine sailing with hunting, it is worth mentioning that wild boar are still to be found in the area of Tabarka and hunting is actively promoted by the tourist office. Better restaurants in the area have wild boar on their menus during the hunting season.

Beautiful beaches E of the port stretch for miles towards the anchorage of Cap Negro, but, there has

Tabarka visitors' quay looking NW towards fishing harbour
Graham Hutt

The port entrance seen from the Genoese fortress

been considerable hotel development. Aside from the fishing fleet there are coral diving boats and a scuba diving club. Shops in the simple village are a short walk away. There is now an international airport nearby.

Diving

Scuba diving here is probably the most colourful and scenic anywhere in the Mediterranean.

The Tabarka Diving Club provides complete facilities for diving. In season they make twice daily excursions to areas close to the port. Training courses are available starting at the elementary level and it is possible to take official CMAS tests. Everything available from diving bottles to a decompression chamber.

History

Tabarka's history goes back to a Phoenician settlement and the name means 'thickly wooded'. In Roman times, marble from nearby mountains was shipped from the ancient port, which then was no more than a causeway to the island. A period of Turkish rule was followed by a short Spanish occupation. In 1542 King Charles V sold Tabarka Island and the coral fishing rights to a Genoese family who constructed the castle and managed to stay for two centuries while the Turks controlled the mainland. After the Second World War and during the French occupation of Tunisia, the present causeway and the port on the east side were constructed. A path leads up to the castle from where there is a splendid view of the village and the miles of beaches. There is no access to the castle itself as it is now closed; a military zone.

Eating out

There are several Tunisian style restaurants around the port and in some, a take-away dinner can be bought. European style dining at the Mimosa Hotel, 15 minutes walk from the port. Hotel de France, Ave. Bourguiba is also recommended.

Transport

There is now an international airport nearby with charter flights which began in summer 2004.

T2 Cap Negro (Anse Budmah) Anchorage

A very pleasant open anchorage sheltered from the N and E, 13M NE of Tabarka.

Location
37°06′N 08°59′E

Distances
Tabarka 13.5M
Galite 26M
Bizerte 53M

Charts
Admiralty *2121*
French *4314, 4219*

The anchorage

Except for a small military settlement and two houses, Cap Negro is uninhabited. There is a small beach with the remains of an old French coral fishing establishment which was chased out by the Bey of Tunis in the 18th century.

PILOTAGE

From a distance the point is not easy to see but when closely following the coastline from Tabarka, the low promontory will be identified. Arriving from Ile de Galite, Jebel Sidi Mohammed at 474m is a good landmark. Approaching from the E, avoid the submerged rocks extending up to 300m from the point.

The S side of the Cap Negro promontory provides good protection in winds from NE to S but is dangerous if the wind shifts to N or W. Anchor in sand in depths of 5–8m, about 200m from the small beach. Left-over swell from the W will make the anchorage uncomfortable.

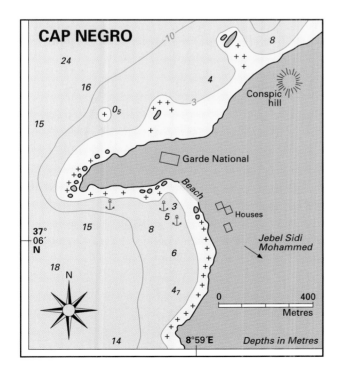

T3 Sidi Mechreg

A small fishing port in the middle of nowhere, of little interest to yachts, on the exposed coast between Tabarka and Bizerte.

Location
37°10′.11N 09°07′.56E

Distances
Tabarka 22M
Bizerte 44M

Charts
Admiralty *2121*
French *4219*

Lights
1. **Jetty head** N 37°10′N 09°07′.5E Fl.R.5s6M
2. **S** Fl.G.4s6M

Communications
VHF Ch16

The harbour

The harbour opened in 1998 and still does not have the facilities promised but is a quiet place where few yachts visit.

PILOTAGE

The coast W of the port is foul and the entrance is prone to silting so approach with care. Make the approach from the NW. The outer breakwater and red light-tower will be seen. The remains of Roman baths, S of the port, make a good landmark. Depths shelve up to the entrance and in onshore winds there is an unpleasant amount of running swell. Depths in the entrance are uncertain, though the authorities report a minimum of 2.5m in the port and entrance.

Berthing

Berth wherever there is space alongside.

Formalities

APIP and Garde National have offices in the port, but this is not a port of entry. ☎ number unknown.

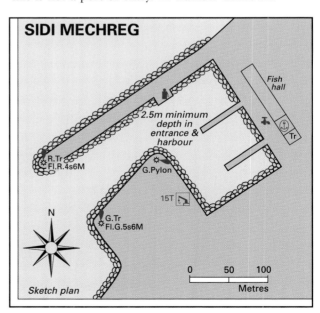

IV. TUNISIA

Cap Negro anchorage approached from the W

Facilities

Water By the fish market.
Electricity In some places along the quay.
Fuel Pump on fuel quay on the N side of the harbour.
Provisions A small shop and hotel with restaurant 1 km from the port.
Telephone APIP in the town.
Repairs 15-ton crane/travel-hoist.

ASHORE

Sites locally

The vaulted remains of a Roman bath house can be seen on the beach 1km south of the port. These are worth a visit – take the road south from the port and 200m past the hotel (1km from the port) follow a track down to the beach. Brushing away the sand over the remains reveals floor mosaics.

T4 Cap Serrat Anchorage

An anchorage well protected from W and NW winds, on the SE side of cape Serrat.

Location
   37°14′N 09°13′.5E
Distances
   Tabarka 29M
   Galite 22M
   Bizerte 37M
Charts
   Admiralty Approach *2121*
   French *4314, 4219*
Lights
Cap Serrat LtHo 37°13′.9N 09°12′.6E
   Fl(2)WR.10s199m24/20M Low black tower, white band
   238°-R-261°-W-238°

The anchorage

This is the most prominent point on the coast between Tabarka and Bizerte. The anchorage E of the cape is surrounded by a rocky coast to the W and deserted beaches to the S and E with white sand dunes in the background. Protection from W to NW and to the S is good. In strong NW winds though, swell rolls around the cape making the anchorage uncomfortable.

PILOTAGE

From the N, the lighthouse on the cape and further E the high sand dunes of Jebel Blida are easy to identify. On the beach about 0.5M from the anchorage is the wreck of a stranded tugboat. The best protection is to be found S of an interesting projection consisting of large symmetrical blocks piled one on top of the other

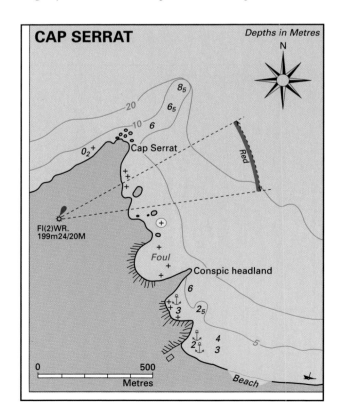

0.8M SSE of the cape. Anchor in depths of about 5m in fine sand with a few, well visible, isolated rocky patches.

ASHORE

Solitude, sand dunes and crystal clear water around the rocks for diving and fishing is all that is here.

T5 Ile de la Galite Anchorage

An anchorage in a bay on the S side of the small island of Galite, 22 miles NNW of Cap Serrat.

Location
37°31′.0N 08°56′.5E

Distances
Tabarka 35M
Bizerte 50M

Charts
Admiralty 2121, 1712
French 3424, 5698

Lights
Approach
1. **Galiton de l'Ouest** 37°29′.9N 08°52′.6E
Fl(4)20s168m24M Black tower, cupola, on grey building
227°-obscd-250° by Ile de la Galite
May appear as Fl(2)20s at a distance
The light on the buoy in the entrance and the lights in the harbour are out of action.

The island

Ile de Galite is the main island of a small archipelago of volcanic origin rising steep from the sea bottom to an elevation of almost 400m. Bizertan sardine and mackerel fishermen work the banks around Galite at night and in season lobster is caught. During the day they use the anchorage and the remaining wall of small harbour on the S side of the island, which was destroyed in a storm some years ago and not rebuilt.

PILOTAGE

By day

Being high and isolated, Ile de Galite and the islets around are visible from a great distance. In strong winds, especially from the NW, avoid passing between Galite and the Galitons l'Est and l'Ouest because of breakers on the shallow banks in the channels.

By night

A night approach is not difficult with the light on Galitons de l'Ouest but lights from the fishermen can be confusing. The large buoy in the entrance to the anchorage should be lit but does not seem to function most of the time (though it is shown to be lit on most charts) and the harbour light is unreliable. There are usually several unlit fishing boats at anchor in the bay.

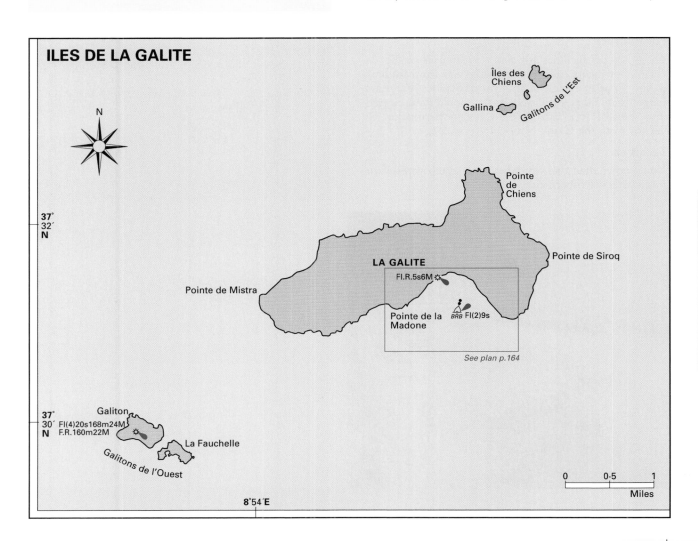

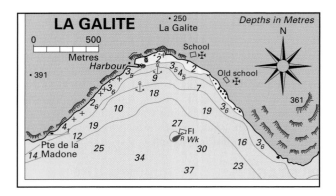

The anchorage

The large bay on the S side provides good protection in NW winds which are common on this part of the coast. Though the remains of a small harbour lie in the NW corner of the bay, occupied by fishing boats or a military vessel, the main breakwater tumbled into the harbour during a storm leaving it foul, with a jetty remaining. The buoy that covers the wreck was moved about 50m SW by the same storm and has not been replaced. The masts of the wreck have been cut and are now reportedly 12m under water. Fairly close inshore good holding is found in sand 3–5m deep. With S winds shelter can be found on the N side of the island which is less steep; care should be taken of isolated rocks along the shore.

Formalities

There are no facilities for entry to Tunisia on Ile de Galite, but yachts calling here on the way from Sardinia to the Tunisian mainland find no difficulties. For stays longer than 24hrs, officially a yacht should have cleared into Tunisia. It is advisable to obtain permission to anchor from the Garde National if possible.

Facilities

None, other than fish which you may catch yourself or trade with the fishermen.

ASHORE

Apart from a Garde National post and small army garrison the island is uninhabited, although the original Franco-Italian inhabitants return to their run-down houses in the summertime. The school and church of their small community are now occupied by cows and chickens. The tranquillity, wild vegetation and splendid views are awe inspiring.

History

Galite was inhabited for centuries by Italians from the island of Ponza near Naples. Fishing was the main source of income for the small community but judging from the fruit trees and spices still found today, they were good farmers too. When Tunisia became independent, the islanders had the choice of becoming Tunisian citizens or accepting a French resettlement offer to become French citizens. Everybody went for the latter option and gradually moved from the island. The last Italians left in 1975.

Sights locally

On the island there are wild figs and cactus fruits. Harpooning is only allowed if you have a licence from the CGP which will prove difficult to obtain because Galite has officially been declared a nature reserve and is well monitored by both military and conservation craft.

Small anchorage on the S side of Galite looking W

2. Bizerte to Cap Bon

T6 Bizerte

There are five harbours in Bizerte, the 'Port de Plaisance' being the yacht harbour. It is well run, a port of entry and easy to enter in any conditions. Formalities are fast and friendly.

Location
37°16′.9N 09°54′.0E (Just S of dique exterior and N mole of fishing harbour)

Distances
Tabarka 65M
Cap Bon 56M

Tides
Usual range less than 0.5 metre, but during February–April Mean Sea Level sometimes falls 0.5m below normal.

Charts
Admiralty *2121, 2122, 1569*
French *4314, 4198 4970, 5791, 5281*

Lights
Approach
1. **Jetée Est N head** 37°16′.4N 09°53′.4E Iso.R.4s24m10M Red tower
Harbour
2. **Jetée Nord head** 37°16′.6N 09°53′.4E F.G.15m4M
3. **Detached breakwater N head** 37°16′.9N 09°53′.5E Fl(2)R.10s10m2M
4. **Detached breakwater S head** 37°16′.5N 09°53′.8E Iso.G.4s15m4M
5. **N breakwater of new fishing port** Fl(2)G.10s12m6M
6. **S breakwater of new fishing port** Q.R.6M not visible from the N

Communications
Harbourmaster ☎ 72436610
VHF Ch 16, 4, 72
Email Bizerte@gnet.tn
www.portplaisance.bizerte.com

The port

Bizerte consists of 5 harbours:
1. The outer harbour (Avant Port)
2. Port de Plaisance (yacht harbour)
3. Old fishing port (in the town)
4. New fishing port (SE of Avant Port) T6a Bizerte Zarzouna
5. Main commercial harbour further up the canal.

Bizerte is one of the major ports in Tunisia and can be entered in any conditions; it is a good port of entry and 'hassle free'. The friendly Port de Plaisance is located in the Avant Port, near the entrance to the channel. The yacht harbour is well run with one long pontoon for visiting yachts, able to accommodate fifty yachts of lengths up to 20m or more. There are some places for larger yachts near the capitainerie.

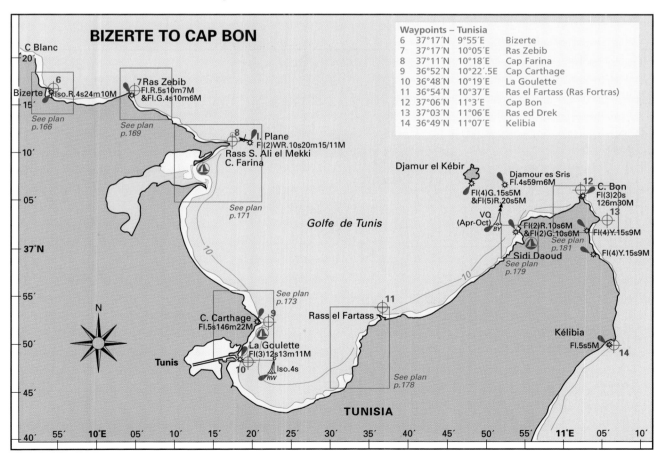

Both commercial and naval docks are situated off the channel leading from the Avant Port connecting to the Lake of Bizerte, where the port of Menzel Bourguiba has one of the biggest shipyards of North Africa.

PILOTAGE

By day

Coming from the W, Cap Bizerte is conspicuous, as are the hotels along the coast on the approach to the port. The half mile long Dique Exterior is easily identified from any direction. Stay at least 0.5M from the shore to avoid Banc de Boberak 2.2M SSE off Cap Bizerte.

By night

Cap Bizerte is not lit but there are three small but prominent peaks and a conspicuous beacon. The coast between Cap Bizerte and the port is low and well lit from apartments and hotels. A night approach to the port can be confusing especially when some of the lights do not work. Look for the lights on the Digue Exterior. From the N and E, the light on Jetée Est behind the dique will be sighted first at around 6 M, rather than the quoted range of 10M.

Warning At The N entrance to the port there is an NE setting current on the ebb and strong tidal currents are experienced in the channel. Even though the tidal range is small it is sufficient to create considerable current due to the large volume of the Lake.

Note Tunny nets usually run NNE from Ras Zebib towards Iles Cani for 3.5–4 miles. (These were not present in summer 2004.)

Berthing

Moor where space is available either side of the long floating pontoon. This is reserved for visitors and can accommodate fifty yachts of all sizes. Lines are tailed to the quay. Be aware of the strong current mentioned above which can sweep the tailing lines under your keel.

Avoid mooring alongside the old concrete jetty beneath the capitainerie to the NE of the port unless there is nowhere else available. It is crumbling and has many nasty protrusions. It is also the fuelling dock and frequented from early morning by local boats. Sometimes during winter NW storms there is little alternative, as the floating pontoon becomes untenable.

Local yachts and long-stay visitors berths are further in, SW of the main pontoon near the yacht club and restaurant where it is shallower.

Anchoring

Anchoring in the Avant Port is possible and comfortable. The best place is N of the yacht club pontoon in depths of 5m or more, just S of Jetty Nord. Closer inshore the bottom is foul and there is an old submerged wall. Close to the entrance of the old fishing port floating nets are set from rowing boats. Use an anchor light because the old fishing port is still in use. The tugboat quay on the starboard side of the channel to the lake looks inviting, but is a prohibited area for yachts, even in bad weather.

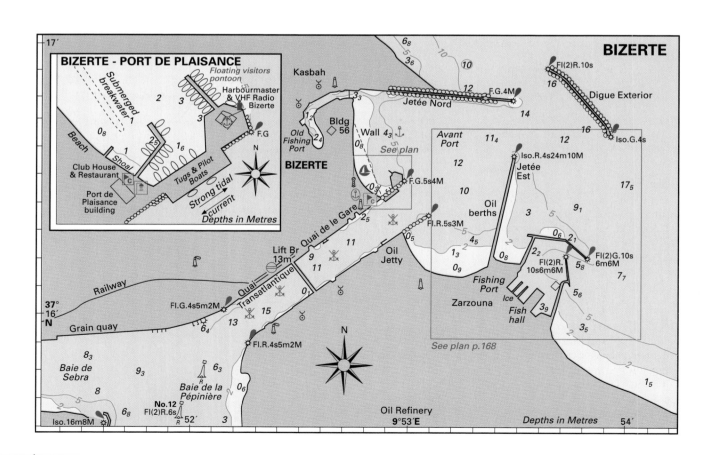

Charges for a 12m yacht

High season May–Oct
  Day TD15.5000
  Week TD100.000
  Month TD300.000
Low season Nov–April
  Day TD 11.000
  Week TD 70.000
  Month TD 215.000
One year: approx 560 TD. Long stays negotiable. Add 10% T.V.A., and another 20% for catamarans and 30% for trimarans.

Formalities

Capitainerie ☎ 02 436610 *Fax* 02 435681
  Port of entry and formalities are handled efficiently.

Facilities

Water and *electricity* Laid to each berth.
Fuel Diesel at main jetty beneath capitainerie N end of quay.
Gas Camping gaz and European type bottles can be filled at the capitainerie.
Provisions Many small shops in the town and a good market near the old port, with another in the new town, including Monoprix (for beer and wine).
Showers Warm showers in the Port de Plaisance building. Several hammams in town (addresses on a little map of Bizerte available at tourist office).
Post office On Avenue d'Algérie off the main square
Telephone Taxiphone in capitainerie .
Bank In the centre of town near the market. 'Change' in capitainerie.
Repairs Small repairs can be arranged through the capitainerie. Wood and metal workshops are in town. For larger repairs and lift-out, go to the new fishing harbour described below.
Wintering Some boats are left afloat for the winter on the inner quayed section near the yacht club.
Laundry In capitainerie.
Weather forecast Available from the Bizerte radio station next to the harbour master's office. If the small radio room is unoccupied, the operator can often be found outside fishing.
Internet facility (Publinet) Follow canal for 100m to shopping mall on right, just before the bridge. The Publinet room is on the ground floor. There are others in the town.

ASHORE

Tourism has not yet touched Bizerte and as the 'Rough Guide to Tunisia' puts it 'Bizerte is one of the most underrated of Tunisia's resorts.' The picturesque old fishing port, with a fixed bridge at its entrance, is featured on many postcards. The view inside has been diminished somewhat by the presence of a large ugly looking 'floating' restaurant built on concrete foundations in the harbour.

History

Bizerte has been one of the great natural ports of the Mediterranean since Phoenician times. The Phoenicians were probably the first to dig a channel between the Lake and the sea. Through the ages it kept its strategic importance under Byzantine, Arab, Spanish and Ottoman rulers. During the French rule the present port

Bizerte yacht harbour seen from yacht club looking N. Visitors' berths on far side   *Graham Hutt*

was constructed and after the Second World War the French held on to Bizerte (on behalf of NATO) while the rest of Tunisia had already become independent. It took a last effort of Bourguiba's army and many deaths to liberate Bizerte on the 15th of October 1963 which is now a national holiday.

Sights locally

Bizerte is a good and safe place from which to explore northern Tunisia. If you do not intend to sail W to Tabarka, visit the spectacular Roman remains at Bulla Regia from here. Wonderful deserted beaches stretch for miles to the north and west, once the new hotel complexes have been passed.

Transport

The main bus station is along the canal past the first bridge and the railway station is a little further on. Hertz car hire in the town.
  For the louage minibus station which provides cheap fast transport to many destinations, including Bizerte, get a taxi across the bridge. Tunis and Carthage are not much more than an hour away by louage and the cost is only TD3.5 per person.
  The station is approx 2km on the main road to Tunis, near the road entrance to the new fishing harbour.

Eating out

An excellent seafood restaurant above the clubhouse in the port (not too expensive). Several Tunisian style restaurants in town where Av. Taieb Mehiri runs into Av. Bourguiba and around Hotel Continental.

IV. TUNISIA

T6a Bizerte Zarzouna

The 'new' fishing port useful for lift-out and repairs.

Location
   37°16'.1N 09°53'.8E

Lights
Harbour
1. **Northern breakwater** Fl(2)G.10s6m6M
2. **Southern breakwater** Fl(2)R.10s6m6M not visible from the N

The port

This port was actually completed in 1987, but remains 'new' to distinguish it from the other ancient fishing port (see Bizerte plan) still in use in the centre of town. It provides good protection in all weather and has extensive repair and haul-out facilities which can handle yachts. The surroundings are not pretty but it is a convenient and cheap place to get repairs and painting done.

Facilities

Water Available at the fish market.
Fuel In the NW corner of the port and fish quay.
Provisions Cafes and basic shops in the port. Several fishermans' chandleries in and around the port.
Repairs There is a 110-ton & 250-ton travel-lift. Prices 10 TD per ton +70 TD chocking up fee. Arrangements for this and other repairs through APIP Director: Homadi Mathlouthi, in the port.

T7 Cap (Ras) Zebib

A small remote harbour 9M E of Bizerte on the E side of Cap Zebib prone to silting, which can take yachts up to 15m when dredged.

Location
   37°16'.N 10°04'.2E

Distances
   Bizerte 9M
   Qhar El Melh 14M,
   Sidi Bou Saïd 31M

Charts
   Admiralty *2122, 1569*
   French *5791*

Lights
1. **East Breakwater** Fl.G G tower approx 7m
2. **West Breakwater** Fl.R R tower approx 7m
3. **Beacon** S of west breakwater Fl.R R metal pylon approx 5m (precise characteristics not known.)

Communications
   VHF Ch 16

The harbour

A harbour completed in 2000 on the Eastern extremity of Cap Zebib. Used by small fishing boats but with room for yachts. The Northern extremity of Cab Zebib is foul and should be given a berth of at least 0.25m. Cap Zebib can be identified by its two conical hills, about 90m high. South of the new port are the derelict and very shallow remains of an old port destroyed in a storm.

PILOTAGE

By day

Approach the port from the SE giving the coast a good clearance. In the immediate approaches there is shoal water SW of the entrance and a red beacon, which should be left to port. The harbour is prone to silting and is regularly dredged. Marker buoys are placed in the channel to avoid the sandbanks and are moved as necessary following storms.

By night

Night entry is not recommended because of unreliable lights, shifting entry channel and nearby shallows.

Berthing

There are two piers in the centre of the port and a quay at the N end. The recommended berths are alongside the N quay or on the N side of the N pier. Depths of 2m or more are found along most of these positions.

Formalities

APIP with charming and helpful Chef de Port, though this is not a port of entry. Other authorities visit the port occasionally.

Facilities

Water At tap by fish market.
Electricity None.
Fuel Diesel obtained from pump on the N quay.
Provisions Shops in village 1.5 km from port.
Repairs 15 ton fixed crane/boat-hoist on N quay.

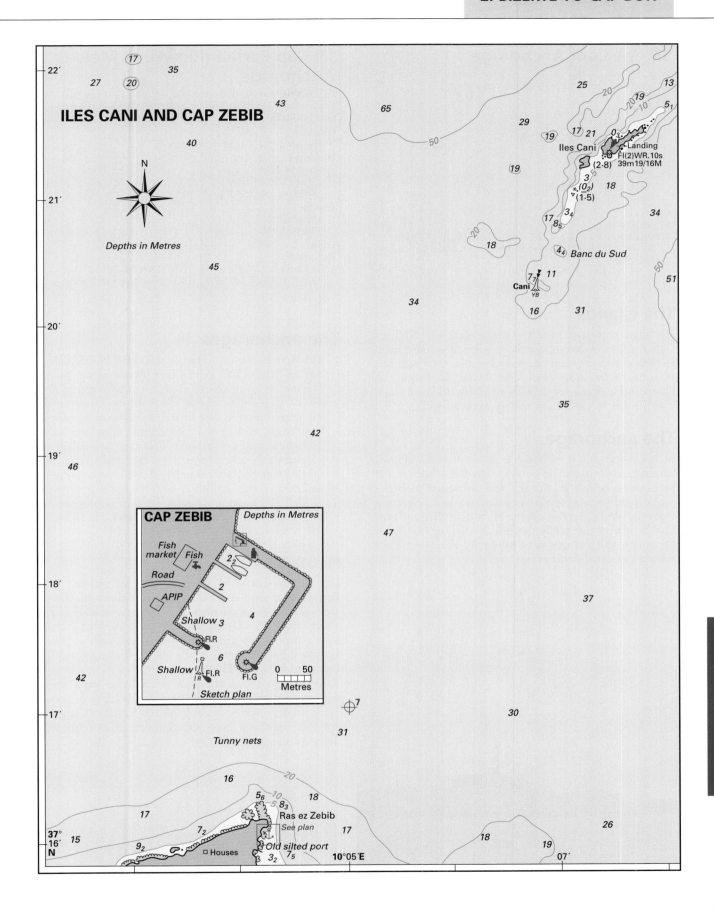

ILES CANI AND CAP ZEBIB

N

Depths in Metres

Iles Cani

Landing
Fl(2)WR.10s
39m19/16M

Banc du Sud

Cani
YB

CAP ZEBIB   Depths in Metres

Fish
market   Fish

Road

APIP

Shallow 3

Fl.R

Shallow   Fl.R

Fl.G

0   50

Metres

Sketch plan

Tunny nets

Ras ez Zebib
See plan

37°
16'
N

Old silted port

Houses

10°05′E

07′

IV. TUNISIA

T8 Iles Cani Anchorage

Two low lying islets 12M from Bizerte, completely exposed to wind and seas and with sparse vegetation.

Location
37°21'.2N 10°07'.4E

Distances
Bizerte 12M
Ghar El Melh 17M,
Sidi Bou Saïd 33M

Charts
Admiralty *2122, 1569*
French *4314, 4198*

Lights
Approach
1. **Iles Canis** 37°21'.2N 10°07'.4E Fl(2)WR.10s39m19/16M 237°-W-177°-R-231° White round tower, black bands, on dwelling

T9 Cap Farina (Ras Ali el Mekki) Anchorage

Cap Farina, between Bizerte and Sidi Bou Saïd has two anchorages, N side at Raf Raf and S of the cape close to Ghar El Melh.

Location
37°10'.6N 10°17'E (just off the cape)

Distances
Bizerte 22M
Ghar El Melh 1.5M
Sidi Bou Saïd 20M

Charts
Admiralty 2122
French 4198

Lights
Approach
1. **Ile Plane** 37°10'.8N 10°19'.7E Fl(2)WR.10s20m15/11M 067°-R-107°-W- 067° White square tower, red bands

The islands

Iles Cani, consist of two low rocky islets 6M NNE of Cap Zebib, completely exposed. Solitude is their main attraction and they can only be visited in good weather. It is an interesting place for diving or fishing. A lighthouse keeper lives with his family on the main islet. The SE side of the largest islet is steep with cliffs.

The anchorage

In good weather it is possible to lie stern-to a small landing close to the lighthouse. The NW side of the islets slopes gently to the sea and is fringed with flat rocks. Either side of the islets provides some protection from the waves. Anchor on the SE side in 15m (or less, further in), in the sandy patches clearly seen between the rocks, using a trip line. Admiralty chart No. 1569 gives good detail of Iles Cani.

The anchorages

1. 3M W from the tip of the cape, on the N side is Raf Raf (37°11'N 10°13'.5E). The beach offers good holding in 3m of coarse sand in settled weather.
2. SW of Cap Farina, about 1M from the point under the ancient fort, is one of the best anchorages along this coast with good protection from the NW prevailing wind. S of the anchorage are miles of untouched beaches formed by the deposits of the Oued Medjerda. This river has shaped the entire area and created the lagoons around the harbour of Ghar El Melh. If caught in strong headwinds on the way N, or if draught does not allow entry into Ghar El Melh, this is an excellent place to anchor.

PILOTAGE

Cap Farina should be given a berth of at least 1M. Beware of a sand spit extending S off the cape. There are several rocky shoals between the cape and Ile Plane which are of no significance in good weather but in strong winds they cause heavy seas and yachts should keep well E of Ile Plane. Watch out for floating nets. The fort provides a good landmark.

Depths in the anchorages around the cape shoal regularly towards the beach and the holding is good. Swell or large waves are rare on the S side. At night a few fishermen may keep you company in an otherwise deserted surrounding.

SE side of Iles Cani looking NW

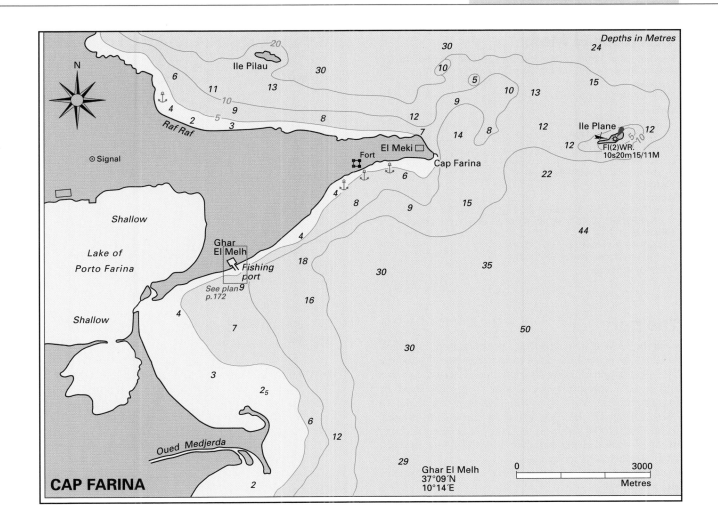

Depths in Metres

CAP FARINA

Ghar El Melh
37°09′N
10°14′E

Remarkable natural pyramid formations NW of Cap Farina
at Raf Raf   *Graham Hutt*

IV. TUNISIA

T10 Ghar El Melh

A small fishing port prone to silting lies 3M WSW of Cap Farina. Very friendly with plenty of room for yachts.

Location
37°09′N 10°14′E

Distances
Bizerte 24M
Sidi Bou Saïd 19M

Charts
Admiralty *2122*
French *4314, 4250 4191, 4198*

Lights
Approach
1. **Ile Plane** 37°10′.8N 10°19′.7E Fl(2)WR.10s20m15/11M
067°-R-107°-W-067° White square tower, red stripes.
Harbour
2. **Eastern breakwater** Fl.G.2s5m3M
3. **Western breakwater** F.R.5m3M

Communications
VHF Ch 16.

The port

Ghar El Melh is a small fishing port situated 3M WSW of Cap Farina N of the delta formed by Oued Medjerda. The port is surrounded by miles of deserted beaches and it is a tranquil place. Today it is only used by fishermen who work in rowing boats in the Lake of Porto Farina. The lake has a shallow entrance to the sea. In summer 2004, the port entrance had been recently dredged to 8m in the entrance and 4m in the channel, enabling yachts to moor inside.

PILOTAGE

By day

Sailing from the N in settled weather, pass between Cap Farina and Ile Plane. In strong NW winds, pass well E of the island. Continue WSW for 2.8M which will bring Ghar El Melh abeam. The port cannot be made out easily until very close because of the lack of buildings. The breakwaters jut out from the beach and they should be given a wide berth because of shifting sand banks. Silting of the entrance has been a problem, though dredging took place in 2004. Two groynes have been built west of the port and the W. breakwater extended to reduce the effects, but dredging will remain a frequent necessity.

Once inside the port there are depths of around 2-3 metres and good protection. Coming from the S, steer roughly between the village of Ghar El Melh and Cap Farina until the harbour is seen.

By night

A night approach is not recommended under any circumstances.

Berthing

Tie up alongside one of the larger fishing boats which are usually moored along the quay NW of the small slipway, at the ends of the two pontoons shown, or next to the slipway.

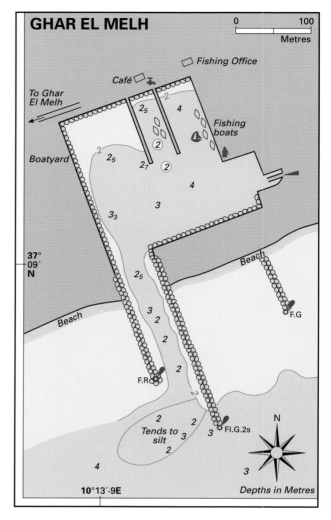

Formalities

There is Garde National post, APIP and *Marine Marchande* post but this is not a port of entry.

Facilities

Water A tap on the quay.

Ghar el Melh looking NE. Pleasant place to await good winds
Graham Hutt

Fuel Diesel is available on the East Quay.

Provisions Fresh bread and a limited selection of vegetables is available from a small shop behind the restaurant. Fish can be bought at the fish market. A good assortment of fresh produce can be found at the market in the village, 5km from the port. It is often possible to get a lift with a pick-up truck.

Post office In the village.

Telephone Taxiphone in the village.

Repairs There is a small boatyard.

ASHORE

The fish market and a few low buildings are the only signs of civilization and not easily seen until close in. The village of Ghar El Melh (formally Porto Farina) is 5km away and makes for an interesting walk if one is not picked up by the occasional passing car. Small plots of land and little islands around the lagoon produce fruit and vegetables. The Turkish fortress in Ghar El Melh, which overlooks the quaint old port, is now used as a school, but its past was less peaceful when it was a notorious pirate's nest. However when the old port silted up it lost its importance.

Eating Out

One small restaurant and a coffee bar in the port.

Transport

A bus to the town runs regularly from the café in the port.

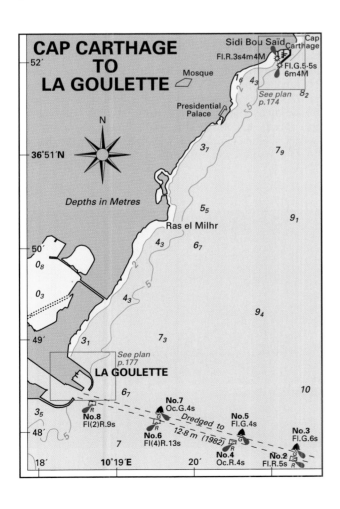

T11 Sidi Bou Saïd

The oldest marina in Tunisia, and port of entry, close to ancient Carthage and the capital. The most picturesque and photogenic village in Tunisia with 380 yacht places, max length 45m.

Location
36°51′.9N 10°21′.3E

Distances
Bizerte 42M
La Goulette 4M
Cap Bon 37M

Charts
Admiralty *2122, 1184*
French *4314, 4250*

Lights
Approach
1. **Cap Carthage** 36°52′.3N 10°20′.9E Fl.5s146m22M White tower with black top in the village
Harbour
3. **SE breakwater** Fl.G.5.5s6m4M
4. **W breakwater** Fl.R.3s4m4M

Communications
http://www.1yachtua.com/Medit-marinas/Tunisia/sidi_bou_said.htm
Harbourmaster ☎ 71741645
VHF Ch 16, 9
Email port.sbs@gnet.tn
Internet (Publinet) In the village of Marsa, though more local facilities are expected.

The marina

Sidi Bou Saïd is the oldest marina in Tunisia, opened in 1980. It is popular as a port of entry and the authorities are well accustomed to foreign visitors and speak French as well as English and Arabic. Many Europeans working in Tunis keep boats here and it is a lively place, especially at weekends. There is an active fleet of small fishing boats just inside the entrance. The setting of the port at the foot of Cap Carthage is very attractive. A stepped footpath leads from the marina up to the famous village of Sidi Bou Saïd, on top of the hill. The marina is usually crowded, but no one is ever turned away. A new and much needed marina complex is soon to be under construction nearby.

PILOTAGE

By day

Coming from the N, Cap Gammarth, the village of La Marsa will be sighted first. Cap Carthage, with two conspicuous wrecks about 500m from the port entrance, provides an unmistakable landmark. Do not venture too far S of the marina, where the presidential palace is located 1M SW of Sidi Bou Saïd. Navigation is prohibited within a radius of 500m of the palace, which is marked with buoys. A huge Tunisian flag will be seen towering above the palace. The Tunisian navy has a patrol boat permanently at sea nearby ready to burst into action should you venture too close. Hotel Amilcar is SW of the port and the minaret of the new mosque lies beyond.

By night

Coming from the N, Cap Carthage light at 146m high is visible at 22M. The large and well lit Hotel Amicar

IV. TUNISIA

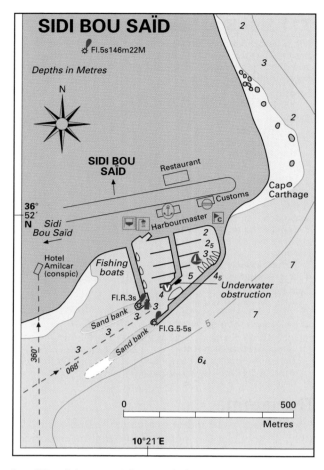

lies SW of the port. The port lights are visible at around 3M.

Night entry is not recommended if this is your first visit. The harbour lights are not entirely reliable and once inside there is little room to manoeuvre.

Entry caution

The entrance to the marina silts up and is not dredged every year. In summer 2004 the sandbank, visible at times and with waves breaking over it, extended some 70m SW of the S mole. Minimum depths in the channel between the bank and the beach are around 3.0m. The channel is unmarked until almost inside the entrance, where some unlit orange buoys are located.

To clear the sandbanks entry is advised as follows. Head N towards Hotel Amicar (Large complex SW of the port) until you can see along the inside wall of the SE mole. Turn on to a bearing of approx 068° towards the marina keeping the length of the inner mole as a transit. Several large vessels and a gunboat are usually moored alongside the wall to assist in identifying this transit. This takes you on a course almost parallel and close to the beach. Keep close to the N breakwater head as you enter as there is a shoal of depth 2.5m in the entrance opposite the fuel berth. Entry in NE to S winds of force 5 or more is difficult due to breakers on the sandbanks around the SE pierhead and with higher winds, entry is not recommended. Under these rare conditions it is better to go to La Goulette. (Currently not useable – Summer 2004 – see under that port.)

Berthing

There are 380 berths, mostly occupied by local motorboats. Tie up alongside the end of the central quay if drawing 1.5m or less. Beware of two underwater obstructions with minimum depth of 1.8m along this quay, as marked on the plan and the other, closer to the W end of the same jetty. Both are the result of poor construction. Alternatively, you may be directed to a finger pier berth or bows/stern-to on the main NE wall. The authorities turn up automatically and a yacht may stay here for a short visit, or the port captain will allocate a longer stay berth. The harbour gets very crowded in summer so be prepared for some very tight manoeuvring sometimes in strong cross-winds. The S mole is reserved for patrol boats from the Garde National, though often room is available for larger yachts further NE along the wall where lines are tailed to the quay. In strong winds from the SE, common in the spring, a considerable swell enters the port but overall, shelter is good. It is very much calmer the deeper into the marina you can berth.

Sidi Bou Saïd viewed from the SE

Charges for a 12m yacht

High season May-Oct
Day TD37.000
Week TD250.000
Month Negotiable
Low season Nov-April
Day TD 25.000
Week TD 170.000
Month Negotiable
Multihulls add 30%
Add 10% TVA

Formalities

A port of entry. All officials are in the port 24hrs a day.

Facilities

Water and electricity On the pontoons for each berth. (new boxes fitted).
Fuel Diesel and petrol from pumps at the end of the W breakwater.
Gas Difficult to get refills. Ask at the capitainerie who will direct you to a shop that may refill camping gas cylinders.
Provisions A small shop in the marina and another just outside the port have fresh bread and a limited assortment of groceries. Magasin Général in the village and a small covered market next to it. A large new *supermarché* in Carthage. A Monoprix and the best market in La Marsa. A new Carrefour has also opened nearby. Although not the most convenient place to go shopping, the colourful central market in Tunis has the best assortment of fruit, vegetable, cheese, meat (including pork and wild boar) and fish that the country produces.

Fresh fish can be bought from fishermen in the port - but bargain!

Duty-free alcohol, cigarettes, perfumes etc. can be ordered through the harbourmaster. Large orders will be delivered to the boat.

Handicrafts can be found in a small market in the village.
Showers In the new harbour buildings. There is also a *hammam* in the village.
Post office In the village.
Telephone and *Fax* In the harbour office.

Sidi Bou Saïd marina in the Gulf of Tunis, from the village above   *Graham Hutt*

Bank In the village, 'change' in the capitainerie.
Repairs 22-ton travel-lift with small high pressure pump in the port. Price about TD 200 for 10–12m yacht, in and out, excluding the high pressure pump and hose.

Maintenance and minor repair work can be carried out. There are two chandleries with limited stock but possibly the best you will find in Tunisia. (but see note in Sailmakers and Sail Repair Facilities section of the Introduction (page 154) re Seamtech who supply all Tunisia). 'General Equipment':
☎ 01743435. Ask for Narges who is keen to help. A caretaker for wintering afloat can be arranged. Work on the hard has to be carried out within a reasonable time period because of limited space. Perkins has an agent in Tunis.
Laundry Available in the town.

ASHORE

History

Sidi Bou Saïd village, above the marina is a place of extraordinary charm and beauty with its narrow streets and white-washed houses with blue studded doors. Founded in 1888 in one of the pavilions of the Bey's palace, it has been – and remains – home to artists, writers and craftsmen. Many famous artists have spent time here, and the Café des Nattes was their favourite meeting place.

Sights locally

This is the best and safest port from which to visit Tunis, Carthage and the Bardo museum. The latter houses one of the world's finest collections of antique floor mosaics, which are arranged in six sections, each reflecting a different era of history, including Greek, Byzantine and Arab-Muslim.

Carthage, once the richest and most desired city in the world, is within walking distance, though the efficient TGM train goes from Sidi Bou Saïd to the centre of Tunis in 30 minutes, stopping at the Carthage ruins.

There is not room here to describe the many attractions of Tunis and Carthage but the travel guides in the reference list cover them well. The Tourist Information office in Tunis is on the Place de l'Afrique, at the beginning of Avenue Bourguiba, about 200m from the TGM station. It provides a wealth of books, photographs, wall posters and CDs covering the whole of Tunisia. Most are provided free.

Nearby, to the E of Tunis, is a new development of Gammarth, which is being built as a special place of beauty to be admired for centuries to come.

Eating out

European-style dining in Le Pirate just outside the marina gate and not too expensive. Many local and tourist restaurants up the steps to the village and more nearby in Marsa.

Transport

The international airport of Tunis is a 20 minute taxi ride from the port (about TD 4). Taxis are available just outside the marina. Car hire can be arranged through the harbourmaster but all big agencies have offices at the airport. Most are negotiable.

T12 la Goulette

A large safe harbour 4M SSW of marina Sidi Bou Saïd and port of entry offering an alternative to the overcrowded and expensive nearby marina.
Note In summer 2004, all pleasure craft were being turned away aggressively, both from the harbour just inside the entrance, and from the canal. No reasons were given and this could just be a temporary inconvenience.

Location
36°48'.5N 10°18'.6E

Distances
Sidi Bou Saïd 4M
Cap Bon 40M

Charts
Admiralty *2122, 1184*
French *4314, 6062, 4222*

Lights
Approach
1. **Jetée Nord SE corner** 36°48'.3N 10°18'.5E
Fl(3)12s13m11M partially obscured by the breakwaters 090°-vis-121°, 215°-vis-035°
2. **Chimney 1M SW of entrance** 36°47'.6N 10°17'.0E
Fl.R.1.5s(hor)102m8M
Harbour
3. **Digue Nord** 36°48'.3N 10°18'.9E
Fl(2)G.10s9m5M
4. **Digue Sud (channel entrance)** 36°48'.4N 10°18'.5E
Fl.R.5s9m6M
5. **Jetée Nord NE corner (entrance to fishing port)**
36°48'.3N 10°18'.5E F.R.13m5M
6. **Ro Ro berth** Fl.G.4s7m6M

Communications
Harbourmaster ☎ 730141
Yacht Club ☎ 736284
VHF Ch 10, 16

The port

La Goulette harbour is situated at the mouth of a 6M long dredged channel which leads through the Lake of Tunis to the capital. It can be entered in all weather conditions and shelter is better than in Sidi Bou Saïd. It is a major commercial port without any great charm, but the town, although a long walk away, is attractive and Tunis is close. A fishing harbour and yacht club is situated N of the entrance to the channel, though Sidi Bou Saïd has always been more popular with foreign visitors. Before La Goulette was closed to yachts, it was an excellent and cheaper alternative. Inside the channel is a ferry terminal and further up, at its end, is the large commercial port of Tunis. There are plans to turn a dilapidated part of the old commercial port in the heart of the city, into a marina. Larger pleasure craft can usually obtain permission to transit the canal and berth in the commercial port of Tunis.

PILOTAGE

By day

Day approach is without any problem, but keep a good lookout for commercial vessels leaving or entering the port. There are always ships anchored in the Bay of Tunis awaiting entry. The main channel leading to the canal is dredged to 12m. The 6M long canal leading to the centre of Tunis is dredged to 8m and well marked along its length.

By night

The entrance buoys and Dique Sud and Dique Nord are well lit and entry presents no problems.

Berthing

The outer end of the 3 pontoons usually has space for visitors' with mooring buoys tailed to the quays. If these are full, take a berth wherever there is space. Moor bows/stern-to. It should be noted, however, that tailed lines are unreliable. If anchoring becomes necessary, holding is good in mud.

Formalities

Port of entry. Police, customs and Garde National, will come from the ferry terminal.

Facilities

Water and *electricity* On the pontoons.
Fuel Diesel available on the fish quay.
Provisions Good market and many shops in the village a short walk from the port. There are also many shops around the port.
Showers Several in the clubhouse.
Post office In the town.
Telephone In the clubhouse.
Bank exchange At the ferry terminal, open 24hrs a day 7 days a week.
Repairs The club hauls boats ashore using a mobile crane. La Goulette has all kinds of repair shops, though locating them is not easy. The yacht club staff are very helpful in finding what is needed. Engine repair and welding facilities are in abundance. There is a small crane but for hauling out, Sidi Bou Saïd is a better option.
Laundry One of the few launderettes in Tunisia is found in La Goulette, in a key copying shop at the bottom of the only tall white apartment building. Price roughly TD 4 for 7kg + TD 1 for drying but there is a washing machine in the yacht club.

ASHORE

Apart from the kasbah fortress built by the Spanish King Charles V in 1535 and its associated history, there are no particular points of interest in La Goulette but it does have a lively atmosphere. It is a convenient base for visits to Tunis and Sidi Bou Saïd. The long canal leading to the city is without interest for yachts until (and unless) the new marina at the end in the city is completed. The commercial port of Tunis, although very close to the city centre, is a dusty and uncomfortable place.

Eating out

Beer and other alcoholic drinks are served on the terrace of the yacht club and the atmosphere is relaxed. The town has several good local style fish restaurants.

Transport

The TGM train to Tunis takes about 10 minutes. A taxi to the airport takes about 20 minutes.

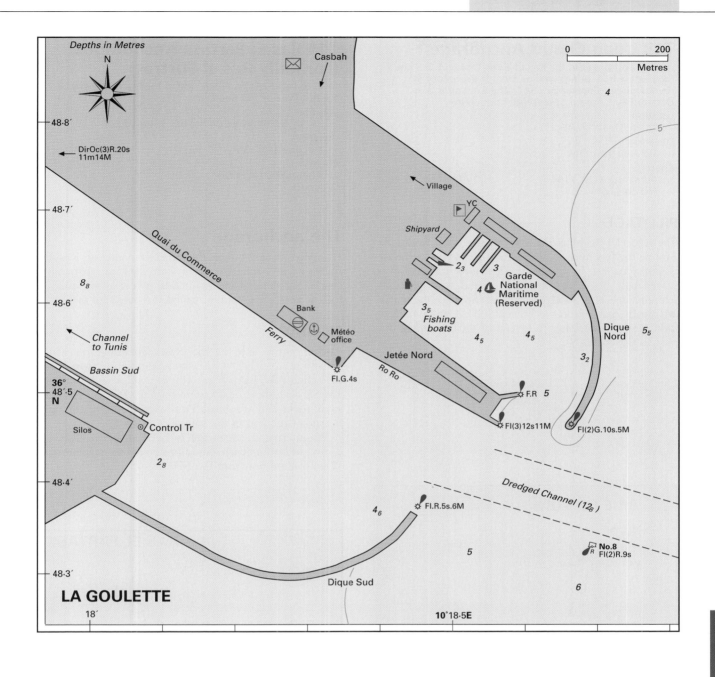

Depths in Metres

N

Casbah

0   200
Metres

4

5

48·8′

DirOc(3)R.20s
11m14M

Village

YC

Quai du Commerce

Shipyard

48·7′

8_8

2_3 3

Garde
National
Maritime
(Reserved)

Dique
Nord 5_5

4

48·6′

Bank

3_5
Fishing
boats

4_5 4_5

3_2

Channel
to Tunis

Météo
office

Ferry

Jetée Nord

Ro Ro

Fl.G.4s

Bassin Sud

36°
48′·5
N

Control Tr

F.R   5

Fl(3)12s11M

Fl(2)G.10s.5M

Silos

2_8

Dredged Channel (12_8)

48·4′

4_6

Fl.R.5s.6M

No.8
Fl(2)R.9s

5

Dique Sud

6

48·3′

LA GOULETTE

18′

10°18·5E

T13 L'eau Chaud Anchorage

A small anchorage in the Bay of Tunis 11M E of Sidi Bou Saïd where hot springs well up from the sea floor in several places. Popular by day, in the evening it is deserted and a place of absolute tranquillity.

Location
36°50′.5N 10°34′.4E

Distances
Sidi Bou Saïd 11M

Charts
Admiralty *2122, 1184*
French *4222*

PILOTAGE

The resort of Korbous 2M S serves as a good landmark. Among the few houses around the tiny bay, a blue house is conspicuous. In moderate N winds protection is surprisingly good. Anchor in 7m sand with rocks. A tripping line is a good precaution. 'Sources thermales' are clearly marked on the French SHOM chart 4222 to indicate the hot springs in several of the bays along this part of the coast.

T14 Ras El Fartass Anchorages (formally Ras el Fortras)

Deserted anchorages either side of the Ras in the Bay of Tunis, 13M E of Sidi Bou Saïd.

Location
36°52′.6N 10°36′.6E (In the bay S side of Ras)

Distances
Sidi Bou Saïd 13M

Charts
Admiralty *2122, 1184*
French *4222*

The anchorage

Formally known under the Spanish name of Ras El Fortras, the name has been corrected on Admiralty charts. Surrounded by mountains, a few goats looking for the scarce vegetation may be the only sign of life.

PILOTAGE

Anchor either side of the Ras, depending on wind direction. Neither give any protection from the prevailing NW. Just off the Ras is a shipwreck. Anchor 1M SE off a short beach with the shipwreck N, in 5-6m sand, rocks and sea weed. Protection from NE through S winds (frequent in the summer), is good.

An alternative anchorage is 1M ESE of the Ras, in 3-4m sand off a beach. Good protection from S through W winds, but not from the NW.

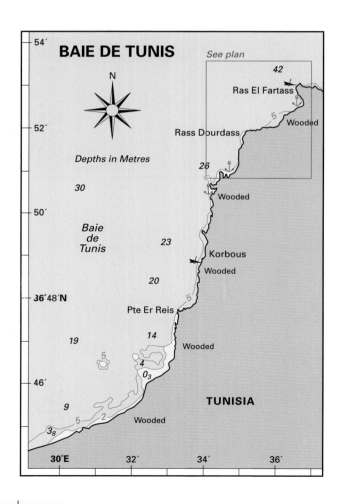

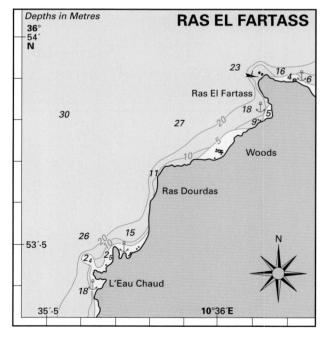

T15 Sidi Daoud

A friendly harbour and port of entry close to Cap Bon, but difficult to negotiate because of shifting sands and nets around the entrance.

Location
37°01′.1N 10°54′.4E

Distances
Sidi Bou Saïd 29M
Cap Bon 8M

Charts
Admiralty *2122*
French *4314, 4191*

Lights
Harbour
1. **N Jetée head** Fl(2)R.10s3m6M
2. **S Jetée head** Fl(2)G.10s3m6M
3. **Directional** white light on white pillar approx 10m at elbow of breakwater

Communications
APIP ☎ 02 294528 VHF 16

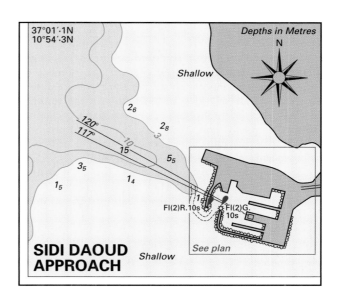

SIDI DAOUD
APPROACH

The harbour

Sidi Daoud is surrounded by shallow water and with onshore winds, quite a sea builds up. Depths within the port must be treated with caution as silting also takes place inside, as well as around the entrance.

PILOTAGE

By day

A line of wind generators form a backdrop to the port making identification easy. The port must be approached from the NW with a final approach from the N along the S going mole, though this changes from year to year.

The coast is shallow with patches of sand, weed and rocks and has depths between 1.0m and 5m within a radius of 1M of the port. Two tunny nets form part of the entrance extending from the coast in a WNW direction. The outer extremities are marked with N cardinal buoys. Entry should be made by going between

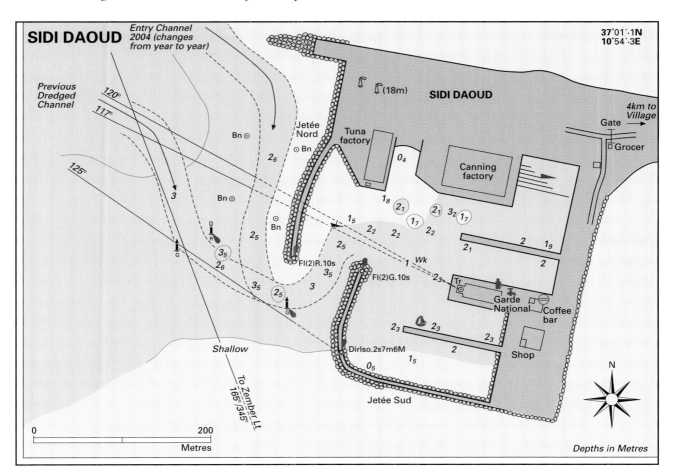

IV. TUNISIA

the N cardinal buoy of the S net, and the W cardinal buoy of the N net. This leads into the channel. In any onshore wind there is a confused sea in the shallows. The actual orientation of the channel and number of buoys in place changes with storms and resultant silting, so charting can only give an indication. In the summer of 2004, there were 4 green buoys marking the channel from the north and two red buoys near the W breakwater. Several earlier reports gave a different number and colour of buoys.

If entry looks confusing, wait for a returning fisherman to guide you in. They are always helpful and friendly here and there is a lot of traffic from the small boats attending the tunny nets.

By night

An approach at night or in unsettled weather is not recommended.

Berthing

Visiting yachts can usually find room on the S pier in minimum depths of 2m. The bottom is covered with thick seaweed and shoals quickly towards the S breakwater. Alternatively, try the N. quay. The fish quay has depths of 2m.

Warning: In the middle of the port midway between the port entry light and the tuna factory lies a dangerous wreck, barely submerged.

Formalities

Garde National and customs in the port, which has been upgraded to a port of entry.

Facilities

Water Water tap near the customs office.
Electricity None available.
Ice Available
Fuel Available in the port.
Provisions A small épicerie at the entrance gate to the tuna factory sells bread and some fresh vegetables. There is a small shop SE of the fish hall. The hamlet of Sidi Daoud is about 4km from the port. El Haouaria, 10km, is the nearest town. Taxi 1TD.
Repairs There is a boatyard and slip. Mechanical repairs are possible.
Post office The first house down the road to the village.
Taxi Comes regularly to the port.

ASHORE

Sights locally

During the tunny season from Apr.1-July it is quite spectacular to watch the 300 to 400kg blue fin tuna being caught in the nets which run 2 miles off the port. The shallow waters make the event a very visible affair. At weekends an excursion boat takes spectators out to the nets. After the tuna have been brought ashore, a long line of women from the nearby village march into the factory to clean the fish. They are then shipped, fresh on ice, to Japan and a few Japanese are there to make sure that the fish are properly packed. The port is surrounded by salt marshes and this is one of the few places along the Mediterranean shores where salicorn (samphire) grows abundantly. Preserved in vinegar this

Sidi Daoud: tuna hauling, some weigh half a ton, most are exported to Japan

makes a delicious salad ingredient or appetizer. Fish are plentiful in the waters around Cap Bon and occasionally good-sized lobsters are caught.

El Haouaria
New port reported, no info available
Location
37°04'.5N 10°58'.6E

A new port reported, as yet unofficially open, and with no information available. Depths of less than 1.5m are reported.

T16 Zembra Island (Djamour el Kébir)

An anchorage on the S side of the Island of Zembra, only for use in an emergency.

Location
37°07′N 10°48′.4E

Distances
Cap Bon 11.5M
Kelibia 27M

Charts
Admiralty *2122*
French *4191*

THE ANCHORAGE

A few white buildings around an old port. These were once used by a sailing club and diving centre. The island is now a military and conservation zone and yachts are not allowed to anchor except in an emergency.

The only place to anchor is on the SW side of the island in a small bay between the light and a rocky protrusion. Protection from N and NW winds is good but anchoring is precarious as deep water extends close up to the beach and the holding is poor. Fishing is prohibited around the island.

T17 Anchorages around Cap Bon

Cap Bon Anchorage
A remote and useful anchorage with good shelter from NE to S winds, in a bay W of a finger on the tip of Cap Bon.

Location
37°04′.9N 11°02′.

Distances
Sidi Bou Saïd 37M
Kelibia 16M

Charts
Admiralty 2122
French 4191

Lights
Cap Bon Fl(3)20s126m30M

PILOTAGE

A small bay with good holding in 4m fine sand, close to the shore, 1M S of the cape. The sandy patches can be easily seen in the crystal clear water. The wind will blow steadily down the steep mountain face but the sea will be flat unless it changes to the NW. Between this anchorage and the anchorage of Ras Ed Drek on the other side of the cape, good shelter can be found in all prevailing wind directions around Cap Bon. There are no facilities ashore, just good snorkelling and fishing around the rocks.

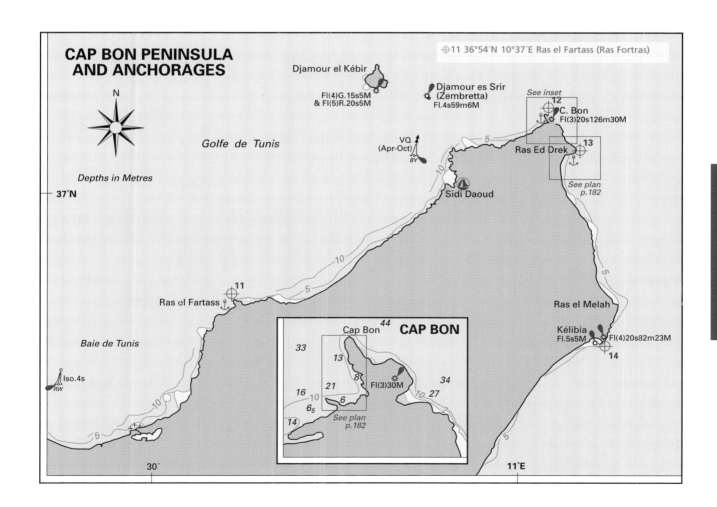

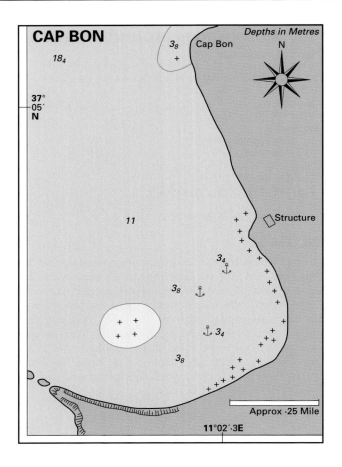

CAP BON

Depths in Metres

18_4

Cap Bon

N

37° 05' N

11

Structure

3_4

3_8

3_8

3_4

3_8

Approx ·25 Mile

11°02'·3E

T18 Ras Ed Drek anchorage

A small shallow harbour of little use to yachts, but with an anchorage off a beach 2.5M S of Cap Bon providing good protection from W to N.

Location
37°02'.3N 11°04'E

The anchorage

The harbour, though completed in 2000 is very shallow and does not encourage yachts. There is, however, a good anchorage off the beach SE of the harbour with good holding if awaiting lighter NW winds to round Cap Bon going W.

PILOTAGE

Lights mark two of the many wrecks along this coast, noted on chart 2122. 4M further S, N and S cardinal buoys have been placed, presumably marking the extent of a protected conservation zone where no fishing is allowed.

Anchoring

Anchor 4-6m in sand between the rocky point and a large wreck, marked by one mast still above water, 400m from the beach. High up on the cape are the remains of an old fortress and towards the S wide sandy beaches, with scattered houses, stretch towards the shore installations of a gas pipeline which is used to export Algerian gas to Italy.

Protection in NE winds is not good as the waves roll around the rocky point on the N side.

ASHORE

Ras Ed Drek marks the area where the mountainous N coast of Tunisia gives way to miles of low sandy beaches and more desert-like conditions stretching 240 miles S to the Libyan border. This is the main tourist coast of Tunisia. Lined with clusters of hotels all the way, there are still plenty of deserted or inaccessible beaches. In 2000 a new harbour was built here, but there was nothing ashore. Little has changed since then.

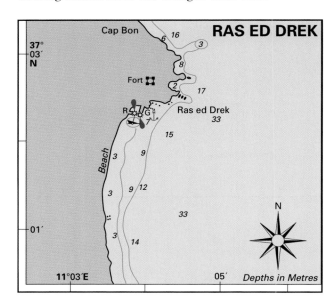

RAS ED DREK

Cap Bon

6 16

37° 03' N

3

8

Fort

2

17

R G

Ras ed Drek

33

15

Beach

3

9

3

9 12

33

3

14

N

01'

11°03'E

05'

Depths in Metres

3. Kelibia to Teboulba

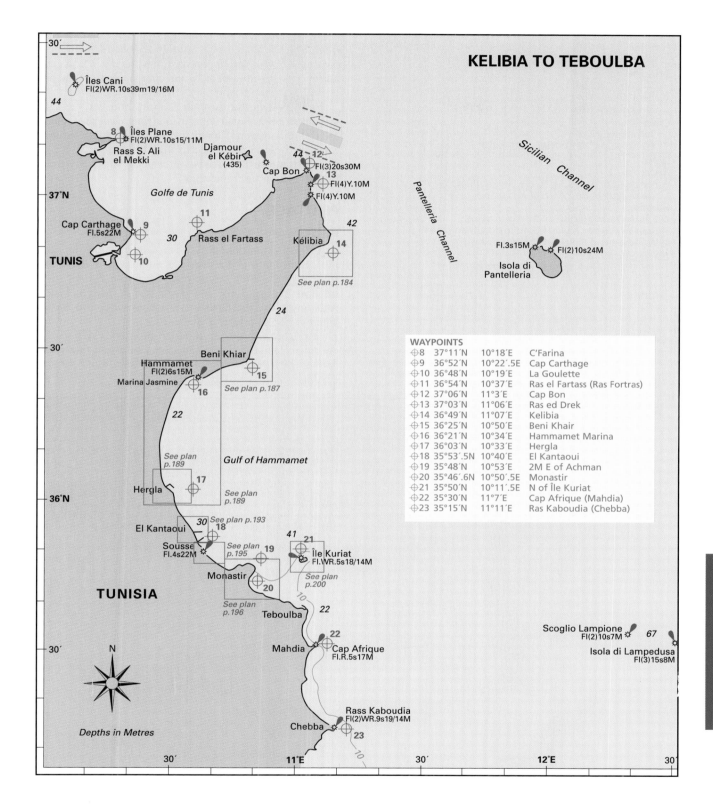

KELIBIA TO TEBOULBA

Îles Cani
Fl(2)WR.10s39m19/16M

44

8 Îles Plane
Fl(2)WR.10s15/11M
Rass S. Ali
el Mekki

Djamour
el Kébir
(435)

44 12
Cap Bon Fl(3)20s30M
13 Fl(4)Y.10M
Fl(4)Y.10M

Sicilian Channel

Pantelleria Channel

37°N

Golfe de Tunis

11

Cap Carthage 9
Fl.5s22M

30

Rass el Fartass

42

Kélibia 14

Fl.3s15M Fl(2)10s24M

Isola di
Pantelleria

TUNIS

10

24

30′

Beni Khiar

Hammamet Fl(2)6s15M
Marina Jasmine 16

15

See plan p.187

22

See plan
p.189

Gulf of Hammamet

36°N

Hergla 17

See plan
p.189

30 See plan p.193

El Kantaoui 18

41 21

See plan
p.195 19

Île Kuriat
Fl.WR.5s18/14M

Sousse
Fl.4s22M

Monastir 20

See plan
p.200

TUNISIA

See plan
p.196

Teboulba 22

N

22

Mahdia Cap Afrique
Fl.R.5s17M

Scoglio Lampione 67
Fl(2)10s7M

Isola di Lampedusa
Fl(3)15s8M

30′

Rass Kaboudia
Fl(2)WR.9s19/14M

Chebba 23

Depths in Metres

WAYPOINTS
8	37°11′N	10°18′E	C'Farina
9	36°52′N	10°22′.5E	Cap Carthage
10	36°48′N	10°19′E	La Goulette
11	36°54′N	10°37′E	Ras el Fartass (Ras Fortras)
12	37°06′N	11°3′E	Cap Bon
13	37°03′N	11°06′E	Ras ed Drek
14	36°49′N	11°07′E	Kelibia
15	36°25′N	10°50′E	Beni Khair
16	36°21′N	10°34′E	Hammamet Marina
17	36°03′N	10°33′E	Hergla
18	35°53′.5N	10°40′E	El Kantaoui
19	35°48′N	10°53′E	2M E of Achman
20	35°46′.6N	10°50′.5E	Monastir
21	35°50′N	10°11′.5E	N of Île Kuriat
22	35°30′N	11°7′E	Cap Afrique (Mahdia)
23	35°15′N	11°11′E	Ras Kaboudia (Chebba)

IV. TUNISIA

T19 Kelibia

16M S of Cap Bon on the E side, Kelibia is a friendly port of entry and a good place to await fair winds for rounding Cap Bon.

Location
   36°50′.1N 11°06′.8E

Distances
   Sidi Bou Saïd 58M
   Beni Khiar 28M
   El Kantaoui 63M

Charts
   Admiralty *2122*
   French *4314, 4315 4183 4191, 4221*

Lights
Approach
1. **Fortress** 36°50′.2N 11°06′.9E Fl(4)20s82m23M White masonry structure with black lantern

Harbour
2. **S Jetée head** Fl(2)8s5m5M White pylon
3. **Spur of S Jetée head** Fl.G.4s5m2M Green pylon
4. **W Jetée head** Fl.R.2s5m2M Red pylon

Communications
   Harbourmaster ☎ 72273639/72273074
   VHF Ch 16

The port

Due to its strategic location on the Cap Bon peninsula, the fishing harbour of Kelibia is a well used port of entry/departure. Despite this, there is only one crowded quay, which is shared by a military vessel and small local pleasure boats which occupy the quay. Whilst the authorities do not seem to encourage yachts, they are friendly, courteous and very efficient.

Protection inside the port is good and entry is safe in almost any weather except in strong easterlies which are not uncommon. Surveillance in the port is good and there are no security concerns. It is often a windy place, with strong north westerlies prevailing, especially from mid-afternoon until midnight.

PILOTAGE

By day

The port is overlooked by a fortress, built on the only hill in the area. This provides an excellent landmark from any direction. If coming from the N stay well offshore to avoid the low cape Ras el Melah. When rounding the S breakwater do not wander too far N where it shoals towards the beach.

Strong easterlies can produce breakers close to the entrance. Take care from late afternoon when the whole fishing fleet, some of them unlit and most towing smaller craft, leaves the port.

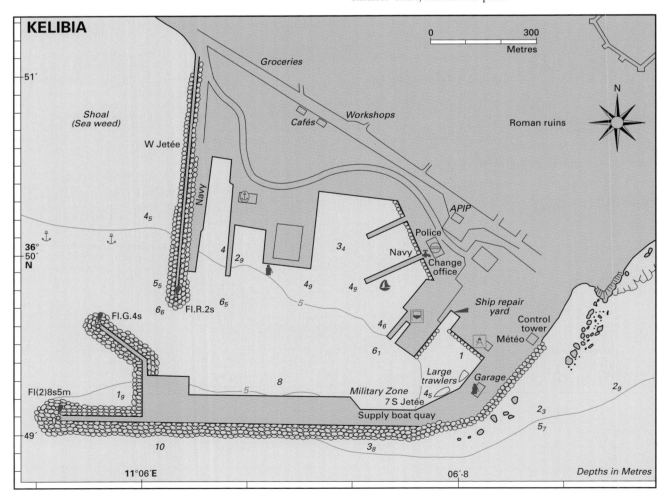

Kelibia harbour from the fortress with a squall sweeping across: common in the afternoons   *Graham Hutt*

Kelibia: always a tight squeeze. The ancient fortress dominates   *Graham Hutt*

By night

No problems. From the N, Ras el Melah has a weak light and the approach light is installed in a small tower on the fortress, which is itself well lit. The port and starboard entry lights are sighted at around 3M.

Berthing

Small locally owned motor boats often use the quay, making it difficult to moor alongside, though they will sometimes move if asked. It is not unusual to have to rack out four deep with smaller vessels on the inside. Lie alongside, either side of the reserved quay. If you manage to get on the inside, a fender board is an advantage to keep off the wooden piles mounted vertically on the concrete quay. The quay on the inside of the S breakwater is reserved for the supply tug servicing the Tazerka oil platform and the W breakwater is used by the Tunisian navy. Anchoring W of the harbour entrance is not recommended since easterlies produce considerable swell, except fairly close to the harbour entrance where it is shallow with thick weed and very poor holding. The port has depths of 4m and more in most places.

Note Be prepared for strong cross-wind gusts as you moor, especially in late afternoon.

Charges for a 12m yacht

High season May–Oct
   Day TD9.350
   Week TD60.000
Low season Nov–April
   Day TD 6.500
   Week TD 35.000
Longer stays negotiable.
Water and electricity per day TD3.

Formalities

Port of entry. Authorities are friendly and well used to visiting yachts.

Facilities

Water Available from a tap at the root of the yacht quay.
Electricity Available from several dilapidated boxes along the quay.
Fuel Diesel from a pump in the SE corner and another one near the fish hall.
Gas The grocery shops along the road to Kelibia will refill camping gas bottles. Other bottles can only be filled if fitted with an open-ended hose.
Provisions Several grocery shops around the port where most basic provisions can be found. Fresh produce from the daily market. Monday is the big weekly market.
Ice Available on the fish quay. Do not use in drinks.
Repairs The 250-ton travel-lift can handle any yacht but there are no specialised yacht facilities. Engine repairs can be taken care of by one of the several workshops around the port.
Post office and *telephone* In the town.
Bank In the town.
Weather forecast: Available at the control tower. VHF 16 then 72. Radio Kelibia for meteorology at approx. 0600 and 1000. Also available from Italy ch 68.
Wintering It is possible to winter here either on the hard or in the water.

ASHORE

History of Kelibia

From ancient times, this has been one of the most important fortifications in the entire Mediterranean because of its strategic location. The original city, Apsis, later renamed Clipea, was built by the Carthaginians in the 5th century BC and was one of the principal cities until the 11th century AD. A major ship building yard was established: a craft that remains on a small scale to this day in the port.

Carthaginians built the original huge fortress. The Romans laid siege to the city by land and sea, which held out for two years before capitulating. Despite the destruction of the fortress in 146BC, several parts of the original wall as well as foundations have been excavated, revealing the layout of the Punic citadel. The end of the first Punic war increased the importance of Kelibia because it protected Roman possessions to the north and therefore became the Italians' first target for landing. Besides protecting the city, the fortress protected the rich surrounding agricultural plains from the raiding Greek pirates based on the nearby island of Zembra.

During the Byzantine period (6th to 11th century), following unification of the Mediterranean after the Roman conquest, little interest was shown in the fortress, and in 580AD the smaller fortress, evident today, was built. This became the last refuge of the Byzantine army following its defeat in Carthage in 698AD. From there the army fled to Pantelleria, falling into the hands of the Arabs.

With the establishment of Muslim rule in North Africa in 7th century AD, the importance of Kelibia as a major military stronghold was again established. The fort became the centre of a ribat (place of learning and home to a teacher) inhabited by ascetic Sufi Muslims who were responsible for controlling the coastline and teaching young Arab volunteers to fight. They were destined, as part of the Aghlabid fleet based in Tunis, to conquer Sicily and the other Mediterranean islands for Islam. Kelibia, Sousse and Sidi Daoud again became major shipbuilding centres during the 10th century from where expeditions against southern Italy set sail.

With the departure of the Fatimid Caliphs to Egypt, the Tunisian naval power under the Zirids collapsed. Kelibia became a target for the Norman fleet established in Sicily in the 10th century. The Normans conquered the city at the end of the 10th century and made it their base in the fight for Tunis.

Successive raids from Sicily caused the population to move 2km inland seeking protection, where the present town is located. The old town at the foot of the hill was finally abandoned in the 13th century. The citadel continued to be maintained by the princes of Tunis and was used until 15th century.

Sights locally

A short walk up the hill to the castle gives a spectacular view of the harbour, as well as north to Cap Bon. This is an excellent place from which to judge the sea conditions to the north and east before leaving the protection of the harbour. The castle itself is interesting to see and entry is only one Dinar.

Just 15km north of Kelibia is the archaeological site of Kerkouane. This Carthaginian village caused great excitement when it was discovered in 1952. Its origins have been dated to the 5th century BC and it was abandoned sometime in the 2nd century BC, after the fall of Carthage. The Romans never reoccupied the site which explains why it is so well preserved. The excavations revealed a complete village and the street plan, drainage systems and even the baths in the houses can still be recognised. The idyllic site on the shore has been enhanced with lovely gardens and a small museum with artefacts found during the excavations; among them some beautiful pieces of jewellery. A taxi from the port reaches Kerkouane in about 20 minutes.

These walls have guarded the nearby town since Carthaginian times   *Graham Hutt*

Eating out

Simple local menu in Le Goeland on the seafront with another eating place, 'Le Petite Pecheur' close to the S exit gate. Two restaurants on the road to Kelibia and many more in the town. Local hotels serve non residents European food if required.

Transport

Taxis provide transportation into the main town, some 2km inland.

T20 Beni Khiar

A small, friendly fishing harbour on the N side of the Gulf of Hammamet, 13M from Marina Jasmine.

Location
36°27′.0N 10°47′.8E

Distances
Kelibia 28M
Marina Jasmine 13M
El Kantaoui 35M

Charts
Admiralty *176*
French *4315, 4314, 4183, 4225*

Lights
Harbour
1. **SE breakwater** Fl(2)G.10s5m6M
2. **SW breakwater** Fl.R.5s5m6M

Communications
Harbourmaster ☎ 7229376
VHF Ch 16

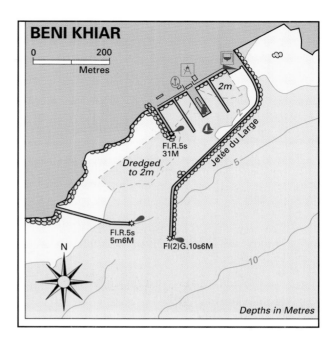

The harbour

A small friendly fishing harbour, prone to silting, in the N of the Gulf of Hammamet. Yachts are welcome and there is sufficient room for visitors. There is a sandy beach E. of the breakwater. Dredging the entrance is a frequent necessity, so the entry depths cannot be relied upon. Usually after dredging 3m depths are found in the entrance.

PILOTAGE

By day

The port is located directly under Ras Maamoura. A brown minaret in the village of Beni Khiar, slightly W of the port and the hotel complexes of Nabeul and Hammamet, further to the W, are conspicuous. When closer, the ice tower in the port will be spotted behind the breakwater.

Dredging was carried out in 2004 and 6 buoys marked the channel, though these looked temporary. Keep close to the E breakwater once near the S section of the breakwater for best depths.

With easterly swell or in strong SE to SW winds, the waves break close to the port entrance on the irregular and shallow bottom 300m SW of the entrance and entry is dangerous.

By night

Not recommended unless recent dredging has taken place because the channel is unlit, though breakwater lights are reported to be reliable.

Berthing

Keep close to the harbour S wall until opposite the first (W) finger pontoon. Visiting yachts usually lie alongside the first pier which has depths of approximately 2.5m at the end, or alongside the fish hall quay where there are 2m depths.

Formalities

Garde National, APIP and *marine marchande* in the port. Not a port of entry.

Facilities

Water Available from a tap at the end of the fish hall.

Fuel Diesel from a pump in the port, petrol has to be carried from the village.

Provisions Bread may be obtainable in the port but anything more has to come from the village of Beni Khiar 3km away, which is well supplied. 2km E a pleasant walk to Maamoura, for basic shops and beach.

Chandlery There is a fishermen's chandlery run by the Fishermen's Cooperative and another chandlery on the road leading to the village approx 1 km from the port. Also some small local shops selling mostly fishing tackle.

Post office, telephone and *bank* In the village.

WCs At the end the of the fish market.

Entrance to Beni Khiar viewed from SE   *Graham Hutt*

Beni Khiar fishing port viewed from entrance light
Graham Hutt

ASHORE

Sites locally

The village of Beni Khiar, 3km further inland, is a weaving centre for bedspreads and carpets. Wandering through the narrow alleys, looms will be found in almost every gap in the wall. Nabeul is only a short taxi ride from Beni Khiar and besides being the seat of the provincial governor, it is Tunisia's capital for fine pottery and stonework. The weekly market on Friday has become a sort of tourist attraction but for yachtsmen it may just be a good place to stock up on fresh supplies. Almost all the pork raised in Tunisia and sold around the capital comes from Nabeul. In summertime an excursion boat makes day trips with tourists from nearby hotels in Nabeul and from Hammamet Marina Jasmine.

Eating out

There is a coffee bar in the port and Beni Khiar has a few simple eating houses. A better selection of restaurants can be found in Nabeul 4.5km from Beni Khiar which has a few tourist hotels.

Carpet making in Beni Khiar

The Gulf of Hammamet

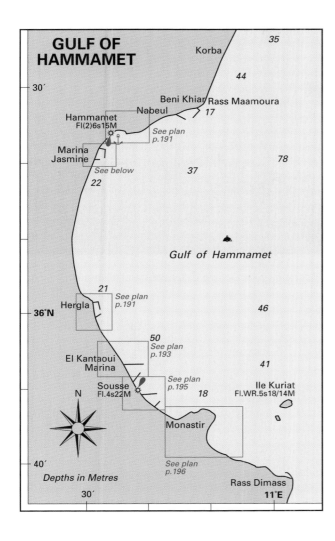

GULF OF HAMMAMET

Depths in Metres

T21 Hammamet anchorage

An anchorage protected from NW winds close to Marina Jasmine, W of Hammamet fortress.

Location
36°23′.5N 10°36′.5E

Distances
Kelibia 35M
Marina Jasmine 4M

Charts
Admiralty *176*
French *4315, 4314, 4183, 4225*

Lights
Lantern on kasbah wall Fl(2)6s17m15M 255°-vis-165° with red sector as marked on plan

The anchorage

Just W of the kasbah fortress of Hammamet is a quite well protected anchorage with a view of Tunisia's oldest tourist development. Beware of fishing nets around the bay. Protection is good even in NE winds, providing they are not too strong and as long as you are able to anchor well into the corner. Anchor in sand, 3–4m with good holding.

A night approach is possible if the kasbah light is working. Note the guidance given by the red sector. An unlit buoy marking a wreck lies SW of the anchorage.

ASHORE

The big hotels, though modest compared with the Spanish Costa del Sol, stretch W along the beautiful beaches of the Gulf of Hammamet. From the sea the aspect is unexpectedly pleasant. Taking a dinghy to the beach places you in the middle of the old town. The medina around the fortress is filled with shops selling Tunisian handicrafts. In spite of the modern tourist development, the area still manages to retain a sense of its history and the fishermen still land their boats on the beach.

Replica pirate galleons: a new tourist industry along this part of the coast
Graham Hutt

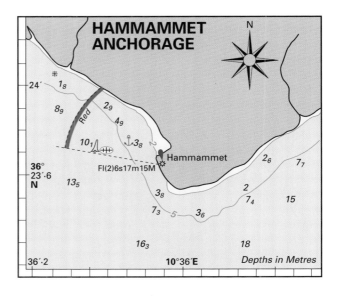

HAMMAMMET ANCHORAGE

Depths in Metres

IV. TUNISIA

T22 Marina Jasmine

A new spacious marina complex for over 700 yachts and port of entry in the N of the Gulf of Hammamet, close to El Kantaoui and Sousse.

Location
36°22′.3N 10°33′.0E

Distances
Sousse 33M
Kelibia 40M

Charts
Admiralty *2122*
French *4314, 4315, 4183, 4191, 4221,4225*

Lights
Lantern on kasbah wall Fl(2)6s17m15M 255°-vis-165°
Marina harbourmaster's office Fl(2)15s17M12M
W breakwater head Fl(2)G.9s10m6M
E breakwater head Fl.R.5s9m6M
Entry light stb Fl(2)G

Communications
Harbourmaster ☎ 72 241111
Fax 72241212
VHF Ch 16
Email contact@portyasmine.com.tn
www.portyasmine.com.tn

Marina Jasmine looking E. Spacious and luxurious
Graham Hutt

The marina

A splendid new spacious marina completed in 2004 with facilities and surrounding infrastructure due to be completed in 2005. Though expensive, the marina rivals anything built anywhere in North Africa. Everything expected of a good European marina will be provided here. Rather soulless in 2004, due to the fact that it had recently opened and was half empty. Because the area is almost non-tidal, water is pumped through the port to keep the water clean and fresh.

PILOTAGE

By day

The marina is clearly visible extending from a long stretch of featureless beach. A hotel complex stretches from the marina S along the beach. The high sea wall is 500m long and easily spotted. To the north is the anchorage and town of Hammamet. Entry in strong E winds may be difficult.

Note A submerged sea wall lies S of the port entry light, marked with yellow buoys. The N cardinal buoy at the N end of the breakwater marks the sea wall, which has a short NW extension.

By night

No problems. The marina and stb entry lights function and the landfall light is clearly visible on the harbourmaster's office.

Berthing

Call the marina on VHF 16 or ch 9 and once inside the entrance you will be met by the marineros in a RIB who take you directly to a berth. Lines tailed to the quay for bows/stern mooring.

Ships' papers are collected and either delivered back to the yacht 20 minutes later, or can be collected from the office.

The marina authorities put new arrivals as far from the marina offices as possible making it a healthy walk round. Mobile staff are very helpful in assisting with berthing and collecting/delivering ships' papers and electricity hook-up cables. (The connections are not standard.)

Wintering 01/10 to 30/04 1200.000
Whole Year TD2100
Water and electricity metred.

Formalities

Port of entry. All facilities and personnel in the marina for entry and departure procedures.

Note Special arrangements can be made for extended stays under 'plombage.' Particularly useful for those

MARINA JASMINE HAMMAMET

Beach Club
Piscine

Ile aux Pêcheurs

Dique Nord

VQ(3)10s4M

BYB

Dique du Large

Sousse

Fl(2)15s 17m12M

Quai d'accueil

N

0   200
Metres

Fl(2)G.9s

Fl.R.5s

Depths in Metres

wanting to leave their yachts here over the winter without having to exit every six months. The period in Tunisia is not counted once the yacht is 'immobilized.' This can theoretically be done in any port, but it is much easier, as here, when the harbour authorities assist with the procedure.

Facilities

Water Available from metered boxes on the quay. (Free in 2004 as meters not fitted.)

Electricity Available from same boxes.

Fuel Diesel from a pump in the port entrance.

Gas Available form chandlery in port.

Provisions Several grocery shops and small supermarkets just outside the marina.

Repairs A 150-ton travel-lift and 40-ton crane. Engine repairs undertaken.

Post office In Hammamet.

Telephone In the marina office and in the hotels around the port.

Bank Just outside the marina.

Weather forecast Available at the harbourmaster's office. Also available from Italian ch 68.

Wintering It is possible to winter here either on the hard or in the water.

ASHORE

Marina Jasmine is part of a new luxury complex seemingly remote, though only 3 miles from Hammamet. Sousse is 32 miles S and a regular bus services the route. Everything is available in Sousse, if unavailable locally.

Eating out

A 'floating' restaurant in the port offering high class and expensive fare. Several tourist restaurants and bars line the beach just outside the marina.

Transport

Enfidah New International Airport is being constructed 20km SW to serve this developing tourist area and is supposed to be operational by 2005.

T23 Hergla

A small fishing harbour in Hammamet bay, between Marina Jasmine and El Kantaoui. Prone to silting.

Location
  36°01′.9N 10°30′.7E

Distances
  Marina Jasmine 21M
  El Kantaoui 11M

Charts
  Admiralty *176*
  French *4315, 4208*

Lights
Harbour
1. **NE breakwater head** Fl(2)G.10s5m6M
2. **SE inner breakwater head** Fl.R.5s9m6M
3. **Nouvelle Jetée Sud head** Fl.R.5s9m6M

Communications
  APIP ☎ 73251464
  VHF Ch 16

The harbour

This small fishing harbour, almost identical to Beni Khiar, lies in the Bay of Hammamet. The village is on a low hill a short walk up steps from the port and amazingly, in view of the large tourist development at El Kantaoui so close by, it is still untouched by visitors.

PILOTAGE

The coast around Hergla is low but the port is made conspicuous by the village, located on the only hill for miles around, with beaches to the N and S. Navigation is further assisted by a tall water tower NW of the port and a minaret in the village. Approach the end of the NE breakwater with caution on a course of 250° in order to avoid rocky ledges N and S of the port. The entrance and inside of the port tends to clog with seaweed as well as becoming silted with sand, but it is dredged regularly. Depths of 2–5m were found at the ends of the second and third piers in summer 2004, though frequently less water is found. Prudence remains

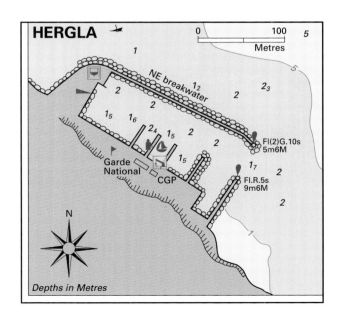

IV. TUNISIA

Hergla entrance from S   *Graham Hutt*

necessary, as the situation can change during storms throughout the year reducing depths considerably. Early in 2004 depths in the entrance were only 1–2m. Approximately 300m N of the root of the NE breakwater, the remains of an Italian naval ship which sank during the Second World War are just visible awash. Beware of fishing nets around the port.

Berthing

Moor near end of finger piers as shown on plan for maximum depths of around 2.5 metres. The port is usually full with fishing boats but yachts are accommodated by their friendly crews. Berth alongside as shown, or moor bows/stern-to one of the quays.

Charges for a 12m yacht

A charge of TD8 per day is made for 12 metre yachts.

Formalities

The port is operated by the APIP. There is a Garde National post but this is not a port of entry.

Facilities

Water Tap on the quay.
Electricity None.
Fuel Diesel on the second quay. No petrol in port or village.
Provisions Shops can be found in the village. Market on Thursdays.
Post office and bank: In the village
Repairs There is a ship and small-boat yard which will organise emergency repairs.

ASHORE

The village is a local centre for the weaving of alfalfa mats which are used in traditional olive presses. Some small local shops sell the alfalfa mats, woven into bowls and other useful shapes, but few tourists seem to come here.

Eating out

Cafés in the village on the hill and a small restaurant in the square below the village.

Hergla harbour from port entry light looking N
Graham Hutt

T24 El Kantaoui Marina

One of the most friendly and attractive marinas in Tunisia, between Marina Jasmine and Monastir, and a port of entry able to berth 340 yachts, with a few places for yachts up to 30m.

Location
> 35°53′.6N 10°36′.3E (Entrance to the dredged channel off marina entrance)

Distances
> Kelibia 63M
> Monastir 14M
> Sousse 5M

Charts
> Admiralty *176, 1162*
> French *4315 4102*

Lights
Approach
1. **Sousse kasbah** 35°49′.4N 10°38′.3E Fl.4s70m22M Metal pylon on white square stone tower
Harbour
Buoys in entrance channel are sometimes lit with green on starboard and red on port side.
2. **NE breakwater** Fl.G.4s9m6M
3. **S breakwater** Fl.R.6s9m6M

Communications
> Marina office ☎ 73348600
> *Fax* 73348506
> VHF Ch 16 and 6
> *Email* portelkantaoui@email.ati.tn
> www.portelkantaoui.com.tn

The marina

The marina of El Kantaoui is located in the centre of a large holiday resort, built in Andalucían style 5 miles north of Sousse. Tourists from nearby hotels and apartments stroll along the quays all year around but because of the spacious layout, yachts can still enjoy reasonable privacy. The marina has a unique self-contained feel to it, quite unlike any other place in Tunisia. Yachts can winter here and it is a good and secure place to leave a boat.

PILOTAGE

By day

The marina is situated immediately S of Cap Ras Marsa, which is hard to distinguish. By day two large pyramid shaped hotels in the complex make the landfall fairly easy. Entrance is through a short buoyed channel on a course of 305°, and the entrance to the port is just to the east of the southernmost hotel, the Hannibal Palace Hotel. In order to avoid the shallows around the entrance, Ras Marsa should be given a berth of at least 0.5M. Yachts drawing more than 3m should approach carefully as the entrance channel tends to silt up and in the past seaweed has been a problem. Note there are rocks to the SW of the dredged channel near the entrance.

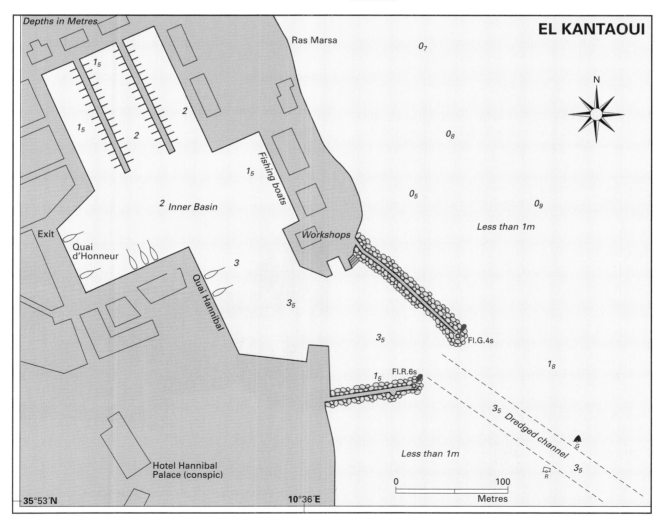

El Kantaoui quay Hannibal viewed from NE   *Graham Hutt*

Entry in most weather conditions is straightforward but strong NE to E winds cause waves to break around the entrance channel making entry inadvisable.

By night

The Sousse light atop the kasbah gives good guidance until the red marina light can be picked up, normally at about 5 miles. Two large floodlit hotels are conspicuous. The breakwater lights are reasonably visible, in spite of the many lights around the marina, because of their isolated position. Hazards in the entrance are the two large buoys marking the entrance channel which are often unlit and, occasionally, nets. On radar Ras Marsa will be seen as the second promontory to the north of Sousse.

Berthing

Mooring lines tailed to the quays are laid all around the marina. Overall protection inside the marina is good although the berths on Quai Hannibal are more exposed to SE wind and waves. Yachts up to 28m and a draught of 3m are accommodated here as well as short-stay visitors. Yachts berth bows/stern-to on tailed lines to the quay all round the marina and alongside finger pontoons in the northern basin. These run SSE from the N wall. They are for boats of up to 12m and will take up to 2.3m draught at the seaward end. Access to these pontoons is through gates, though they are rarely locked.

Charges for a 12m Yacht

Despite the neat and tidy upmarket atmosphere the charges are still very reasonable, though greatly increased since 2001.

See website for full list of charges www.portelkantaoui.com.tn/english/plaisance/rates.htm

Formalities

A port of entry where formalities are dealt with efficiently. Officials are on duty 24hrs a day.

Facilities

Water and *electricity* Laid on the quays for each individual berth.

Fuel Diesel and petrol available from pumps on the service

El Kantaoui marina: very pleasant gardens around the port
Graham Hutt

quay next to the travel-lift. Kerosene from a service station outside the marina.

Gas Available at the boatyard.

Provisions A good assortment of groceries, wine and beer is available from two supermarkets (including a Magasin Général) in the port. Not a great choice of fresh vegetables but the market in Sousse is close.

Showers On the S side of the inner basin. Clean and reserved for yachts.

Post office and *banks* In the marina.

Telephone Coin telephones in the post office but they are also used by many hotel guests.

Repairs A 40-ton travel-lift, with very experienced staff. Rates are competitive by Mediterranean standards. Price about TD120 for 10-12m in and out excluding high pressure hose. Winter guests get a considerable discount on hauling out. The boatyard is small and exposed, so perhaps not a good place to be on the hard during winter. The ship chandler has a better assortment of air mattresses than yacht spares.

Laundry Reasonably priced washing and dry cleaning in the marina.

Weather forecast From the capitainerie.

ASHORE

The marina itself is interesting, having been designed along the lines of the ancient villages found in Andalucía, with cobbled narrow winding streets, flower gardens and palm trees. The quays are lined with shops, restaurants and terraces and in the evening it is a lively place. Yachtsmen can use the swimming pools and participate in the nightly entertainment of the nearby hotels. The location is good for excursions inland, which leave from the hotels and there is good transport to the centre of Sousse, just 8km away. English is widely spoken around the port.

There is a tourist information office in the marina which can be helpful in planning excursions, which in winter time can be made at quite attractive prices. The 18 hole golf course has an international reputation. A sports centre with tennis courts and horseback riding is nearby.

Eating out

An abundance of restaurants cafés and bars around the marina cater to the needs of vacationers and yachtsmen. For cheaper fare, take a taxi to nearby Hammet-Sousse or Sousse.

Transport

International flights at Monastir (25km) or Tunis (150km). Buses (hourly service to Sousse) and taxis leave just outside the marina. Rent-a-Car has an office with cars opposite the Magasin Général. (Around TD 80 per day including full insurance and unlimited mileage. Cheaper for longer term rental.)

T25 Sousse

A large, dirty and uninviting commercial port between El Kantaoui and Monastir with nothing to attract yachts. A port of entry.

Location
   35°49´.5N 10°39´.1E

Distances
   El Kantaoui 5M
   Monastir 10M

Charts
   Admiralty *176, 1162*
   French *4315, 4226*

Lights
Approach
1. **Kasbah** 35°49´.4N 10°38´.3E
   Fl.4s70m22M Metal pylon on white square stone tower
Harbour
2. **Jetée Abri head** Oc.WR.4s12m10/6M 135°-R-180°-W-045°
   Red pylon, white base
   Emergency light Fl.WR
3. **Epi Nord head** Iso.G.4s10m8M 258°-vis-112° Green conical tower
4. **Epi Sud head** Fl.R.5s10m8M Red conical tower
Communications
   ☎ 73 225755
   VHF Ch 16 (24hrs)

The port

With the nearby marinas of El Kantaoui, Monastir and Marina Jasmine, all with repair facilities within easy reach, there is very little reason to visit Sousse. The port has 3 basins and the small basin in the NW corner of the commercial port can be used by yachts. It is very dusty in E winds, which are common in spring and summer and it becomes very uncomfortable with the wind blowing into the entrance. The fishing port S of the commercial basin offers good protection but is full and not very clean. There are plans to turn the main commercial harbour into a large yacht basin, but this is unlikely now in view of the construction of nearby Marina Jasmine. The north section of the port is used by patrol boats.

PILOTAGE

By day

Straightforward by day and night. The slightly elevated kasbah fortress with its tower dominates the Sousse skyline and is well visible from seaward. A thermal

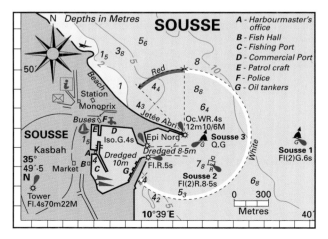

IV. TUNISIA

power station with red and white striped chimney, 2.5M SE of Sousse is another good landmark. Entry is via a buoyed channel dredged to 9m.

By night

The 22M range light on the tower of the kasbah provides very good guidance. The entrance channel is without hazards, the buoys are lit and are reliable. Enter on a course due W. The red sector of the light on the N mole shows the extremity of the N side of the channel.

Berthing

Yachts may find a berth alongside a fishing boat on the E pier of the fishing port. Commercial rates apply here. In case of an emergency the small basin can also be used with the discomforts mentioned before. Depths are uncertain in this basin, though there is 4m in the entrance. Yachts are not welcomed in the port and charges have consequently been reported as very high.

Formalities

A port of entry with all officials in the port.

Facilities

Water Taps near the fish hall of the fishing port.
Fuel On the quay.
Provisions Good provisions are available, all within a short distance from the port. Monoprix on Avenue Bourguiba and two markets in the kasbah.
French charts are available from the office of the Service Topography on Avenue Bourguiba opposite the Monoprix.
Post office and *telephone* Close to the port on Avenue de la Republique.

Banks Many in the town with ATM cash facilities.
Repairs Good engine repair facilities can be found around the port along Avenue Mohammed V and in the street behind it. Roto diesel on the road to Monastir near the southern railway station undertakes good quality fuel system repair work.

ASHORE

History

Sousse has been an important city to every civilization that has occupied this part of North Africa because of the fertile land of the Sahel region around it. After independence, Susa, the old Arabic name still used today, became the third city of Tunisia with textiles and tourism as the key economic activities.

Sights locally

Several monuments illustrate the rich history and the museum in the kasbah has an excellent collection of mosaics.

The street opposite the fishing port is lined with hardware, spare parts and engine repair shops.

The weekly market is on Sundays, but for a real camel market, as the tourist brochures describe it, one has to go further south.

Eating out

Sousse is the city in Tunisia where tourism began, thus many good and reasonably priced restaurants can be found. Good listing in the *Rough Guide*.

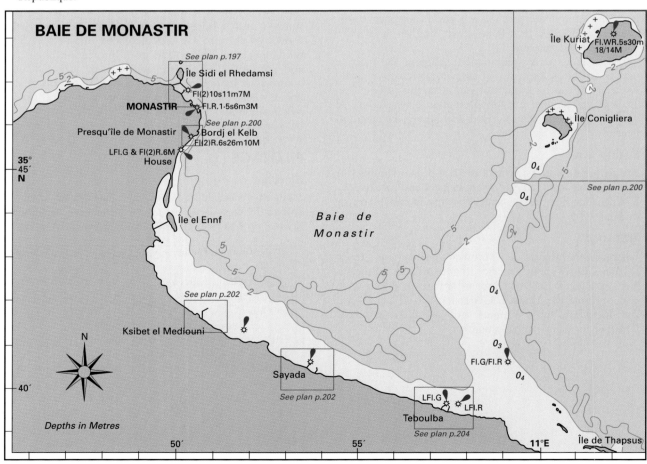

T26 Marina Cap Monastir

Probably the best loved and most frequented marina in Tunisia, located mid way down the E coast. It is a port of entry and has been a popular wintering spot for two decades.

Location
35°46´.7N 10°50´.3E

Distances
Malta 188M
Kelibia 65M
El Kantaoui 14M
Mahdia 25M

Charts
Admiralty *176, 1162*
French *4315, 4226*

Lights
Approach
1. **Île Kuriat** 35°47´.9N 11°02´.0E
Fl.WR.5s30m18/14M 053°-W-348°-R-053° Emergency light F.WR
Harbour
2. **Bordj el Kelb** Fl(2)R.6s26m10M 197°-vis-355°
3. **Old Fishing Hbr shelter mole head** Fl.R.1.5s6m3M
4. **New Fishing Hbr Entrance** LFl.G.10s12m5M and Fl(4)R.15s12m5M
5. **Marina E side** LFl(2)G.10s8m6M
6. **S breakwater W side** Fl(2)R.10s8m6M
7. **E breakwater head** Fl(2)10s11m7M

Communications
Harbourmaster ☎ 73462305
Fax 73462066
Email mansour.chaabane@planet.tn
www.marinamonastir.com
VHF Ch 16 monitored by marina office and police during office hours.

The marina

Monastir is one of the older established marinas in Tunisia and a popular place to winter afloat. It is also a popular landfall when coming from the E and a port of entry. The marina has been formed by joining two islands with the shore and protection is excellent in all wind directions. Entry can be made in all weather

Monastir marina looking across from the NE breakwater
Graham Hutt

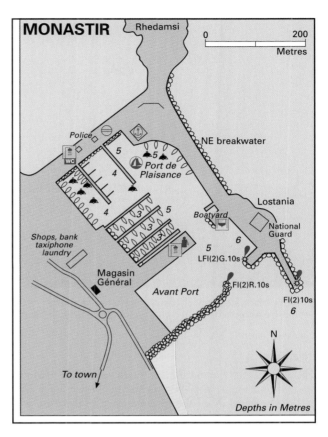

conditions and the double breakwaters, with good depths in the marina, effectively prevent swell from entering. Services in the marina, overseen by an obliging harbour master, were some of the best in Tunisia, though show signs of aging now.

PILOTAGE

By day

Coming from the E, stay far enough N to avoid the tunny net laid N of Kuriat Island and the shallows between it and the mainland. The net is put out every year from April-July. The light on the buoy marking the N end of the net is unreliable. Coming from the SE there are two possible channels between Kuriat Island and the island closer to the mainland, Conigliera. These are not as charted. The northern passage is used by fishermen and shallow draught tourist boats, but depths vary considerably from that recorded on the SHOM charts and the buoys are rarely in position. In summer 2004 they were not present at all. See notes on Kuriat and Conigliera Island for more information.

The lighthouse on Kuriat and the ruins of an old fish factory on Conigliera are the only landmarks in this low lying area which has a hazy atmosphere in summer, usually clearing as the sun goes down. Once past Kuriat, the approach is straightforward, with several minarets and the Ribat just to the south of the marina, serving as good landmarks.

The tunny nets directly N of Monastir and marked on Admiralty chart 1162 are no longer laid but bottom nets with marker buoys are present in the area.

Monastir marina entrance from SE. Note fuelling jetty
behind freighter left   *Graham Hutt*

By night

The entrance to the marina, although narrow, is without hazards and night entry is possible. In the bay enclosed by Île Rhedamsi, N of the marina, floating fish nets are often laid at night. The harbour lights function reliably but are obscured from N to W by the two islands; a lit buoy should be in position 1M NNE of the marina entrance, though this is not always working. The breakwater lights are difficult to see until very close because of the background lighting, despite claims on the chart of 6M visibility.

Berthing

The outer basin is used by a few small fishing boats but is otherwise empty. The boatyard is to the right of the entry into the main basin and an abandoned freighter has lain opposite since 1996. Yachts over 12m are normally directed to berth bows/stern-to to the NE breakwater where there are buoys to attach to. There is space for very large yachts at the NW end of this quay near the harbourmaster's building. For yachts less than 12m the 3 piers in the south of the port and the W quay have tailed lines for fore-and-aft mooring.

The two piers in the NW of the harbour have short finger pontoons and lines to sinkers. Smaller visiting yachts are most likely to be directed to these 2 piers. The N side of the N Pier is most affected by any swell that enters the harbour. If arriving at night, or in doubt as to where to berth, moor on the end of the fuelling quay, behind the freighter at the left side of the entrance.

Charges for a 12m yacht

See website for full list of charges.

Formalities

Port of entry with 24hrs service. Formalities are handled efficiently. The harbour office and police monitor VHF Ch 16 during office hours.

Facilities

Water and *electricity* Laid on the quays for each berth.
Fuel Diesel and petrol from pumps on the service quay. Paraffin available from the Mobil station in town.
Gas Boatyard takes care of filling gas bottles.
Provisions Between the Monoprix, Magasin Général and the market, excellent provisions are usually available. All are within 10 minutes walking distance of the marina. There is a smaller Magasin Général at the entrance to the marina. Alcoholic beverages can be ordered.
Ice Can be arranged by marina personnel.
Showers Showers and a bath tub are in the facility on the N side of the marina. These have undergone renovation during 2004, though are still inadequate for a marina of this size.
Post office Main office next to the Monoprix.
Bank A user-friendly bank in the marina's shopping arcade and several in the town centre.
Telephone Taxiphone at entrance to the marina. Phone lines can be supplied to berths.
Repairs Boatyard with 30-ton travel-lift which can undertake most repairs; limited space for wintering ashore but it is now possible to haul-out for extended periods. The yard is situated on the outer end of the E mole of the entrance to the marina. Run by Mohamed Ben Mrad, who speaks good English and previously worked in Italian boatyards.

    'Elite Services' have an office in the N corner of the marina and can undertake electrical and electronic repairs and installations: Cap Marina Local 11BP 5000 Monastir. ☎ 03 449037 *Fax* 03 461211. Fritz Demmer. See also Monastir New Fishing Harbour.
Sail repairs See note in introduction.
Laundry Arranged by marina personnel. Dry cleaning available in the town about 200m past the Magasin Général.
Weather forecast A daily bulletin is posted in the capitainerie.

Wintering notes

It is necessary to book very early to reserve a place for wintering. Pay a deposit if possible, because the harbour office often 'loses' the booking paperwork if sent by fax or email. Turning up will usually result in a place being found, but it becomes a tight squeeze. See below for alternative arrangements in the fishing harbour.

ASHORE

History

Monastir is a typically ancient Arab town dating from the C10th with citadel, ribat and the kasbah. The marina, next to the site of Ruspina of the Romans, is a blend of tourist hotels, Islamic shrines and the beautiful old walled Arab quarters. The C10th mosque is well preserved and used.

The fact that Monastir is the birth place of former President Bourguiba makes this a town of particular importance. His mausoleum with twin gold domed minarets, just above the port, is without doubt the most spectacular of all new architecture in Tunisia and well worth a visit. Just outside the port the other monument is the Ribat. Its style is peculiar to a period in North African history when the Muslims were under regular attack from Christians based in Sicily. It served a religious as well as military purpose. In times of war it was a fortress and in peacetime the fighters studied the

Qu'ran in bare cells around the central court, not unlike the Madressas in Morocco. Here they prepared themselves for 'jihad.' (Holy war). There is a small museum inside with Cufic script on parchment and some Fatimid glassware. Monastir International Films uses the Ribat as a set and some well known films with biblical connections have been shot here. Large parts of the old town have been taken down to show off the new monuments and the result is a pleasant, open town centre with lots of greenery.

Sights locally

The marina complex has shops, apartments and several restaurants. Except during summer months the atmosphere is relaxed and quiet, though the marina is full by the end of October. The nearby islands N of the marina are still in their natural state and the pleasant town centre of Monastir is only five minutes walk from the marina. Excursions inland can easily be arranged.

Tennis courts on Rhedamsi island, N of the marina and built as part of the Hotel Mediterranean complex, now lie derelict. Monastir has an 18 hole golf course. The tourist information office is located opposite Magasin Général and carries a good selection of brochures and maps.

It should be noted that there is a distinct climatic difference from Monastir and S. It is much warmer and not as subject to the constant storms which batter Cap Bon and the N coast during winter. This makes visits to the desert and further inland very pleasant during winter months.

Eating out

Several restaurants with seafront atmosphere and at reasonable prices are in and around the marina. Le Roi de Couscous in the centre opposite Bourguiba statue is good value. Hotel Yasmin 3km N of the marina has good European and Tunisian cooking.

Transport

The international airport at Skanes is 8km from the marina. The train to Tunis takes under 3 hours and from there to its international airport is another 30 minutes. Buses, train and louages to Sousse take between 20–30 minutes. Car hire can be arranged through the capitainerie and also via a rental office in the marina. Major hire companies have offices in the airport and will deliver and collect cars from the marina. Transport by taxi to Tunis airport can be arranged for Dh50 and takes 2 hours.

Air ticket prices at the 'resident' rates can be obtained from 'Skanes Travel' a few hundred metres N of the Medina in the Kairoun road.

Monastir Old Fishing Harbour

This ancient fishing harbour, 2M S of Monastir is now silted and unusable except by small fishing boats.

T27 Monastir (New) Fishing Harbour

A large fishing harbour 1.5M S of Marina Monastir, underused and welcomes yachts, especially for wintering. An excellent and cheaper alternative to Marina Monastir.

Location
   35°45′.3N 10°50′.4E

Charts
   Admiralty *176, 1162*
   French *4226*

Lights
Approach
1. **Bordj el Kelb** 35°45′.6N 10°50′.3E Fl(2)R.6s26m10M
   White tower black bands 197°-vis-355°
Harbour
2. **E breakwater** LFl.G.10s12m5M
3. **W breakwater** Fl(4)R.15s12m5M
Communications
   VHF Ch 16, 9.

The harbour

The harbour, situated between Bordj el Kelb and the old customs pier to the S was completed in 1988. The harbour is large for today's needs and despite Tunisia's growing fishing fleet the harbour is under-used leaving room for visiting yachts. There is very little of interest other than excellent protection and boatyards with full repair facilities. Although not as well set up for yachts as Monastir, it is a useful alternative if space or facilities at Monastir are fully booked. There is plenty of space afloat and ashore and in 2004 several yachts were hauled out for the winter. The yard is keen to attract more work and is competent to undertake all mechanical repairs, welding, painting etc. Sand and grit blasting can be arranged here. All prices are cheaper than in Monastir.

PILOTAGE

By day

The harbour is SSW of Monastir Marina which is easily identified by the large fortress near the entrance. Passing the old fishing port S of the marina, continue S for a further 1M where Borjiel Kelib light structure will be seen. The entrance is just S of this light.

By night

The light on Borjiel Kelib is usually functional and entry in all but strong E to SE winds is not difficult.

Berthing

Berth as directed by the harbourmaster on arrival or negotiate place in advance.

Facilities

Water and *electricity* Available on the quay and ashore.
Fuel On the quay.
Provisions There is a chandlery, shop (basic provisions) café and a restaurant in the port. All facilities in Monastir, 3 km away.
Repairs A 250-ton travel-lift, and high pressure washer.
Yards Chantier Yasamine, ☎ 73447510, Chantier Naval, ☎/*Fax* 73 467122, Mr Ali Bedoui (home ☎ 73 461820).

IV. TUNISIA

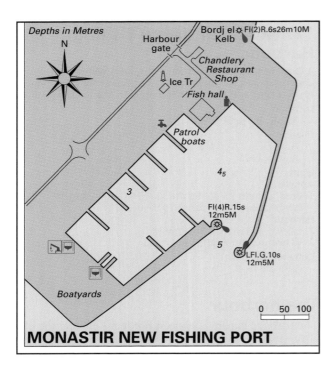

Depths in Metres
N
Harbour gate
Bordj el Kelb ☆ Fl(2)R.6s26m10M
Chandlery Restaurant Shop
Ice Tr
Fish hall
Patrol boats
4₅
3
Fl(4)R.15s 12m5M
5
☆ LFl.G.10s 12m5M
Boatyards
0 50 100

MONASTIR NEW FISHING PORT

Chantier Naval and Elite Yacht Services joined forces to create full services for visiting and wintering yachts. They have a WC and shower block and run a minibus service regularly into town. Elite is run by a German, Fritz Demmer who speaks good English. Elite ☎ 73 449037 *Fax* 73 461211.

Monastir: Mausoleum of Bourguiba L, behind Cemetry of Sidi Mazeri　　　　　　　　　　　*Graham Hutt*

T28 Ile Kuriat and Ile Conigliera Anchorages and Passage

These low-lying islands 9M E of Monastir are part of the extensive shallows forming the SE extremity of the Bay of Monastir.

Location
　35°47′.9N 11°02′.0E (Kuriat lighthouse)

Distances
　Marina Monastir 9M

Charts
　Admiralty *1162*
　French *4226*

Light
Ile Kuriat lighthouse (35°47′.9N 11°02′.0E)
　Fl.WR.5s30m18/14M 053°-W-348°-R-053° Emergency light F.WR

Anchorages

The area is typical of the shallow sailing grounds going S from Monastir to the Libyan border. There are several places to anchor around the shores of both Ile Kuriat and Conigliera islands. Use the chart, wind direction and a good eye on the depth sounder, along with a sharp look-out on the bow, to determine the best places to anchor given prevailing conditions. The bottom is exceptionally clear.

Except for the lighthouse keeper on Kuriat island and fishermen during the tunny season, the islands are uninhabited. Several small fishing vessels leave their nets on the S of Kuriat Island in summer. The islands' solitude makes for a pleasant day trip from Monastir and tourist boats visit daily.

In good weather the wind direction is quite predictable. In the morning the sea breeze starts from the NE and changes to SSE during the course of the

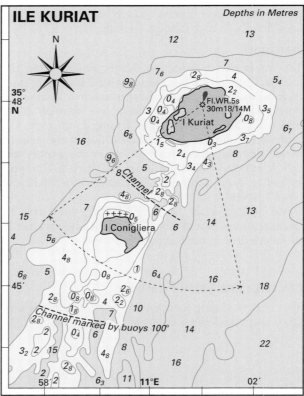

ILE KURIAT　　　　　Depths in Metres

day, dropping at sunset. Slightly hazy conditions, with a visibility of 6M, are normal in the summer.

A wooden landing jetty marked on some charts on the SE side of Kuriat, was not in place summer 2004. It was formerly used to discharge supplies for the lighthouse. Fishing boats beach along the shore. Depths along the old landing vary from 1m to 2.5m but there are a few shallow patches in the unmarked approach with less than 1m.

S of the SE tip of Ile Conigliera is a short landing where a shallow draught replica pirate galleon from Monastir anchors while tourists wade ashore to the island.

PILOTAGE

Between the islands and mainland

There are theoretically 3 passages across the shallows between the islands and S of Ile Conigliera:

1. A dredged channel close to the fishing port of Teboulba, (described under the port).
2. An unmarked passage between Kuriat and Conigliera.
3. A buoyed natural channel 1.5M SW of Conigliera.

There were no buoys marking any of these channels in summer 2004 and only shallow draught fishing boats and day tripping tourist boats were observed using the northern channel between Kuriat and Conigliera. None were using the passage south of Conigliera. It is reported that fishing boats regularly tie up to the buoys when they are in place, dragging them to 'more convenient' spots. I spoke with many yachtsmen in 2004, who had tried using the channels – some on several occasions. All reported going aground, though one had subsequently made it through after several attempts. (1.8m draught.)

Navigation in this area is complicated by the fact that, aside from the lighthouse on Kuriat and the remains of an old fish factory on Conigliera, there are few landmarks and the area is often shrouded in mist.

Although there are undoubtedly channels between the islands which the more adventurous may like to probe, my advice it to take the extra hour to go around Kuriat Island, rather than attempting 'a short-cut.' Shifting sands, ancient charts and unreliable markings – when they are in place – make these channels hazardous at the very least. British and French charts covering the islands show considerable differences and neither are correct in the placement of contour lines or depths.

A tunny net is usually laid N of Kuriat from April to July but was not in place summer 2004. When in use, the net is more than 3M long and well visible with blue floating balls along its full length. Four boats with short masts are permanently moored in the middle to haul the tunny from the 'death chamber'. The N extremity is usually marked with a N cardinal buoy. Passage between this type of net, the island and mainland, is usually impossible.

ASHORE

There is nothing here except the delight of a short and quiet sailing excursion from Marina Monastir.

It is reported (Summer 2004) that this area is now a military zone.

T29 Ksibet El Mdeiouni

A fully occupied fishing boat quay projecting N, 6M SE of Monastir. Of little use to yachts.

Location
35°41´.5N 10°50´.8E

Distances
Monastir 6M
Mahdia 19M

Charts
Admiralty *176, 1162*

Lights
Breakwater Fishing harbour jetty head Fl.G.4s10m6M

The harbour

A very small fishing harbour consisting of a single breakwater with protection only from the W and NW. It is crowded and shallow and there is nothing of interest or merit ashore. It is likely that this jetty is the beginning of a larger, and more protected harbour development in the future.

PILOTAGE

By day

A meandering channel marked by 4 pairs of red and green buoys leads to the breakwater on a course of 348°. Depths in the channel are not known, though it is regularly dredged.

By night

The Fl.G breakwater light was functioning in summer 2004, as were the channel markers. Approach not recommended by night because of the shallow and crowded quay. Note that the coast is also very shallow for 1.5M offshore in all directions, except in the channel.

Berthing

Stern/bows-to if there is space.

Formalities

Officials at entrance to harbour but this is not a port of entry.

Facilities

Water and *fuel* Available on the quay as indicated.
Repairs 10-ton crane and small boat hoist.

ASHORE

Sights locally

The facility is on a long stretch of beach with small fishing communities and a thriving home carpet industry.

Eating out

There are some small very cheap fish restaurants on the road which passes through the harbour.

IV. TUNISIA

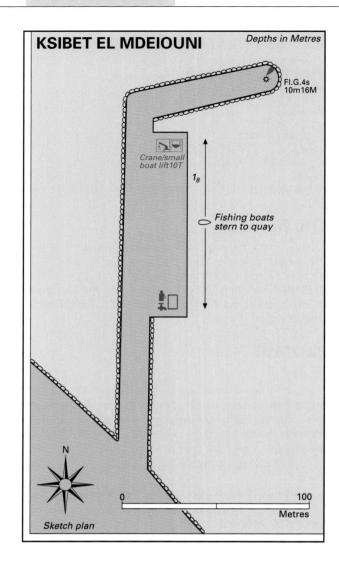

KSIBET EL MDEIOUNI Depths in Metres

Fl.G.4s
10m16M

Crane/small
boat lift10T

1₈

Fishing boats
stern to quay

N

0   100
                                  Metres

Sketch plan

T30 Sayada

A small fishing harbour off a shallow coastline accessed through a buoyed channel, 7M S of Monastir.

Location
35°40´.5N 10°53´.6E (White light end of N breakwater)

Distances
Monastir 7M
Teboulba 3M

Charts
Admiralty *1162*
French *4226*

Lights
1. **Light N of harbour** Fl.2s
2. **NW jetty head** Fl.G.4s7m5M green stone tower
3. **NE jetty head** Fl(3)R.12s7m6M red stone tower
4. **2 pairs of R and G lit buoys** mark dredged channel

The harbour

This small and busy fishing harbour S in the Bay of Monastir, provides income for local fishermen who supply the tourist hotels further N. In spite of its insignificance, there is more activity here than in the new fishing harbour of Monastir. Octopus, prawns and sardines are caught in season. The harbour is crowded with small fishing boats. Yachts are welcome here, although few visit.

PILOTAGE

By day

The surrounding coast is very shallow and the dredged channel leading to the entrance extending 0.5M is marked only by two pairs of lit buoys. The area silts frequently and channel depths are uncertain, though they are dredged to 3m.

By night

Not recommended due to shallows and uncertain depths.

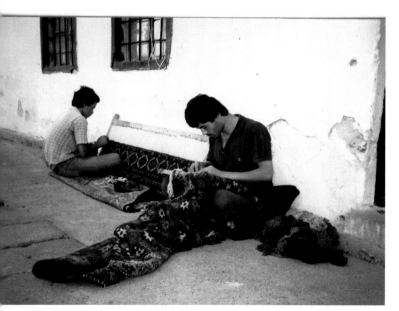

Carpet industry in Ksibet el Mdeiouni

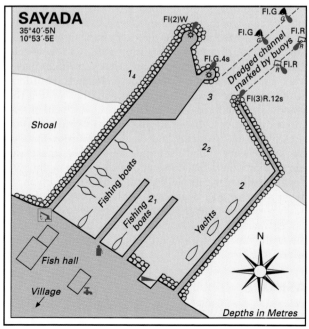

SAYADA
35°40´.5N
10°53´.5E

Fl(2)W

Fl.G
G

Fl.G
G

Fl.R
R

Dredged channel
marked by buoys

Fl.G.4s

Fl.R
R

1₄

3

Fl(3)R.12s

Shoal

2₂

Fishing boats

2

Fishing
boats

2₁

Yachts

2

Fish hall

N

Village

Depths in Metres

Fishing port of Sayada looking N   *Graham Hutt*

Berthing

Depths once inside the port are around 2m, with 3m in the entrance. There are places for yachts along the SE breakwater as shown.

Formalities

Garde National and *marine marchande* are situated just outside the harbour. This is not a port of entry.

Facilities

Water and *diesel* In the harbour.
Banks, *PTT* and *shops* In the town.

Thriving boat building industry in Teboulba   *Graham Hutt*

T31 Teboulba

A busy fishing port surrounded by shifting sands in the S of the Bay of Monastir, 9M S of the marina. Though recently extended, there is little room for yachts.

Location
  35°39′.6N 10°57′.5E

Distances
  Monastir 9.5M
  Mahdia 16M (via dredged channel)

Charts
  Admiralty *1162*
  French *4226*

Lights
Approach
1. **Secondary channel No.1** 35°40′.6N 10°59′.1E
   Fl.G.6s3m2M on green column
2. **Secondary channel No.2** 35°40′.6N 10°59′.2E
   Fl.R.6s3m2M on red column
Harbour
3. **W breakwater head** LFl.G.10s7m5M Green stone tower
4. **E breakwater head** LFl.R.10s7m5M Red stone tower
Communications
  ☎ 73479495
  VHF Ch 16 (0730–1330, 1500–1745)

The port

This is an ancient port used by an active fishing fleet which was enlarged with new breakwaters and quays in 1990. The port offers a nice change of scenery from the marina in Monastir and is a good base from which to explore the shallows on the SE side of the Bay of Monastir. The port offers excellent protection but unfortunately there is little room for visiting yachts.

PILOTAGE

By day

The channel was silted in 2004, though shallow draught fishing boats were using it with ease. The channel is 65m wide and runs 175°/355° for a length of 0.7M. It is marked by 2 pairs of buoys. Minimum depth in the channel is supposed to be 3.5m and only in the last 500m; depths of less than 2m are found outside the channel. The edge is soft sand and mud. A course of 150° for 2.6M from buoy no 4 in the group of buoys marking the Fosse de Teboulba leads to the beginning of the dredged channel. From this position, steer to the port entrance on a course of 175°. From this same position a dredged and buoyed channel branches off to Ras Dimas across the shallows. The accuracy of this information cannot be confirmed because of frequent silting in the channel following storms.

By night

Night entry not recommended

Berthing

Berthing is possible, but there is very little space.

Formalities

Garde National and CGP. Not a port of entry.

Facilities

Water and *ice* In the fish market.

IV. TUNISIA

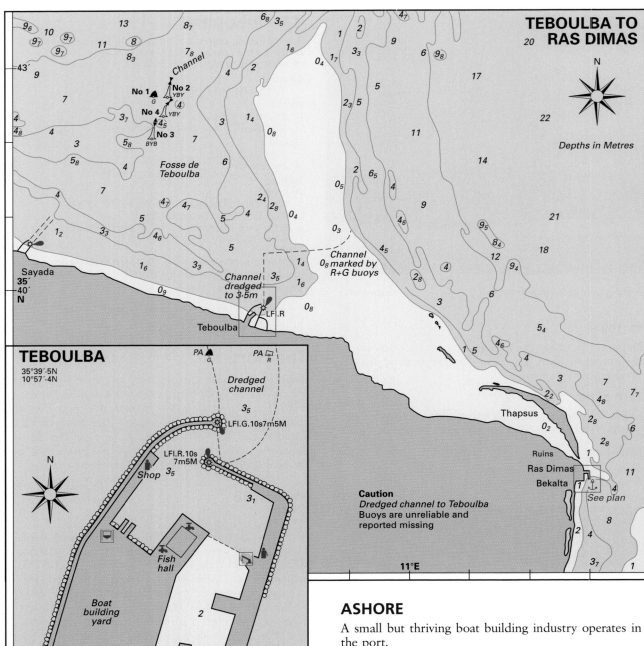

TEBOULBA TO RAS DIMAS

20

Depths in Metres

TEBOULBA
35°39'·5N
10°57'·4N

LFl.G.10s7m5M

LFl.R.10s
7m5M

Shop

Fish
hall

Boat
building
yard

Ice

Garde
National

Teboulba
3km

Depths in Metres

0   50   100

Caution
*Dredged channel to Teboulba
Buoys are unreliable and
reported missing*

11°E

Fuel On the W and E quays.

Repairs Boatyard with 130-ton travel-lift, and engineers at port entrance.

Provisions Lively market in the town 3km from the port. It is a busy place with many shops, garage and hardware stores. One may be able to catch a ride with a fishmonger or taxi. There is a chandlery and café in the port.

Post office and *bank* In the town.

ASHORE

A small but thriving boat building industry operates in the port.

The town is some 3 km inland and is worth a visit, if only to get a taste of everyday life unchanged by tourism. It is dominated by a huge mosque with lively market around it. The minaret is the tallest in the entire area. Soukrine, the village between the port and Teboulba town is of little interest and has one small shop.

Eating out

Restaurant du Plaisir and Restaurant Populair in Teboulba are places without a menu. If you do not object to eating whatever the chef decides to cook, this is a great and original place to eat. You will be unlucky if the bill reaches 2 TD for a splendid meal!

T32 The channel from Teboulba to Ras Dimas

Location
35°41′.N 11°57′.6E (approximately NW entrance of the channel)

Communications
VHF Ch 16 (0730–1330, 1500–1745)

A channel has been dredged for the Teboulba fishermen who work around Ras Dimas and provides a short-cut compared to the Conigliera channel for their shallow draught boats. It branches off from the entrance channel to Teboulba at 090° and the course to steer is 085°/265°. Depths vary from 1.5m to 2.75m and the width is about 40m. It is marked by green and red buoys of which several pairs were missing in 2004. With careful navigation, shallow draught yachts can safely pass through it as the sides are well visible. In the middle section, depths outside the channel are about 0.5m. Late in the afternoon the channel is marked by the lively traffic of fishing boats on their way out from Teboulba. Be careful in the narrow parts where there is not much room to pass. Special care has to be exercised at the eastern end where the channel bends about 045° to the N for the last 600m. In the last 200m, the channel sides are not well visible, follow the light green path.

Warning Lateen rigged fishing boats work on the shallows around the channel and from a distance in the mirage their masts can be mistaken for the perches of the channel. These boats often draw less than 0.5m.

T33 Bekalta harbour and anchorage

A small shallow harbour on the tip of Ras Dimas between Marina Monastir and Mahdia.

Location
35°37′.4N 11°03′E

Distances
Monastir 14M
Mahdia 7M

Lights
1. **W breakwater** R light on red tower approx 7m
2. **E breakwater** G light on green tower approx 7m
Characteristics unknown.

The harbour

This small fishing harbour on the S side of Ras Dimas suffers from silting and seaweed. Rendered unusable by seaweed shortly after construction, this has been a constant problem since.

PILOTAGE

Ras Dimas, a low rocky promontory joins with the Thapsus sandbank to the NW, the shoal of which extends submerged ESE for some distance offshore. When approaching from the N the shallow extension of the cape should be given a berth of 1M. Entry to the harbour must be made from the S but depths in the entrance are uncertain. There is a strong E going current around this cape.

Berthing and anchorage

The harbour is always crowded and entry is not recommended, though space for a small yacht may be found on the end of the S pontoon.

In fair weather, anchor in coarse sand SE of the harbour entrance, just S of the ridge sandbank.

Formalities

None in port.

Facilities

Fuel, *water* and *café* In the port.
Provisions The village 2 km away has a shop. Bekalta, 5 km away, has a garage, shops, telephone and railway station.

ASHORE

History

Ras Dimas, a low rocky promontory, is the site of the old Roman settlement of Thapsus, of which a few traces can still be found.

Sights locally

The tranquil surroundings are attractive with sandy beaches lined with a few palm trees and a few scattered houses. In spring time the area around the port is particularly beautiful with many wild flowers in full bloom and the current flowing gently through the narrow channel separating Ile de Thapsus from the mainland.

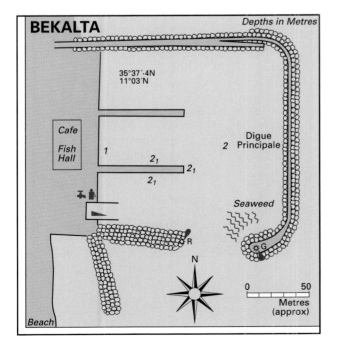

BEKALTA

Depths in Metres

35°37′.4N
11°03′N

Cafe

Fish Hall

Digue Principale

Seaweed

R

G

N

Beach

0   50
Metres
(approx)

IV. TUNISIA

4. Mahdia to Port de la Louata

T34 Mahdia

A popular harbour for yachts coming from the E, and the nearest to Lampedusa Island. A port of entry always with room for yachts, offering a friendly reception.

Location
35°30′.0N 11°04′.2E

Distances
Monastir 25M
La Chebba 17M
Lampedusa 75M

Charts
Admiralty *3403*
French *4315, 4227, 4086*

Lights
Approach
1. **Cap Afrique** 35°30′.4N 11°04′.8E Fl.R.5s26m17M White pylon, red top, on dwelling
2. ♦ **card buoy off Cap Afrique** 35°30′.1N 11°05′.8E Fl(3)10s
Harbour
3. **E breakwater outer spur head** Fl(2)G.10s6m6M
4. **New breakwater head** Fl(2)R.10s4m6M
5. **E breakwater S head** Fl.2s
6. **E breakwater inner spur** F.G.6m3M
7. **Terre-plein Ouest, corner** F.R.5m3M
Note these are as observed in summer 2004, but are not the listed characteristics so may change.

Communications
Harbourmaster ☎ 73281695
VHF Ch 16

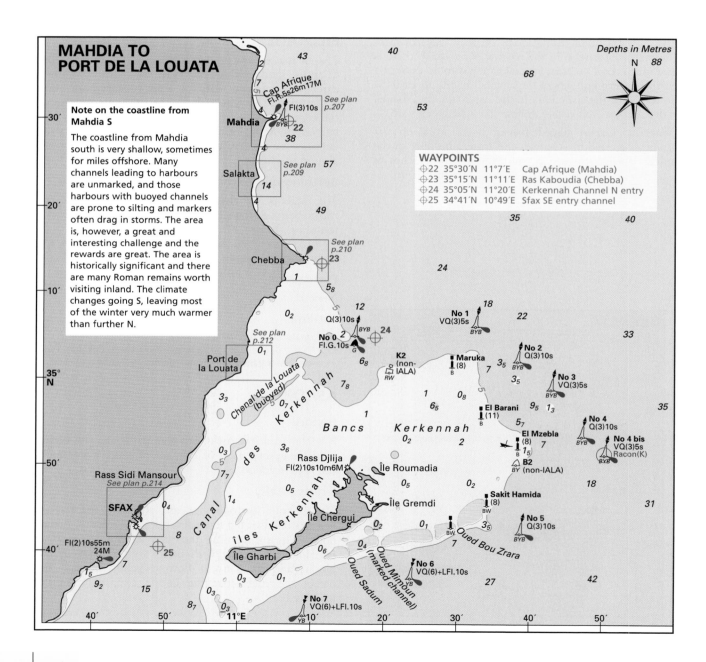

MAHDIA TO PORT DE LA LOUATA

Depths in Metres

Note on the coastline from Mahdia S

The coastline from Mahdia south is very shallow, sometimes for miles offshore. Many channels leading to harbours are unmarked, and those harbours with buoyed channels are prone to silting and markers often drag in storms. The area is, however, a great and interesting challenge and the rewards are great. The area is historically significant and there are many Roman remains worth visiting inland. The climate changes going S, leaving most of the winter very much warmer than further N.

WAYPOINTS
⊕22 35°30′N 11°7′E Cap Afrique (Mahdia)
⊕23 35°15′N 11°11′E Ras Kaboudia (Chebba)
⊕24 35°05′N 11°20′E Kerkennah Channel N entry
⊕25 34°41′N 10°49′E Sfax SE entry channel

The harbour

Mahdia is the second largest fishing port of Tunisia with a history going back to Phoenician times. Several thousand families live off its activities. Recently the port has been enlarged with a new breakwater to accommodate the growing fishing fleet and further developments are planned. The picturesque medina on the narrow peninsula is directly adjacent to the port and the market is close by. Entry is safe in any weather, and protection inside is good except during strong S winds. This is the nearest port to Lampedusa and a good port of entry. The quay reserved for yachts at right angles to the fish hall, is noisy in the mornings, but it is interesting to be in the middle of all the activity. Mahdia is the most accommodating harbour for yachts south of Monastir. Although primarily a fishing port, it is well worth visiting. There were plans to build a marina here, but they seem to have been shelved, although the area reserved for this is in the W corner of the port and is dredged.

PILOTAGE

By day

Straightforward without any offlying dangers. The ruins and lighthouse of Cap Afrique will be seen when coming from the N and E. Seas break on the shallow and irregular bottom between the cape and the E cardinal buoy marking these shallows. This buoy has been known to drift W during storms, so check your depths and keep well to the E of the buoy. A factory complex S of the port for processing ground olive pips will be seen. In strong SE winds the entrance can be rough.

By night

Night entry is possible as the harbour lights function reliably and the port is reasonably well lit. (Though note light characteristics are not as listed or as on the charts.) Cap Afrique light seems to be reliable.

Berthing

Depths in the entrance are around 4.5m. The quay at the SW end of the fish hall under the police building is reserved for visiting yachts. Keep fenders low because there is a protruding ledge just on the water line. In

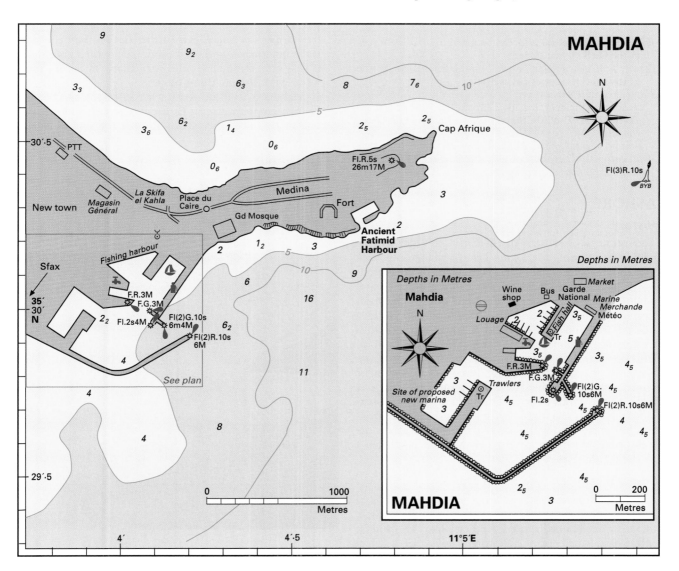

strong S or SE winds, a holding-off anchor is useful. The daily movements of fishing vessels produce some wash along this quay. There is an underwater projection in the middle of the quay, where boulders have slipped. A painted warning 'Don't stop here' marks the hazard. Depth alongside is 2.6–3.0m.

Charges for a 12m yacht

TD 11.650 per day inclusive.

Longer stays are negotiable. Yachts have wintered here and rates need to be negotiated in advance.

Formalities

Port of entry. Offices of police and capitainerie at the reserved yacht quay. Customs offices in town. All officials will call at the yacht soon after arrival.

Facilities

Water From a tap on the W side of the fish hall.
Fuel Diesel from pump on the E breakwater opposite the yacht quay. Petrol from Shell station at the mosque.
Provisions Good daily market next to the port and an excellent and very interesting weekly market on Fridays. Wine can be found in an inconspicuous store next to Restaurant Le Lido on the main road along the water front. A Magasin Général is on Avenue Bourguiba.
Post office On Avenue Bourguiba 600m from the port.
Banks Several directly outside the port.
Telephone International calls can be made from a booth next to the Shell service station.
Repairs Emergency engine repairs can be carried out but no specific yacht facilities are available.
Travel hoist 250 tons.
Chandlery 'Equipment Maritime' in the Av. Fashat Hached (☎ 03 695237) on the Sfax Road W of the port, has basic chandlery, but can undertake electronic repairs and is a Furuno agent. Contact Abdallah Jomaa.
Weather forecast Daily bulletin available from the Météo office next to the *marine marchande*.

ASHORE

History

The strategic location of Mahdia on the narrow peninsula accounts for a long history which goes back to a Phoenician trading post. The remains of the present fortifications were built by the Fatimid ruler Mahdi around 915. He rebuilt the city into one of the most formidable fortresses of the Mediterranean with a massive wall enclosing a Grand Mosque, a palace with military installations and the harbour. After the Fatimids left, the fortified city was taken by Christians from Sicily, reconquered by Islamic forces and later, after unsuccessful sieges by French, English and Genoese, taken by the Turkish corsair Dragut in 1547. Dragut was defeated three years later by the Spanish and to avoid another corsair from threatening their ships again, the walls were blown up. Since then Mahdia has been a peaceful fishing port.

Sights locally

Take a walk through the old city, starting at the 'Skifa El Kahla' (Tunnel of Darkness) the entrance to the medina, to feel what it once must have been like. The tourist office is located in the restored house of a local

Rounding the breakwater into the large port of Mahdia
Graham Hutt

Marabout (a holy man, usually a Sufi Islamic teacher) directly behind it. Place du Caire is a delightful little square which is best enjoyed in the shade of a tree with a cup of tea. Around it, several small jewellery shops line the narrow covered alleys. Further out on the peninsula is the big fortress and old Fatimid port with a graveyard; it is a very tranquil setting, particularly in spring time when wild flowers are in bloom.

Mahdia is well located for a visit to the spectacular Roman amphitheatre in El Djem, 42km inland. This is one of the most spectacular Roman remains in North Africa.

Eating out

A pizzeria and several European-style restaurants (serving wine) along the water front. Restaurant Le Medina next to the market serves typical reasonably priced Tunisian dishes.

Busy streets outside the port   *Graham Hutt*

T35 Salakta

A small shallow fishing port 7M S of Mahdia, on the southern side of Ras Salakta, providing shelter from the NW winds for yachts up to 12m.

Location
   35°23′.3N 11°02′.8E

Distances
   Mahdia 7M
   La Chebba 11M
   Monastir 50M

Charts
   Admiralty *3403*
   French *4315, 4227*

Lights
Harbour
1. **S breakwater** Green light believed to be Iso.4s
2. **W breakwater** Red light believed to be Iso. Both on short round metal poles

Communications
   Harbourmaster ☎ 666415
   VHF Ch 16, 24

The harbour

A small fishing port situated on the S side of Ras Salakta. Prone to silting, depths in the entrance vary from year to year and can be less than 2m. Depths in 2004 were 3m in the entrance and 2.5m in the port. The harbour is always full of fishing boats and is not used to visiting yachts.

PILOTAGE

By day

When approaching from the N, give Ras Salakta a wide berth to clear the partially submerged rocks extending from the E corner and the end of the S breakwater. Safe entry is then made from the S. Keep an eye out for fish nets. The ruins of an old breakwater extend from the coast 500m SW of the entrance. When entering, stay close to the starboard breakwater to avoid shallow seaweed patches.

A tower on the fish hall roof is conspicuous.

By night

Entry in rough weather and at night is not recommended.

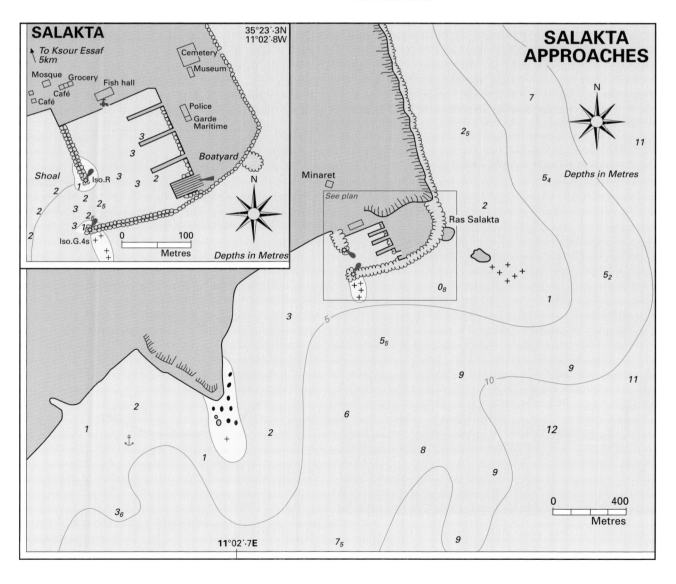

IV. TUNISIA

Berthing

Tie up alongside or with a stern anchor to the first or second pier as convenient. Further N inside the port depths are uncertain. The basin is small but there is room for a few visiting yachts with a maximum length of 12m.

An alternative is to anchor W of the entrance in front of the beach in fine sand with reasonable protection from waves. There are rocks S in this small bay.

Formalities

Police and Garde Maritime. Not a port of entry.

Facilities

Water and *ice* In the harbour.
Provisions Limited provisions from a shop in the harbour. PTT and a few basic shops in the village. A better assortment in Ksour Essaf 5km from Salakta.
Post office and *bank* In Ksour Essaf.
Repairs A boatyard building traditional wooden fishing boats has a 17-ton slip and 1-ton crane. Some mechanical repairs can be undertaken. Yachts can be lifted here.

ASHORE

The village, adjoining the harbour, is located on the site of Roman Sullecthum but the ruins are hardly worth mentioning. There is a little museum in the port with local finds and the Christian catacombs of Arch Zara, although not spectacular, are interesting. They are located inconspicuously in the middle of a field some 3km from the harbour and a guide is necessary; take a torch. The spectacular Roman amphitheatre in El Djem is 31km away.

Eating out

No restaurants in Salakta, only a coffee bar.

Fishermen of La Chebba use shallow draught lateen rigged boats
Graham Hutt

T36 La Chebba

A large and friendly harbour in a remote area of shallows, 17M S of Mahdia.

Location
  35°13′.7N 11°09′.8E
Distances
  Mahdia 17M
  Sfax 46M
Charts
  Admiralty *3403*
  French *4315, 4227*
Lights
Approach
1. **Tour Khadidja** 35°14′.0N 11°09′.4E
   Fl(2)WR.9s28m19/14M 135°-W-325°-R-135° White metal tower with red bands and inverted triangular topmark
2. **Starboard buoy No.0 entrance channel** Fl.G.10s
Harbour
4. **NE breakwater** Fl(2)G.9s8m6M Green tower
5. **SE breakwater** Fl.R.6.5s8m6M Red tower
Communications
  Harbourmaster ☎ 643044
  VHF Ch 10, 16

The harbour

The fishing harbour of La Chebba consists of a large basin protected by breakwaters, dredged in the shallows of Ras Kapoudia. La Chebba is the last port before the Kerkennah Islands and as such, a good departure point. The sea here is called Baher Maïte in Arabic, meaning 'dead sea' because even strong winds do not cause big waves. These are the fishing grounds of the traditional

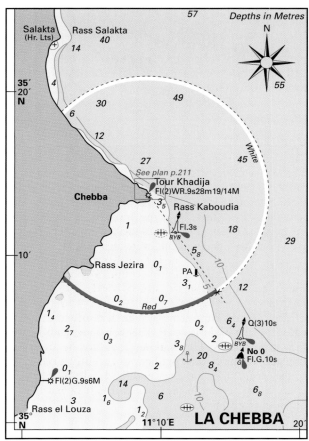

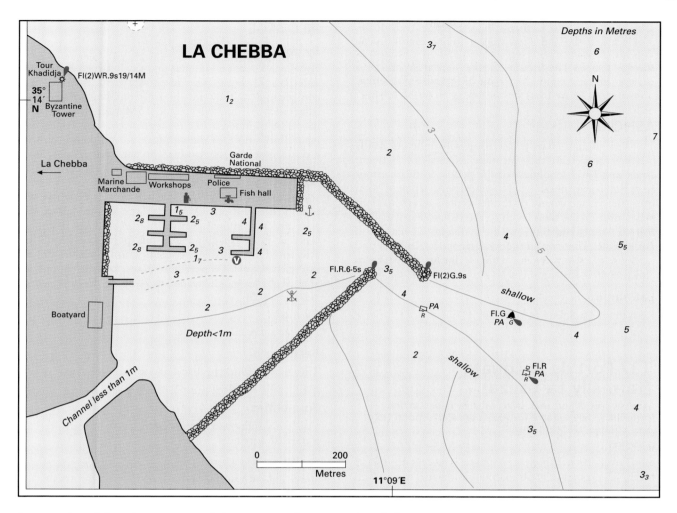

lateen sailing fishing boats. Most of them operate from the Kerkennah Islands and La Louza, but a few of them, mostly octopus fishermen, work from La Chebba. The harbour is not accustomed to yachts but the locals are friendly in accommodating visitors.

PILOTAGE

By day

The red and white bands of the metal tower of Tour Khadidja with its strange top-mark, is visible at around 5M. The Byzantine tower next to it and the harbour buildings are all good landmarks in an otherwise featureless low coast. N of the harbour low houses line the beach. The two buoys marking the entrance channel are prone to dragging, but were marking the channel correctly in 2004. 3.5-4m is found in the channel. The bottom is irregular near the entrance of the channel which makes it rough in strong winds. Although the tidal range is not very noticeable, it causes some current in the harbour, particularly at the entrance, as the SW corner of the basin is open. This helps maintain depths but nevertheless the harbour has to be regularly dredged. Accurate tidal predictions are difficult to make as they seem to be irregular and the height of the water is more noticeable during rises and falls of barometric pressure than tides.

By night

Night entry is possible but not recommended due to the few (and unreliable) entry lights and uncertain depths.

Berthing

Visiting yachts are usually accommodated on the outside of the first pier lying either alongside or stern-to but beware of the cross current which flows underneath the quays. There is room for about 10 yachts. In an emergency anchor directly E of the first pier in 2-5m fine sand.

Formalities

Police, garde national and *marine marchande*. Not a port of entry.

Facilities

Water Available from a tap at the ice tower.
Electricity None.
Ice Available on the quay.
Fuel Diesel from a pump. Depth at this section of the quay is approximately 2m. Petrol has to be carried in jerry cans from La Chebba.
Provisions Basic provisions available from 2 small shops in the port. Frequent louages to the village, where all provisions and facilities can be found.
Post office and *bank* In the village.
Repairs Engine repairs can be made by a competent mechanic with workshop in the port and there is a welder, a

IV. TUNISIA

blacksmith and a hardware shop. Boatyard with 50-ton winch and slip and 1-ton crane repairing timber fishing boats.

Weather forecast The friendly *marine marchande* official is happy to have customers for his daily report and he may even come by with an express delivery on his Mobylette.

ASHORE

The surrounding coast is low lying with miles of sandy beaches and scattered vacation homes for affluent Tunisians. The friendliness of the people in this harbour is perhaps explained by its remoteness, situated 4km from the village. Many of the fishermen return to their boats after taking their catch to the fishmongers, grilling fish on simple barbecues with the ubiquitous tea pot in the middle. There is a canning factory for sardines and octopus; giant prawns are caught during the summer and prepared for shipment to Europe.

Eating out

Restaurant La Sirène in the port.

T37 Port de la Louata (formally La Louza)

A small port almost exclusively used by lateen sailing fishermen, only suitable for yachts drawing around 1m or less. Located 32M N of Sfax.

Location
35°02´.5N 11°02´.1E

Distances
La Chebba 23M
Sfax 32M

Charts
Admiralty *3403*

Lights
Harbour
1. VQ(3)R.6s5M
2. Fl(2)G.10s5M

Communications
Harbour master ☎ 896091, ☎ 223717
VHF Ch 16

The harbour

A small fishing harbour in the very shallow coastal waters S of La Chebba. It has the largest fleet of the traditional Lateen rigged sailing fishing boats operating in Tunisia. Entry is restricted to yachts drawing little more than 1m. The port itself is 0.5M offshore, at the end of a long dike in deeper water which has low breakwaters to protect it. Large waves cannot build up in the shallow sea around it. The primary attraction of La Louata is the lateen-rigged fishing boats sailing in and out of the port during the busy octopus season (March and April). An old pierhead 1.3M S from the harbour, near the hamlet of La Louza, is still used by a few fishermen who wade through the water to get to their anchored boats. Few yachts are likely to visit the harbour, but the Tunisian National Tourist Office lists it as having room for ten visiting yachts. Five is more realistic.

PILOTAGE

By day

Port de la Louata is situated midway between Ras Batria and Ras El Luza. The ice tower and fish hall are conspicuous as they are the only buildings in the low-lying area. A sandbank about 0.5M from the entrance has to be rounded at the northern extremity. Four small white buoys ENE of the entrance are supposed to mark a passage across the sandbar. French chart No. 4236 is the only one showing the area in detail, though it does not mark the port. Note that it dates back to 1884 with some corrections in 1928. The low breakwaters have the usual green and red light structures. Depths inside the port are not known exactly but around the fish hall there is 1.5m–2m. Obviously this port should only be attempted by suitable boats in good weather during daylight hours. If uncertain about how to come in, anchor in the shallow water surrounding the port, where depths are 2m.

By night

Not recommended.

Berthing

The quay around the fish hall can accommodate a few yachts with a maximum length of 12m.

Formalities

Garde maritime and *marine marchande* in the port. Not a port of entry.

Facilities

Water and *ice* Available in the port.

Provisions There are two shops for basic provisions in the port and freshly butchered grilled lamb is available on the quay out of paper bags. There is a small chandlery for fishermen in the port. The nearest town is Jebiniana some 10km inland. PTT, 2 shops and a petrol station in La Louza. Hezeg has basic shops.

Fuel On the quay as indicated on port plan.

Repairs There is a small crane on the quay north of the fish market.

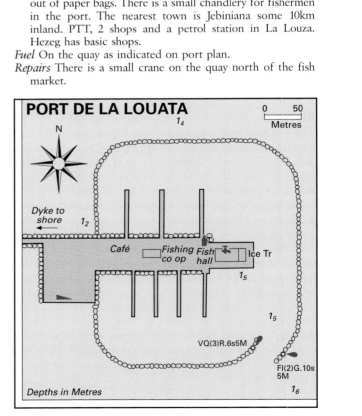

PORT DE LA LOUATA

5. Sfax to El Ketef

T38 Sfax

The largest fishing harbour in Tunisia and a large commercial port of entry. Located half way down the E coast of Tunisia W of the Kerkennah Islands.

Location
34°43´.0N 10°47´.0E (pair of entry buoys: Sfax 7 and Sfax 8 marking channel)

Distances
La Chebba 46M
Maharès 23M
Gabès 75M
Houmt Souk 62M

Tides

MHWS	MHWN	MLWN	MLWS
1.7m	1.1m	0.8m	0.3m

Charts
Admiralty *3403, 1162*
French *4315, 4237, 4238, 4228*

Lights
Commercial Port
Approach
1. **Ras Tina** 34°39´.0N 10°41´.1E Fl(2)10s55m24M White tower, red bands, white dwelling
2. **Six pairs of lit buoys** marking the dredged deep water channel leading to the commercial harbour.
Commercial Harbour
3. **Quai du Commerce** DirOc(2)8s18m13M 319°-intens-325°
Fishing port
4. **Buoy N of detached breakwater** Fl(2)G.7s
5. **Detached breakwater NE head** Iso.R.6s4m10M Red tower
6. **N breakwater head** Fl.G.4s4m10M Green tower
7. **S breakwater head** Fl.R.5s4m10M Red tower

Communications
Harbourmaster fishing port ☎ 296888 *Fax* 296816
Harbourmaster commercial port ☎ 225644
VHF Ch 16, 14

The port and fishing harbour

Sfax is the second major city of Tunisia after Tunis and the major industrial centre of the country. The large commercial port is not suitable for yachts and it should only be entered for clearing customs if necessary. In bad weather it offers little shelter as it is very open. The 'Bassin des Voiliers' marked on the French and British Admiralty charts is reserved for the Tunisian navy and ferries to the Kerkennah Islands.

The fishing harbour SW of the commercial port affords excellent protection and is slightly more accommodating to yachts although there is little room for visitors. It is the largest fishing harbour on this side of the Mediterranean, and is not very clean. In S winds, smog from nearby industry blows over it. In spite of its disadvantages, Sfax is an interesting place to spend a few days, but it is not used to visiting yachts.

PILOTAGE

By day

Entry is easy by day and night. The buildings and factories in the commercial harbour and the tall white control tower at the entrance are conspicuous in an otherwise flat coast. Entrance is by a dredged deep water channel which is marked with ten pairs of lit buoys. Beware of current up to 2 knots across the channel. From the fifth pair of buoys, marked Sfax 7 and Sfax 8 a dredged channel branches off to the fishing harbour. A detached breakwater protects this harbour which should be entered from the E, as a sandbar has formed around the SW end. The main channel is dredged to 11m and depths either side vary between 2.2m and 9m. The branch to the fishing harbour is dredged to 5m.

By night

The occulting light at the end of the commercial port is visible for 13M. It is in transit with the channel which is well marked with lit buoys as indicated.

Berthing

To clear customs, tie up at the quay below the directional light in the commercial port. After clearing, move to the fishing harbour if there is space to avoid high port charges. It was reported in 2004 that there was no room in the fishing harbour and yachts were allowed to berth along the N side of the Quai du Commerce.

Formalities

Port of entry. Clear customs first in the commercial harbour. Customs, police, garde nationale and *marine marchande* also in the fishing harbour.

Facilities (Fishing Harbour)

Water Has to be carried in jerry cans from various taps around the fish hall and restaurants.
Electricity Available in some places around the harbour.
Fuel From a pump in the fishing harbour.
Provisions Fresh produce available in the fishing harbour and a weekly market on Fridays.
Post office and *bank* In the fishing harbour.
Repairs Welders, blacksmiths, engine repair shops, paint, antifouling and hardware available in the fishing harbour. Two 250-ton and one 150-ton travel-lift and several shipyards, for repairs of steel fishing vessels and construction of large wooden fishing boats.
Weather forecast From the Météo office on the N side of the fish hall.

Eating out

Several eating houses along the quay. Good and high class restaurants in town.

Transport

Sfax has its own airport.

ASHORE

The city of Sfax is 3km away and the road to it passes through dismal surroundings. The port is a town in itself, with grocery shops, eating houses, stores with ships' supplies, a bank and even a mosque as well as repair shops, ship yards and three large travel-lifts.

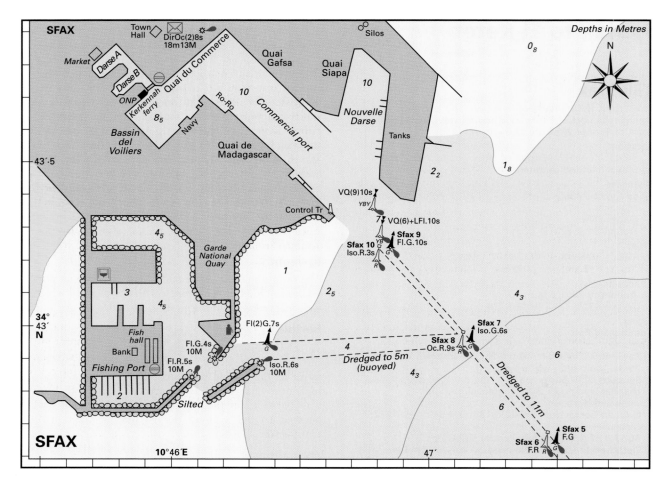

SFAX

Town Hall

Market

DirOc(2)8s 18m13M

Darse A

Darse B

ONP

Kerkennah ferry

Quai du Commerce

Quai Gafsa

Silos

Quai Siapa

0_8

Depths in Metres

N

10

Commercial port

Ro-Ro

Navy

8_5

Bassin del Voiliers

Quai de Madagascar

Nouvelle Darse

10

Tanks

2_2

1_8

43'·5

Control Tr

VQ(9)10s

YBY

7 VQ(6)+LFl.10s

Sfax 9 Fl.G.10s

Sfax 10 Iso.R.3s

YB

G

R

4_5

Garde National Quay

1

2_5

4_3

34° 43' N

3

4_5

Fish hall

Bank

Fl.G.4s 10M

Fl.R.5s 10M

4_5

Fl(2)G.7s

G

Iso.R.6s 10M

4

Dredged to 5m (buoyed)

Sfax 8 Oc.R.9s

R

G

Sfax 7 Iso.G.6s

G

Dredged to 11m

6

4_3

6

Sfax 5 F.G

Sfax 6 F.R

R

G

2

Silted

Fishing Port

SFAX

10°46′E

47′

History

The modern town, rebuilt after heavy bombardments in the Second World War, is attractive and quite sophisticated but at the same time it has a large medina which is not overrun by tourist shops.

Sights locally

Compared with the other big cities in Tunisia, Sfax has not been affected much by tourism. Sfaxians are renowned for their entrepreneurial skill and probably do not need the revenues from tourism. There is a good Archaeological and a Popular Arts Museum of which the Rough Guide gives an enthusiastic and detailed account. Whether all of this is enough to overcome the inconveniences of visiting by boat is a personal matter.

Kids having fun near Sfax   *Graham Hutt*

T39 The Kerkennah Islands

Comprised of two principal islands 10M E of Sfax, this is a low-lying place of tranquillity amongst very friendly and hospitable people who see few tourists.

Charts
 Admiralty *3403, 1162*
 French *4315, 4235, 4237*

The islands

A group of sandy islands 10M from the mainland coast and a world away from busy Sfax. Vegetation is sparse: mainly wind-blown palm trees, some scattered fig trees and small vegetable gardens. Their greatest attraction is their solitude and the simple, unchanged way of life of hospitable people.

The islands have in the past been a place of exile. During the recent struggle for independence, Bourguiba was interned here until he escaped to Libya from Kraten on the NW corner of Ile Chergui.

The group consists of two main islands, Ile Rharbi and Ile Chergui, separated by a narrow channel, and two small uninhabited islets off the E coast. Much of the land is less than 3m above sea level and the highest point is 20m. They sit among the Kerkennah Banks, of sand, mud and weed, which extend 35 miles from the coast between Ras Kapoudia and Sfax, and are separated from the mainland by the Canal des Kerkennah.

The main activity is fishing on the sandbanks. Traditionally the fish are caught in charfias, traps made of palm tree fronds permanently planted in the sea bed. Long lines of these palm fronds stretch from the beach out to sea and serve to divert the fish to a chamber with fish nets around its circumference. Typically one charfia brings in 1000kg of fish per month. Small rowing or lateen rigged sailing boats are used to empty the nets daily. Two thousand sailing and rowing boats are still in use around the islands together with a slowly increasing number of powered boats. The sailing boats are mostly used from the beaches whereas the powered boats operate mainly from the new fishing port of Najet at Kraten. Fishing by the ancient method of net-throwing is also used.

PILOTAGE

Navigation around the islands is tricky, but less exacting for yachts drawing less than 1.5m which do not mind going aground. Landmarks are few and far apart in the Kerkennah region and accuracy of the French charts cannot be relied on as no proper surveys have been made in recent years. (Some, no more recently than 100 years ago.) SHOM chart *4237* is the most useful and

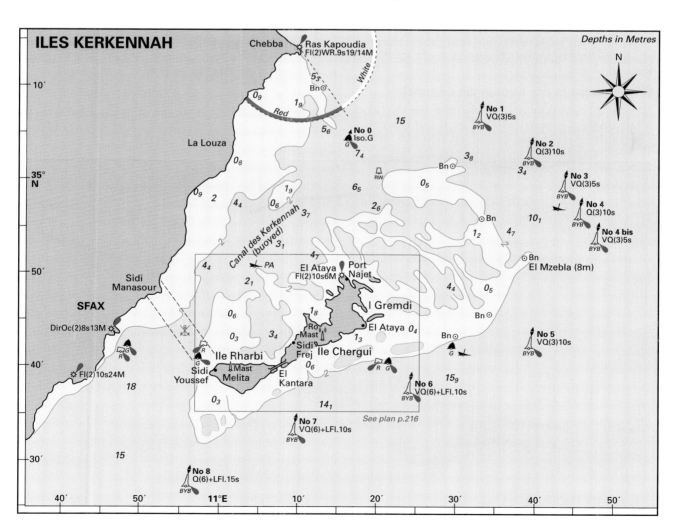

IV. TUNISIA

detailed, but GPS WGS 84 coordinates will be out by over half a mile.

Land features such as buildings, new ports and antennae which could provide useful navigational aids are missing. On the other hand, serious grounding can be avoided by proper timing of the tides which are significant here. There is an amazing difference in tidal range even within a few miles.

The seaward edges of the Kerkennah banks are fringed with shoals and marked by lit buoys and beacons. The shallower parts are intersected by numerous steep-sided channels called *oueds* (river) in Arabic. The banks, in common with similar shoals off the Tunisian coast, possess the remarkable characteristic of reducing swell. This is due to the gradual slope of the bottom and thick seaweed which covers it. In many of the oueds a yacht can anchor safely providing it has proper ground tackle. The area does not require special anchor gear other than mentioned under 'Yacht and Equipment'.

The main shipping route leads around the banks which are well marked with large buoys and beacons though their lights are unreliable. It is worth checking the situation at the *marine marchande*. The alternative route to the S is through the Kerkennah Channel, between the islands and the mainland. This channel is reasonably well buoyed and is used by small coastal ships. Care is required around some beacons which are planted on the shallow sea bed just outside the channel.

South from La Chebba the tidal range increases rapidly and current in the channel has to be taken into account.

Tidal streams in the Kerkennah Channel

There is no tidal flow chart of the area but the flood comes across the banks from NE or E and enters the Kerkennah Channel from either end. The ebb stream sets in the reverse direction. Thus, when proceeding on the edge of the banks or in the Kerkennah Channel, caution must be exercised as the tidal stream may set directly on to the banks.

On the eastern extremity of the banks the tidal streams turn at the time of local high and low water and the maximum rate, at about half tide, does not exceed 1 knot. In the Kerkennah Channel the tidal streams are stronger and may attain a rate of 1.5 knots. They turn 2-3 hours after local high and low water and attain their maximum rate shortly before the time of high or low water. They set equally through the channel and meet at about the middle of it, where they are irregular.

Tides for Kerkennah Islands

The tides (taken from the British Admiralty Tide Tables) for the ports in the Kerkennah Islands are as follows (Time based on HW Gibraltar)

	MHWS	MHWN	MLWN	MLWS	HW	LW
Kerkennah Banks, E point	0.8m	0.4m	0.4m	0.2m	1:05	0:55
Kraten (estimated)	1.1m	0.7m	0.5m	0.2m		
Bordj el Hassar/ Sidi Frej	1.2m	0.8m	0.6m	0.2m	+2:10	+3:15
Sidi Youssef (estimated)	1.3m	0.9m	0.7m	0.3m		
Kerkennah Banks, S point	1.4m	0.9m	0.7m	0.3m	+0:35	0:10
El Abassia (near Ataya)	1.1m	0.7m	0.5m	0.3m	+0:43	+1:52
Sfax	1.7m	1.1m	0.8m	0.3m	+0:50	+1:15

French charts, taken together with the general information available on tidal streams, for instance Admiralty Tide Tables, may provide more clues.

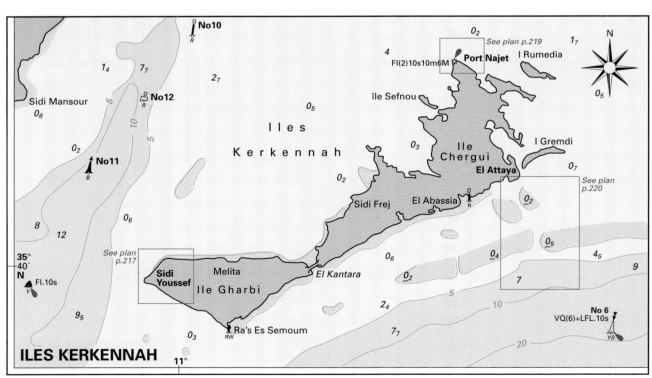

ILES KERKENNAH

THE ANCHORAGES

There are three small fishing harbours and anchorages around the Kerkennah Islands. With the exception of Sidi Youssef, none of the harbours has a properly buoyed approach. It is possible to anchor in many places in and around the banks as the seas will be calm in almost any weather. Drying sandbanks extend for some distance S of the islands, as noted on the chart. The prevailing E winds will generally favour anchoring on the NW side of the islands.

Net throwing: a traditional fishing method for thousands of years
Graham Hutt

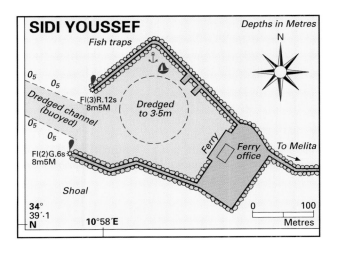

T40 Sidi Youssef

This small harbour principally for the ferry from Sfax, 10M away, is the only port in the Kerkennah Islands which is relatively easy to enter for normal draught yachts.

Location
34°39′.3N 10°57′.5E

Distances
Sfax 10M
La Chebba 45M
Maharès 30M

Charts
Admiralty *3403, 1162*
French *4315, 4235, 4237*

Tides

MHWS	MHWN	MLWN	MLWS
1.3m	0.9m	0.7m	0.3m

Lights
Approach
No.1 34°39′.7N 10°56′.8E Iso.G.4s7m5M Green and white bands
No.2 (close to No.1) Iso.R.4s7m5M Red and white bands
No.3 LFl.G.10s7m5M Bn
No.4 F.R.7m5M Bn stripes.

Harbour
1. **N breakwater** Fl(3)R.12s8m5M
2. **S breakwater** Fl(2)G.6s8m5M
3. **Dir Lt** DirOc(2)WRG.9.6s9/7M

Communications
Harbourmaster ☎ 281154
VHF Ch 16

The harbour

This small harbour on the W point of the Kerkennah Islands comes to life when the ferry from Sfax arrives. The 4m high concrete wall running the entire length of both breakwaters, provides good shelter. The basin is small and has no quays. With some improvising, smaller yachts can lay bow-to the N breakwater if sufficient room is left for the ferry to swing.

PILOTAGE

The palm trees on the island will be spotted first, and the port only when close, as the few buildings are low. Using chart BA 3403, (to WGS84 datum) the waypoint for the first pair of entrance buoys is 34°39′.858N 10°56′.827E. Entrance is through a narrow channel dredged to 4.5m, about 1.5M long on a course of 112°. The channel is marked by a green and a red buoy at the entrance and 2 more buoys. Yachts should stay well in the centre and it is advisable not to share the channel with the ferry. Beware of a strong cross current of around 2 knots.

Berthing

There are no quays on the N breakwater but there is a dilapidated wooden landing and the remains of another which can be used to tie a bow-line, using a dinghy to get ashore. The ferry produces considerable wash. When laying the kedge keep in mind that the ferry needs a large turning circle to leave the port. There is no ideal place to avoid obstructing the ferry but moored in as close to the E breakwater as possible is the best.

Formalities

A small Garde National post but not a port of entry.

Facilities

There are virtually no facilities other than a little stall in the summer season which caters for the needs of passing ferry passengers. The nearest village where some provisions are available is Melita, 5km from the port. Buses are available after the arrival of the ferry six times a day. Taxis are practically non existent.

Water (and WC) At Café du Port.

Provisions Melita has basic shops, hardware store, café and PTT.

T41 Sidi Ferruch pier and anchorage

A quiet anchorage on the NW side of Ile Chergui, the main island, half mile N of a tourist development.

Location
34°41′.372N 11°08′.046E (Root of pier/breakwater)

Charts
Admiralty 3403, 1162
French 4315, 4235, 4237

Tides

MHWS	MHWN	MLWN	MLWS
1.2m	0.8m	0.6m	0.2m

The anchorage

Sidi Ferruch, on the NW coast of Ile Chergui, is the only part of the Kerkennah Islands with some modest tourist development. A few low-key hotels line the beach, from which a pier extends from Hotel Cerana 550m into deeper water. It is only accessible to yachts drawing half a metre or less.

PILOTAGE

Approach is best started from buoy 12 in the Kerkennah Channel. Steer for the small fortress at Bordj el Hassar, close to Sidi Ferruch until 2–3M from the shore, then a course can be set for the pier. Beware of strong tidal streams which set across the banks.

Berthing

The pier was formerly frequented by small boats that supplied the islands before the ferry port of Sidi Youssef was built. It is now used by tenders supplying the oil platform approximately 3M offshore. Tie up at the end bows-to where the minimum depth is approximately 1.5m at low water. Alternatively anchor further out in minimum of 2-2.5m with good holding. Beware of uncharted shallow patches in the N part of the anchorage. Protection during the common E to SE summer winds is good.

Facilities

Basic provisions Are available in Ouled el Kassem, a hamlet on the main road to Remla, about 4km from Sidi Frej.

Fishing In the summer some fishing boats make excursions to see the traditional fishing method with charfias. Note that several grounds around these shores are now conservation areas where fishing is prohibited.

Transport

Bicycles can be hired at Hotel Cercina which also serves good meals.

T42 Ramla

Location
34°42′N 11°12′.5E (approximately)

Ramla is the capital of the islands with a pier running approximately 250m out to sea, but with only 0.5m depth at its end. It is of little use to yachts.

Facilities

Water and *diesel* Are available at the root of the pier.

PTT pharmacy, bank, garage and *shops* In Ramla.

T43 Port Najet (En-najet or Kraten)

The main fishing harbour of the Kerkennah Islands, located close to the NW of Ile Chergui. Yachts are welcome in this friendly port but approach is restricted to shallow draught yachts.

Location
34°49′.8N 11°15′.4E

Distances
La Chebba 27M
Sidi Youssef 24M

Tides (approx)

MHWS	MHWN	MLWN	MLWS
1.1m	0.7m	0.5m	0.2m

Lights
Approach
1. **Ras Djila (NW point of Ile Chergui)** 34°49′.7N 11°14′.8E Fl(2)10s10m6M

Harbour
2. **East jetty head** Fl(2)R.10s7m5M
3. **W jetty** Fl.G.7s5M and Fl.G
4. **El Kraten fishing harbour** Fl(2)G.10s10m8M and Fl.R.5s10m5M

Communications
Harbourmaster ☎ 487450
VHF Ch 16

The harbour

The main fishing harbour of the Kerkennah Islands, welcomes yachts, though only shallow draught yachts will make it in. The harbour and entrance have been dredged to depths of 2m, but silting is a constant problem and depths therefore are uncertain.

PILOTAGE

There are no buoys and apart from the minaret of Kraten, which is not marked on the chart and the ice tower in the port, there are no landmarks. Beware of small banks of sand and seaweed on this part of the coast; octopus fishermen lay their pots in them.

French chart No. 4237 indicates the approach from buoy K4 in the Kerkennah Channel. A track of 141° for 6.5M will bring the harbour abeam. This chart, like most

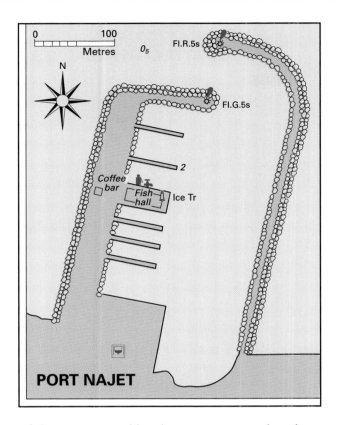

PORT NAJET

of the area is very old and no recent surveys have been undertaken in this area. Avoid the bank which extends approximately 1M N of Ras Djila.

Berthing

There is room for a few visiting yachts (maximum length 12m) which can tie up wherever convenient.

Formalities

APIP in the port. Will provide weather forecasts on request.

Facilities

Water Available from a tap near the fish market.
Fuel Diesel from a pump.
Provisions Limited provisions available in the small village approximately 3km from the harbour. There is a coffee bar and small shop in the harbour.
Repairs A boatyard and slip in the S corner of the harbour.

T44 El Attaya

A small thriving fishing harbour located in the NE side of Ile Chergui, the main island of the Kerkennah group.

Location
   34°43´.4N 11°17´.7E

Distances
   Sidi Youssef 37M
   Sfax 40M

Tides

MHWS	MHWN	MLWN	MLWS
1.1m	0.7m	0.5m	0.3m

Lights

Harbour
1. **Red and green lights** on outer breakwaters.
2. **Red light** on inner breakwater (characteristics unknown)

The harbour

El Attaya is a small thriving harbour in a forgotten corner of Ile Chergui with a large fleet of sailing and motor fishing boats.

PILOTAGE

Entrance to the harbour is via a 4M long natural channel, Oued Mimoun, of which the last part has been dredged. Two sets of buoys mark the entrance to the channel and palm fronds are planted randomly further on. Once the entrance buoys are located it is best to rely on 'eye-ball' navigation as the channel is visible, though in rough seas the visibility of the sea water is reduced and the river course is difficult to determine. Entry is best started at low water when the drying parts of the banks around the oued are visible. Depths vary from a minimum of 4.5m to a maximum of 12m and the sides are steep. The dredged 60m wide channel leading into the harbour is 700m long on a course of 005°. Depths are 3.5m. The breakwaters protecting the harbour are low. The antenna from the radiobeacon N of the harbour and a large factory hall near the harbour are conspicuous. Once in the oued, between the banks, there are plenty of places to anchor and holding is good.

Berthing

Tie up anywhere as convenient.

Formalities

APIP are helpful and will supply weather forecasts daily.

Facilities

Water Available at SE end of the fish hall.
Fuel From the fuel quay as indicated on the harbour plan.
Provisions One shop in the harbour. Basic shops and PTT in El Attaya 2 km away.
Repairs A boatyard with 100-ton travel-lift and 10-ton crane, building and repairing fishing boats.

ASHORE

The picturesque setting of the old anchorage W of the harbour makes a nice afternoon walk. On the road to Remla, there is a museum dedicated to Bourguiba's escape from the island to Libya. It contains several letters Bourguiba wrote, the house he sheltered in and the boat he used for his escape from the French occupation forces.

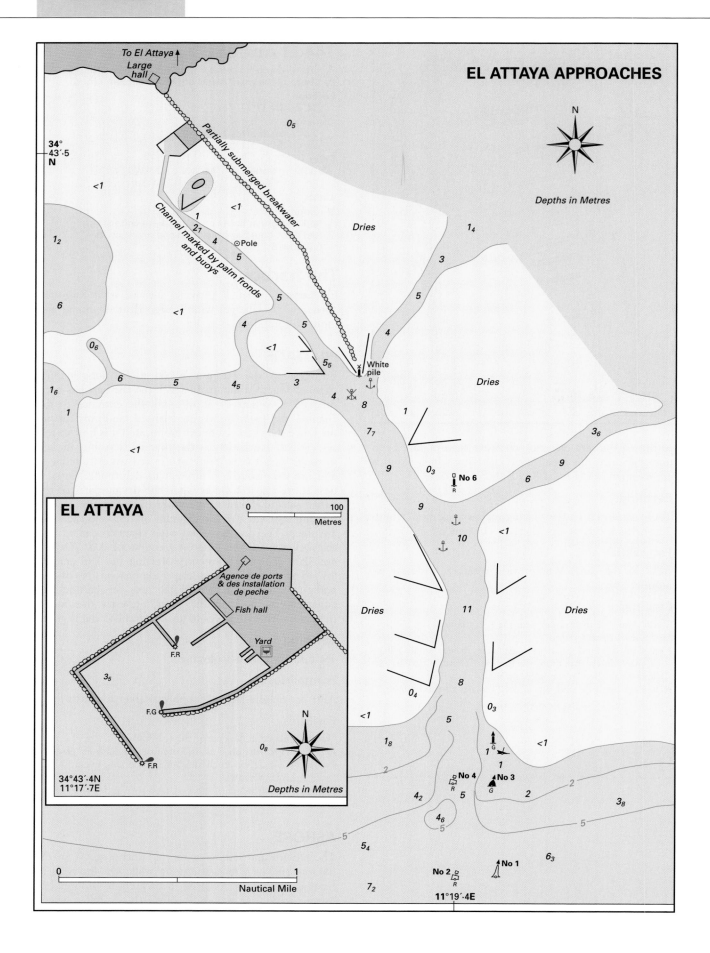

EL ATTAYA APPROACHES

Depths in Metres

To El Attaya
Large hall

34°
43´·5
N

Partially submerged breakwater

Channel marked by palm fronds and buoys

Dries

Pole

White pile

Dries

No 6

Dries

Dries

EL ATTAYA

0   100
Metres

Agence de ports & des installation de peche

Fish hall

Yard

F.R

F.G

F.R

34°43´·4N
11°17´·7E

N

Depths in Metres

No 4
No 3
No 2
No 1

0   1
Nautical Mile

11°19´·4E

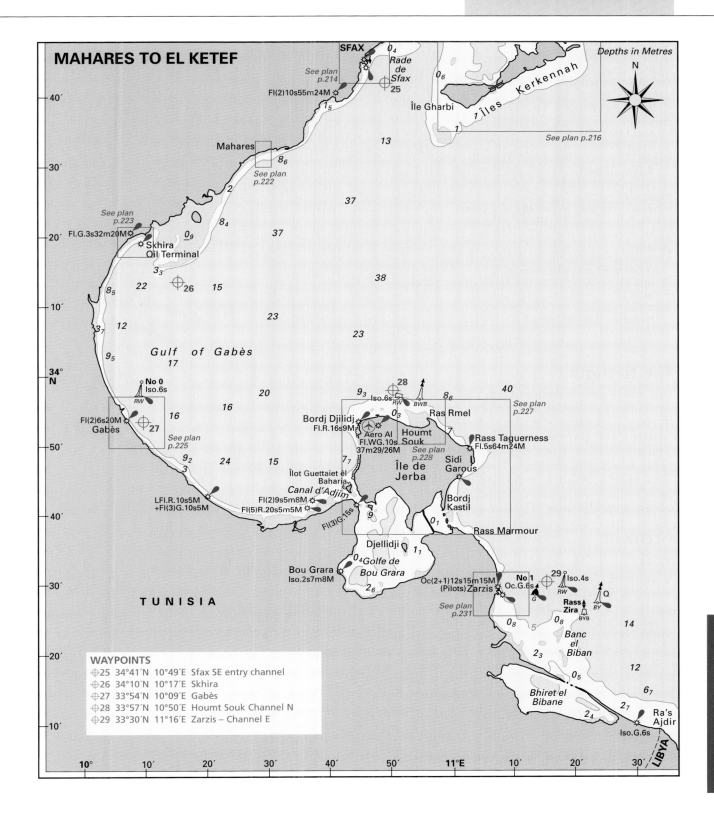

MAHARES TO EL KETEF

Depths in Metres

SFAX

Rade de Sfax

See plan p.214

Fl(2)10s55m24M

25

Île Gharbi

Îles Kerkennah

See plan p.216

13

Mahares

See plan p.222

8₆

2

37

8₄

See plan p.223

Fl.G.3s32m20M

Skhira Oil Terminal

0₉

37

3₃

38

22

15

26

8₅

23

12

23

3₇

Gulf of Gabès

9₅

17

No 0
Iso.6s

RW

9₃

28

Iso.6s

RW

BWB

8₆

40

See plan p.227

34°
N

20

16

16

Fl(2)6s20M
Gabès

27

0₃

Bordj Djilidj
Fl.R.16s9M

Ras Rmel

See plan p.225

Aero Al
Fl.WG.10s
37m29/26M

Houmt Souk

7

Rass Taguerness
Fl.5s64m24M

See plan p.228

9₂

24

15

7₇

Île de Jerba

Sidi Garous

3

Îlot Guettaiet el Baharia

Canal d'Adjim

Bordj Kastil

LFl.R.10s5M
+Fl(3)G.10s5M

Fl(2)9s5m8M
Fl(5)R.20s5m5M

Fl(3)G.15s

9

0₁

Rass Marmour

Djellidji

1₁

Bou Grara
Iso.2s7m8M

0₄ Golfe de Bou Grara

2₆

No 1
Oc.G.6s

G

29

RW

Iso.4s

Q

BY

Rass Zira

BYB

14

Oc(2+1)12s15m15M
(Pilots) Zarzis

See plan p.231

0₈

5

0₈

TUNISIA

Banc el Biban

2₃

12

Bhiret el Bibane

0₅

6₇

2₇

Ra's Ajdir

Iso.G.6s

2₄

LIBYA

WAYPOINTS

⊕25 34°41′N 10°49′E Sfax SE entry channel
⊕26 34°10′N 10°17′E Skhira
⊕27 33°54′N 10°09′E Gabès
⊕28 33°57′N 10°50′E Houmt Souk Channel N
⊕29 33°30′N 11°16′E Zarzis – Channel E

10°   10′   20′   30′   40′   50′   11°E   10′   20′   30′

IV. TUNISIA

T45 Maharès

A small fishing harbour 21M SW of Sfax with little room for yachts, accessed through a dredged channel.

Location
34°30´.5N 10°29´.8E

Distances
Sfax 21M
Gabès 50M

Charts
Admiralty *3403*
French *4315, 4239*

Tides

MHWS	MHWN	MLWN	MLWS
1.7m	1.1m	0.8m	0.3m

Lights
Harbour
1. **Maharès** 34°30´.8N 10°29´.9E DirF.WRG.9m3M
   Lit Bns mark entrance channel
2. **No.1** 34°30´.7N 10°29´.8E Q.G.8m3M (green pylon)
3. **No.2** Q.R

Communications
Harbourmaster ☎ 290543
VHF Ch 16

The harbour

This small fishing harbour in a very shallow area is built away from the land at the end of a short dyke. The entrance is through a dredged channel which ends between low, partially submerged breakwaters. The fishing harbour is active with little room for visiting yachts. It is a good jumping off point for Gabès or the island of Jerba. Maharès has benefited considerably from the re-opening of the Libyan border and as it is on the main road to Sfax. Many Libyans stop here to shop.

PILOTAGE

By day

A TV antenna NE of the port is visible from a distance of around 3M and closer in, the mosque minaret will be seen. The dredged channel to the harbour is not buoyed. Being in the correct position at the beginning of the channel is therefore essential. Time has to be allowed to take accurate bearings – 356° through the centre line of the entrance channel to the minaret and 016° to the radio mast. Beware of the low breakwaters which are partially submerged at HW. Minimum depth is 1.8m at LW in the channel and 1.5m in the harbour itself.

By night

Approach the harbour using the narrow white sector of the leading light. The four harbour lights placed at either end of the two breakwaters extending from the entrance, show the breakwaters' position S when submerged.

Berthing

Tie up anywhere as convenient. The harbour officials have not in the past welcomed yachts as it is overcrowded with fishing boats. The tourist authorities, however, state that there is room for 7 visiting yachts with a maximum length of 14m.

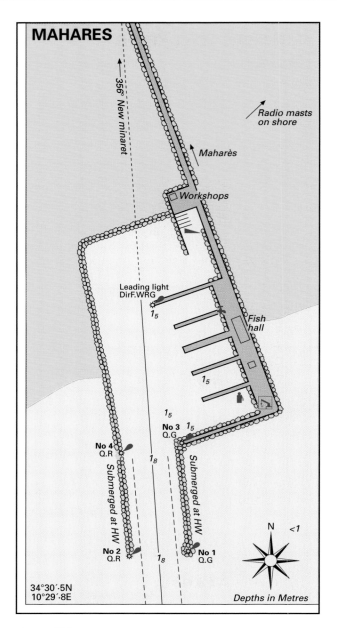

Formalities

Garde National and *Marine Marchande*. Not a port of entry.

Facilities

Water From a tap on the quay.
Fuel Diesel pump on the first pier. Petrol from a service station on the main road close to the harbour.
Provisions Good assortment from several shops close to the harbour and one small shop inside the harbour.
Post office and *telephone* In the town past the railroad tracks.
Bank Several along the main road.
Repairs A yard for small wooden fishing boats has a 15-ton winch and a 1-ton crane. Mechanical repairs undertaken. The village has several hardware stores.

ASHORE

Eating out

A good choice of restaurants and cafés along the main road from Sfax to Gabès.

The Gulf of Gabès

T46 La Skhira Khedima

Location
34°18´.4N 10°08´.4E

Tides

MHWS	MHWN	MLWN	MLWS
1.1m	1.4m	1.0m	0.5m

Lights
End of oil terminal F.R.5M

An oil terminal with a 1.5M long jetty projecting SE, 3M N of La Skhira. Of no use to yachts but included here for navigational purposes and for use in an emergency.

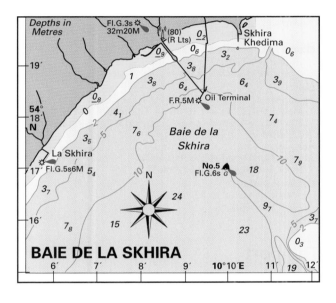

T47 La Skhira

A small overcrowded fishing harbour 25M from Gabès and 3M SW of the large oil terminal jetty noted. Yachts have not been welcome here because there is no room to accommodate them.

Location
34°17´.0N 10°05´.9E (Breakwater light)

Distances
Sfax 50M
Gabès 25M

Tides

MHWS	MHWN	MLWN	MLWS
2.1m	1.4m	1.0m	0.5m

Charts
Admiralty *3403, 9*
French *4316, 6325*

Light
Harbour end Fl.G.5s6M

The harbour

A small fishing harbour in an unattractive part of the coast, 3 miles SW of the commercial terminal at La Skhira Khedima. The harbour is well used by small and medium sized fishing boats. Exact depths are not known. Harbour officials claim there are minimum depths of 2m inside the port. All available space is taken by fishing boats, resulting in yachts being unwelcome visitors. Depths are uncertain in the harbour.

PILOTAGE

By day

From the N, the commercial quay of Skhirra Khedima will be seen. A buoy 1M S of the end of the quay is also a good marker. The fish market, breakwater and lights, together with the apartments on the cliff 200m behind the port are conspicuous.

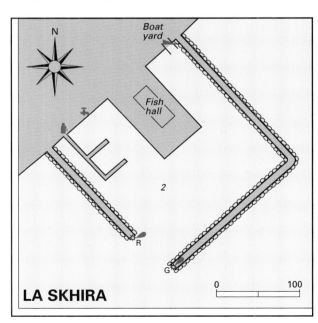

IV. TUNISIA

By night

Skhira Khedima terminal jetty light 3M NE of the harbour (F.R) has a range of 5M and the lit buoy marked No5 (F.G.6s) E of the harbour will also be seen.

Berthing

Alongside a fishing boat or vacant space on the quay, but expect to be moved.

Formalities

Garde National just outside the port. Not a port of entry.

Facilities

Water Available from a tap on the quay.
Fuel From a pump on the quay or petrol from 2 garages in the town.
Provisions Two small shops in the harbour for basics only. A selection of shops and cafes in the town.
Post office, telephone and *banks, PTT* taxiphone and 2 banks in the town.
Weather forecasts Available from the office (believed to be APIP) at vehicular entrance of the harbour.

ASHORE

The town of La Skhira has all facilities including a station and is on the main Sfax to Gabès road. It is 1km from the harbour, past a development of luxury apartments built for the foreign engineers working at the phosphoric acid plant. There is much new building going on.

T48 Port Ghannouch

Location
33°55′.6N 10°06′.8E

Tides
MHWS	MHWN	MLWN	MLWS
2.1m	1.4m	1.0m	0.5m

A large phosphate commercial port 2M N of Gabès. Not for use by yachts but included for navigational information.

T49 Gabès

A large and accessible, though busy, port in a tuna fishing area 75M S of Sfax and close to Chenini oasis. A port of entry.

Location
33°53′.7N 10°07′.3E Light on E breakwater

Distances
Sfax 75M
Houmt Souk 43M

Tides
MHWS	MHWN	MLWN	MLWS
2.1m	1.3m	1.0m	0.3m

Charts
Admiralty *3403, 9*
French *4316, 4240, 4241*

Lights
Approach
1. **Main light** 33°53′.6N 10°06′.8E Fl(2)6s13m20M 124°-vis-304° White 8-sided tower, black top R lights on pylon 0.9M SW

Harbour
2. **Jetée Nord head** Fl(2)G.9s10m6M
3. **Jetée Sud head** Fl.R.6.5s10m6M

Communications
Harbourmaster ☎ 5270367
VHF 16 (24hr)

The port

The busy fishing port of Gabès is situated near the large oasis of Chenini. The port is big but there is not much room for visiting yachts. In winter time, local depressions develop over the Gulf of Gabès and strong winds are frequent, mainly from SW to W or from NE to E and occasionally gales are recorded.

The Gulf has rich fishing grounds and in mid-March when the prawn and tuna season begins, fishermen from all over Tunisia come for the tunny fishing for which large trawl nets are used.

The large commercial port of Ghannouche, 3M N of the fishing port, is far from the city and not suitable for yachts.

PILOTAGE

By day

The coast around Gabès is low but the port is not difficult to approach. There are no offlying dangers and the industrial complex around the commercial port is conspicuous from a great distance. The breakwaters of the fishing port are high with large light structures.

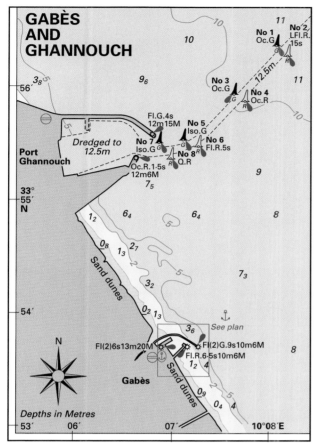

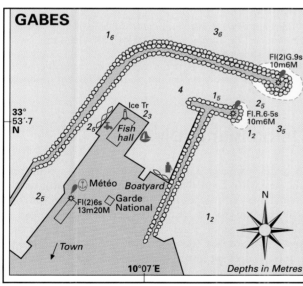

Silting takes place around the entrance and positioning the yacht mid-channel is important. The entrance is dredged regularly to 4m, but silts quickly to below 2m.

By night

Night entry is not recommended.

Berthing

The most likely place to find a space is on the quay NE of the fish hall, alongside the Garde National patrol boat. Most berths are needed from early morning for fishing boats.

Formalities

Port of entry. Friendly and helpful officials.

Facilities

Water From the fish market.
Electricity Not available.
Fuel Diesel pump in the port, petrol from service station in town.
Provisions Many small shops and a good local market for fresh produce, meat and fish. Magasin Général and wine shop in the town. The port has 2 shops, including a fruit and veg shop, and a café.
Post office, telephone and *banks* On Ave Bourguiba.
Repairs A boatyard with 200-ton travel-lift. Timber and mechanical repairs possible.
Laundry On a slightly hidden corner of Avenue Farhat Hached.
Weather forecast Posted in arabic at NE end of the fish market.

ASHORE

The pleasant town of Gabès is a short walk from the port and has good shops to provision, restaurants and hotels of all categories. It is also a good base for excursions into the desert.

History

Gabès was originally a Phoenician settlement, later becoming the most southern port of the Roman Empire in Africa. The most important religious monument is the new Mosque of Sidi Boulbaba, named after the marabout (holy man) who brought peace and prosperity in the 7th century. Nearby is an old mosque with a beautifully decorated inner courtyard, well worth visiting.

The relics of its Spanish, Ottoman and Arabic conquerors were destroyed between the French bombardment in 1904 and the Second World War, after which most of the present town was built.

Sites locally

A main attraction of Gabès is the large Chenini oasis where one can still find a classic haven of peace and shade under the tall date palms. Bicycles can be hired at the youth hostel or alternatively one can rent a horse drawn carriage.

Another interesting excursion is to visit the desert regions in the south. The most popular trip is to the underground Berber dwellings in Matmata. Staying in one of the pit hotels is a unique experience. Haddej, close to old Matmata, is less visited and gives a good idea what these underground villages were like. Take a torch to see olive presses and family dwellings and the pit house used for marriage ceremonies.

From Matmata a picturesque but rough trail leads to Toujane, one of the most isolated Berber villages, built on two sides of a steep gorge in arid and wild mountains. The area was a battle ground in the Second World War. Other interesting places in the same area are the extraordinary Berber village of Chenini (visit early in the morning before the tour buses arrive), Douirat and a hotel in converted storage rooms in Ksar Haddada.

The shortest way from Gabès to the true beginning of the Sahara is via the oasis of Douz. The piste route S of Douz to Sabria El Faouar loops through the desert and to isolated oases; in normal circumstances four wheel drive is not necessary.

Other worthwhile excursions are across the Chott el Djerid to the large oases of Tozeur and Nefta, though these are popular destinations for tourist buses. The drive through the desolate salt pans of the Chott is a very special experience and it opens the way to another interesting desert trail to the Seldja Gorge via Tamerza.

In three days several of these places can be visited by car but a week or more will not be wasted. The landscape is spectacular and a glimpse of the unique and almost unchanged lifestyle of the Berbers over 2000 years, is a highlight of a visit to Tunisia. The Rough Guide covers these excursions extensively.

Eating out

A wide selection of restaurants ranging from European style to the most simple Tunisian eating houses, in the town.

Transport

Major car rental agencies have offices in town as well as a Land Rover hire agency.

T50 Zarat

A small and shallow harbour at the S end of the Gulf of Gabès near Ajim, built out into the sea on a dyke with the village 5km away. Only of use to shallow draught yachts less than 12m.

Location
  33°42'.0N 10°21'.8E

Distances
  Gabès 17M
  Ajim 19M

Tides

MHWS	MHWN	MLWN	MLWS
2.1m	1.3m	1.0m	0.3m

Charts
  Admiralty *3403, 9*
  French *4316, 4242*

Lights
Harbour
1. **NE breakwater head** Fl(3)G.10s6m5M
2. **SW breakwater head** LFl.R.10s6m5M

The harbour

A small recently built fishing harbour in an isolated part of the coast between Gabès and Ajim. The port is situated near the site of an old tuna factory, Sidi Marmora. The new village of Zarat is some 5km from the port close to the main road along the coast. Depths in the harbour are not more than 1.5m at LW.

PILOTAGE

Approach is straightforward. A hill behind the port rises to 45m and the white tower of an old tuna factory on it is conspicuous. The harbour buildings are the only structures on the shore for miles.

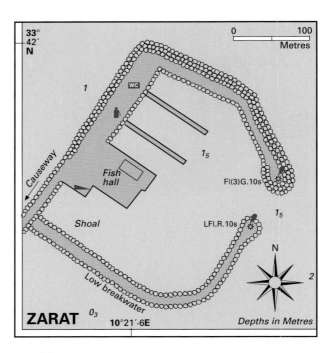

Berthing

Tie up where convenient on the two N piers. The part SW of the fish hall is very shallow. Not for yachts over 12m long.

Formalities

No authorities except for CGP representative.

Facilities

Water and *diesel* Available in the harbour.
Provisions The village has basic shops, cafés, hardware stores, PTT and bank.
Repairs A boatyard and 15-ton slip. There is a small crane on the quay. Timber repairs and some mechanical repairs are possible.

Jerba Island (Djerba)

A large, low-lying island rising not more than 30m from the sea with 2 small harbours and one nearby on the mainland, only accessible with very shallow draught yachts. Due to its natural beauty, year-round warm climate and wide sandy beaches, Jerba was a logical place for tourist development and it has become Tunisia's most successful endeavour in this field. In spite of the considerable number of visitors every year, the island has remained relatively unspoilt and the number of tourists is never objectionable except perhaps in mid-summer. Most of the hotels are concentrated on the NE coast and because none of them are massive, they blend in with the surrounding landscape.

T51 Houmt Souk

Considered the capital of Jerba, this small harbour on the N coast of the island is famous for sponge and octopus fishing. A port of entry with room for yachts up to 20m.

Location
33°53′.3N 10°51′.3E

Distances
Sfax 50M,
Gabès 43M
Zarzis 42M

Tides
MHWS	MHWN	MLWN	MLWS
1.7m	1.2m	1.0m	0.7m

Charts
Admiralty *3403*
French *4316, 4244*

Lights
Approach
1. **Bordj Djellidj** 33°53′.1N 10°44′.6E Fl.R.5s16m9M White 8-sided tower, black top, on building
2. **Ras Tourgenes** s33°49′.3N 11°02′.7E Fl.5s64m24M White tower, red bands
3. **Houmt Souk** 33°53′.1N 10°51′.2E Oc(2)7s9m14M 080°-vis-320° (existence doubtful) F.R on radio mast 0.5m SE
4. **No.0** R/W buoy in entrance channel Iso.6s
Harbour
5. **W breakwater head** F.G
6. **E breakwater head** F.R
Note Lights correct for colour but periods may differ.

Communications
Harbourmaster ☎ 650135
VHF Ch 16

The harbour

Houmt Souk is the only harbour on the island easily accessible to yachts. Over the years the fishing fleet, many of them not from the island, has outgrown the small port but yachts can usually find a berth alongside a fishing boat or the Garde National patrol boat. Protection in the port is good but occasionally the quays flood in the winter when the sea level is raised by N winds.

PILOTAGE

By day

The N coast of Jerba is fringed with banks of sand and seaweed which extend up to 4M from the shore. Entrance to the port is through a buoyed channel, dredged in 2004 to 4m, 4M long on a course of 184°. Stay well in the centre as depths shoal around the buoys. Beware of strong tidal streams which transverse the channel. The N extremity is marked with a single buoy, well visible, but note that it is not in line with Oc the centre of the channel, which is marked by several pairs of buoys. Do not confuse the palm fronds on the drying banks around the channel for buoys. The basin is protected by low breakwaters which are almost flooded at HW.

Landmarks on the N coast are from W to E:

The flood stream sets W and the ebb stream sets E. Visibility is often reduced to 5-6M during summer.

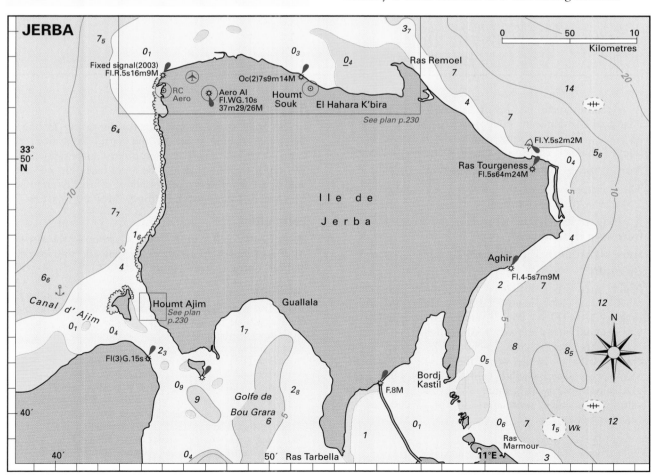

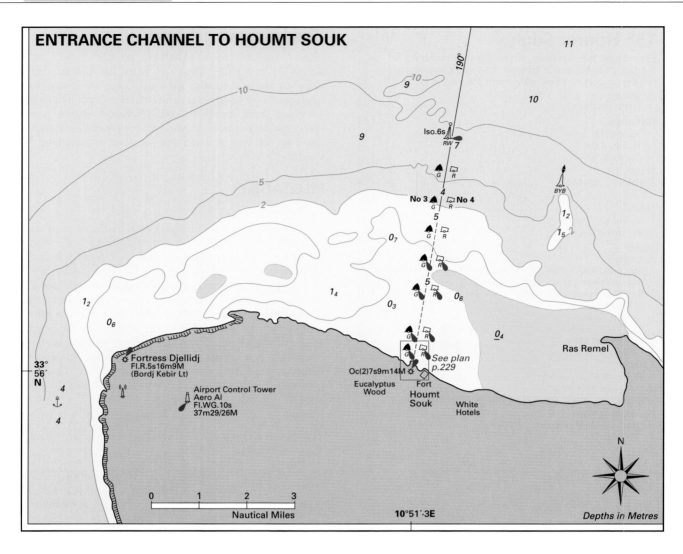

ENTRANCE CHANNEL TO HOUMT SOUK

A telecommunications tower approx. 50m high just inland of the harbour. If approached on a bearing of 188/190°. This will bring you to the entrance of the buoyed channel. This tower can be seen almost 10M off.

A small fortress with light tower at Bordj Djellidj.

The control tower of the airport (best landmark and 1.5M away form the harbour).

A group of eucalyptus trees and the Bordj El Kebir fortress in the harbour.

Some white hotels E of the harbour.

By night

Night entry is not difficult if the lights are functioning reliably. Ras Tourgueness lighthouse is visible with a range of 24M (Fl.5s). Jerba '0' landfall buoy is lit (Iso.6s) and channel buoys are with flashing lights.

If lights are obscure, anchor either close to the entrance of the channel or on the W side of the island SSW of the Bordj Djellidj light in depths which shoal gradually towards the shore. With the predominant summer easterlies, protection on the W side of the island is better.

Berthing

In the outer basin visitors can usually tie up to one of the larger fishing boats or the patrol boat from the Garde National. There is a temporary anchorage on the W side of the outer basin. The inner basin has no quays and, apart from being very shallow, is usually crammed with small fishing boats. Harbour dues are very low.

Formalities

Port of entry. Police in the town, Customs at the airport. APIP and *marine marchande* just outside the vehicular harbour entrance are helpful.

Facilities

Water Two water taps in the SE corner of the outer basin.
Electricity None readily available.
Fuel Diesel on the quay as indicated on harbour plan.
Repairs A boatyard with slip.
Provisions The village, 2km from the harbour, has a good local market and a Magasin Général. There is a small grocery shop, Magasin du Port, and a fruit stand about halfway between the harbour and village. English language newspapers are available in a book shop next to the main post office. There is a café in the harbour.
Post office, telephone and *banks* In the village.
Weather forecast From Djeban Airport ☎ 650109 (24hr)

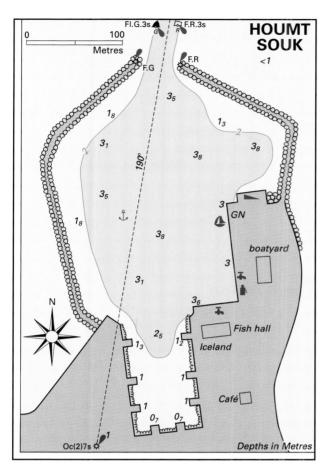

HOUMT SOUK

Depths in Metres

ASHORE

The village is one of the most pleasant along the Tunisian coast and if only for this reason, well worth a visit. The interior of the low-lying, semi-desert island is interesting and, because it is flat, well suited for exploration by bicycle.

Perhaps the special atmosphere of Houmt Souk is explained by the different population of Kharijites and Jews, who lived on the island for centuries. However, as is often the case with enterprising islanders, Jerbans have moved away from their island and settled on the mainland of Tunisia. Many of them operate grocery corner shops which are therefore called 'Djerbans'. There are still a few synagogues on the island but over the years most Jews have moved to Israel. In spite of these changes and the influx of tourists, Houmt Souk remains a charming place with its covered souks, narrow streets and shaded squares.

Eating out

A benefit of the tourist development in Jerba is that Houmt Souk has a wide choice of restaurants. Restaurant Haroun, just outside the port, with a French trained chef, has excellent fish specialities.

Transport

The major car hire agencies have offices in Houmt Souk.

T52 Ajim

A small fishing harbour and ferry terminal on a promontory into the channel between Jerba and the mainland, exposed to the SE. A strong tidal stream makes this harbour difficult to negotiate.

Location
33°42′.8N 10°44′.5E (End of breakwater)

Distances
Gabès 35M
Houmt Souk 33M

Tides

MHWS	MHWN	MLWN	MLWS
1.2m	0.7m	0.5m	0.1m

Charts
Admiralty *3403*
French *4316, 4242*

Lights
Approach
1. **Passe Ouest** 33°42′.1N 10°36′.3E Fl(2)9s4m7M Tank on masonry base
2. **No.1 buoy** in port channel Fl(3)G.15s7M Green and white horizontal stripes on metal tripod
3. **No.2 buoy** black and white horizontal stripes on metal tripod
4. **No.3 buoy** – as No.1 light, unknown
5. **No.4 buoy** – as No 2. light, unknown
Harbour Fl.G.5s, Fl.R.5s

Communications
Harbourmaster ☎ 655002

The harbour

The small jetty at Ajim, which is used by the ferry to Tarf el Djorf on the mainland, was upgraded to a fishing harbour but without enclosing the facility to the E. The harbour does not have breakwaters as it is between the drying banks of the Canal d'Ajim. This channel separates the island of Jerba from the mainland and leads to the Bahiret el Bou Grara, an enclosed gulf. The Gulf of Bou Grara is barred on the E side by a causeway which connects the SE point of Jerba with the mainland. Strong tidal streams flow through the Canal d'Ajim and the entrance is very difficult to negotiate. At least one yacht is known to have made the passage but not without running aground. The challenge is probably the only good reason to visit Ajim because the village, although not unattractive with its white-washed houses, is without any particular interest.

PILOTAGE

Two natural channels, Passe Nord and Passe Ouest, respectively 3 and 4M W of Tarf el Djorf, lead to Canal d'Ajim. Neither is clearly buoyed and certain buoys may be missing or displaced. Buoyage is particularly confusing where the two channels merge with the main channel. In the entrance channels the tidal stream can reach a spring rate of 3 knots and in the main channel off Ajim, 5 knots. An unmarked rocky bank in the middle of the channel, 1.5M W of Tarf el Djorf with depths of 1m, has to be avoided. E of this bank the deep water is clear of dangers. From Canal d'Ajim a short dredged and buoyed channel leads to the harbour. There are two pairs of buoys marking the channel,

IV. TUNISIA

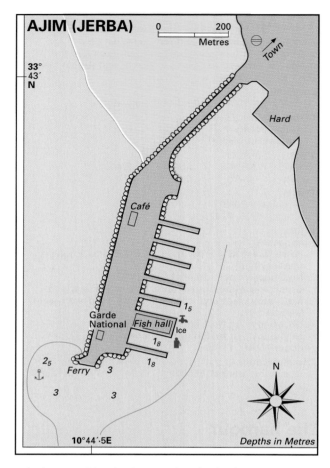

AJIM (JERBA)

33°
43′
N

Town

Hard

Café

Garde
National Fish hall Ice

1₅

1₈

2₅ Ferry 3 1₈

3 3

10°44′·5E Depths in Metres

N

which is used by the ferry and is dredged to 3m. Depths in the port are around 1.5m at MLWS. The fishermen of Ajim use these channels everyday as they go to their fishing grounds in the Gulf of Gabès but most of their boats do not draw more than 0.75m.

Berthing

The pier S of the fish hall has depths of around 1.2m. Stay as close as practical to the quays since the E side of the port is shallow. Alternatively anchor SW of the ferry landing; good holding in sand and seaweed, but approach carefully as exact depths are uncertain. It is difficult to find a berth here.

Formalities

Garde National only.

Facilities

Water and *diesel* On the fish quay.
Provisions Only a café in the port. A selection of shops in the village plus PTT., bank and garage (diesel and petrol).
Repairs A small crane on the quay. Boatyard on the beach behind the port with a 17-ton winch.

T53 Bou Grara

Similar to Ajim, a projecting jetty which, in the bay S of Jerba with strong currents and displaced or absent buoyage, makes this small harbour a challenge to negotiate.

Location
33°32′.3N 10°41′.3E

Distances
Ajim 15M

Tides
MHWS 0.8m MHWN 0.5m MLWN 0.5m MLWS 0.3m

Charts
Admiralty *3403*
French *4316, 4245*

Light

Harbour
Iso.2s7m8M

The harbour

A very small fishing harbour, similar in layout to Ajim and Zarat, set in an idyllic location in the remote SW corner of the Gulf of Bou Grara. Tall palm trees against a background of sandy cliffs and (rare nowadays) women and children searching for shellfish off the beach, create the perfect setting for a picture postcard. Visiting this port by sailing yacht presents the same sort of problems as visiting Ajim: shallow depths and strong tidal streams. From Ajim onward, the Gulf has sufficient depths for any yacht, but there are no buoys to mark the dangers. However with careful 'eye-ball' navigation and a suitable boat, a visit to Bou Grara is possible and will be a unique experience.

PILOTAGE

Entrance to the Gulf of Bou Grara is as described under Ajim. French chart No. 4245 is required to cross the Gulf but buoyage in the channels marked Chenal Balise is far from certain. The port buildings at the end of a long pier and a water tower and minaret in the village, 1km inland on low sandy cliffs, are conspicuous.

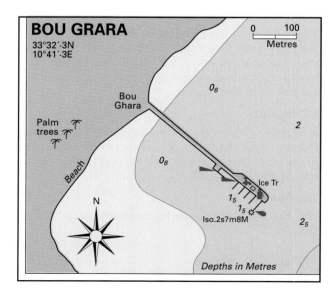

BOU GRARA

33°32′·3N
10°41′·3E

0 100
Metres

Bou
Ghara

0₆

2

Palm
trees

0₈

Ice Tr

Beach

1₅

N 1₅
Iso.2s7m8M 2₅

Depths in Metres

Berthing

Tie up where convenient. The harbour, dredged to 1.5m at MLWS, is usually not crowded.

Formalities

Garde National and APIP.

Facilities

Water and *diesel* In the harbour but no petrol anywhere.
Electricity None.
Provisions Only the most basic provisions are available in the hamlet of Bou Grara, 1km away. There is a small shop in the harbour.
Repairs A boatyard and small slip.

ASHORE

History

Though isolated today, Bou Grara has an interesting history. The Phoenicians were the first to establish a trading post in Bou Grara, then called Gightis and the Romans took control after the campaign of Julius Caesar in 40BC. The Gulf of Bou Grara was a perfect natural harbour for their large fleet and the port was an important link in their trading route which went from Carthage via Puppet (Hammamet), El Djem and Tacape (Gabès) to Gightis and from there further S to Cydamus (Ghadames, in Libya). As a result of silting, the port lost its importance and during the Arab invasions in the 7th century it was destroyed. Since that time, the site was covered until excavated in 1906.

The Roman ruins of Gightis are 2km from the port at the intersection of the road from the village with the main road between Djorf and Medenine and are well worth a visit.

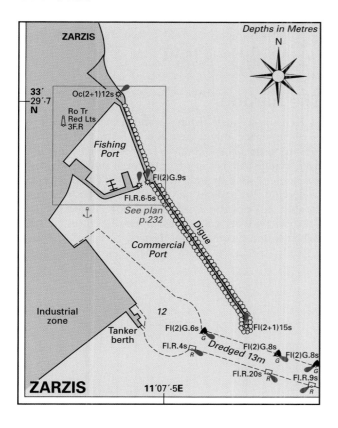

T54 Zarzis

The last useable port of entry and departure in Tunisia, 30M from the Libyan border.

Location
33°29′.9N 11°08′.5E

Distances
Sfax 77M
Houmt Souk 42M
Libyan border 30M

Tides

MHWS	MHWN	MLWN	MLWS
1.0m	0.7m	0.5m	0.2m

Charts
Admiralty 3403
French 4316, 4245

Lights
Approach
1. **LtHo near customs house** 33°29′.7N 11°07′.2E Oc(2+1)12s15m15M 180°-vis-090° Emergency light F.R.10M Obstn light on mast 3M WNW White 8-sided tower, black top
2. **The dredged deep water entrance channel** is marked with 6 buoys Fl(2)G.8s, Fl(2)G.8s, Fl(2)G.6s and Fl.R.9s, Fl.R.20s, Fl.R.4s

Harbour
3. **New breakwater head** Fl(2+1)15s11m12M Red and white tower
4. **Entrance fishing port** Fl(2)G.9s8m6M Green tower
5. **SW breakwater fishing port** Fl.R.6.5s10m6M Red tower

Communications
Harbourmaster ☎ 5 680304 (0830–1300, 1500–1800)
Control tower ☎ 5 680850.
VHF Ch 10, 16 (24hr)

The commercial port and harbour

Zarzis is the most southern port of Tunisia and a useful port of entry on passage from the eastern Mediterranean. Also a good base to explore the Ksars in the South. The government has ambitious plans to develop Zarzis into a commercial port for oil and fertilizer products but a falling demand in world markets has delayed the construction of a potassium sulphate plant and consequently the new port, where a huge breakwater, quays and port buildings, finished in 1989, remain little used. The main activity is in the old fishing harbour which is busy. Yachts rarely visit this far S. Protection is good and with the new breakwater entry can be made in any weather.

Note It is only 30M from the Libyan border and it is wise to stay well clear of Libyan territorial waters. Although things are changing in Libya, it is still likely that a yacht may expect a hostile reception.

PILOTAGE

By day

The coast N of Zarzis is backed by a chain of low hills, faced with cliffs, beginning about 2 miles N of the town. The coast S of Zarzis, towards the Libyan border at Ras Ajdir, is low and backed by several lagoons. When approaching from the E, avoid the shallows around Banc el Biban which extend up to 12M from the shore. The huge breakwater is probably the best landmark.

IV. TUNISIA

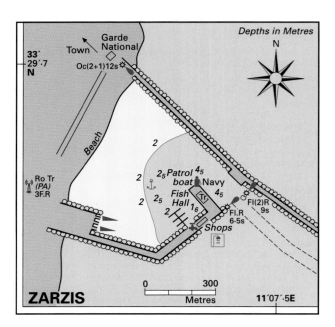

Zarzis harbour viewed from the SSE

By night

At night, approach the entrance to the fishing harbour from the main port carefully as the starboard breakwater projects SW a considerable distance beyond the green light.

Berthing

Proceed N through the commercial port to the fishing harbour. The most likely place to find room is around the fish hall, alongside the patrol boat at the NW end of the fish quay. Although the APIP recommended the small finger piers, these are usually crowded and depths are no more than 2m. In strong northerly winds, waves build up in this relatively large harbour. Alternatively anchor in the NW of the commercial port. The basin shoals gradually towards the beach in the NW corner. Keep the tidal range in mind.

Formalities

Port of entry. Take paperwork ashore if anchored.

Facilities

Water Several water taps around the harbour.
Electricity None easily available.
Showers & WC As indicated on the plan.
Fuel Diesel pump in the harbour. Petrol from the town.
Provisions A good market, a Magasin Général and many small shops in the centre of the town, a good walk (3km) from the harbour. There is a café, grocery and fruit & vegetable shop in the harbour.
Post office, telephone and *bank* In the town.
Repairs A boatyard and slip, workshops for mechanical repairs and Perkins agent.

ASHORE

Several new hotels line good beaches N of the town but they lack the surroundings and atmosphere of Jerba.

Eating out

In most of the Mediterranean, the grouper (mérou in French) has disappeared but not so in Zarzis. This delicious fish can be found in the better restaurants.

Transport

Avis and Hertz have offices in the hotel area N of the town.

T55 El Ketef

A small fishing harbour 3M from the border with Libya, currently forbidden to yachts. This is expected to change in the near future and is therefore mentioned here, though no details are yet available.

Location
  33°11′.1N 11°29′.3E
Distances
  Zarzis 30M
Tides

MHWS	MHWN	MLWN	MLWS
1.0m	0.6m	0.6m	0.3m

The harbour

El Ketef is a small fishing harbour in the middle of nowhere, near a minor cape Ras el Ketef, 3M from the Libyan border. The harbour is built at the end of a long dyke/bridge-like pier in order to reach sufficiently deep water and is used by small fishing boats. There are plans to develop this harbour and it will undoubtedly become useable and possibly a substantial port as the political situation with its eastern neighbour improves. A new village is under construction nearby.

V. PANTELLERIA AND THE PELAGIE ISLANDS

Pantelleria Island

Introduction

Situated half way between Sicily and Tunisia and close to the Italian Pelagie Islands, Pantelleria is not part of the same group, though it is an Italian island. It is quite different to Lampedusa (Pelagie) because of its volcanic origins. The fertile soil on the terraced slopes is intensely farmed and even though tourism has grown considerably in the last 10 years, agriculture is still a major source of income. Capers and grapes are the main crops, enabling Pantelleria to produce some good red and white wines. For yachtsmen cruising or wintering in Tunisia, Pantelleria is only a few hours away and an excellent place to stock up with wines, spirits and supplies where there is less choice in Tunisia.

The island has two ports, the main harbour of Pantelleria in the NW corner and the smaller Porto Scauri on the W coast.

History

Known human habitation goes back as far as the 18th century BC and the ruins of a Neolithic village from that time are found near Mursia, only a few kilometres from Pantelleria port. The island has been under the influence of all the great Mediterranean empires but the Arabs were the first to start cultivation of the rich soil and they built the typical dammuso houses near their fields, still found all over the island. After the Arab period, Pantelleria was taken by the Normans and since that time it has been ruled from Sicily. During the Second World War the Allied Forces heavily bombed the island before they could advance from North Africa to Sicily and Pantelleria town was completely destroyed.

Ashore

Tourism has not reached an objectionable scale and outside of Pantelleria town the island is still rural and pretty. There are good diving spots around the island and this is an important attraction for the mainly Italian visitors.

International Travel

The Siremar ferry serves Pantelleria from Trapani, Monday to Saturday and daily in the months of July, August and September. The daily hydrofoil from Trapani to Kelibia (May-Oct.) also stops in Pantelleria. There are daily flights from Palermo and Trapani all year around. In summer time the town is teaming with Italian holidaymakers.

P1 Pantelleria Port

Situated 57M SW of Sicily and 45M E of Kelibia, Pantelleria is a day sail away from either, and good place to stop en route from both.

Location
36°50′N 11°56′.5E

Distances
Kelibia, Tunisia 40M
Malta 120M

Tides
Insignificant

Charts

	Approach	Port
Admiralty	2122, 3327	193
French	4315	5023
Italian	947, 948	

Lights
Approach
1. **Punta San Leonardo** 36°50′.1N 11°56′.7E Fl.3s21m15M Yellow building Reserve light range 8M Fl.R.2.5s on radio mast 1.6M SSE
2. W end Fl.Y.2s8m5M Yellow × on framework tower
Harbour
3. **Porto di Pantellaria outer breakwater** head Fl.G.5s7m3M
4. **Molo Cidonio Dir Lt 232°** DirIso.WRG.2s8m7M 213.5°-G-228.5°-W-235.5°-R-258.5°
5. **S head** 2F.G(vert)7m3M Green post
6. **Molo Nasi head** 2F.RG(vert)8m4M Red post, green bands

Communications
VHF Ch 16, 14

The port and its harbours

An active and not particularly attractive port but an interesting contrast with Tunisia. There are several areas where visiting yachts can moor: an old harbour, a newer one and the main mole. The lively quays in the old harbour are lined with shops and restaurants. The port is used by a small fishing fleet as well as occasional freighters and the Siremar ferry.

In recent years new quays have been built in Porto Vecchio and Porto Nuovo. Several times work has begun but nothing ever seems to get finished, with the resultant destruction by storms or disrepair of whatever was achieved. Until completed, protection from the prevailing NW winds will remain poor and finding a safe place to moor, difficult. Swell from the NW enters Porto Vecchio.

The floating pontoons for visiting yachts installed in Porto Nuovo offer better protection but they are further from the town centre and a long dusty walk through abandoned boats used by the illegal immigrants who land on the island. Not a pretty sight. Despite this, it is still well worth a visit to the island.

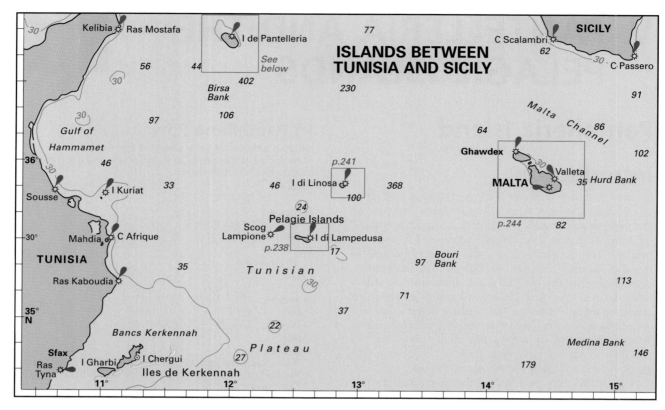

ISLANDS BETWEEN TUNISIA AND SICILY

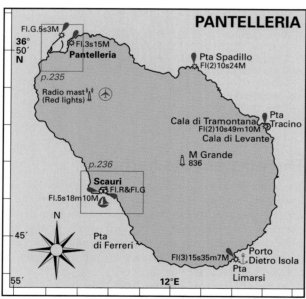

PANTELLERIA

Reasonable supplies are available in the town. With NW winds over force 7, Porto Nuovo is the only safe port on the island as in these conditions swell also enters Porto Scauri.

PILOTAGE

By day

The island is over 800m high and Pantelleria is the only major town in the relatively flat NW corner. In strong NW winds, which are frequent in summer, beware of overfalls in the entrance. The long breakwater consists of concrete boxes ballasted with rocks. It has never been completed, and is often in need of repair following storms. Once rounded, there is some protection from NW winds under the wall until a mooring can be found. Depths in the entrance are around 16m.

By night

A night approach should be done with caution. Although the end of the moles are lit, the lights are unreliable. Even with the breakwater complete, it is a surprisingly confusing entrance, partly because the breakwater is built at differing heights and parts are often awash in strong NW winds.

Berthing

Porto Vecchio This is the old harbour within the port and on the town quay. Beware of the partially submerged remainders of an old breakwater in the middle of the entrance. Depths are between 1.5m and 2m.

Porto Nuovo At the S end of the port there are pontoons behind an E-W mole. Rocks barely awash extend from this mole, which is itself being extended. The southern half of the entrance is shallow. Safe entry is made by rounding the N breakwater at a distance of between 10m and 25m. Do not enter in strong NW winds. There is a lot of old ground tackle near the jetties.

In good weather, the best berth is on your own anchor stern-to the quayed N breakwater in Porto Vecchio. Draught permitting, smaller yachts can tie up stern-to the E quays. In strong NW winds, swell makes its way into Porto Vecchio, rendering it intolerable. Under these conditions the safest berth is on the new

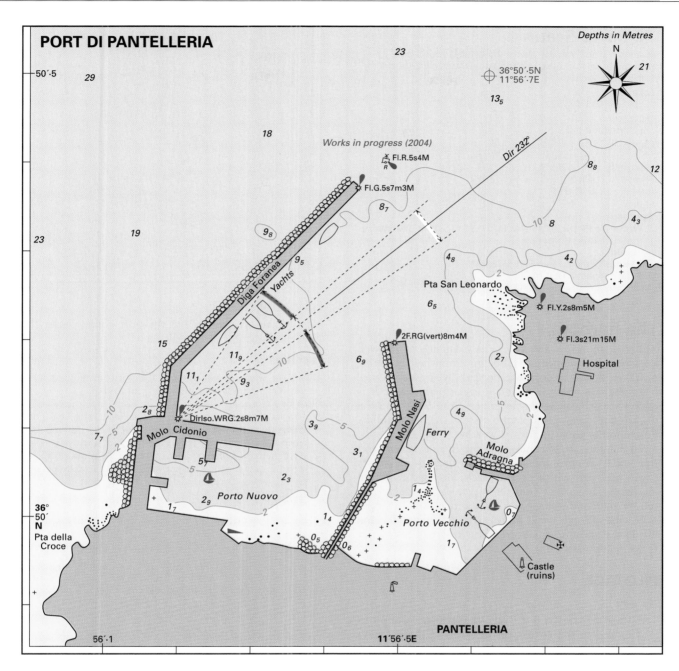

PORT DI PANTELLERIA

Depths in Metres

floating pontoons or on the quay (mooring lines planned) in Porto Nuovo.

Alternatives are to lay alongside the main breakwater, which is usually unoccupied. Although the concrete is rough, the NW winds will push you off.

Another alterative is to anchor off the main breakwater in 9–13m sand keeping clear of the ferry.

Charges

There has been no charge here in the past, but this will change if facilities are improved.

Facilities

Water Two taps on the quays.
Electricity None, though boxes have been fitted for many years without being connected.
Fuel From two service stations around Porto Vecchio.

Provisions Reasonable choice from several shops and a supermarket.
Post office and *banks* In the town with ATMs.
Repairs Limited possibilities but several repair shops for outboards and inflatables.

Formalities

No formalities are required.

ASHORE

The islanders, though detached, are not unfriendly.

Eating out

Several restaurants around the port, though not cheap.

Transport

Car hire in town.

P2 Porto Scauri

A small harbour on the SW of Pantelleria Island only suitable in settled weather and usually with little room for visiting yachts.

Location
36°46′N 11°57′.5E

Distance
Pantelleria 6M

Charts

	Approach	Port
Admiralty	2122, 3327	193
French	4315	5023
Italian	947, 948	

Lights
Approach
1. **Punta Tre Pietra** 36°46′.1N 11°57′.5E Fl.5s18m10M White metal column on pedestal
Harbour
2. **Marina W mole head** Fl.R.3s7m3M
3. **E mole head** Fl.G.3s7m3M

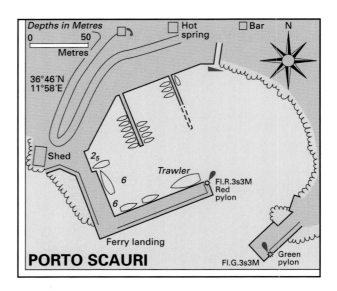

PORTO SCAURI

The harbour

Although by no means a port its existence is not well known and it appears to be an unfinished planning mistake. Italians refer to the port as `Marina di Scauri' but there is nothing here and it is not maintained. It is mainly used by transient fishermen from Sicily and the occasional yacht that appreciates the tranquillity. Protection is good in normal weather.

In summer, holidaymakers bathe in one corner and the small floating pontoons, with gutted electricity boxes and taps which do not work, are used to tie up inflatables and small craft. However if tranquillity is a requirement and not supplies, it is a nice stop. In strong NW winds (Force 7 and more) swell rolls around Punta Tre Pietra and into the port. Entry in strong SW winds is not recommended.

PILOTAGE

By day

The small harbour is not easily visible from seaward as it is tucked in the corner of the bay and there are no buildings. A deserted white hotel with domed arches on top of Punta Tre Pietra is conspicuous from W to S.

By night

A night approach is not difficult as there is good street lighting to accommodate the fishing boats. Lights on the end of the breakwaters were functioning in summer 2004 though this is apparently unusual.

Berthing

Tie up alongside or with a stern anchor to the W or S quay. The floating pontoons are for the small fishing boats and do not accommodate yachts. The first pontoon and the inner part of the SE breakwater have both been badly damaged by storms. The ferry landing is not in use. If caught in strong N or SW winds, lie along the S quay with a breast anchor or stern-to the W quay but neither will be very comfortable due to the swell.

Formalities

No officials whatsoever but the port comes under the Italian jurisdiction of Pantelleria.

Facilities

Water The warm spring water in the port can be used for a shower or laundry but it is not fit to drink.
Electricity None.
Provisions There are no shops or other facilities in the port. However in the pleasant little village of Scauri on top of a steep hill (15 minutes' walk from the port) there is a baker, an alimentari, a pizzeria and a trattoria. A visit is worth the effort if only for the pleasant walk. When there are enough fishing boats, bread is delivered to the port in a small truck.

The Pelagie Islands

Introduction

The Italian islands of Lampedusa, Linosa and Lampione are grouped together as the Pelagie Islands although geologically they are quite different. Lampedusa and Lampione are both low, flat, limestone islands situated on the edge of the Tunisian continental shelf, while Linosa is volcanic, rising steeply from the sea bottom as the most southern volcano in a chain that begins north of Sicily at Mount Etna.

The rocky islet of Lampione, only 700m long, has been uninhabited since the lighthouse keeper left following automation. A small landing built during the Second World War is used today by the occasional diving boat, but there is no safe anchorage on the island. Lampedusa and Linosa were both inhabited in ancient times but there are no historic remains. In the past century, Lampedusa has turned into a barren island, bereft of practically all vegetation through careless soil management. It is hard to imagine that in 1800 the island had trees, fertile soil and wild boar. It now has around 4000 inhabitants. A Loran station, operated by a small US navy crew, is located on the W end near Capo Ponente and when the American air force bombed Benghazi and Tripoli in 1986 the Libyans retaliated with an attack on this installation, which failed.

Lampedusa has in recent years been the point where illegal migrants, mostly from North Africa head for, in small unseaworthy boats. This has become a big problem for the Italian authorities who used to ship them on to Sicily. The problem has become so big that the resentment built up in Italy over the migrant issue has led to a more permanent camp being set up on Lampedusa, which is currently said to contain between 10,000 and 18,000 migrants camping out in appalling conditions. Tourists are kept away from this area and most visitors remain ignorant of the situation.

The fertile lava soil of Linosa proved less vulnerable to erosion than Lampedusa and supports a variety of vegetation. In the 1880s, the Italian government sent convicts to the islands, much to the dislike of the inhabitants but today the Linosans, who number less than 500, live a peaceful existence. Fishing in this unpolluted part of the Mediterranean is the most important economic activity. Some income is made from tourism during the summer months and the terraced slopes between the dead craters are still farmed.

P3 Lampedusa Island

25M SW of Linosa and half way between Malta and Tunisia, Lampedusa is the main island of the Pelagie group. A pleasant harbour and last opportunity for stocking up on Italian wines and pasta before reaching Tunisia.

Location
  35°29′.6N 12°36′E (Mid way between headlands leading to harbour)

Distances
  Monastir 90M
  Malta 100M

Tides
  Less than half metre

Charts

	Approach	Port
Admiralty	3327, 2124	193
French	5023	

Lights
Approach
1. **Capo Ponente** 35°31′.1N 12°31′.2E Fl(3)15s110m8M White metal pillar on pedestal 290°-vis-222° Iso.R on radio mast 740m E
Note Several red lights in the top and green lights near the base of the radio tower for the Loran C station near Capo Ponente will be more visible from a distance.
2. **Capo Grecale** 35°31′.0N 12°37′.9E Fl.5s82m22M White 8-sided tower on dwelling 112°-vis-075°
Harbour
3. **Punta Maccaferri** Fl.G.3s17m8M
4. **Punta Guitgia** Fl.R.3s14m8M
5. **Punta Favalore** breakwater head Fl.R.5s7m7M
6. **Health Office Pier** F.R.7m3M
Communications
  VHF Ch 16, 9

The port

This busy port is home to a fishing fleet, the Italian military, a freighter dock and a well used ferry terminal as well as many tourist boats in summer. It retains a peaceful atmosphere and is well worth the stop, being conveniently placed between Malta and Tunisia. It is easy to enter in most weather and there are no clearing formalities.

PILOTAGE

By day

The island is surrounded by stark, dark, low cliffs and rocky outcrops. Coming from the W the island looks almost deserted but closer in, the town will be seen on a low hill in a bay between headlands.

By night

Coming from the E, the light on the NE tip of Capo Grecale with a range in excess of 22M will be seen. The SE tip of the island is not lit. From the W, Capo Ponente light is difficult to spot being far weaker than the higher lights of the Loran station, which will be seen well before the lighthouse. With onshore winds the sea builds up and runs through the entrance of the harbour. Once close in, the harbour lights will be seen as shown and are reliable.

V. PANTELLERIA AND THE PELAGIE ISLANDS

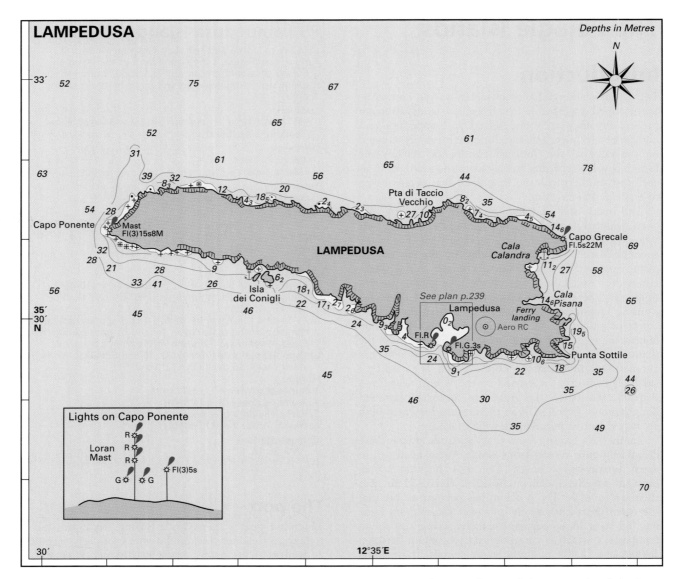

LAMPEDUSA

Depths in Metres

Capo Ponente
Mast
Fl(3)15s8M

Pta di Taccio Vecchio

LAMPEDUSA

Cala Calandra

Capo Grecale
Fl.5s22M

Cala Pisana

Isla dei Conigli

See plan p.239

Lampedusa

Ferry landing

Aero RC

Fl.R

Fl.G.3s

Punta Sottile

Lights on Capo Ponente

Loran Mast

R
R
R
G   G   Fl(3)5s

N

Note Depending on the wind direction, the daily ferry to Sicily sometimes runs a mooring line to the end of the Favalore breakwater, effectively blocking the entrance. The ferry usually docks between 0800-1000. Similarly Cala Guitgia is occasionally blocked for a day or two by the mooring line of the fuel tanker discharging near the fuel reservoirs.

Berthing

There is not much room for visiting yachts in the port but room can usually be found on the harbour wall beneath a hotel as marked. Depths along the quay are around 2-3m. An alternative is to try the inside of the west (Favalore) breakwater where the military boats moor, or on the E side of the harbour near the hydrofoil berth.

Anchoring

The bay Cala Guitgia, just W of the entrance is the best place to anchor in 3-4m soft sand. Holding is poor. Cala Palma and Cala Salina are very full with fishing boats, with lines everywhere.

Lampedusa yachts moorings looking SE   *Graham Hutt*

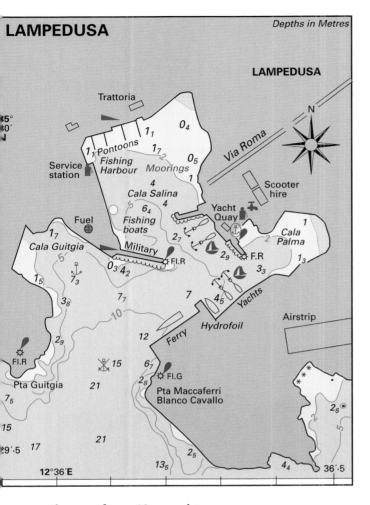

Charges for a 12m yacht

€ 15/day, paid at the nearby harbourmaster's office. (If you choose to pay – the authorities do not seem bothered.)

Lampedusa anchorage off Isola dei Conigli   *Roberto*

Formalities

None. Customs and police are present and very friendly but do not visit yachts and seem totally disinterested in their presence.

Facilities

Water A tap on the jetty is used by the diving charter boats and can be used at night. Water quality is good as it is delivered from the mainland but there is also low purity local water on the island which is not for drinking.

Electricity Power is available by arrangement with local boats who obtain a hook-up at night from the nearest lamppost.

Fuel From the service station a short distance from the quay. Another service station in Cala Salina near the fishing boats has a depth of 2.3m and can be used.

Provisions Good provisions are available from a large Standa supermarket (opening hours 0830–1300 and 1700–2130) at the other end of the village and several smaller supermarkets along Via Roma. Photo and diving shops and several gelaterias in Via Roma.

Post office In the fifth block on Via Guglielmo Bontiglio, a right from Via Roma (towards the end).

Telephone Several card telephones. GSM mobile phones work well here.

Bank Three banks in Via Roma with ATM's.

Repairs Emergency engine repairs. 25-ton slipway.

ASHORE

Many Italians are attracted by the good diving in the unpolluted waters around Lampedusa.

Eating out

Numerous trattorias around Cala Salina and in the village.

Transport

Cars and scooters May be hired near the service station in Cala Palma and in town, though they are very expensive.

Ferries Daily ferry service to Porto Empedocle, Sicily and several times weekly to Trapani. Hydrofoil service to Porto Empedocle on Monday and Thursday between 1 June and 30 September.

By air Flights to Palermo all year around and to Rome in summer.

Anchorages around Lampedusa

Isola dei Conigli

There are pleasant anchorages on the W and E side of this small island on the S coast of Lampedusa with shelter from NW to NE. The island is not easily identified as such because it is almost attached to the shore. Beware of rocks on a bank 200m off the S side of the island. Good anchorage on either side in about 6m, sand.

Lampedusa: one of many small anchorages along the S coast *Graham Hutt*

Cala Calandra

Location
35°30′.8E 12°37′.6E

A quiet, pretty anchorage tucked in the NW corner of Cala Creta on the E side of Lampedusa. Shelter from SW to NW. Anchor in sand, 6–10m.

Cala Pisana

Location
35°30′.2N 12°37′.5E (Mid entrance to bay).

Not a very picturesque anchorage but snug with good protection in case of strong westerlies. Only suitable for small yachts. There is a shallow emergency ferry landing on the S side. Do not proceed too far beyond this landing as the bay shallows gradually towards the head. Anchor in sand, 4–6m.

Crystal clear water in these rocky bays *Roberto*

The

P4 Linosa Island

A small volcanic island 25M NNE of Lampedusa, with a jetty on the N and two on the S side with an anchorage on the E, all suitable for small yachts.

Location
35°52'.1N 12°51'.7E (Just S of entrance to Scala Veccio harbour)

Distances
Lampedusa 26M
Malta 85M

Charts

	Approach	Port
Admiralty	3327, 2124	193
French	–	5023

Lights
Approach
1. **Punta Arena Bianca** 35°51'.2N 12°51'.5E Fl.5s9m9M
   White square stone pillar and hut 276.5°-vis-150°
2. **Punta Beppe Tuccio** 35°52'.2N 12°52'.6E Fl(4)20s32m16M
   White round tower and dwelling 107°-vis-345° (arc varies with distance from light, at 6M 103°-vis-346°)

The harbours and anchorages

From a distance, Linosa looks similar to Pantelleria but is much smaller. The slopes between the dead craters are farmed and the island looks surprisingly green from the S. The N coast is more rugged and steep, with large areas covered by black lava rocks.

There is no harbour or anchorage with good all around shelter but that need not prevent a visit in settled weather. Surprisingly, for such a remote island, the daily ferry drops off many visitors during the summer but life in the small village is not much affected.

Scalo Vecchio is a very small picturesque open harbour with two jetties next to the village. The ferry landing provides the life line for the island.

Vittorio Emanuelle just over 1M NW is a single ferry jetty but open to the prevailing NW winds.

A single jetty has recently been added to the N of the island for ferries.

Anchorages on the E side of the island N and S are marked on the plan.

PILOTAGE

With an elevation of 200m, the island is easily identified. There are no off-lying dangers.

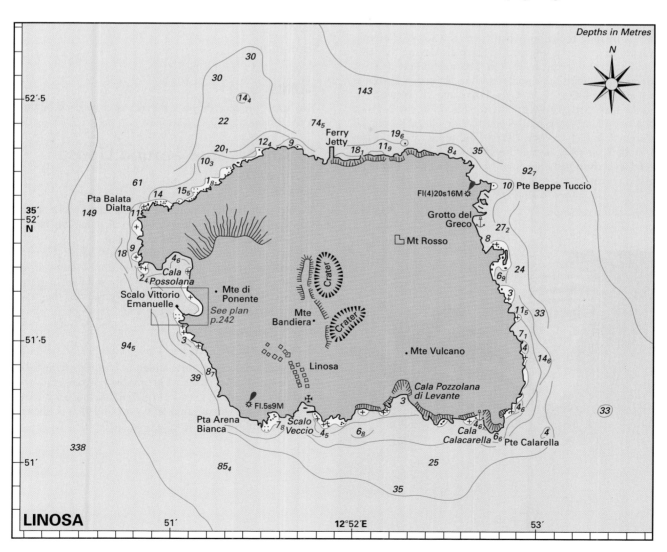

V. PANTELLERIA AND THE PELAGIE ISLANDS

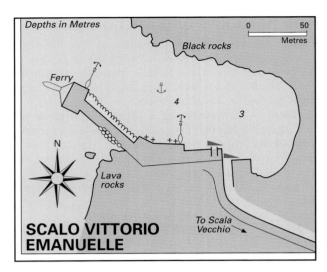

SCALO VITTORIO EMANUELLE

Just room for a couple of yachts in Linosa harbour
Graham Hutt

Berthing

In settled weather one or two yachts can lie bows/stern-to the short quay in Scalo Vecchio. However there is not much room to drop anchor and the bottom is rocky. A safer option is to anchor in Scalo Vittorio Emanuelle, 1M NW. The large pier constructed for the ferry provides some additional protection but a swell from the NW makes the anchorage uncomfortable. Most of the quay on the inside of the pier is unusable because of submerged rocks but when there is no swell running, yachts can tie up at the end of the pier, leaving the ferry landing free for the hydrofoil. The anchorage is 3–5m deep, rocks, with reasonable holding. A further option is to anchor 400m N in Cala Pozzolana di Ponente in sand, with better protection from the NW swell. From the ferry landing, a road leads to the village (about 20 minutes' walk). A new ferry landing jetty has been installed mid-way along the N side of the island, for ferries to drop passengers when strong winds blow from the S sector.

Signs of life on Linosa   *Roberto*

Charges

None.

Formalities

None

Facilities

Two small grocery shops, a butcher and two restaurants in the village.

P5 Anchorages around Linosa

Grotto del Greco

35°52′.1N 12°52′.6E

A remote anchorage among rugged volcanic rocks 500m S of the lighthouse of Beppe Tuccio. A house on top of Mt. Rosso can provide a useful bearing.

The underwater caves in the N part of the bay are attractive to snorkel around. The bottom is large rocks with poor holding, 8–12m deep, only suitable in good weather. With no wind and leftover swell from the NW, the anchorage is uncomfortable.

Punta Calcarella

35°51′.4N 12°52′.6E

A beautiful anchorage surrounded by steep rocks off the SE corner of the island. The sandy bottom shallows gradually towards the head of the bay, making anchoring easier and more secure than in Grotto del Greco. Shelter from NW to NE.

Lampione

This small uninhabited island is bereft of vegetation and without a safe anchorage, but makes a photogenic landmark in this area of the Sicilian Channel.

Lampione W Jetty of the small harbour   *Graham Hutt*

Lampione: a good landmark between Malta and Tunisia
Graham Hutt

VI. MALTA

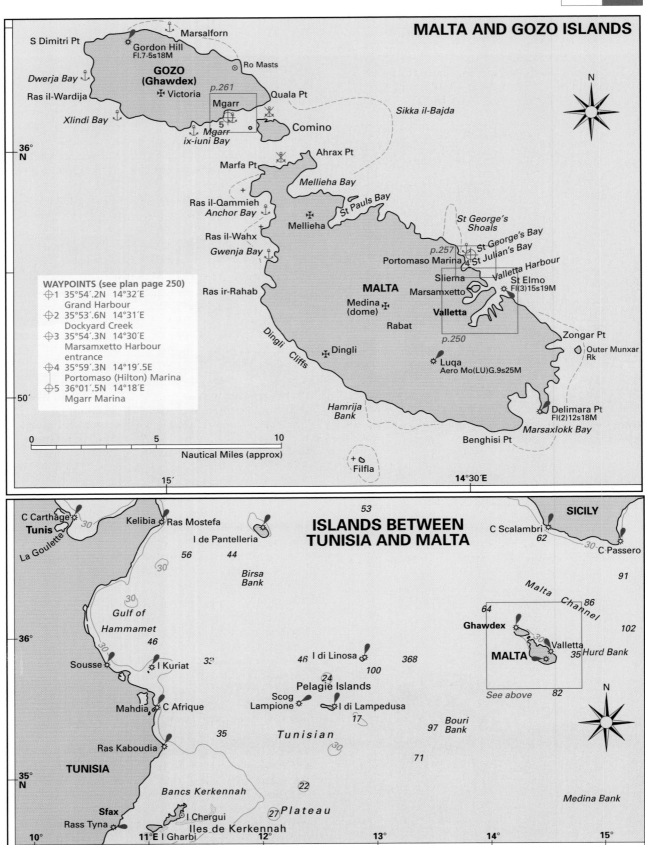

MALTA AND GOZO ISLANDS

S Dimitri Pt

Marsalforn

Gordon Hill
Fl.7·5s18M

Ro Masts

**GOZO
(Ghawdex)**

Dwerja Bay

Ras il-Wardija

✠ Victoria

Quala Pt

p.261

Mgarr

5

Xlindi Bay

*Mgarr
ix-iuni Bay*

Comino

Sikka il-Bajda

N

36°
N

Marfa Pt

Ahrax Pt

Mellieha Bay

Ras il-Qammieh
Anchor Bay

St Pauls Bay

St George's
Shoals

Mellieha

St George's Bay

Ras il-Wahx

p.257

St Julian's Bay

Portomaso Marina

Valletta Harbour

Gwenja Bay

Sliema

Marsamxetto

St Elmo
Fl(3)15s19M

WAYPOINTS (see plan page 250)
⊕1 35°54'.2N 14°32'E
    Grand Harbour
⊕2 35°53'.6N 14°31'E
    Dockyard Creek
⊕3 35°54'.3N 14°30'E
    Marsamxetto Harbour
    entrance
⊕4 35°59'.3N 14°19'.5E
    Portomaso (Hilton) Marina
⊕5 36°01'.5N 14°18'E
    Mgarr Marina

Ras ir-Rahab

MALTA

Medina
(dome)

Rabat

Valletta

p.250

Zongar Pt

Outer Munxar
Rk

Dingli Cliffs

✠ Dingli

☼ Luqa
Aero Mo(LU)G.9s25M

50'

*Hamrija
Bank*

Delimara Pt
Fl(2)12s18M

Benghisi Pt

Marsaxlokk Bay

Filfla

0   5   10

Nautical Miles (approx)

15'

14°30'E

**ISLANDS BETWEEN
TUNISIA AND MALTA**

53

SICILY

C Carthage

Tunis

Kelibia Ras Mostefa

30

I de Pantelleria

La Goulette

C Scalambri
62

30

C Passero

56   44

*Birsa
Bank*

91

30

Malta Channel

86

64

30

Gulf of
Hammamet

Ghawdex

102

36°

Sousse

I Kuriat

46

33

46 I di Linosa

368

30

Valletta

35 Hurd Bank

MALTA

100

24

Pelagie Islands

See above

82

N

Mahdia C Afrique

Scog
Lampione   I di Lampedusa

17

*Bouri
Bank*

97

35

Tunisian

71

35°
N

TUNISIA

Bancs Kerkennah

22

Medina Bank

Sfax

Plateau

27

Rass Tyna

I Chergui

Iles de Kerkennah

11°E I Gharbi

12°

13°

14°

15°

10°

Introduction

The Maltese Islands lying S of Sicily are located almost exactly in the centre of the Mediterranean. They are included here because this convenient proximity ensures Malta's enduring legacy of thousands of years as a stop - over when coming or going from the Eastern or Western Mediterranean.

The group consists of the main island of Malta, with a population of 400,000, Gozo 30,000 and the tiny Comino Island between the two. There are also the

Hypogeum. Strange Neolithic temples about which little is known   *MTA*

uninhabited islets near St Paul's Bay and Fifla, a few miles to the W of the island. The latter is a nature reserve where landing is prohibited.

Malta is a fascinating archipelago with well preserved evidence of a very long history of civilisation going back to pre-historic times. The strategic location of the

St.Pauls Catacombs   *MTA*

islands has resulted in some of the best fortifications in the world and many conquests by different civilisations over the centuries. Well-preserved historic remains all over the islands testify to Malta's historical importance and now comprise some of the main attractions of the islands.

HISTORY

Pre-history (5000 to 700BC)

Malta also boasts some of the best preserved prehistoric remains in the world. They are something of a mystery, but date from the 'Temple period' around 5000BC. Temples at Ghar Dalam, Taxien and Hagar Qim are wonderfully preserved examples of this period about which little is known.

Phoenician and Carthaginians (700 to 200BC)

Phoenician and Carthaginians occupied the islands from around 700 to 200BC and tombs testify to their presence and wealth. There are many Punic period rock-cut tombs, but little remains of their contents.

The Romans (218BC to AD300)

Following the Punic wars, the Romans captured Malta and built roads, bridges and temples, the finest of which is a villa complex at Rabat. The detailed description of St Paul's shipwreck on the N coast of the island recounted in the Bible, was a remarkable historic and well-documented event during this period.

The Arabs (870 to 1090AD)

Arab forces conquered Malta in 870, though the Maltese did not convert to Islam. Remaining staunchly Christian, as they do today, they lived together in peace for 300 years before the Normans invaded. Evidence of this period remains in the architecture of the city of M'dina and in the Maltese language, which is 70% Arabic in construction and vocabulary.

Middle Ages (1090 to 1530)

Following the Norman conquest in 1090, Malta was effectively ruled from Sicily. The Arabs were expelled in 13th Century. As Sicily changed hands, Malta came under Aragonese and Castilian rule, followed by more intensive attacks from North African Muslims, until the Knights came to the rescue.

The Knights of St John (1530 to 1798)

In 1523 the Knights of St John were expelled from Rhodes and were looking for a base. The Emperor Charles V offered them Malta, in exchange for them defending it against Turkish Moslem raiders, who already controlled most of the E Mediterranean and wanted to move W. They immediately began fortifying Valletta and some of the greatest architectural monuments are still largely intact after two great sieges.

The First Great Siege (1565)

In 1565, Suleiman the Great of Turkey sought to inflict the 'Final solution' on Malta which stood in the way of the Jihad (holy war) and amassed a force of 138 warships and nearly 40,000 troops with heavy artillery to overrun the fortifications. This fleet, reinforced with more ships and troops from Dragut, a notorious North African pirate based in Tunisia, were facing a garrison of a mere 600 Knights and less than 10,000 ground troops. The scale of horrors during this siege were legendary and included Turkish troops returning rotting captured Maltese corpses, tied to crosses, by floating them into the harbour. The Knights responded by catapulting the decapitated heads of Turks back. The siege went on through one of the hottest summers on record. A force to assist the Maltese finally arrived from Sicily and the Turks, with the loss of most of their force, retreated. Very few ships or men arrived back in Turkey.

French and British Rule (1798)

Following two centuries of peace, the Knights departed after Napoleon arrived in 1798. Britain took possession of Malta in 1814, following a very unpopular rule by the French. Malta became the principal Mediterranean base for its warships and the infrastructure was developed with major dry docking facilities, ensuring a strong economy for the islands.

The Second Great Siege (1942)

During the Second World War, Malta was key to strategy for the Mediterranean fleets and the main refuelling and supply base for allied forces in North Africa who were attempting to overturn the advances of Rommel and the German army. In 1941 and 1942 German and Italian bombers blitzed Malta in order to stop supplies from reaching the island. Approximately 15,000 tons of bombs were dropped in 3,000 raids. 1,500 civilians were killed. Several convoys were destroyed en route with the loss of many men and supplies during this time. A breakthrough came with the arrival of a tanker in 1942, following heavy bombardment and the sinking of most of the protecting convoy.

Recent History

Post-war Malta

Malta became self-governing following the war with its economy derived from its facilities as a major refit base for the Royal Navy and the American fleet until the early 1970s. Facilities matched some of the best dockyards in the world with several dry docks and a

Grand Harbour looking towards Floriana from Dockyard Creek
Graham Hutt

highly skilled workforce ensuring the economy and stability of the island. This all gave way to a preferential alliance with Libya under the elected premiership of Don Mintof in 1971, following which the bases and their facilities went into decline and ruin, along with most of the associated businesses.

A reliance on trade with Libya became an important part of the island's economy, with passenger ferries arriving daily from Tripoli. Malta provided one of the only possible destinations for Libyans during the embargo on flights out of the country. Initiatives with the USSR, China and other communist block countries brought little prosperity or hope to Malta and labour unrest and turmoil throughout the islands resulted. Following elections in 1984, a new leader and government was elected and Malta began bouncing back. It never regained its position as a service base for shipping on such a scale, and the many hundreds of businesses and industries in the old dockyards still lie derelict. These are now being put to other uses or their buildings restored. Low class charter tourism became the mainstay of the economy, though several modern high-class hotels and excellent restaurants have now been built. Now that Libya has opened up to the world and its airports are again operating, Malta can no longer rely on Libyan tourism.

Current affairs and the EC

Having entered the EC in mid 2004, many changes are taking place in Malta, which will particularly affect the tourist sector and yachting over the coming years. Already new marinas have begun operating, roads are being improved and European standards are being introduced in many sectors. With the assistance of the EC, the tourist sector is likely to be the main beneficiary. One negative consequence for yachts on which VAT has not been paid, is that Malta loses its status as a place for non EC yachts to spend more than the prescribed time in Europe without having to pay VAT.

General Information

Socio-cultural guidelines

Language

Maltese and English are the official languages although Italian, French and German are widely spoken. Maltese has Arabic roots but uses the Roman alphabet.

Religion

Most Maltese are Roman Catholic with their own brand of Catholicism. This becomes very evident in summer when the feasts of the saints in each village and town take place. These are huge and colourful occasions with fireworks and the whole village turning out to see figurines of the saints or the Virgin Mary paraded along the streets on brightly painted floats. The festivities begin around midday and last well into the night. Each village tries to outdo the next as the tens of thousands of pounds worth of pyrotechnics go up to noisy cheers along with, no doubt, the prayers of the faithful.

Maritime Information

Weather

Very hot and dusty in summer, very windy and often with torrential rain in winter, sums up my experience of Maltese weather, visiting over a 40 year period with long spells living on the island. Temperatures can be very different to Sicily and Tunisia, despite their close proximity. The prevailing wind is NW throughout the year. In summer this wind usually starts with a gentle breeze around midday rising to force 4 or 5 and suddenly dies off as the sun sets. There is often a very hot humid three week period with a light S wind or none at all, during July or August. This is the only time Malta becomes unbearable.

In winter a very cold gale force NE occasionally blows, the gregale, which can last for several days. The principal harbours are open to this direction and it can be most unpleasant.

Weather forecasts

The continual Italian forecast in English and Italian on VHF ch 68 can be heard around Malta and gives conditions for the entire central and E Mediterranean area. VHF Channel 12 and 04 also give local weather for a 50M radius of Malta at 0803, 1803 and 2303. All Maltese marinas post weather information daily. These are derived from internet sources. Malta airport will usually oblige with a forecast on ☎ 5004 3848/5004 3858. For a general forecast with an excellent British Met Office synoptic chart go to http://meteonet.nl/aktueel/brackall.htm and www.bbc.co.uk/weather/coast/pressure/ or www.sto-p.com/atol
Also try
www.maltaweather.com
www.maltaairport.com

Planning your cruise

Time Zone

Central European time is used with the hour changing to UT + 1 hour from the last Sunday in October to the last Sunday in March.

Money

Malta has its own currency, the Maltese Lira (Lm) but is expected to change to the Euro in the near future. Banking hours are Mon–Thur 0830-1230, Fri 1700-1900, Sat 0830-1200.

Approach to Malta and Gozo

The Maltese Islands are low-lying with a maximum elevation of 240m but the approach is not difficult by day or night as the coast is free from off-lying hazards, with the exception of Fifla Island S of Malta, which is unlit. The passages between Gozo, Comino and Malta are free of dangers and well-marked. Marsamxett and Grand Harbours, though huge, are not clear until actually in the entrance because of the high fortresses guarding the entry. Concentrated hotel complexes along the coast identify the towns and the most conspicuous landmark coming from the E is the Hilton Tower, a blue skyscraper which dominates St Julian's Bay.

CRUISING GROUNDS

With its central location in the Mediterranean, Malta is much used by yachts on their way to and from Tunisia and Sicily, and those moving Westwards from Crete. The islands are more a stopping-off, repair and refuelling base as well as an excellent place to lay-up for the winter, rather than a cruising ground.

A great change has taken place on the islands in recent years. Not so long ago there was hostility from the government to yachtsmen and a special – and very difficult to obtain permit was necessary to anchor anywhere around the islands. The few moorings were mostly occupied and finding anywhere safe to winter was very difficult.

The political scene changed through the 90s and yachts were encouraged, but lack of facilities still made finding a mooring difficult. Just prior to EC entry in 2004, new marinas were built in anticipation of a boom and Malta is indeed now booming, with infrastructure and every facility to accommodate and encourage yachtsmen not only to pass through on their way somewhere, but to stay, cruise the islands, winter here: even make this their base for seasonal cruising.

Wintering in Malta

Malta has always been a popular place for wintering, with its international airport and relative cheapness as compared with Europe, becoming increasingly so as marina facilities improve. Shore hard-standing facilities are limited, but these too are being increased.

Harbour charges

Tariffs seem to change with great regularity. Few of the printed price lists seem to agree with what is on the internet. Some prices are quoted in Euros and fluctuate with the exchange rate, whilst others are quoted in Maltese Pounds. To avoid confusion, and because of the ease with which anyone can look up this information on the marina internet web sites, this information is not included here. Full and updated price lists for all lengths of yachts will be found along with available discounts at the internet addresses given under 'Communications' for each harbour/marina.

Security

There are no particular security issues in Malta. Other yachtsmen are more likely to cause a problem than the locals, who are typically very honest. However, problems of theft outside the main marinas in Lazaretto Creek and Ta'xbix have been reported.

Availability of supplies

Just about anything is available in Malta and all within a reasonable distance, wherever you are moored. See under 'Facilities' on page 257.

Water quality has improved dramatically over the years and electricity is available at every marina berth.

Senglia creek. Land exit from Grand Harbour Marina
on left
Graham Hutt

Yacht repair facilities

Because Malta was traditionally a major shipyard centre and has been run down by the navies, spare capacity abounds. A suggested list is given on page 258. Most manufacturers of any marine product are represented on the island somewhere. There is nothing that cannot be made, modified or repaired here. The Maltese are masters at improvisation and repair and have served the great navies of the world for many years.

Entry formalities

Before joining the EC, yachts announced their arrival to Valletta Port Control on VHF Ch 12 to receive clearing instructions prior to berthing. Normally yachts were directed to Marsamxetto Harbour but late at night or during the weekend yachts were requested to proceed to Grand Harbour to clear customs. Since mid-2004, there has been some confusion, since technically there is no longer any need for EC yachts to report to the customs authorities when coming from another EC country. The authorities were, however, still insisting on the old routine in January 2005. This will be resolved in due course, most probably with each marina taking particulars and reporting to customs, rather than yachts having to report.

Currently three main Customs and immigration facilities exist: in Grand Harbour, at the entrance of Msida Marina and in Mgarr Marina, on Gozo Island.

Visas

Until now there have been no problems for almost any nationality in Malta. With its entry into the EC, there may now be restrictions on North Africans and some other nationals, but this was still being hammered out in late 2004, because Malta wanted to retain its links and special relationship with North Africa, especially Libya.

Pets onboard

In the past the Maltese authorities engaged a very strict policy and would not allow any vessels with pets aboard to berth or even anchor around the Island. Another consequence of EC membership, is that this ruling is being revised. Now, as in other EC countries, pets need 'chipping' and a passport showing recent vaccinations.

Agents

Harbour and marina authorities in Malta insist that yachts moored shall at all times be under the charge of a master or a person duly authorised to assume full responsibility for the yacht. Arrangements can usually be made with staff in the marinas. This may be a rule dating from times when all facilities were full and if an owner returned to find his berth occupied, there were few options but for the visitor to be expelled. With more room available now, this may be unnecessary.

Internet

Internet cafés are numerous, especially in the tourist areas. Grand Harbour Marina intends to connect facilities to every yacht and with wireless facilities now easily available, the other marina no doubt will be providing the same facilities in due course.

Mobile phones

For a small price a SIM card can be purchased from any of the many phone shops around the tourist areas in Malta and also from some newspaper shops. This enables calls from abroad to be received without charge to you. Phone cards can also be purchased to make international calls at a much cheaper rate than by dialling direct, either from a local phone or mobile.

Mail in Malta

Mail can be forwarded to marinas in Malta in advance of a yacht visiting and will be held for up to a month. Use the yacht's name and the marina name and address. Mailing addresses are all listed on the internet. (see Communications for URL)

Tourist information

Malta's history is long, rich and varied from Prehistoric times, as noted under 'History.' It was well fortified by the Knights Hospitallers, who used it as their base in 1530–1798 and the ancient fortifications and facilities were used during the second world war. Apart from the books recommended in the appendix, it is worth seeing 'The Malta Experience', a mult-visual, multi-language show on the history of the islands, at the Mediterranean Conference Centre, Merchant's Street, Valletta. It is shown weekdays every hour between 1000 and 1600. There are many sites well worth a visit, including one of the oldest known temples in the world, dating from pre-historic times and some spectacular caves. The tourist office in Valletta town centre has maps and information on all the sites and is worthwhile visiting before beginning your tour. Mdina is an ancient and very beautiful town with spectacular architecture and fine restaurants. Its narrow streets are usually deserted around sunset. The old fort of St Angelo, guarding the entrance of Grand Harbour is also worth a visit, especially if you are berthed in Grand Harbour Marina. The excellent and cheap bus service operates throughout the island, giving access to all the sites, which are never very busy. Since the late 1970s Malta has primarily been sold as a package holiday resort, with its beaches as the main attraction. Few tourists seem interested in venturing out of their hotels to explore its rich history.

Business hours

Mon–Sat 0830–1245 1430–1730. Some small shops close for lunch between 1300 and 1600 and remain open later in the evening.

Eating out

Malta does not have a tradition of haute cuisine but the tourist trade has encouraged many good restaurants. In Paceville (about 20 minutes by bus from Gzira) there is a wide choice and there are fast food shops closer. The hospitable Valletta Yacht Club in Fort Manoel has good bar and dining facilities in one of the nicest locations on the island. Above the casino in Grand Harbour Marina is an excellent restaurant and surprisingly inexpensive.

Transport

Bus There is an extensive bus service. The old, colourfully decorated buses are being replaced and connect just about any point on the island. It is well worth getting to know the system as it offers a cheap and very effective, frequent service. Safety while travelling is assured by the presence of a statue of the Virgin Mary in every bus, whilst many drivers even move over to make room for her presence! Less than a pound takes you around the whole island. Get to know the routes, which are well-publicised and run every few minutes from many locations. Taxis, in comparison, are quite expensive, as are carrozzis, the horse-drawn carriages which have reappeared to please the tourists. Sadly, the hundreds of colourful dghaisas (pronounced die-soes) which provided the main cross and inter-harbour transport, have all but vanished following the withdrawal of the Royal Navy from Malta. Some however have recently been refurbished and are returning to service.

Car hire All the main European agencies are represented, along with some local ones. Prices are quite cheap and negotiable.

A ferry service links Malta main island with Gozo and this runs very frequently throughout the day.

International travel

Air Luqa is the international airport on the island offering several fights every day to London and other destinations in the United Kingdom and Europe. Tunisavia (☎ 682234) flies three times a week to Tunis and once a week to Sfax as well as Monastir in summer.

Sea There is a weekly ferry to Naples, a service to Reggio Calabria and Syracuse and a catamaran service to Pozzallo and Catania.

More information

An amazing amount of information can be obtained about the facilities Malta has to offer on the internet. Type into a search engine 'Malta marinas' and see what comes up!

http://www.noonsite.com/Countries/Malta/MsidaMarina

Tides

These are insignificant, being less than 0.5m.

Important note on waypoints and co-ordinates

Please refer to the important note regarding waypoints in the Introduction, page 12.

VI. MALTA

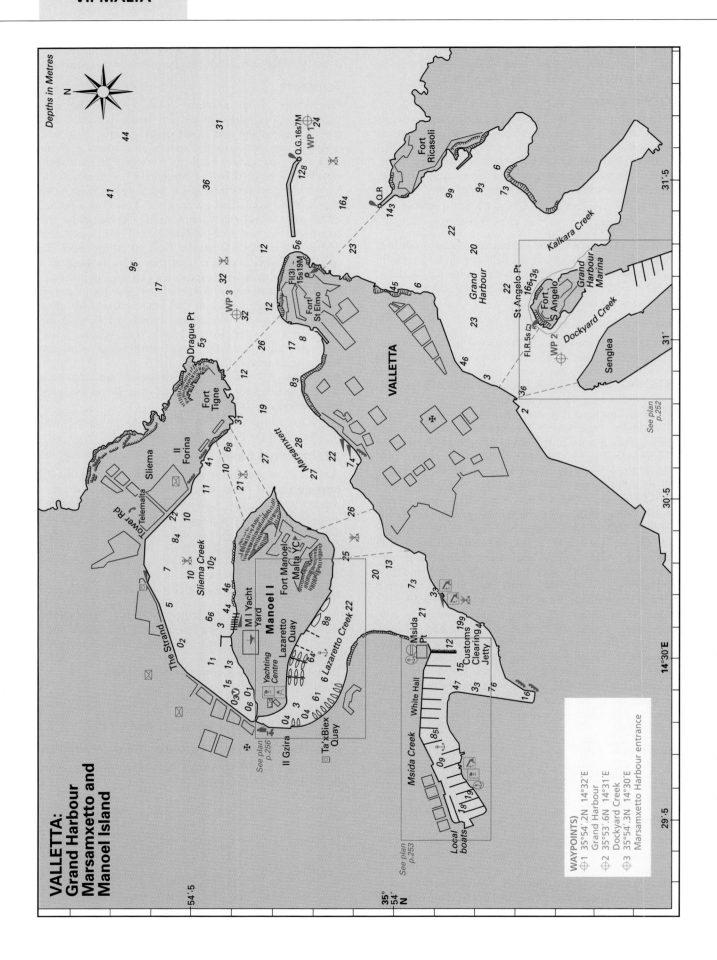

VALLETTA:
Grand Harbour
Marsamxetto and
Manoel Island

Depths in Metres

N

WAYPOINTS)
⊕1 35°54'.2N 14°32'E
   Grand Harbour
⊕2 35°53'.6N 14°31'E
   Dockyard Creek
⊕3 35°54'.3N 14°30'E
   Marsamxetto Harbour entrance

Harbours and marinas around Malta

MA1 Grand Harbour

A large and very safe harbour in all conditions with a new marina.

Location
35°54´.2N 14°32´.E (E end of St.Elmo mole)

Grand Harbour is the main commercial harbour of the island and one of the best and largest natural harbours in the world. Whereas in the past, few facilities existed for yachtsmen, the new and prestigious Grand Harbour Marina has opened, tucked into the old Naval victualling section of Vittoriosa, just East of Fort St Angelo, 1M SE inside the entrance of Grand Harbour.

Distances
Monastir 185M
Kelibia 180M
Lampedusa 107M
Crete 450M.

Tides
Insignificant

Charts

	Approach	Port
Admiralty	2124, 2537, 2538, 2623	974, 177

Lights
Approaches
Delimara Point (SE end) Fl(2)12s35m18M R lights on chimney 0.7M N
Giordan (NW corner of Gozo) Fl.7.5s180m18M
Grand Harbour Approach
1. **St Elmo** 35°54´.2N 14°31´.2E Fl(3)15s49m19M Metal framework tower on Fort St Elmo
2. **St Elmo breakwater head** Q.G.16m7M White round tower, red band on E side
3. **Ricasoli breakwater** Q.R.11m6M 120°-obscd-157° Metal structure on white round stone tower, red bands on E side F.R radio mast 0.5M SE

Communications
VHF Ch 16

PILOTAGE INTO GRAND HARBOUR

By day

The ancient limestone structures all around the coast blend into the surroundings, making identification difficult from seaward. The entrance is not easily recognized until the detached mole, Fort St Elmo and the fort on Ricasoli are identified. The gap at the W end of St Elmo detached mole just under the fort has depths of 5m, though an old iron bridge linking the mole to the mainland collapsed there some years ago. In rough seas use the E entrance, where ⊕1 is located. Beware of large passenger liners and ships turning within the entrance to round St Elmo mole. Coming from the E they are difficult to spot until in the entrance. This harbour is safe to enter in any weather conditions.

By night

A very easy entry at night. St Elmo light (Fl(3)15s) is visible at 19M and Ricasoli light at 6M. Fort St Angelo, which lies at the W end of the marina is well flood-lit, though without a navigation light apart from a Fl R buoy marking a ledge below the fort and entrance to Kalkara Creek.

Formalities

All yachts currently must call at the customs point in Grand Harbour, Marsamxett Harbour or at Mgarr in Gozo to clear customs on entry. See further note under 'Entry Formalities', page 248.

Grand Harbour Marina viewed from Floriana   *Graham Hutt*

MA2 Grand Harbour Marina

This splendid and well protected new marina is tucked 1M inside Grand Harbour. It can accommodate 250 yachts, including some moorings for yachts up to 100m. Very friendly and helpful staff: a safe and suitable marina for both visiting and wintering.

Location
35°53′.6N 14°31′E (Entrance to Dockyard Creek)

Communications
Harbourmaster ☎+356 21 800700
Fax +356 21806148, 21 800900.
VHF Ch 13
Email info@ghm.com.mt
www.cnmarinas.com

The marina

Opened in 2003, the marina will be fully operational by the beginning of 2005, though some facilities, including the harbourmaster's offices, will not be in their permanent position until late 2005. The staff are very friendly, efficient and helpful and with facilities for yachts up to 100m. The marina is well protected from all directions and offers winter berthing facilities. This marina is the best option at present for yachts visiting Malta. It has room, facilities and is excellently run by manager Anna Tabone and her staff.

PILOTAGE

Before rounding Fort St Angelo, call on VHF 13 any time of day or night and a RIB from the marina will meet you and direct you to a berth, assisting with mooring if necessary. WP2 takes you to the entrance of Dockyard Creek.

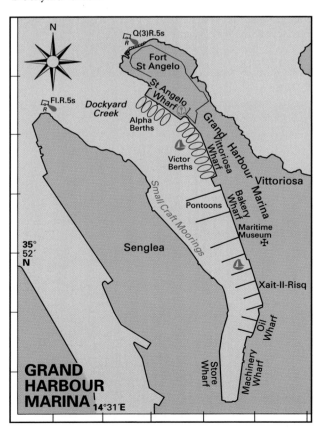

GRAND HARBOUR MARINA

Berthing

Yachts up to 15m will be directed to a pontoon berth at the S end of the marina where finger berths allow alongside berthing either stern or bows-to. Larger yachts (over 20m) use stern lines to the quay near the office at the N end of the marina. Whilst there is plenty of room to manoeuvre, there is a policy by the staff always to offer assistance with the RIB.

Charges

Full and updated information available on the web or by contacting the marina on email given above.

Formalities

There should be none for EC citizens entering Malta coming from an EC country, but in summer 2004 all vessels were still being first directed to the main Customs house on the NW side of the harbour, half a mile beyond the old Customs House below the Barracca Gardens. All the marinas should eventually have their own facilities for yachts, as in the EU countries.

Facilities

Water Metered, excellent quality.
Electricity Metered.
Fuel On G pontoon. Pipes are being laid with metered outlets for larger yachts moored on the main quay.
Repairs Small yard in nearby Kalkara Creek with laying-up and repair facilities for yachts, and large yards at Marsa where work on any size yachts can be undertaken. French and Dockyard Creeks contain dry docks and facilities for repairing large commercial vessels.
  Full lift-out and yacht repair facilities on Manoel Island, on the N side of Valletta.
Engine and *mechanical repairs* Engineers call at the yacht.
Provisions Local market Tuesday. Everything available for re-stocking just a short walk out of the marina and up the hill behind the bus depot. Many more shops and supermarkets in the locality. The nearby Chain supermarket in Fgura will deliver to yachts.
Internet Connection will be supplied from the office.
See end of section for a more detailed list of services and supplies available in Malta.

ASHORE

In the marina itself is the Museum of Maritime History and an art museum. The latter hosts special events at weekends, including concerts. St Angelo fort, at the N end of the marina, gives a fascinating glimpse of the amazing fortress and is home to the Knights of St John who survived the siege. The local town of Birgu has a fascinating history and also houses the Inquisitors Palace, which is open to the public as a museum.

Eating out

Above the Casino in the port is an excellent restaurant which is not expensive compared with other similar facilities.

Transport

A frequent bus service links the area to the main bus terminus in Valletta. Bus no 1, 2, 3, 4 and 6 all go to and from Valletta from outside the marina.

MA3 Marsamxetto Harbour

Well protected natural harbour, a short distance N of Grand Harbour on the Valletta side. Host to 3 marinas and the main Maltese yacht repair facilities of Manoel Island.

Location
35°54′.4N 14°30′.0E

Charts
Admiralty *974*
Italian *917*

Lights
Marsamxetto Harbour Approach
4. **Dragut Point** has been extinguished for some years
5. **Msida Marina Jetty head** Q.G.5m2M

Communications
VHF Ch 16

PILOTAGE INTO MARSAMXETTO HARBOUR

By day

From any direction the fort of St Elmo and the breakwater across Grand Harbour to the S of the entrance of Marsamxetto, are the most prominent features on entry. ⊕3 is at the entrance.

By night

St Elmo light, though obscured from afar by high background lights in the town, is easily identified once closer in. There is no light on Tigne fort, but the looming blackness to starboard as you enter makes mid channel entry easy to identify. The land lights of Manoel Island and the old Quarantine Hospital will be seen as you enter.

Berthing and anchoring

Berthing arrangements are described under each facility. Anchoring is possible both N and S of Manoel Island as indicated, but note that charges for anchoring are no cheaper than a marina berth.

Facilities

Fuel The main fuelling facility for yachts is a floating platform near the end of the creek leading to Msida Marina. This can be duty free by arrangement with customs if over 400L is required. EC rules may change the price and duty free facilities, but this had not been changed in early 2005.

MA4 Msida Marina

Msida Marina, near to Floriana town, has 700 yacht berths, with some moorings up to 18 metres. It is conveniently located close to Valletta with customs facilities on entry.

Location
35°53′.8N 14°30′.E (Customs berth)

Charts
Admiralty *974*

Communications
Berthing Master ☎ 21332800 *Fax* 21332141.
VHF Ch 09
Email info@mma.gov.ma
www.mma.gov.mt
http://www.noonsite.com/Countries/Malta/MsidaMarina

The marina

This Malta Maritime Authority owned marina is run with very few staff, so do not expect any help with mooring whatever the weather. The breakwater at the E end serves as the customs quay, and makes the marina safe and comfortable from any wind direction. The main road from Msida to Valletta runs around the marina and it is very noisy on the S side where other roads converge with heavy traffic as they near Floriana en route for Valletta. Most of the berths have permanent occupants and it is consequently quite difficult to get a berth for more than a day or two in summer, though sometimes longer term stays are possible if you do not mind being moved around from day to day. In winter many boats are hauled, so there is no problem for long term wintering berths. Each pontoon is accessed with a key and security is excellent.

The Malta Maritime Authority also formerly owned the Manoel Island berthing facilities, but this is now in private hands and described separately.

PILOTAGE

By day

There are no special problems. From the entrance of the main harbour, (WP3) continue SE until the breakwater is seen. Depths in the entrance are from 12m to 17m.

By night

The green light at the end of the breakwater is easily identified and the area is well lit with floodlights.

Berthing

Moor first at the S end of the breakwater, where several berths are marked for guests with lines tailed to the quay. This area is owned by the Customs Authorities

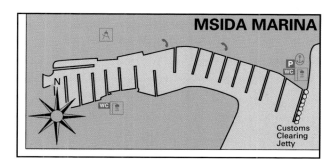

Msida Marina looking E. Ship Restaurant left of customs
jetty and fuel barge beyond   *MTA*

and their office is a short walk along to the N end of
the quay. If arriving by day, on completion of clearing
formalities in the customs and immigration office, visit
the marina office next door and a berth will be
allocated. At night, all offices are closed, and there are
no marina staff on duty.

Charges

Look up the internet site above for the latest
information with a full list of charges for all lengths of
yacht. A 30% surcharge is levied on yachts with crew
living aboard.

Formalities

Yachts should call on VHF channel 9 to receive berthing
instructions by day or moor at the customs jetty as
indicated under 'Berthing.' For more information see
further note under 'Entry Formalities', page 248.

Facilities

Water and *electricity* Available on pontoon. Metered for yachts
over 18m.
Showers and *toilets* Facilities both sides of the marina, though
it can be a long walk, depending on which pontoon the
yacht is berthed.
Fuel From floating facility just outside marina.

See page 257 for more facilities.

ASHORE

See under Tourist Information.

Eating out

The nearest and most interesting place is a harbour
restaurant and bar housed in an old timber ship, the
Black Pearl, next to the marina office. Built in 1909 it
serves good food and fine wines and makes for a
different atmosphere overlooking the marina. A chilly
breeze can blow across her open decks in the evenings
so take a shawl or jacket.

Chinese, Indian and other speciality restaurants as
well as normal European fare are to be found further
round in Gzira, or in Valletta.

Msida Marina from the E. Customs jetty, ship restaurant and
harbourmaster bottom of picture   *MTA*

MA5 Manoel Island Marina (Lazaretto Creek)

This new marina has been developed from the remains of
the Msida Marina facilities on the SW side of Manoel
Island. A very convenient location for all facilities ashore
and afloat, being a short walk to the tourist centre of
Gzira, yet far enough away to eliminate noise from the
town.

Location
  W end of Lazaretto Creek
Communications
  Marina Office ☎ 21338589/21330982 *Fax* 2134 1714
  VHF Ch 12
  www.melitamarine.com and
  www.manoelislandmarina.com
  Email melita@onvol.net and
  info@manoelislandmarina.com

The marina

Formerly belonging to the Malta Port Authority and
operated by Msida Marina, this new facility, located on
the SW side of Manoel Island is now owned by Melita
Marine and has been developed with the recent
addition of pontoons to accommodate many more
yachts. More will be added to the E during 2005. The
infrastructure will finally be completed with the
addition of a new breakwater at the E end to minimise
the surging that takes place during NE gregale gales
which have always been a problem here in Marsamxett
harbour in winter.

PILOTAGE

As for Msida Marina. Once in the harbour, head SW for
Lazaretto Creek and follow the S side of Manoel Island,
where the marina will be seen. Depths are from 22m to
a minimum of 3m at the far end of the marina. (But
don't venture near the bridge where shallower depths
are found.)

VI. MALTA

Berthing

Call on Ch 12 and a berth will be allocated on a pontoon. At night when staff are not present, other options are the customs berth in Msida Marina or anchoring mid-stream S of the marina. This latter facility is expected to be withdrawn during 2005 as pontoons will extend from both sides of the creek, restricting swinging room.

Charges

Different rates are quoted in Lm and Euros. Check with the web sites above for updated information.

Formalities

As for all harbours of Malta, currently under review. See further note in introduction under 'Entry Formalities', page 248.

Facilities

Water and *electricity* Available on each pontoon.
Showers and *toilets* Facilities behind marina office.
Fuel From floating facility near Msida Marina.
See page 257 for more services and facilities in Malta.

ASHORE

Gzira town is just across the Manoel Island connecting bridge and is a hub of tourist activity with many bars, restaurants (including Royal Malta Yacht Club) and shopping facilities.

Transport

A bus service runs along the main road every few minutes, heading for Valletta bus centre, from where hundreds of buses operate throughout the island. Do take the opportunity to see the island and its sights which are plentiful and unique.

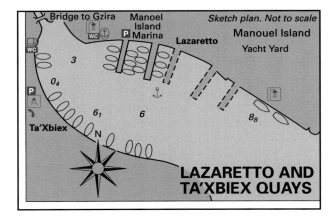

LAZARETTO AND TA'XBIEX QUAYS
Sketch plan. Not to scale

MA6 Ta'Xbiex Quay moorings, (Lazaretto Creek)

Moorings at the SW end of Lazaretto Creek on the SW Ta'Xbiex side provide facilities for yachts moored stern or bows-to up to 25m length. Separation from the main road with gardens and walkways makes this a pleasant place in all but the severe gregale winds.

Communications
www.manoelislandmarina.com
Email melita@onvol.net and
info@manoelislandmarina.com

Berthing

There is no reception quay and berthing must be arranged in advance by contacting the berthing master on VHF ch 9 at Msida Marina or visit the office when clearing customs on entry. There is no reliable ground tackle here – use your own anchor. Ancient anchors, heavy ground chains, chains and lines litter this end of the harbour. Any lines tailed to the quay are unreliable. Drop anchor well out to avoid old ground chain and always use a tripping line. The bottom is mud and holding is good provided you don't select an area still littered with discarded ironwork.

An alternative is to anchor temporarily in the middle of the creek, though this is now discouraged with swinging room restricted now that pontoons have been placed on the Manoel Island side. Anchoring charges are the same as for mooring in the marinas.

Facilities

Water and *electricity* Available on jetty.
Showers and *toilets* On jetty.
Fuel From floating facility near Msida Marina.
See page 257 for more services and facilities in Malta.

Formalities

As above for Manoel Island Marina. Moorings in Ta'Xbiex belong to the Malta Maritime Authority and are managed by the Msida Marina office. See further note under 'Entry Formalities', page 248.

Wintering

It becomes very rough here during the NE gregale winds, although once the breakwaters are in place on the N side of the Creek at Manoel Island Marina, things should improve.

If leaving a yacht for the winter, the best option is hauling out in Manoel Island, or remaining afloat in one of the other marinas.

MA7 Manoel Island Malta Yacht Yard, (Sliema Creek)

A few alongside berths at Manoel Island Pier and some moorings for boats waiting to slip at the yard or after launching.

Communications
☎ 334453 *Fax* 343900
Email miyy@global.net.mt

The yard

Formally owned by the Admiralty, this yard is now under the management of Malta Dry Docks and caters mainly for yachts of all sizes. It has excellent facilities and can undertake anything from yacht building to repairs on yachts with any hull construction. Winter lay-up can also be arranged here.

For short stays, the management insist on all work being carried out by its own staff. However, for longer stays they are negotiable on this. Though living aboard is not technically allowed, it can be arranged for the first week following lift out, and for the final week before return to the water. In practice, the yard is negotiable both on prices and rules. It is a busy yard offering some of the best yacht yard facilities in the Mediterranean and at reasonable prices.

A large life-raft and dinghy servicing facility operates within the yard, catering for most manufacturers.

Facilities

Water and *electricity* At the pier.

Other facilities and services around Marsamxett Harbour (Msida, Ta'XBiex and Manoel Island)

Fuel A fuel barge selling duty free diesel is moored 300 metres to the ENE of Msida Marina entrance. Petrol and lubricants are also stocked. This is the best and most convenient way of fuelling. The alternative is to order delivery of duty paid fuel by tanker through the marina or your agent or direct from the Service Station very close across the Island bridge.

Provisions Good provisions are available, although fruit and vegetables (available from visiting trucks) are seasonal and limited. Carefully check the prices, weights and quantities dispensed by the truck owners. Also check for fruit about to turn rotten which he may slip in, especially if the vendor knows you are leaving! Excellent bread and very good, cheap frozen meat from Ireland, Australia and New Zealand. Not much fish which mostly goes to the restaurants. The best supermarket and well worth the walk (20 minutes) is the Tower Self-Service Store on Tower Road in Sliema. They will deliver to the boat if a sizeable order is placed. There is a good butcher, Charles close by. There are some small shops on the Strand close to Manoel Island Bridge with a limited range but cheerful service.

Duty free Alcoholic beverages can be ordered through the yacht agents. Allow 2–3 days for delivery.

Post office Next to the Health Centre in Gzira and signposted from the Strand.

Bank Several banks near the bridge to Manoel Island and more in Valletta.

Medical The Health Centre in Gzira is 10 minutes' walk from Manoel Island and is good for uncomplicated medical problems. If X-rays or special tests are required, it is better to go to St Luke's hospital in Msida. In normal circumstances services are free of charge.

Laundry Around the corner from RLR chandlery and another laundrette on the Strand shortly before Tower Road. Facilities are planned for the marina.

MA8 Portomaso Marina

A new marina under the Hilton Hotel on the W side of St Julian's Bay. This is suitable for those wanting a very up-market marina in luxury surroundings.

Location
35°55′.2N 14°29′.7E (Harbour entrance)

Communications
☎ 21387803, 79495768 *Fax* 21389655, 21410183
VHF Ch 09
Email info@portomasomarina.com
www.portomasomarina.com

The marina

Set in St Julian's bay at the base of the huge Hilton hotel tower and surrounded by luxury apartments, this is certainly the most prestigious place to be in Malta, if not the most attractive. The marina is fully booked most of the time, so do not turn up without prior arrangement. Holding tanks are a must here and are checked. The sight of any discharge, however slight and whatever it is, apparently brings the marina management running to the scene with a bill, and immediate sailing orders. To see the extensive list of prohibitions and rules in this marina, look up the "Marina Rules" on their web site listed above.

PILOTAGE

By day

The Hilton hotel itself being several stories high and with blue tinted glass, provides the best landmark from any direction. The actual port is not seen until quite close so use WP4. The grey stone walls blend into the surrounding rocky coast. Head for the Hilton until the entry is seen. Entry is dangerous during strong NE gregale winds.

By night

The marina entrance is lit, as is the S headland of St Julian's Bay.

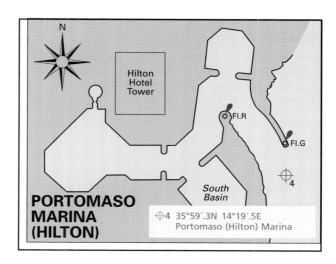

VI. MALTA

Portomaso Marina entrance from SE. The Hilton Tower is
unmistakable from any direction   *Graham Hutt*

Berthing

Contact the marina manager in advance for berthing.
Note that the marina is usually full and cannot often
accept visiting yachts except by prior arrangement.

Charges

Check out the web site for latest full price information
for all lengths of yachts.

Formalities

Currently customs formalities must first be dealt with in
Grand Harbour, Msida Marina or Mgarr until EC law is
put into operation, following which it should be
unnecessary for yachts coming from the EC to clear
customs. See further note under 'Entry Formalities', page
248.

Facilities

Water and *electricity* Available on each berth.
Showers and *toilets* Excellent and clean facilities.
See below for more information on Services and
Facilities in Malta.

ASHORE

St Julian's Bay is one of the most pleasant areas of Malta,
especially in the evenings. Many fine restaurants and
bars surround the bay, offering a wide variety of food
and entertainment. The bus route goes around the bay
and runs every few minutes throughout the day and
evening. Do take a trip to Valletta, from where further
buses can be taken to every far corner of the island.

YACHT SERVICES IN MALTA

Yacht Agencies

RLR/Yachtcare Services, Gzira
    ☎ 21331192/21331996 *Fax* 21344615. Agencies for
    Musto, Raymarine, Sebago, Crewsaver, Volvo Penta,
    Johnson, Evinrude, Marlow Ropes and Zodiac.
    Yacht Care is a subsidiary, specialising in the care
    and maintenance of yachts. Brokers and boat
    builders. Also a large chandlery.
S&D Yachts Ltd, Guiseppe Cali St, Ta'Xbiex Gzira
    ☎ 21320577/21331515/21339908 *Fax* 21332259.
    Yacht brokers and agents, charter management,
    engineering, consultants, registrations, guardianage.

Agents for Tohatsu, Rotostay, Gib-Sea, Westerly Marine.

Nautica, Sliema ☎ 21342286/7 *Fax* 21342228 Small company offering brokerage and chartering. Chandlery in Gzira listed below.

Chandlers/Electronics/Services

D'Agata Marine/Nautilus Services Ltd, Gzira. Chandlery and importer of Force and Cruise n'Carry outboards, Plastimo, Extensor International paints, Wilks fendering, Imray pilots etc.

Gauci Borda Ltd, The Strand, Gzira/Msida. ☎ 21364255/21340491 *Fax* 21343604 Good assortment of chandlery and hardware.

International Marine Centre Ltd, Gzira. Well-assorted chandlery and importer of a wide range of products: Avon Inflatables, ITT/Jabsco, Lavac, Blake, Whale, Henderson, Simpson Lawrence, Aqua Signal, Frigoboat, Morse Controls, Vire, VDO, Aqua Marine, Sestrel

Camilleri Marine, Gzira. Chandlery and importer of Mercury, Morse, Shurflo, Guidi brass hardware, Inox-Mare stainless steel hardware etc. Specialist in welding/bending of stainless steel pipes, etc.

Data Marine Ltd, Gzira. Representative of Navico, SeaFresh, Neco Micrologic.

Fabian Enterprises, Gzira. Electronic repairs and supplier of communication equipment and electronic components.

Medcomms Ltd, Gzira. Electronics specialists. Sales and service of Cetrec, Furuno, Magnavox, Navionics, Sailor, Seafarer, Thrane & Thrane, Thomas Walker, SAIT/Skanti, Swiftech and V-tronic.

Medway, Gzira. Engine specialist and 'Jack of all trades' including stainless steel. Saab engines representative.

Nautica Ltd, Gzira. Chandlery and importer of Vetus, Bombard, Davis, etc., Yamaha outboards and generators.

Ripard, Larvan & Ripard Ltd, (RLR) Gzira. Wide range of chandlery items and importers of many nautical products: SPSystems, Lewmar, stainless hardware and yacht fittings, Mase, Sikkens, International paints, Musto, VDO, Autohelm, Zodiac, Jabsco, Hood, Norseman Gibb, Johnson outboards, Volvo Penta, Simpson-Lawrence and Imray pilots.

Ronnie's Marine Services, Gzira. Engine/transmission specialist, engine spares, paints and very helpful in other matters. Tomos Outboards representative.

Portomaso Marina looking E from the Hilton Hotel tower.
Graham Hutt

Zarb Stores Ltd, Luqa. Chandlery with yachting hardware and accessories. Suzuki importer.

Thos. C. Smith & Co Ltd, Valletta. Stockist of Admiralty charts and publications.

Gaetano Bondin, Mellieha ☎ 21472302 Refrigeration. Handles Taylor professional ice making machines.

Action Sails, Cannon Road, Qormi. ☎ 21623511 Sail makers.

Marine Services Ltd, Sliema. Young company specialising in boat care and maintenance.

Dolphin Forge, Msida Galvanising, welding, shot-blasting on site, reconditioning of prop shafts.

Shipyards

Manoel Island Yacht Yard, Gzira ☎ 21334453/4, 21334320 *Fax* 21343900. The largest facility for yacht repairs, maintenance, refitting, conversions, osmosis treatment for GRP hulls etc. Owned by Malta Drydocks, who deal with commercial vessels or very large yachts. Conveniently located on Manoel Island, it has a 40-ton travel-lift and room for about 240 yachts on the hard and seven slips for yachts or commercial vessels up to 60m and 500-tonnes' displacement. Anything larger can be accommodated in Malta Dry Docks in the Grand Harbour http://www.maltadrydocks.com.mt/
For rates and more information see http://www.yachtyard-malta.com/

Kalkara Boatyard Co. Ltd, Kalkara ☎ 21661306 Yacht yard with winter storage on the hard and mobile crane for boats up to 50 tons. Lifting and storage rates are about the same as Manoel Island Yacht Yard but fewer restrictions. Specialists in laying teak decks and joinery work. Close to Grand Harbour Marina.

Guzi Azzopardi, Marsa. ☎ 21234200. Boat Builders and Consultants

Bezzina Ship Repair Yard Ltd, Marsa ☎ 21824138/21826283. Mostly for merchant vessels but they have worked on large private yachts up to 65m.

Cassar Enterprises Ltd, Marsa ☎ 21225764 *Fax* 21229761 One of the few yards, aside from Malta Dry docks, that does dry grit blasting.

GOZO ISLAND

Gozo has a very different character to Malta Island. Though only a short sail across the Comino channel, it is a peaceful island without the incredible traffic chaos of the main island. It relies on fishing and tourism, the latter derived from day-trippers arriving by ferry throughout the day. They do not, however, impede the relaxed and friendly atmosphere amongst the people.

Looking N to Gozo: a spectacular coastline   *MTA*

MA9 Mgarr Marina

Updated from a fishing harbour to a marina, on the SE side of Gozo, Mgarr is the only marina on the island. Space for 208 yachts and a port of entry. Wintering is possible here.

Location
36°01´.5N 14°18´.0E

Charts
Admiralty *974, 2537, 2623*

Communications
Harbourmaster ☎ 558856/7 Fax 562672
VHF Ch 16, 12
http://www.mma.gov.mt/yacting_mgarr_marina.htm

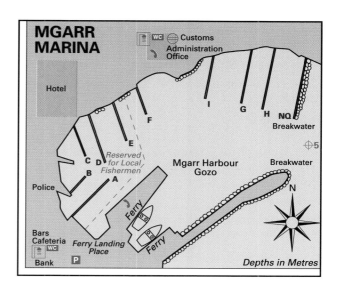

The marina

A pretty fishing and ferry harbour, now rated as a marina, with more pontoons having been added. Mgarr is Gozo's main port for car and passenger ferry services between the islands. There are frequent services from Cirkewwa across the Comino channel and a ferry service from Marsamxetto. Yachts must keep clear of them in the harbour and approaches.

PILOTAGE

By day

Though its close proximity to Comino and Malta makes pilotage unmistakeable, the main identifying feature is the ferry which scuttles across the 2.5 miles between Malta and Gozo every few minutes, arriving at the ferry dock in Mgarr. These ferries represent the only hazard on entry.

By night

The entry lights are easily identifiable as is the light on Ras I Irqieqa on the SW tip of Comino (Fl.R.7m2M).

Berthing

There are pontoons in the NE corner or as directed by the berthing master on entry.

Marina charges

A full list of prices for all lengths is provided at

Mgarr harbour   *MTA*

VI. MALTA

http://www.mma.gov.mt/yacting_mgarr_marina.htm
(or type into a search engine 'Malta marinas').

Anchoring in Mgarr Harbour

There is now insufficient room to anchor within the marina.

Formalities

This is a port of entry/departure. A customs and immigration office is situated in the marina and it may be more convenient to clear out here rather than in Marsamxetto.

Facilities

Water and *electricity* Available on each pontoon.
Showers and *toilets* Facilities available.
Fuel From the nearby petrol station.
Provisions From the nearby village.

ASHORE

Gozo is a quiet, peaceful place and a relaxing contrast to the bustle of Malta, notwithstanding the ferry traffic. Shops and restaurants, ice and fuel can be found in the village.

Transport

A car and passenger ferry runs across to Malta Island frequently, from where a bus to the capital Rabat (Victoria) and Valletta can be taken.

There is a helicopter service to-and-from the island from Luqa airport.

Melilla Bay: good shelter in quiet surroundings in the NE corner *MTA*

MA10 Anchorages around Malta Island

(Anti-clockwise from Valletta).
The NE coast of Malta slopes gradually to the shore and is indented with numerous bays. Due to ease of access, this part of Malta has the most tourist development. In the summer months many local boats use these bays and consequently few, if any, are secluded. They all offer good protection from the W to SE and the anchorages are mostly sand or soft mud with seaweed in patches. Coordinates are given for the entrance to the bays mentioned. No charges are levied for anchoring in these bays.

St Julian's Bay
35°55′.2N 14°29′.8E

A wide pleasant bay built up all round. Good protection except in E and NE winds and holding with room to swing. St Julian's and its neighbouring Balluta Bay are surrounded by restaurants and pubs. No stern-to moorings.

St George's Bay
35°55′.7N 14°29′.5E

A very good anchorage and alternative to St Julian's in E and NE winds, but surrounded by terraces and restaurants. A very busy tourist spot in summer and popular for watersports. If you like noise and bustle, this is the place.

Qala ta' Sn Marku
35°56′.9N 14°27′.0E

A quiet and peaceful bay to the SE of Salina Bay. Good holding. No services. If proceeding from here to Salina Bay give the Ghallis Rocks a wide berth.

Salina Bay
35°57′.0N 14°29′.5E

Derives its name from the salt pans situated at the head of the bay which is shallow but with good holding. The NW side is covered with hotels and restaurants and there is a water sports centre. Avoid a wandering sandbank at SW end of bay, in line with Coastline Hotel.

St Paul's Bay
35°57′.3N 14°23′.7E

A large bay around which Malta's major tourist area has grown up which is noisy until the early hours. There is good holding and several small bays offer safe anchorages. Small boat moorings occupy some of Mistra Bay on the N side. The cliffs between Mistra Bay and St Paul's Island afford a quieter anchorage, sheltered from W and NW.

St Paul's Island, marked by a conspicuous statue to the saint, is the site of his shipwreck while en route to Rome from Anatolia in AD60. This provided the opportunity to convert the islands to Christianity. The passage between St Paul's Island and the mainland should only be attempted by dinghy.

Mgiebah or Selmun Bay
35°58′.0N 14°22′.0E
A shallow bay open to the N and holding in soft sand. No road access.

Anchor Bay: with Mellieha Bay on far side

Mellieha Bay
35°59´.0N 14°22´.5E

The largest bay on the NE coast. It has one of the largest sandy beaches in Malta with many watersport facilities but some quiet anchorages along the N shore. Beware of a shoal patch and submerged rock in the middle.

Armier Bay
35°59´.5N 14°21´.5E

A large sandy beach with three restaurants, also known as the White Lido. If a quieter ambience is desired, Little Armier Bay just to the W is more tranquil. Both bays are open to the NW and the prevailing breeze.

Ramla Bay
35°59´.4N 14°20´.6E

Ramla Bay is dominated by a large hotel complex on the W side. The bottom is hard and sandy in the middle of the bay with weed and rocks at the sides. A watersports area.

Paradise Bay
35°59´.2N 14°19´.9E

Paradise Bay faces WNW and is open to the prevailing winds. A pretty bay with a small hotel and private beach. Soft sandy bottom.

Anchor Bay
35°57´.7N 14°20´.4E

A small, attractive bay on the NW coast surrounded by steep hills, exposed to westerly winds. Approach carefully as the narrow entrance has submerged rocks on both sides. An unused ferry boat landing is located on the S side. The bottom is rocks with weed and sand patches. The village at the head of the bay was built by a film company for the Popeye cartoons. It is regularly visited by tour groups, either by boat or bus.

Ghajn Tuffieha
35°55´.9N 14°20´.4E

The largest sandy beach in Malta and popular. Sandy, regular bottom.

Gnenja Bay
35°55´.6N 14°20´.5E

A wide, beautiful bay in unspoilt surroundings, open to the NW. Small fishermen's cottages line the steep S shore and the beach at the head is frequented by swimmers at weekends but is quieter than Ghajn Tuffieha. The sandy bottom shoals gradually towards the head of the bay.

Gnenja Bay: clear waters

Fomm Ir-Rih Bay
35°54´.5N 14°20´.3E

A quiet if not desolate bay, open to the NW, just S of Gnenja Bay. Good holding but not comfortable with swell from the NW when the waves are reflected off the steep cliffs on the S side.

The SW coast of Malta consists of steep and dramatic cliffs which are well worth a sightseeing passage to visit. Unfortunately if offers no shelter. The only place that can be visited is:

Blue Grotto
35°49´.3N 14°27´.4E

It is not recommended to go into Wied iz-Zurrieq to visit the Blue Grotto, and the water is too deep to anchor outside. It is better to stay underway and visit by tender. A number of small boats based in Wied iz-Zurrieq will be doing the same.

Fifla
35°47´.3N 14°24´.5E

This island lying 2.5 miles S of Malta is a bird sanctuary and prohibited area. It was used as a target for many years by the Royal Navy and Fleet Air Arm and no doubt a quantity of unexploded ordnance still remains.

VI. MALTA

Marsaxlokk Bay

35°50′N 14°33′.3E

There are three bays within Marsaxlokk which is the second commercial port of Malta. There are still some quiet anchorages along the NE shore although the new power station casts a blight over the scenery. The bay offers good protection from prevailing wind directions. Beware of shallow patches both on this side, and SE from the fort in the middle of the bay (marked with a beacon).

Marsaxlokk The biggest fishing port of Malta, is located in the N corner of the bay. A picturesque village with some good restaurants, shops and services. Using the large scale chart (No.36) it is possible to get to one of the jetties at Marsaxlokk drawing up to 2.2 metres.

Qajjenza A south facing bay to the W of the fort with good holding.

Birzebugia A popular summer resort. There is a small jetty on the W side to which a few yachts can secure stern-to. Shops and restaurants ashore.

To the SE of Birzebugia lies the commercial and freeport of Kalafrana which will be of little interest to yachtsmen.

Il-Hofriet (Peter's Pool)

35°50′.3N 14°34′E

Two pleasant quiet bays divided by a narrow spit, protected from SW through N to NE but open to the SE. Anchor in sand patches. Depths shoal gradually towards the head of the bay. Both anchorages are deserted and have no road access.

The transmitters of Deutche Welle (German World Service) overlook the bay and have been known to play havoc with yacht electrics. DW usually starts transmitting at 1400.

Il-Hofret (Armchair) bay on E coast

MA11 Anchorages around Gozo
(Anticlockwise from Mgarr)

Marsascala Bay

35°52′.0N 14°34′.5E

A small bay surrounded by the village with good protection from N to S through W. Shoals abruptly towards the head. Good holding. Numerous small boat moorings. Beware of the Munxar reef to the SE.

There are good fish restaurants, bars and pubs ashore. Grocers, butchers and greengrocers are within walking distance.

Marsascala Bay:

Tac-Cawl Rocks

36°01′.6N 14°19′.0E

A small bay surrounded by high rocks but good holding. 2 yachts would be a crowd.

Gebel tal-Halfa

Facing SE this is a beautiful little bay behind a big rock but very small and quickly crowded.

Marsalforn

36°01′.8N 14°15′.7E

Good anchoring in a bay open to the N. The fishing village of Marsalforn is built around the bay and has been swallowed up to some extent by tourism. Usual services ashore. A small and shallow fishing port is located on the E shore.

Qala Dwejra

36°02′.9N 14°11′.2E

An interesting and beautiful anchorage in an almost

circular bay surrounded by steep hills on the W side of Gozo. The entrance is partially closed off by Fungus Rock and entrance to the bay is by a narrow passage N and a wider one S of the rock. Anchorage is on rock and sand 5–12m. Good shelter from N to S through E.

An enchanting place whose only sounds at night are the wash of any swell against the cliffs, goat bells and owls.

Dwejra Inlet
36°03′.3N 14°11′.4E

A half mile to the N of Dwejra Point lies a tunnel through the cliffs to an inland bay. This is only accessible by road or through the channel. Anchoring outside is just possible in 25m; otherwise go by dinghy from Qala Dwejra or lie off. Dinghies can get through the tunnel or it is possible to swim through. Be very careful if there is any swell which can fill the tunnel, with unfortunate results for any dinghy and occupants in it.

Between Qala Dwejra and Xlendi are the highest and most impressive cliffs in Malta, rising vertically for up to 500 feet from the sea. There are no off-lying dangers and a close passage along them is impressive.

Xlendli Bay
36°01′.7N 14°12′.8E

Formerly a fishing village in a small narrow bay on the SW side of Gozo. It is open to the SW with a shallow area at the entrance (see chart 195). Beware of a rock, which is 1m awash, off the N point of the bay almost in the middle of the entrance. The S shore of the bay is clear of any dangers to yachts. Very little swinging room. Only suitable for small craft.

It is now a popular resort and the inner end of the bay is much cluttered with small boat moorings. There is

still room to anchor outside the moorings. It is noisy in summer. Shops and restaurants ashore.

Mgarrix-Xini Bay
36°01′N 14°16′.5E

A peculiar, deep and narrow inlet cut out of the limestone cliffs on the S coast of Gozo. The entrance is marked by a tower on the E side and a wied (Maltese for river) flows into the natural bay. Good holding and almost all round protection except from the S. Space is very restricted and it may be necessary to take a line ashore. There is a small beach at the head but beware of a rock with 1.5m and shoal patch on the western side near the head.

MA12 Anchorages around Comino

Santa Marija Bay
36°01′.3N 14°16′.5E

Good holding but much frequented by watersports from the Club Nautico.

San Niklaw Bay
36°01′.3N 14°19′.9E

Good holding but fronted by a large hotel with a private beach.

Blue Lagoon
36°01′.1N 14°19′.3E

One of Malta's loveliest bays and heavily crowded by tour boats and people at weekends, public holidays and during the summer. Reasonable holding if you can find

Looking NW to Gozo and Comino   *MTA*

VI. MALTA

a space. Most of the tour boats go bows-to on the Comino side to disgorge the hordes. Nevertheless a sheltered and peaceful anchorage at night and out of season. The entrance from the S should not be used by deep draught yachts without great care. The depths are marginal and changeable.

Dwejra natural arch on a spectacular rocky coastline   *MTA*

Comino: anchoring in the clear waters around the small island   *MTA*

APPENDIX

1. CHARTS AND BOOKS

Chart agents

Before departure – British Admiralty and Spanish charts from Imray Laurie Norie & Wilson Ltd, Wych House, The Broadway, St Ives, Cambs PE27 5BT ☎ 01480 462114, *Fax* 01480 496109 www@imray.com. However in the case of Spanish charts, stocks held are limited and it may take some time to fill an order. It may be simpler to order directly from the Instituto Hidrográfico de la Marina, Tolosa Latour 1, DP 11007 Cádiz ☎ (956) 59 94 12, *Fax* (956) 27 53 58 and pay by credit card.

Gibraltar

Gibraltar Chart Agency, 11a Block 5 Watergardens, Gibraltar

☎ +350 76293 *Fax* +350 77293

email gibchartag@gibtelecom.net

www.gibchartagency.com

Spain (Algeciras)

SUISCA SL

Avda. Blas Infante, Centro Blas Local 1, 11201 Ageciras, Cádiz

☎ +34 902 220007 *Fax* +34 902 220 008

email barcelona@suiscasl.com

www.suiscasl.com

Admiralty charts

Chart	Title	Scale
9	La Skhirra, Gabès and Ghannouch with approaches	
	Gabès and Ghannouch	30,000
	La Skhirra	50,000
	Gulf of Gabès	100,000
36	Marsaxlokk	10,000
45	Gibraltar harbour	3,600
91	Cabo de Sao Vicente to the Strait of Gibraltar	350,000
142	Strait of Gibraltar	100,000
	Tarifa	25,000
144	Gibraltar	10,000
165	Menorca to Sicilia including Malta	1,100,000
176	Cap Bon to Ra's At Tïn	1,175,000
177	Valletta harbours	7,500
178	Ports in Algeria	
	Port de Beni Saf	10,000
	Port de Ghazaouet: Port de Mostaganem:	
	Port de Ténès	12,500
	Approaches to Beni Saf	125,000
193	Islands in the Sicilian Channel	
	Isola di Linosa	25,000
	Isola di Lampedusa	35,000
	Isola di Pantelleria	50,000
	Porto di Lampedusa;	
	Porto di Pantelleria	75,000
194	Approaches to Malta and Ghawdex (Gozo)	100,000
211	Plans in the Maltese Islands	
	Channel between Malta and Ghawdex	25,000
	Il-Bajja ta'San Pawl	12,500
	Il-Bajja tad Divejra	4,000

Chart	Title	Scale
	Il-Port ta' L-Imgarr	3,000
	Il-Bajja ta Marsalforn	4,000
	Il-Bajja tax-Xlendi	4,000
252	Cap Corbelin to Cap Takouch	300,000
580	Al Hoceïma, Melilla and Port Nador with approaches	
	Al Hoceïma Melilla and Port Nador	10,000
	Approaches to Al Hoceïma	50,000
	Approaches to Melilla and Port Nador	60,000
773	Strait of Gibraltar to Isla de Alborán	300,000
812	Oran and Mers-el-Kebir	10,000
822	Approaches to Oran, Arzew and Mostaganem	120,000
838	Port of Arzew	15,000
855	Approaches to Alger and Skikda	
	Skikda	10,000
	Golfe de Stora	25,000
	Baie D'Alger	30,000
856	Oued Sébou to Casablanca	150,000
860	Approaches to Casablanca and Mohammedia	50,000
861	Mohammedia and Casablanca	
	Rade de Casablanca	12,500
	Mohammedia	15,000
862	Al Jadida, Jorf Lasfar, Safi and approaches	
	Safi	12,500
	Al Jadida	17,500
	Jorf Lasfar	20,000
	Approaches to Al Jadida and Jorf Lasfar: Approaches to Safi	150,000
863	Plans on the NW coast of Morocco	
	Anza and Agadir	12,500
	Apps to Essaouira	150,000
	Essaouira	12,500
	Cap Rhir to Agadir	175,000
	Laâyoune	30,000
	Apps to Anza and Agadir	50,000
	Apps to Laâyoune	175,000
1162	Sfax and Sousse with approaches	25,000
	Port de Sfax: Port de Sousse	25,000
	Approaches to Sfax: Approaches to Sousse	125,000
1184	Baie de Tunis	65,000
	La Goulette and Tunis	25,000
1440	Adriatic Sea	1,100,000
1448	Gibraltar bay	25,000
	Puerto de Algeciras	12,500
1567	Approaches to Annaba	25,000
	Annaba	10,000
1569	Bizerte and approaches	50,000
	Port de Bizerte and Goulet du Lac:	
	Port de Menzel Bourguiba	15,000
1710	Cherchell, Dellys and Bejaïa	
	Port de Cherchell	10,000
	Port de Dellys	12,500
	Port de Bejaïa	15,000
1712	Plans on the coasts of Algeria and Tunisia	
	Port of Jijel: Port de la Calle	12,000
	Collo anchorage	25,000
	Mersa Toukouch	25,000
	Port de la Calle	12,000

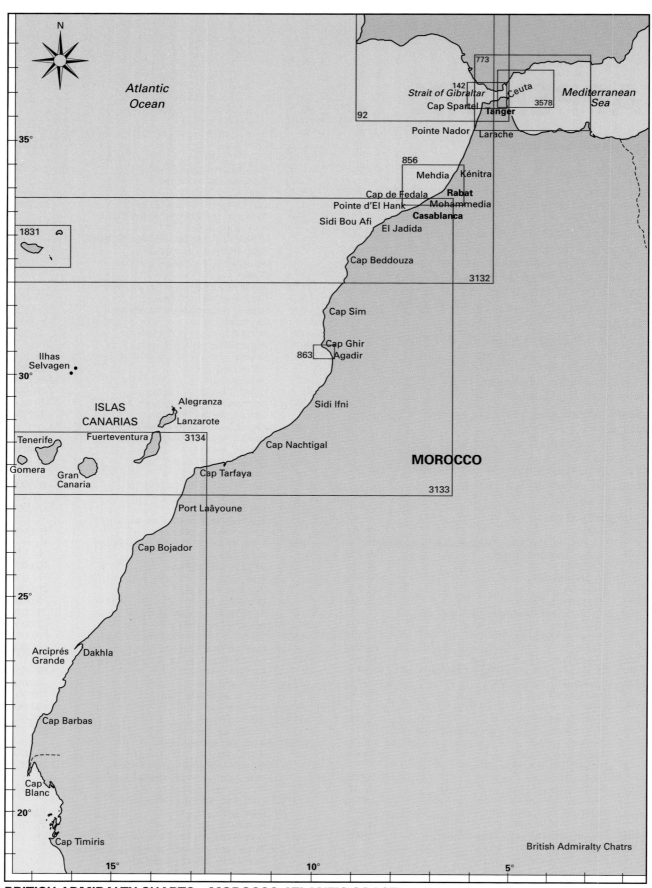

BRITISH ADMIRALTY CHARTS – MOROCCO ATLANTIC COAST

Chart	Title	Scale
	Tabarka	25,000
	Île de la Galite	75,000
1909	Île Plane to Cherchell	300,000
1910	Cherchell to Bejaïa	300,000
1912	Tanger with approaches, Larache and Oued Sébou	
	Tanger: Larache	10,000
	Oued Sébou	20,000
	Approaches to Tanger	25,000
2121	Ras el Hadid to Îles Cani	300,000
2122	Bizerte to Capo San Marco	300,000
2123	Capo Granitola to Capo Passero	300,000
2124	Isola di Lampedusa to Capo Passero including Malta	300,000
2437	Cabo Quilates to Oran	300,000
2537	Ghawdex (Gozo), Kemmuna (Comino) and northern part of Malta	50,000
2538	Malta	50,000
2555	Alger	10,000
2717	Strait of Gibraltar to Barcelona and Alger including Islas Baleares	1,100,000
2742	Puerto de Ceuta	10,000
3132	Strait of Gibraltar to Arquipélago da Madeira	1,250,000
3133	Casablanca to Islas Canarias	1,250,000
	Ilhas Selvagens	100,000
3403	Cap Afrique to Misratah	500,000
	Zuwarah	25,000
	Abu Kammash	30,000
	Az Zawiyah	40,000
3578	Eastern approaches to the Strait of Gibaltar	150,000
4301	Mediterranean Sea – western part	2,250,000

French charts

Service Hydrographique et Océanographique de la Marine

Chart	Title	Scale
1619	Mouillages de Tarifa	10,000
1700	Baie de Tétouan	25,000
1701	Tanger et ses atterrages	20,000
	Cartouche: Port de Tanger	10,000
1711	Côte Nord du Maroc	307,000
3023	De Djidjelli à Collo	100,000
3024	Du cap Toukouch au cap Rose	100,000
3029	Du cap Sigli à Djidjelli	100,000
3030	D'Alger à Cherchell	101,000
	Cartouches: Bou Aroun	5,000
	Chiffalo	5,000
3036	De Dellys au cap Sigli	102,000
	Cartouche: Port Gueydon	5,000
3043	D'Alger à Dellys	100,000
	Cartouche: Courbet-Marine	5,000
3061	Du cap Bougaroni au cap Axin	100,000
3202	De Cherchell à Ténès	101,000
3234	De la Point Kef el Assfer au cap Ténès	99,500
3405	D'Alger à la frontière de Tunisie	584,000
3424	Du cap Rose au cap Nègre	125,000
3678	Côte de l'Algérie (1ère feuille), d'Alger à la frontière du Maroc	596,000
4086	Al Mahdïyah	15,000
4087	Tabarca	15,300
4102	Sousse	25,000
	Cartouche: Port de Sousse	10,000
4129	Du cap Serrat au cap Blanc	61,600
4183	Tunisie côte Est, ports et mouillages	
	Cartouche: Rade de Kelibia	25,000
	Port de Kelibia	7,500
	Rade d'Hammamet	25,000
4191	De Ras-al-Fortas à Kelibia	61,700
4198	Du ras Enghela au cap Farina, baie et lac de Bizerte	61,100
4208	De Ksar Menara à Sousse	63,500
4219	Du cap Roux au cap Serrat (Tabarka et cap Négro)	61,700
4221	De Kilibia à ras Mamour	62,100

Chart	Title	Scale
4222	Du cap Kamart au Ras-al-Fortas (Golfe de Tunis)	61,900
4225	De Kurba à la Sebkha Djiriba (Golfe d'Hammamet)	63,000
4226	Du ras Marsa au ras Dimas (Golfe de Sousse et de Monastir)	62,800
4227	Du ras Dimas au ras Kapudia	63,300
4228	De Sfax à Maharès	63,600
4235	Du ras Kapudia au ras Ungha (Iles et bancs Kerkennah)	152,000
4236	Du ras Kapudia à Sidi Makluf (Partie Nord du canal de Kerkennah)	63,500
4237	De Sidi Makluf à Sfax (Iles Kerkennah)	63,500
4238	Sfax	25,000
	Cartouche: Port de Sfax	10,000
4239	De Maharès à la Skhirra (Golfe de Gabès)	63,900
4240	De la Skhira à Gabès (Golfe de Gabès)	64,100
4241	Gabès (ancienne Tacape)	25,000
4242	De Gabès au Bordj Djilidj (Golfe de Gabès)	64,300
4244	Du Bordj Djilidj à Sidi Garus (Partie Nord de l'île de Djerba)	64,200
4245	De Sidi Garus à Zarzis, Bahiret el Bou Grara	64,400
4247	De Zarzis au ras Ashdir (Bahiret el Biban)	64,700
4250	Du cap Farina au cap Carthage (Delta de Medjerda)	61,800
4314	De Bône à Tunis	328,000
4315	De Tunis à Sfax	335,000
4717	De Gibraltar à la pointe del Sabinal	250,000
	Cartouche: Port de Motril	10,000
	Mouillages de la Herradura, Los Berengueles, Almu nécar, Belilla et Salobrena	80,000
4970	Lac de Bizerte	25,000
5023	Iles au Sud de la Sicile	
	Cartouches: Ile de Pantelleria	30,000
	Port de Pantelleria	7,500
	Port de Lampedusa	10,000
	Ile de Linosa	30,000
	Ile de Lampedusa	30,000
5281	Port de Bizerte et goulet du Lac	10,000
5617	Port d'Alger	10,000
	Cartouche: Mouillage de la Pointe Pescade	10,000
5638	Baie d'Alger	30,000
	Cartouche: Mouillage de La Pérouse	10,000
5640	Port de Dellys	10,000
5641	Port de Bejaia (Bougie)	15,000
5669	Port d'Annaba (Bône)	10,000
5670	Abords de Bône	25,000
5696	Port de Mostaganem	10,000
5697	Rade de Casablanca	10,000
5698	Ile de La Galite	27,500
5699	Port de Tipaza et baie de Chenoua	10,000
	Cartouche: Port de Cherchell	10,000
5708	Port de Ténès	10,000
	Cartouches: Baie des Beni-Haouas - Mouillage de Sidi Djilani	10,000
	Baie et mouillage de Térarénia	10,000
	Baie des Souhalias - mouillage de Kef Doumia (Kef el Haouaci)	10,000
5787	Abords de Philippeville (Skida)	25,000
	Cartouche: Port de Philippeville (Skida)	10,000
5791	De Bizerte aux îles Cani	25,000
5864	Ports et mouillages sur la côte Nord du Maroc. Cartouche:	
	A – Baie de Al Hoceïma	120,000
	B – Port de Al Hoceïma	15,000
	C – Afraou	5,000
	D – Baie Tramontane	15,000

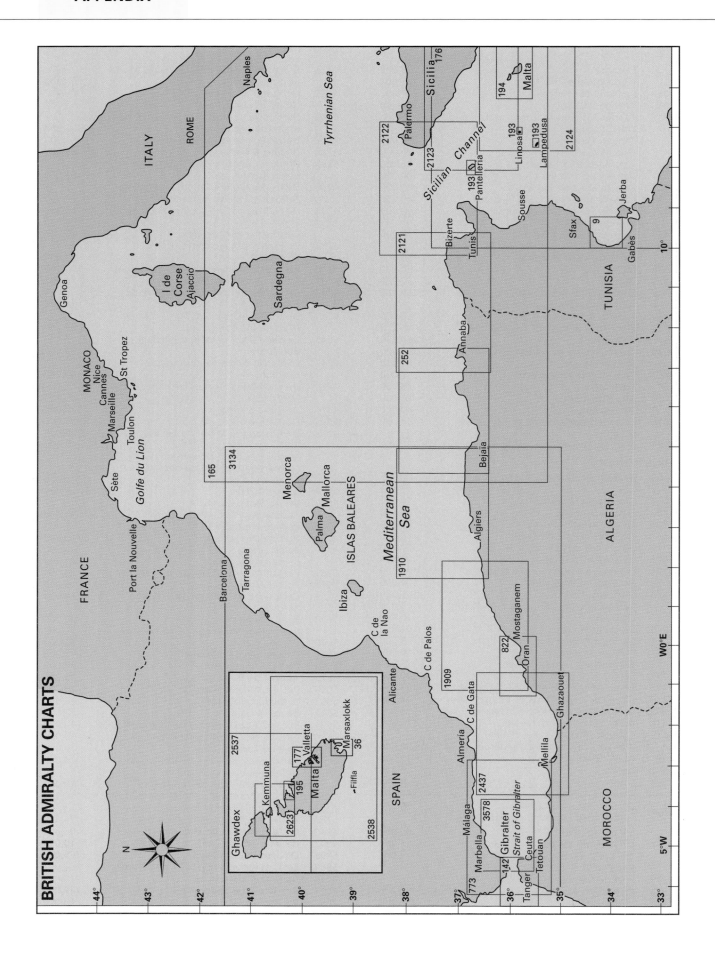

BRITISH ADMIRALTY CHARTS

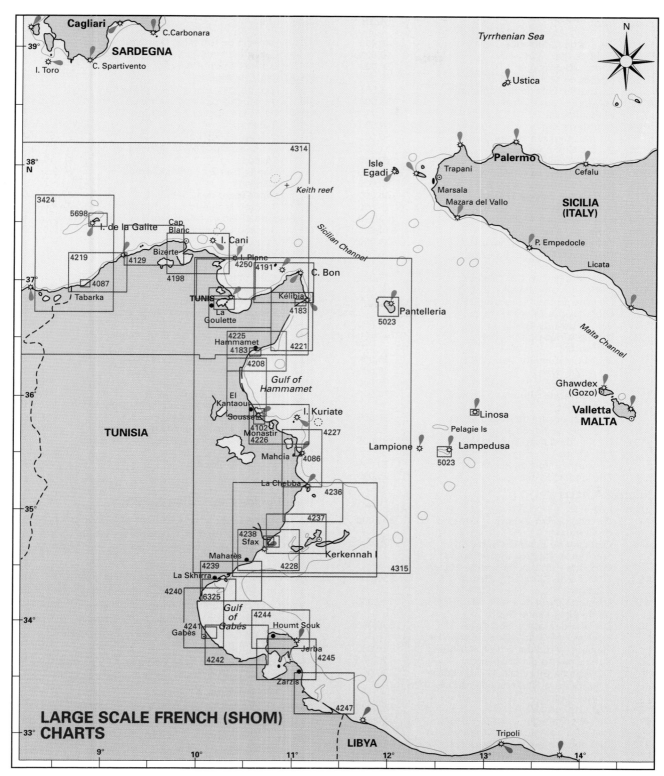

Chart	Title	Scale	Chart	Title	Scale
	E – Ile Alboran	20,000	5940	De la Tafna au cap Sigale	101,000
	F – Ports de Melilla et de Nador	11,200	5942	Iles et récifs de Cani	10,000
	G – Iles Zafarines et port de	15,000	5948	D'Arzew au cap Figalo	101,000
	Ras Kebdana		5951	Du Cap Ferrat à la pointe Kef el Asfer	100,000
5873	Port de Nemours	10,000	5955	Rade et port d'Agadir	10,000
5876	Ile Rachgoun, embouchure de la Tafna	10,000	6011	Des îles Zafarines à la Tafna	102,000
	Cartouche: Béni-Saf	10,000	6062	Ports de la Goulette et de Tunis	20,000
5886	Iles Habibas	10,000	6070	Port de Sidi-Abdallah	10,000
	Cartouche: Mersa Ali Bou Nouar	10,000	6103	Rade de Safi	10,000

NORTH AFRICA   **271**

Chart	Title	Scale
6111	Abords de Casablanca	49,900
6119	Rade de Mazagan	10,000
6120	Abords de Mazagan	50,000
6142	Abords de Mohammédia	15,000
	Cartouche: Port de Mohammédia	5,000
6145	De Moulay Bou Selham à Mohammédia	153,000
6169	Abords de Safi	50,600
6170	Du cap Magazan au cap Cantin	156,000
6178	Du cap Ghir à Agadir	51,600
6204	Rade d'Essaouira (Mogador)	10,000
6206	Du cap Hadid au cap Sim	51,100
6226	Du cap Cantin au cap Sim	158,000
6227	Du cap Sim à l'Oued Massa	160,000
6325	Baie de la Skhira ou des Sur-Kenis	35,000
6570	Mer d'Alboran, feuille Sud	203,000
6606	Canal de Sicile	674,000
6611	Entrée de la Méditerranée	674,000
7015	De Gibraltar aux îles Baléares (f.s. E 3)	1,000,000
7026	Baie de Algeciras (f.s. ES 445A)	25,000
7042	Détroit de Gibraltar (f.s. E 105)	100,000
7300	De cabo de São Vicente au Détroit de Gibraltar (f.s. ES 44)	350,000
7503	Baie et port de Ceuta	10,000
7524	Du cap Afrique à Mikratah	494,00
	Cartouche:	
	A - Abu Kammash	30,000
	B - Az Zawiyah	40,000
	C - Zuwarah	25,000
7550	Du Détroit de Gibraltar à Kenitra	324,000
	Cartouche:	
	A - Embouchure de l'Oued Sebou	30,000
	B - Cours de l'Oued Sebou	30,000
7551	De Kenitra au cap Beddouza (cap Cantin)	331,000
	Cartouches: Port de Rabat	20,000
	Port de Jorf Lasfar	25,000

Spanish Charts

Chart	Title	Scale
44	De cabo de San Vicente al Estrecho de Gibraltar	350,000
44C	Costa Sur de España y Norte de Marruecos. De Broa de Sanlúcar a Estepona y de Larache a cabo Mazarí	175,000
45	Estrecho de Gibraltar y Mar de Alborán	350,000
45A	De punta Carnero a cabo Sacratif y de punta Cires a cabo Negro	175,000
46	De cabo de Gata a cabo de las Huertas y de cabo Milonia a cabo Ivi	350,000
	Plano inserto: Puerto de Ghazaouet	10,000
50	Rada y puerto de Casablanca	10,000
105	Estrecho de Gibraltar. De cabo Roche a punta de la Chullera y de cabo Espartel a cabo Negro	100,000
181	Rada y puerto de Agadir	10,000
215	De cabo Trafalgar a punta Europ y de Ceuta a Kenitra (Port Lyautey)	350,000
216	De Kenitra a cabo Beddouza (Cantín)	350,000
	Planos insertos: Puerto de Rabat	20,000
	Puerto de Jorf-Lasfar	25,000
217	De cabo Safí a Sidi Ifni	350,000
254	Rada y puerto de Safí	10,000
	Puerto de Es-Suira (Mogador)	10,000
431	Bahía de Alhucemas	25,875
	Plano inserto: Puerto de Villa Sanjurjo	5,356
432	De cabo Abduna a puerto de Melilla	50,000
433	De Ras Tleta Madari (Cabo Tres Forcas) a Ras Cantara Run	50,000
	Plano inserto: Freu de los Farallones	10,000
434	De Ras Quiviana a la desembocadura del río Muluya	50,000

Chart	Title	Scale
445	Estrecho de Gibraltar. De punta Camarinal a punta Europa y de cabo Espartel a punta Almina	60,000
445A	Bahía de Algeciras	25,000
445B	Bajo de los Caberos e Isla de Tarifa	2,500
446	De la bahía de Tánger a Asilah (Arcila)	52,500
447	De Asilah (Arcila) a El Aaraich (Larache)	52,500
451	De punta Leona a cabo Mazarí	50,000
453	De Punta Europa a la torre de las Bóvedas	50,000
	Planos insertos: Fondeadero de Estepona	12,500
	Fondeadero de la Sabinilla	12,500
527	De cabo Mohammedia (Fedala) a cabo El Jadida (Mazagán)	160,000
529	De cabo Cantín (Beddouza) a cabo Sim	160,000
530	De Es-Suira (Mogador) a Agadir	160,000
	Planos insertos: Fondeadero de cabo Sim	51,060
	Fondeadero de Tafelneh	51,241
	Bahía de Imsouane	51,446
532	Del río Asif Solguemat al río Asaca	75,000
4331	Puerto de Melilla	5,000
4341	Islas Chafarinas y Ras El Ma (Cabo del Agua)	10,000
4451	Bahía de Algeciras - zona oeste	10,000
4452	Bahía de Algeciras - zona este	10,000
4461	Bahía y puerto de Tánger	15,000
	Puerto de Asilah (Arcila)	10,000
	Barra y puerto de El Aairaich (Larache)	10,000
4511	Bahía y puerto de Ceuta	10,000
5271	Aproches de Mohammedia (Fédala)	15,000
	Plano inserto: Puerto de Mohammedia (Fédala)	5,000
5320	Puerto de Sidi Ifni	6,000

Travel guides and other books

Do consult some of the excellent guidebooks on North Africa, both for further information on the ports and for places you may want to visit on excursions from them.

The Rough Guide to Morocco Mark Ellingham and Shaun McVeigh, Harrap-Columbus is probably the best general guide on Morocco and is written with enthusiasm. It has detailed information on travel, hotels, costs, sights and history. Indispensable when travelling inland.

The Rough Guide to Tunisia Peter Morris and Charles Farr, Harrap-Columbus, of the same excellent quality as their guide on Morocco.

Morocco, Algeria & Tunisia: a travel survival kit Geoff Crowther and Hugh Finley.

Lonely Planet The best alternative to the individual Rough Guides on Morocco and Tunisia. Not quite as detailed as the Rough Guides but it probably has the best coverage on Algeria for which there is no specialised guide in English.

A Guide and History of Morocco Nina Banon (Societe Nouvelle)

Marreucos (Guias Acento) and *Morocco Handbook* Anne and Keith McLachlan (Passport Books) are also excellent publications.

Italian Islands Dana Facaros & Michael Pauls (Cadogan Books). Amongst coverage of all the Italian Islands including Sardinia and Sicily, it has a good section on

Pantelleria and the Pelagie Islands.

Road maps

Road maps are indispensable when making a journey inland, one of the attractions of visiting North Africa, but they are difficult to find there.

RV Reis and Verkehrsverlag *World Maps* cover Morocco, with another covering all of Northwest Africa. These are available in most petrol filling stations in Spain and France. Roger Lascelles map of Morocco is also excellent. Also available are Hallwag or Kummerly & Frey's maps of Morocco.

Michelin's map 172 covers Algeria and Tunisia and is more detailed than the maps produced by the Tunisian Cartographic Office.

Cookery books

Mediterranean Seafood Alan Davidson (Penguin). A handbook with all the names of Mediterranean fish, crustaceans and molluscs in several languages and over 200 recipes from Mediterranean countries. Indispensable in the markets and fishing harbours with their unfamiliar fish. The recipes are practical and do not require ingredients exotic to the Mediterranean.

Mediterranean Cookery Claudia Roden. It contains 250 delicious and easy recipes of traditional Mediterranean cooking prepared with locally available ingredients.

Further reading

Italian Waters Pilot Rod Heikell (Imray Laurie Norie & Wilson)

Imray Mediterranean Almanac Editor Rod Heikell and Lu Michell. Two yearly

Votre Livre de Bord-Mediterranée (Bloc Marine)

Mediterranean Pilot (NP 45) Vol. 1 British Admiralty.

Mediterranean Cruising Handbook Rod Heikell (Imray Laurie Norie & Wilson)

Atlantic Islands RCC Pilotage Foundation (Imray Laurie Norie & Wilson)

Atlantic Spain and Portugal RCC Pilotage Foundation (Imray Laurie Norie & Wilson)

Mediterranean Spain – Costas del Sol & Blanca. RCC Pilotage Foundation (Imray Laurie Norie & Wilson)

A Bridge and Galley Guide to Tunisia Ann P. Maurice and Bryan E. Lockyear. Out of print.

Guide Practique de Sardaigne et Côtes de Tunisie Jacques Anglès. (Edition du Pen Duick)

Fodor's North Africa. A guide to Morocco, Algeria and Tunisia. Reprinted in 1989.

Traveller's Guide to North Africa (IC publications). The history, economy and culture of Mauritania, Morocco, Algeria, Tunisia, Libya and Egypt.

The Travellers' Guide to Malta and Gozo Christopher Kininmonth.

The Haj, Leon Uris. A fictitious account of Arabic lifestyle and values based on historical events. (Doubleday and Company, Garden City, New York.)

On the shores of the Mediterranean Eric Newby. (Penguin.) His journey through the Mediterranean countries.

The Lemon Mohammed Mrabet translated by Paul Bowles. An account of life in Tanger under international rule.

The Sheltering Sky Paul Bowles. A couple's travels in Morocco.

Midnight Mass Paul Bowles. Several short stories set in Morocco.

Berlitz Guide to Algeria.

It will be advantageous to obtain the books required from Europe, as they are difficult to find in the Maghreb, except for some of the titles in Morocco.

2. COASTAL RADIO STATIONS

Times are UT
MOROCCO
Tanger (CNW) 35°49′N 05°48′W
RT (MF) Transmits on 1911, 2182, 2635kHz. Receives on 2182kHz (H24)
Traffic lists on 1911kHz at 0740, 1140, 1540, 1740
VHF Transmits and receives on Ch 16 (H24), 24, 25, 26, 27.
Al Hoceïma 35°10′N 03°58′W
VHF Transmits and receives on Ch 16 (H24), 23, 25, 27, 28
ALGERIA
Ghazouet (7TE) 35°04′N 01°09′W
VHF Transmits and receives on Ch 16 (H24), 24, 25, 26, 27, 28
Traffic lists Ch 28 at 0303, 0703, 0903, 1103, 1303, 1503, 1703, 1903, 2103, 2303
Oran (7TO) 35°46′N 00°33′W
RT (MF) Transmits on 1735, 2182, 2586, 2719kHz. Receives on 2182kHz
Traffic lists on 1735 at every even H+35
VHF Transmits and receives on Ch 16 (H24), 24, 25, 26, 27, 28
Traffic lists on Ch 25 at 0303, 0703, 0903, 1103, 1303, 1503, 1703, 1903, 2103, 2303
Arzew 35°43′N 00°18′W
VHF Transmits and receives on Ch 16 (H24), 24, 25, 26, 27, 28
Traffic lists on Ch 27 at 0303, 0703, 0903, 1103, 1303, 1503, 1703, 1903, 2103, 2303
Tenès 36°30′N 01°19′E
VHF Transmits and receives on Ch 16 (H24), 24, 25, 26, 27, 28
Traffic lists on Ch 24 at 0333, 0733, 0933, 1133, 1333, 1533, 1733, 1933, 2133, 2333
Alger (7TA) 36°40′N 03°18′E
RT (MF) Transmits on 1792, 2182, 2691, 2775kHz. Receives on 2182kHz
Traffic lists on 1792kHz every odd H+03
VHF Transmits and receives on Ch 16 (H24), 24, 25, 26, 27, 28, 84, 87
Traffic lists on Ch 84 at 0330, 0730, 0930, 1130, 1330, 1530, 1730, 1930, 2130, 2330
Bejaia 36°45′N 05°05′E
VHF Transmits and receives on Ch 16 (H24), 24, 25, 26, 27, 28
Traffic lists Ch 26 at 0333, 0733, 0933, 1133, 1333, 1533, 1733, 1933, 2133, 2333
Skikda 36°53′N 06°54′E
VHF Transmits and receives on Ch 16 (H24), 24, 25, 26, 27, 28
Traffic lists Ch 25 at 0303, 0703, 0903, 1103, 1303, 1503, 1703, 1903, 2103, 2303
Annaba (7TB) 36°54′N 07°46′E
RT (MF) Transmits on 1911, 2182, 2775kHz. Receives on 2182kHz
Traffic lists on 1911 at every even H+50.
VHF Transmits and receives on Ch 16 (H24), 24, 25, 26
Traffic lists on Ch 24 at 0303, 0703, 0903, 1103, 1303, 1503, 1703, 1903, 2103, 2303

TUNISIA
Bizerte 37°17′N 09°53′E
RT (MF) Transmits on 2182, 1687.4, 2210kHz. Receives on
2182kHz.
VHF Transmits and receives on Ch 16 (0700–1900), 23, 24
Tunis 36°54′N 10°11′E
RT (MF) Transmits and receives on 1768.4, 2182, 2670kHz.
Receives on 2182kHz
Traffic lists on 1768.4kHz at 0250, 0450, 0950, 1350, 1750,
2150, 2350
VHF Transmits and receives on Ch 01, 10, 12, 18, 21, 25, 26,
16
Kelibia 36°50′N 11°07′E
VHF Transmits and receives on Ch 16 (0600–1800), 26, 28
Mahdia 35°31′N 11°04′E
RT (MF) Transmits on 1696.4, 1771, 2182kHz. Receives on
2182kHz
VHF Transmits and receives on Ch 16 (H24), 27, 28
Sfax 34°44′N 10°44′E
VHF Transmits and receives on Ch 16 (0600–1800), 02, 22, 24

3. GLOSSARY

Weather forecast terms

French	English
prévisions météo	weather forecasts
abondant	heavy
affaiblissement	decrease
agité(e)	rough
amélioration	improvement
anticyclone	anticyclone
apercu	short summary
après midi	afternoon
assez fort	rather strong
augmentant	increasing
aujourd'hui	today
averse	shower
avis	warning
avis de coup de vent	gale warning
basse pression	low pressure
en baisse	falling
banc de brouillard	fog bank
beau	fair, fine
belle (mer)	smooth
bon(ne)	good
en bordure	on the border, edge of
brouillard	fog
brise	breeze
brise de mer	sea breeze
brise de terre	land breeze
bruine	drizzle
brume légère	haze
brume mouillée	mist
brume sèche	haze
brumeux	hazy, misty, foggy
calme	calm
centre	centre
comblant	filling
coup de vent	gale
courant	current/airflow
couvert	overcast
creusant	deepening
cyclonique	cyclonic
demain	tomorrow
se déplacant	moving
dépression (bas)	depression (low)
devenant	becoming
direction	direction
se dispersant	dispersing
dorsale	ridge
éclair	lightning
éclaircie	bright interval
échelle de Beaufort	Beaufort scale
état de la mer	sea state
est	east
étendu	extensive
extension	extending

faible	slight, weak
force du vent	wind force
en formation	building
fort	strong
fraîche	fresh
frais	fresh
fréquent	frequent
front	front
front froid	cold front
front chaud	warm front
gelée	frost
grain	squall
grand frais	near gale
grêle	hail
en hausse	rising
haut	high
houle	swell
isolé	isolated
jour, journée	day
au large	at sea
léger	light
légère	light
légèrement	lightly
lentement	slowly
locale	local
matin	morning
mauvais	poor
même	the same
mer	sea
mer forte	rough sea
modéré	moderate
se modérant	moderating
néant	none
neige et pluie	sleet
noeuds	knots
nord	north
nuages	clouds
nuageux	cloudy
nuit	night
orage	thunderstorm
orageux	stormy
ouest	west
ouragan	hurricane
passagèrement	temporarily/passing over
persistance	continuing
perturbation	disturbance
pluie	rain
pluvieux	rainy
précipitation	precipitation
pression	pressure
prévision	forecast
probabilité	probability, chances of
prochaine	following
profond	deep
rapidement	quickly
rafale	gust
recul du vent	backing
région	area
ressac	surge, backwash
rester, restant	remain, stay
sans nuages	cloudless
situation générale	general synopsis
suivant	following
sporadiques	scattered
stationnaire	stationary
sud	south
temps	weather, time
tempête	storm
tonnerre	thunder
vagues	waves
valable	valid
variable	variable
vent	wind
vent frais	strong breeze
vent à rafales	gusty
virement	veering
visibilité	visibility

voilé	cloudy/overcast
zone	area
Sea state	*Wave height*
Peu agitée	Slight (0.5-1.25m)
Agitée	Moderate (1.25-2.5m)
Forte	Rough (2.5-4m)

Terms found in French Charts

jusant	ebb tide
flot	flood tide
marnage	max. range of the tide

Terms used in custom clearing and other formalities

acier	steel
allant a/destination	going to/destination
année de construction	year of construction
bois	wood
chantier	ship yard
combien de cheveaux	horse power
date et lieu de naissence	date and place of birth
delivré	issued (date)
douane	customs
d'ou vous venez?	where do you come from?
destination	destination
equipage	crew
expire le	expires on
fabriqué de	constructed in (date)
heure d'arrive	hour of arrival
heure de départ	hour of departure
jauge brut/net	tonnage gross/net
largeur	width
lieu de l'emission	place where issued
loch	log
longueur	length
marque	brand name
matricule	registration (country)
moteur	engine
né le	born on
nom du bateau	name of the boat
numero d'immatriculation	registration number
passagers	passengers
pavillon	flag/nationality
proprietaire	owner
polyester	grp/polyester
port d'attache	port of registration
venant de/provenance	coming from
puissance	horse power
renouvellé	renewed

sondeur	echo sounder
tirant d'eau	draught
tonnage	tonnage

Sample Crew List and Boat Data
Nom du Bateau (name of the boat):
Nationalité (nationality):
Port d'attache (port of registration):
Matricule (registration number):
Longueur (length):
Largeur (width):
Tirant d'eau (draught):
Jauge brut/net (tonnage gross/net):
Année de construction (year of construction):
Chantier (shipyard):
Moteur (engine):
Provenance (coming from):
Destination (going to):
Date d'entrée (date of entry):
Date de sortie (date of departure):

Proprietaire ou skipper (owner or captain)
Né le (date born):
à (place):
No. de passport (passport number):
Délivré le (date of issue):
par (by whom):
Renouvellé (renewed until):
Expire le (date of expiry):

No. de visa (visa number):
Délivré le (date of issue):
par (by whom):

Profession (profession):

Addresse du proprietaire (owner's address):
Passagers (number of passengers):

The same data for the crew as for the owner or captain.
Equipement (equipment):
Radio (VHF, radios and transmitters):
Radar (radar):
Marque (brand):
Sondeur (echo sounder):
Type (model No.):
Loch (log), Satnav, Loran, etc.

Index